New Worlds, New Lives

Globalization and People of Japanese Descent in the Americas and from Latin America in Japan

ASIAN AMERICA

A Series Edited by Gordon Chang

The increasing size and diversity of the Asian American population, its growing significance in American society and culture, and the expanded appreciation, both popular and scholarly, of the importance of Asian Americans in the country's present and past—all these developments have converged to stimulate wide interest in scholarly work on topics related to the Asian American experience. The general recognition of the pivotal role that race and ethnicity have played in American life, and in relations between the United States and other countries, has also fostered this heightened attention.

Although Asian Americans were a subject of serious inquiry in the late nineteenth and early twentieth centuries, they were subsequently ignored by the mainstream scholarly community for several decades. In recent years, however, this neglect has ended, with an increasing number of writers examining a good many aspects of Asian American life and culture. Moreover, many students of American society are recognizing that the study of issues related to Asian America speak to, and may be essential for, many current discussions on the part of the informed public and various scholarly communities.

The Stanford series on Asian America seeks to address these interests. The series will include work from the humanities and social sciences, including history, anthropology, political science, American studies, law, literary criticism, sociology, and interdisciplinary and policy studies.

New Worlds, New Lives

Globalization and

People of Japanese Descent

in the Americas

and from Latin America

in Japan

Edited by

Lane Ryo Hirabayashi

Akemi Kikumura-Yano

James A. Hirabayashi

Stanford University Press, Stanford, California, 2002

International Nikkei Research Project coordinated by

the Japanese American National Museum

Published with the assistance of a grant from

The Nippon Foundation

Stanford University Press
Stanford, California
©2002 by the Japanese American National Museum
Printed in the United States of America

Library of Congress Cataloging-in-Publication Data

Hirabayashi, Lane Ryo
　　New worlds, new lives: globalization and people of Japanese descent in the Americas
and from Latin America in Japan / edited by Lane Ryo Hirabayashi, Akemi Kikumura-
Yano, and James A. Hirabayashi.
　　　　p.　cm. — (Asian America)
　　Includes bibliographical references and index.
　　ISBN 0-8047-4461-0 (cloth: alk. paper) — ISBN 0-8047-4462-9 (pbk. : alk. paper)
　　1. Japanese—Ethnic identity—America.　2. Japanese—America—History.
3. Japanese—America—Social conditions.　4. America—Ethnic relations.
5. Globalization—Social aspects.　6. Japan—Relations—America.　7. America—
Relations—Japan.　I. Hirabayashi, Lane Ryo.　II. Kikumura-Yano, Akemi.
III. Hirabayashi, James A.　IV. Series.
　E29.J3 N49　　2002
　305.895'607—dc21　　　　　　　　　　　　　　　　　　2001008166

This book is printed on acid-free, archival-quality paper.

Original printing 2002

Last figure below indicates year of this printing:
11　10　09　08　07　06　05　04　03　02

Typeset at Stanford University Press in 10/12.5 Minion

Acknowledgments

We would like to thank, first and foremost, The Nippon Foundation for their generous support of the International Nikkei Research Project, coordinated by the Japanese American National Museum, and the first two books the project has produced: *New Worlds, New Lives* and *Encyclopedia of Japanese Descendants in the Americas: An Illustrated History of the Nikkei.*

In addition, Mr. Francis Y. Sogi has given us wise advice and counsel. As always, Ms. Irene Hirano is very deeply appreciated by every one of the participants in the International Nikkei Research Project. She has always believed in the importance of collaborative research and in establishing ties with Nikkei communities and institutions in the Americas, in Japan, and beyond.

Two staff members who made the INRP run on a day-to-day basis are, first, Ms. Satomi Takeda, Project Coordinator, who helped coordinate INRP research efforts, and Dr. Masayo Ohara, INRP Research Specialist, who worked to interpret and to translate much of the correspondence and many of the drafts the project entailed, which was not an easy task.

Lane Ryo Hirabayashi is grateful to all who helped him with *New Worlds, New Lives.* Only a few of them can be mentioned here. At the University of Colorado, Ms. Antonia Green, Ms. Katherine Martínez, and Ms. Karen Moreira did rapid work on the initial translations of chapters 16, 5, and 8. Ms. Joan York and Joanne Hirabayashi provided invaluable assistance and advice in regard to editing the initial manuscript. Two of his then–graduate students, Sawa Kurotani-Becker and Kenichiro Shimada, as well as colleagues Marilyn C. Alquizola and Evelyn Hu-DeHart, offered helpful advice on topics germane to this anthology that was much appreciated.

At Stanford, we are deeply indebted to Professor Gordon Chang, and to Ms. Muriel Bell and the staff of Stanford University Press, as well as Sharron Wood for her copyediting and John Feneron, Stanford University Press production editor. Their advice, support, and enthusiasm for this aspect of the project energized us.

Finally, we are deeply grateful to our families—immediate, extended, and international—for their love and support.

Lane Ryo Hirabayashi

Akemi Kikumura-Yano

James A. Hirabayashi

Contents

Preface

The main focus of *New Worlds, New Lives* is the impact of globalization on the identities of "Nikkei"—that is, people of Japanese descent living outside Japan.* Since by 1990 over 90 percent of all Japanese emigrants were living in either Latin America or North America (Canada and the United States), we decided that during the first cycle of the International Nikkei Research Project (INRP) we would focus primarily on the Americas as our geographic unit of analysis.† Doing so, however, entailed one significant twist. During the 1980s and 1990s, large numbers of Latin Americans of Japanese descent— perhaps on the order of 300,000 by 1991—had returned to Japan in order to seek employment as temporary workers, or *dekasegi*.‡ Other reasons will appear below, but these were the key reasons for our focus on the Americas.

*We offer our definitions of key terms—including Nikkei, Nikkei identities, community, globalization, and so forth—in chapter 2. Also in chapter 2 we explain in more detail why globalization became the central theoretical framework for *New Worlds, New Lives*.

†For more details on this topic, see Iyo Kunimoto, "Japanese Migration to Latin America," in Barbara Stallings and Gabriel Szekely, eds., *Japan, the United States, and Latin America: Toward a Trilateral Relationship in the Western Hemisphere* (Baltimore, Md.: Johns Hopkins University Press, 1993), 99–121. For a current overview also see Mike Douglass and Glenda S. Roberts, eds., *Japan and Global Migration: Foreign Workers and the Advent of a Multicultural Society* (New York: Routledge, 2000). For a general historical survey pertaining to Asians, see the work of Evelyn Hu-DeHart, e.g. "The Study of the Asian Diaspora in the Americas: Latin America and the Caribbean," paper presented at the "Colors of the Diaspora" conference, Apr. 23–25, 1992, University of Colorado at Boulder.

‡Describing them with the term Nikkeijin (people of Japanese descent from overseas), Yoko Sellek discusses dekasegi in her chapter, "Nikkeijin: The Phenomenon of Return Migration," in Michael Weiner, ed., *Japan's Minorities: The Illusion of Homogeneity* (New York: Routledge, 1997), 178–210.

From the beginning, we were intrigued by a series of questions. First, what does it mean to be of Japanese ancestry in the Americas? Second, are there any attributes or characteristics that such persons generally share through time and across space? Third, what significant differences are there between people of Japanese descent in the Americas, and what kinds of conditions explain why these differences have developed? Finally, since we were born in the United States, are people of color, and are anthropologists who have traveled extensively, we had a corollary question. What, specifically, would the Japanese American experience look like if we were to reexamine it in terms of the myriad groups of Japanese immigrants who arrived during different times and in different places throughout the Americas?

Beyond this, we acknowledge that our approach in *New Worlds, New Lives* is indelibly influenced by our ties to the Japanese American National Museum in Los Angeles and its unique approach to collecting, conceptualizing, and presenting data. The mission of the Japanese American National Museum, the only museum in the United States expressly dedicated to sharing the story of Americans of Japanese ancestry, is to make known the Japanese American experience as an integral part of America's heritage in order to improve understanding and appreciation of America's ethnic and cultural diversity. The National Museum was established with the central focus on the Japanese American community, its history, and its present condition so that future generations can learn from this experience, and so that Japanese Americans in particular can better chart their futures by reinterpreting the past in light of their perceptions of their experience as Americans.

The concept of a community-based, community-oriented museum is a critical part of the National Museum's philosophy. Through participatory engagement, communities are empowered to define and interpret their own experiences. Local communities, institutions, and individuals (including scholars, artists, and designers) preserve, document, interpret, and present their own stories through exhibitions, publications, educational materials, and public programs. At all levels of the enterprise, partnerships are the key feature of this process.*

The International Nikkei Research Project extends the National Museum's philosophy and program beyond the United States in order to explore the rich and diverse cultures of Nikkei around the world. The main mission of the project is to increase and share knowledge about Nikkei on a global basis in order to foster greater understanding between peoples, communities, and nations in

---

*See *Japanese American National Museum Quarterly* 11 (Spring 1996), a special double issue entitled "Partnerships—Communities and Collaborations," for additional information about the museum's unique methodology.

the Americas, Japan, and other countries throughout the world. The goal here is to document Nikkei experience as perceived by the Nikkei themselves, within the national, transnational, and global contexts, and to make this data available to all interested parties via the National Museum's Hirasaki National Resource Center. So the INRP works very much in the same spirit of collaboration and partnership that has always characterized the activities of the larger museum. Not surprisingly, then, the INRP has also prioritized insiders' points of view in studying the impact of globalization on Nikkei identities. Thus, whether our collaborators happen to be of Japanese descent or not, or university professors or not, they are uniformly persons who have had intimate, long-term ties to the communities and to the Nikkei who make them up. In addition, many contributors have also played roles as activists in or as advocates for the Nikkei community with which they are associated. That this principle guided the selection of participants has made *New Worlds, New Lives* especially rich in terms of insights that are based on combinations of scholarly, applied, and activist endeavors.

The Americas as a Case Study

As mentioned above, *New Worlds, New Lives* focuses on "the Americas," by which we mean both South and North America. Besides the fact that by 1990 over 90 percent of Japanese emigrants living outside Japan were in the Americas, we had four reasons for this emphasis.

First, there were and are tremendous logistical problems when trying to conceptualize comparative research on the scale that the INRP intends. The Americas seemed like a good place to begin because—unlike other comparable geographical areas—it seemed feasible in terms of the number of languages. Thus, in every case we were able to complete our review of the literature and our own chapters in four languages: Portuguese, Spanish, Japanese, and English. Even so, the linguistic dimensions of this first phase of the project have often been formidable.

Second, the Americas were an attractive site because of the dekasegi, that is, the people of Japanese descent in Latin America who began to return to Japan as temporary laborers in the 1980s and 1990s.* The dekasegi phenome-

---

*For the record, the term is *dekasegi* in Japanese, *dekasegui* in Spanish, and *dekassegui* in Portuguese (Akemi Kikumura-Yano, personal communication, 2000). We have left the term as the author originally spelled it and have not imposed uniformity in spelling throughout the text. As readers will note by comparing the accounts of the dekasegi experience in Part Three, it is not altogether certain whether the experience is basically the same, or whether assertions along these lines are essentialist. Chapter 16, by Marcelo Higa, probably makes this point most insistently.

non seemed to present a perfect opportunity to study the issue of changing identities, and—because of the new kinds of linkages between transnational migrants who moved back and forth between Latin American countries and Japan—whether globalization was having a marked impact on Nikkei and Japanese proper.

Third, Latin America is the site of major populations of *Uchinanchu*, that is, people of Okinawan descent (Okinawa is a southern prefecture of Japan). Because of their historically marginalized status as residents of a semicolonial region of Japan who were seen as lesser than mainland Japanese (or *Naichi*), Okinawans represent an interesting permutation of Japanese identity.* Moreover, we already knew that there were efforts underway as early as the 1980s to create linkages between Okinawans on a global scale. Thus, all of the following invited examination of this case as an integral part of INRP's efforts to study Nikkei identities in the Americas: 1) the diasporic dimension of the Okinawan immigration experience, 2) their subcultural affinity—which is a matter of oppression, as well as historic, linguistic, and regional affiliations—and, 3) their efforts to establish and maintain contact with each other globally, and with the home prefecture.

Finally, readers will note that we have given a greater emphasis to Latin American case studies within the Americas. There is already a solid literature on many aspects of the Japanese American experience on the mainland as well as in Hawai'i, and the literature on Japanese Canadians grew rapidly in the 1980s and 1990s. Thus, while three of the chapters include information about Nikkei in North America, these offer a comparative perspective on Nikkei in the Americas as a whole. In addition, although there have been many studies carried out concerning the Nikkei in Latin America, a good deal of this research has been published in Spanish, Portuguese, or Japanese and so is not widely accessible to an English-speaking audience. One of the main purposes of putting together this anthology is to remedy that and promote a broader perspective on the evolving nature of Nikkei identities.

The Selection of INRP Participants and Research Topics

Based on the criteria described above, eighteen scholars from seven different countries were invited to conduct original research on topics related to Japanese immigrants and their descendants in the Americas. The selection was also intended to include countries where there were the largest and most

*A compact but accessible introduction to Okinawan history and identity is available in Koji Taira, "Troubled National Identity: The Ryukyuans/Okinawans," in Michael Weiner, ed., *Japan's Minorities: The Illusion of Homogeneity* (New York: Routledge, 1997), 140–77.

significant concentrations of people of Japanese descent by the mid-1990s: Brazil (620,370), the United States (760,370), Peru (55,472), Canada (55,111), Argentina (29,262), Mexico (14,735), Paraguay (6,054), and, of course, Japan, where there were some 233,254 Brazilians of Japanese descent, approximately 40,394 Peruvian Japanese, 3,300 Argentine Japanese, and 1,466 Paraguayan Japanese, among others.*

As previously indicated, we drew from the Japanese American National Museum's institutional affiliations in order to identify potential contributors. In many cases, these were persons who were tied to other museums, institutes, or programs that had past and present collaborative relationships with the Japanese American National Museum.† In most cases we also prioritized the selection of scholars who had close working ties with Nikkei individuals and organizations in the community in question, and individuals who had given emphasis to insiders' viewpoints on the Nikkei experience. In other cases, certain participants came to our attention because of their advocacy work on behalf of community members.

Participants were invited to address one of three broad research topics, according to the specifics of the country or case(s) with which they were familiar.‡ The first topic was historical perspectives on migration and the ini-

---

*These statistics appear in the INRP publication *International Nikkei Research Project: First Year Report* (Los Angeles: Japanese American National Museum, 1999), 14–16; for the different sources for these data, mostly from Japanese-language publications, see note 1, on p. 14. Note that Brazil has the largest number of people of Japanese descent in the Americas, but that this fact is partially hidden because of the Japanese Brazilians living temporarily in Japan.

†*New Worlds, New Lives* will be followed by the INRP's publication of Akemi Kikumura-Yano, ed., *Encyclopedia of Japanese Descendants in the Americas: An Illustrated History of the Nikkei* (Walnut Creek, Calif.: AltaMira Press, 2002), which focuses on the history and development of Nikkei communities in Latin America. The encyclopedia will be complementary to this anthology and provide a good deal of background and resources for further reading. There is a definite overlap between the contributors to *New Worlds, New Lives* and the encyclopedia because the same community-based museums, cultural programs, and associations were targeted in order to recruit potential contributors to these two INRP projects. In addition, readers can consult a recent publication by INRP participant Gary Mukai that presents some of the key case studies in a curriculum package suitable for sixth- to twelfth-grade students: Gary Mukai and Rachel Brunette, *Japanese Migration and the Americas: An Introduction to the Study of Migration* (Stanford, Calif.: Institute for International Studies, 1999).

‡INRP definitions of terms and project guidelines were fairly extensive, yet clearly provisional and evolving. The latest of many versions was handed out to INRP participant scholars at the last general "assessment and planning meeting." It is simply titled *International Nikkei Research Project*, and dated June 24–26, 1999 (Los Angeles: Japanese American National Museum). It was divided into eight chapters, including chapter 5, "Research Framework." Each chapter was translated into Japanese, Span-

tial establishment of Nikkei cultures and societies in the Americas.* A second broad topic had to do with the formation of, and linkages between, Nikkei communities in the Americas, including subtopics such as social institutions, the family, religion, education, politics, and economics. Third was the different forms of new migration, including post–World War II immigrants, guest workers, businessmen on tours of duty, and so forth. We also sought contributors who would be able to address the future prospects of Nikkei communities.

As the INRP project evolved, some of the initial participants chose to leave for a range of reasons. A number of new participants were added during the second year in order to ensure coverage of key countries or topics. In any case, readers should appreciate that many of the research projects were developed in tandem so that authors working on specific themes were often able to conduct a dialogue over the course of one or two INRP meetings, as well as at other professional meetings or conferences.

In addition, readers should note that this anthology lacks a separate chapter about people of Japanese descent in Mexico. Tragically, Dr. Maria Elena Ota Mishima, an INRP scholar and an internationally recognized expert on Mexican Japanese, died prematurely in 2000 before she was able to complete her proposed chapter. Because of the collaborative setup of the INRP project—which entailed two meetings and both collective and dyadic discussions of our research projects—we felt it best not to try to add a substitute chapter on Mexico, as that author would not have had the benefit of the time and the meetings that the rest of the project members had access to.

In sum, what we were striving for in assembling *New Worlds, New Lives* was to present an interdisciplinary, multifaceted portrait of people of Japanese descent in the Americas. We wanted readers to be able to compare, for example, the Peruvian Japanese experience through the eyes of an anthropologist, a demographer/historian, and a journalist—all of whom are Peruvian. In addition, readers who are interested in specific topics such as Nikkei women's experiences can read and compare chapters focusing on a range of countries, including Canada, Peru, the United States, and Brazil. It is in this respect that *New Worlds, New Lives* achieves its best success. The excitement

---

ish, and Portuguese. All meetings and workshop sessions were also conducted with simultaneous interpretation into Japanese, Spanish, and English, as all INRP participants spoke one of these three languages fluently.

* Although *New Worlds, New Lives* features many contemporary accounts, we also solicited a number of historical pieces because we wanted to establish a diachronic perspective on the evolution of Nikkei identities. The INRP and *New Worlds, New Lives* were specifically informed by the pioneering historical research of Professor Yasuo Sakata, as well as the innovative research of the historian Shigeru Sugiyama.

comes precisely from juxtaposing different perspectives and analyses of Nik-kei identities in the same country, or thematically across a number of coun-tries, all of which were generated from insiders' points of view.

Although we provided stipulative definitions from the beginning as well as a list of suggested topics, participants were quite free to develop their re-search projects in any way they chose. We realized that this might cause some difficulties in stitching this anthology together, but we believed very strongly that this approach was consistent with one of the INRP's key priori-ties: to produce a set of chapters about Nikkei identities that highlighted in-siders' points of view. One of the most significant controversies within the INRP developed as a direct result of this approach. In the end, although each author presented information about community formations, half of the re-search papers raised substantive challenges to the general applicability of the concept of "Nikkei" to people of Japanese descent in the Americas. Some re-searchers even argued that changes in the 1980s and 1990s were so profound that it was no longer possible to characterize all people of Japanese descent overseas as such. Thus, one of the greatest challenges that we faced as an editorial team was not only explicitly recognizing this controversy, but coming up with a theoretical framework that would do justice to it and allow us to account for the different positions among the contributors regarding the applicability of the term "Nikkei" to the people of Japanese descent in the Americas.*

Organization of the Anthology

New Worlds, New Lives is divided into four parts. The first three parts be-gin with a brief introduction by one of the three principal academic advisers for the INRP—Eiichiro Azuma, Lloyd Inui, and Richard Kosaki. These in-troductions detail themes raised in the Preface and in chapter 2, and intro-duce the individual chapters in more detail.

After Azuma's introduction, Part One begins with a chapter by our col-league Harumi Befu, which presents a global overview of Japanese emigra-tion that will help readers contextualize the histories of people of Japanese descent in the Americas. Following that, we—the editors—discuss *New Worlds, New Lives'* focus on the evolving nature of Nikkei identities. In order to assess recent developments, the editors delineate five propositions con-cerning how Nikkei identities and communities are being transformed by globalization. These propositions provide an orienting framework that will help readers to make their own judgments as to whether or not Nikkei iden-

---

* We present and discuss this framework in detail in chapter 2, below.

tities are actually changing in the new millennium and, if so, whether globalization is having an impact in this regard.

Parts Two and Three reflect the fact that the state of Nikkei identities in the new millennium can be evaluated, from the beginning, in terms of a series of conjunctions versus disjunctions.* Conjunctions have to do with continuities and with the fact that, even given massive global economic changes, Nikkei individuals and communities are basically able to reproduce themselves fairly effectively. Disjunctions, on the other hand, indicate a situation in which ethnic reproduction writ large is not occurring; rather, the disjoining (in the sense of connections, or parts, being severed) of what was once a whole is the predominant trend. The division into these two parts was a substantive one, given that approximately half of the INRP scholars stressed conjunctions, while the other half highlighted open disjunction or situations that implied disjunction.

Once we have presented the eighteen case studies featured in *New Worlds, New Lives*, we return in Part Four to the five propositions concerning the impact of globalization on contemporary Nikkei identities. On this basis, we also discuss the implications the International Nikkei Research Project has for future research in the Americas and beyond.

Lane Ryo Hirabayashi
Akemi Kikumura-Yano
James A. Hirabayashi

*The anthropologist Arjun Appadurai highlighted the importance of "disjuncture" in his widely cited article "Disjuncture and Difference in the Global Cultural Economy," *Public Culture* 2 (Spring 1990): 1–24. We use this term in chapter 2 in a related fashion but without drawing from Appadurai's five "landscapes."

Contributors

Editors

LANE RYO HIRABAYASHI, Senior Editor, is Professor of Asian American and Ethnic Studies at the University of Colorado, Boulder, where he is also a graduate faculty in the Department of Anthropology. His books and anthologies include *Cultural Capital: Mountain Zapotec Migrant Associations in Mexico City* (1993), *Inside an American Concentration Camp* (1995); *Migrants, Regional Identities, and Latin American Cities* (1997), *Teaching Asian America* (1998), and *The Politics of Fieldwork: Research in an American Concentration Camp* (1999).

AKEMI KIKUMURA-YANO, Coeditor, is an anthropologist and Director of the International Nikkei Research Project. She has curated exhibits at the Japanese American National Museum, including "Issei Pioneers: Hawai'i and the Mainland, 1885–1924," "In This Great Land of Freedom: Japanese Pioneers of Oregon," and "The Kona Coffee Story: Along the Hawai'i Belt Road." She is the author of several books, including *Through Harsh Winters: The Life of a Japanese Immigrant Woman*, and *Promises Kept: The Life of a Japanese Immigrant Man*.

JAMES A. HIRABAYASHI, Coeditor, received his Ph.D. from the Department of Social Relations at Harvard University. Subsequently, he was Professor of Anthropology, the Dean of Ethnic Studies, and the Dean of Undergraduate Studies at San Francisco State University. Over the years, in his spare time, he has acted in many plays staged by the Center Players and the Asian American Theater Company in San Francisco. His latest project, a study of how four Hirabayashi cousins responded to the mass incarceration of Japanese Americans during World War II, will be published in 2002.

Principal Academic Advisers

EIICHIRO AZUMA is an Assistant Professor of History and Asian American Studies at the University of Pennsylvania and specializes in Japanese American history, immigration/emigration, and U.S.–Japan relations.

LLOYD INUI is Professor Emeritus at California State University, Long Beach, where he was the founding member and director of the Asian American Studies Program and held positions in the Department of Political Science and the Asian Language Program.

RICHARD KOSAKI is credited with the establishment of the public community colleges in Hawai'i. He is Chancellor Emeritus of the University of Hawai'i at Manoa and President Emeritus of Hawai'i Tokai International College. As a Special Assistant to the Governor of Hawai'i, he dealt with international and educational matters.

Chapter Contributors

KOZY KAZUKO AMEMIYA is a Research Associate at the Japan Policy Research Institute, University of California at San Diego.

MAKOTO ARAKAKI is Associate Professor at the Okinawa Christian Junior College.

RAÚL ARAKI is a Researcher at the Museo Conmemorativo de la Inmigración Japonesa en el Perú.

HARUMI BEFU is Professor Emeritus of Cultural Anthropology at Stanford University.

MARCELO HIGA is Associate Professor of Global and Inter-Cultural Studies at Ferris University in Yokohama, Japan.

MASAKO IINO is Professor of History and American Studies at Tsuda College, Japan.

EMI KASAMATSU is Professor of Philosophy at the National University of Asunción, Paraguay.

AUDREY KOBAYASHI is Professor of Geography at Queen's University, Canada.

TERUKO KUMEI is Professor of American Culture and History at Shirayuri College, Japan.

JEFFREY LESSER is a Professor of History and Latin American Studies at Emory.

DORIS MOROMISATO MIASATO is a writer and editor for the newspaper *Perú Shimpo*.

NAOMI HOKI MONIZ is Associate Professor of Portuguese at Georgetown University.

EDSON MORI is with the World Bank in Washington, D.C.

AMELIA MORIMOTO is Director of Research at the Museo Conmemorativo de la Inmigración Japonesa en el Perú.

MASATO NINOMIYA is Professor of Law at the University of São Paulo in Brazil.

STEVEN MASAMI ROPP is an Assistant Professor, Asian American Studies Department, California State University, Northridge.

YASUKO TAKEZAWA is Professor of Anthropology at the Institute for Research of Humanities at Kyoto University.

New Worlds, New Lives

*Globalization and People of Japanese
Descent in the Americas and from
Latin America in Japan*

PART ONE

The Impact of Globalization on Nikkei Identities

Introduction

EIICHIRO AZUMA

Although the era of mass emigration from Japan is over, many persons of Japanese descent are scattered around the globe at the beginning of the new millennium. One estimate has it that by 1993, there were some 1,650,285 living in countries other than Japan. Among them, some 816,034 resided in North America, while another 737,642 lived in Latin America. Large-scale overseas migration from Japan dates back to 1868, the year that marks Japan's entry into the modern world system. Becoming part of the global network of labor, capital, and transportation, the Japanese suddenly found themselves in the middle of rapid socioeconomic changes, which created opportunities for a rural population ready for both domestic and international migration.[1]

Meiji Japan, however, did not allow its subjects to lawfully seek employment overseas until 1885. In 1886, the governments of Japan and Hawai'i concluded the Immigration Convention, which brought contract laborers (kan'yaku imin) to the sugar plantations for the next nine years. Approximately twenty-nine thousand Japanese obtained three-year labor contracts under this agreement. Thousands of Japanese also arrived in other South Pacific destinations for similar contract work.

The end of the nineteenth century saw the earliest attempts to place Japanese immigrants in Central and South America. In 1893 a group of Japanese governmental officials, politicians, and intellectuals organized the Colonization Society and called for the creation of Japanese settlements overseas. They argued that Meiji Japan, like other modern, industrially developing nation-states, would need to expand abroad in order to gain access to larger markets to which to export its surplus population and commercial goods. The society's pet project of 1897 was an attempt to establish an agricultural colony in Mexico. The plan did not succeed, but it marked the beginning of Japanese immigration to Latin America, followed in 1899 by the departure of 790 people to Peru as contract laborers.

In Part One of *New Worlds, New Lives* we present two chapters that offer an introduction to the intricacies of migration from Japan to the Americas. From the beginning, these two chapters reveal complex migration patterns that, in and of themselves, produced diversity in the experiences of Japanese emigrants and their descendants outside Japan.

The anthropologist Harumi Befu opens Part One by offering a historical overview of the dispersal of Japanese emigrants on a global basis. Noting that out-migration from Japan goes back to at least the fifteenth century, Befu acknowledges that the bulk of Japanese emigration to the Americas occurred during the late nineteenth and early twentieth centuries.

Befu next proposes that, in terms of global patterns of migration, there are at least eight different categories of Nikkei, each type arriving in a different destination at a different time, and for a distinctive set of reasons. Befu refers to the emigrants in each of these categories as "Nikkei" and specifies that, although they interact with each other in "complex ways," they recognize each other as such. In terms of his conceptualization of this affinity, Befu's analysis revolves around the idea of globalism. For Befu "globalism" refers to a complex set of processes having to do with Western incursions into Japan during the late nineteenth century, but also to Japan's technological and military development during the Meiji era, in an effort to stave off conquest or colonization by the West. And if, as Befu argues, globalism can be thought of as the movement of capital, knowledge, and other resources from the center to the periphery, and back again, then Japan's entry into the global economy was as both an "exploited" country, and, if one thinks of Korea between the early 1900s and 1945, an "exploiting" country.

The second chapter in Part One, by Lane Hirabayashi, Akemi Kikumura-Yano, and James Hirabayashi, expands upon themes delineated in the preface, as well as those introduced by Befu. The authors posit that since the 1970s globalization—which is actually a multifaceted set of processes, simultaneously economic, technological, cultural, and political, which result in new levels of interconnectedness—has had a profound impact on the world.[2] Hirabayashi, Kikumura-Yano, and Hirabayashi cite a range of theorists in order to identify how globalization affects cultural identities in general. They draw specifically from the work of Stuart Hall in order to develop five propositions in order to conjecture how globalization may be shaping Nikkei identities, in the Americas in particular. These propositions offer readers a framework for considering the historical and contemporary case studies that are presented in Parts Two and Three of *New Worlds, New Lives*, and the editors evaluate their merits in the concluding chapter.

Notes

1. The first part of this introduction draws from my research, in both English- and Japanese-language sources, for the INRP project. These points have appeared in a somewhat different form in the publication *International Nikkei Research Project: First Year Report* (Los Angeles: Japanese American National Museum, 1999). Readers may also find a recent survey useful: Roger Daniels, "The Japanese Diaspora: The New World, 1868–1990," *Pan Japan* 1 (Spring 2000): 13–23.

2. This definition of globalization is derived from Robin Cohen and Paul Kennedy, "Thinking Globally," in *Global Sociology* (New York: New York University Press, 2000). Cohen and Kennedy also characterize globalization as entailing the compression of time and space and the increase of cultural interactions, common problems, "fast-expanding interconnections and interdependencies," transnational organizations, and global social movements. All of these then act upon each other in a "reinforcing and magnifying" fashion.

CHAPTER ONE

Globalization as Human Dispersal

Nikkei in the World

HARUMI BEFU

Japan's Initial Globalization

Most globalization theorists acknowledge that globalization—at least its Western version—had its beginnings in the late fifteenth century.[1] If globalization is a process, as it most certainly is, then historicizing globalization is mandatory for its full understanding. In this spirit, this paper reformulates Japan's modern history in the framework of globalization. Using globalization as the key operational construct, I revisit Japanese history and reframe it in terms of human dispersal as an aspect of globalization.

If Western globalization began toward the end of the fifteenth century, then Japan's globalization also may be said to have begun about the same time. By the fifteenth century Japanese pirates were already sailing the coasts of East and Southeast Asia.[2] In the sixteenth century, Japanese ships were frequenting China and Southeast Asia, carrying silver, swords, and other goods for trade. From 1604 to 1635 as many as 341 permits, called *shuinjo*, were issued by the Tokugawa government to 106 individuals to license foreign trading. These Japanese trading boats were engaged in capital accumulation as much as European boats were. Merchants in Sakai who amassed wealth through trading with Southeast Asia in those days were the equivalent of the merchants of Venice.

With these Japanese ships going back and forth, Japanese communities naturally sprang up all over Southeast Asia. Some of these "Japan towns" had populations in the thousands. Manila in the Philippines, Ayuttaya in Thailand, and Hoian in Vietnam still retain memories, if not remnants, of Japanese residence of those days.

All this overseas expansion of Japanese trading and movement of the Japanese came to an abrupt halt in the 1630s due to Japan's prohibition of overseas trading—except with Dutch and Chinese merchants, and only through Nagasaki. The Tokugawa government also issued a total ban on overseas travel and prohibited the Japanese then living in Southeast Asia from returning to Japan. This seclusion policy was, of course, motivated by the government's fear of excessive missionary activity by Jesuits and the eventual colonization of Japan by European powers, as had happened in the Philippines. In Huntington's terms, this was the first veritable "civilizational clash" between Japan and the West, whereby European civilization threatened Japan's civilizational integrity.[3]

The Second Initiative for Globalization

Japanese territorial expansion through the invasion of Korea had been contemplated from the early years of the Meiji era. In Year One of Meiji emigrant laborers, known as *Gannen-mono*, had left Japan for the Kingdom of Hawai'i, resuming Japan's initiative for human dispersal that had been interrupted in the seventeenth century. Since then, dispersal of the Japanese through emigration has continued into the postwar era. They dispersed not only to North and South America, but to Southeast Asia, continental Asia, Taiwan, Sakhalin, and Micronesia. This dispersal was in large measure a state policy, in part to alleviate domestic population problems, and in part to establish ethnic Japanese foundations in colonial and occupied territories.

The story of Japanese migration to North America is relatively well known and will be left to other papers in this volume. The migration to North America began earlier than that to South America, though not by many decades. The earliest Japanese emigrants to Latin American countries arrived just before the turn of the twentieth century, as well as decades later. Konno and Fujisaki show the earliest Japanese settlers in various Latin American countries as follows: Mexico 1892, Peru 1899, Chile 1903, Cuba 1907, Argentina 1907, Brazil 1908, Panama 1915, Bolivia 1916, Colombia 1921, Uruguay 1930, Paraguay 1930, and Venezuela 1931.[4] Altogether Japan sent 244,334 emigrants to Latin America before 1945. By now there are more Nikkei— Japanese emigrants and their descendants—in Latin America than in North America.

In total, however, more Japanese left for parts of Asia and Micronesia as part of the second wave of human dispersion, that is, in the period from 1868 to 1945, than for both North and South America put together. This dispersion of Japanese in Asia and Micronesia has been all but forgotten because those who left for these parts of the world have mostly either died there or returned to Japan. And most of the latter, too, are by now dead. Thus the history of Japanese dispersion in these parts of the world is now, for most Japanese, just a thing of the past to be forgotten.

This fact should not deter us from appreciating the scope of the dispersion of the Japanese that took place during this period. Before the end of the nineteenth century—at about the same time many Japanese were leaving for South America—Japanese emigrants had already begun going to the Philippines, primarily as construction workers to help build roads in Luzon and Mindanao. During the First World War, due to the demand for local products from Mindanao, emigration to Mindanao increased greatly. Some twenty thousand Japanese lived in Davao at that time. Japanese newspaper publishers, Shinto shrines, Buddhist temples, schools, hotels, clubhouses, and other institutions flourished to the extent that Davao was dubbed "Little Japan."[5] Like most emigrants to North and South America, these construction workers did not initially plan to stay in the Philippines very long. But eventually most of them stayed and married local women. When the Pacific war began and the Japanese army invaded the Philippines, these men were recruited by the Japanese army to take part in the war effort. This meant, first, participating in the atrocities against local civilians for which the Japanese army is now infamous, and, second, near the end of the war, fleeing from the advancing Allied forces into the jungle and mountains.[6]

The media have widely publicized the "comfort women" the Japanese government and military recruited in its colonies and occupied areas in the 1930s and 1940s. We should not forget that Japanese comfort women were also recruited, and very often kidnapped, mostly from the southern regions of rural Japan. They were recruited from the early twentieth century—before the time of non-Japanese comfort women—to be sent to various parts of Southeast Asia.[7] They were assigned—and confined—to brothels to satisfy the sexual desires of Japanese men, both civilian and military, settled or stationed in the area, or passing through it, as graphically depicted in Tomoko Yamazaki's *Sandakan Brothel No. 8.* [8] In Singapore, a major hub for Japanese trading, just before the turn of the twentieth century already nearly nine hundred prostitutes were reported.[9] Similar prostitution quarters were known in Sumatra, Borneo, Malay, Batavia, and elsewhere throughout Southeast Asia. The untold misery that these women suffered was at the foundation of Japan's southern expansion.

Emigrants also went in large numbers to Micronesia upon Japan's acquisition of this area as the League of Nation's trust territory after Germany lost the group of islands as its colony as a result of defeat in World War I. At the peak of emigration, Japanese workers far outnumbered the local population on some of the islands. Here again, as in the Philippines, many Japanese men married local women, producing offspring with Japanese names. Fortunately, here the Japanese treatment of local populations was relatively benign, and most of Micronesia did not turn into a battlefield, relieving the Japanese there from going through the hardships the Japanese in the Philippines had to experience. Again, the Japanese here had to return to Japan in 1945, but they left their children in Micronesia. These offspring with Japanese names are Nikkei, just like so many half-blooded Nikkei who are known as *hapa* in North and South America, as well as in Hawai'i.

As soon as Japan began to acquire colonies—Taiwan with the Sino-Japanese war of 1894–95, Sakhalin Island as a result of the Russo-Japanese war of 1904–5, Korea in 1905 with a rather dubious treaty—these colonies began to be peopled by Japanese, a good portion of whom were sent by the Japanese government. Japanese dispersion was similarly seen in the areas occupied by the Japanese army, including Manchuria—which had been established by a puppet government—coastal China, and insular and continental Southeast Asia. Some emigrants, especially to Manchuria, went as farmers, enticed from eastern and northern Japan by the Japanese government, only to be betrayed and suffer unimaginable hardship. Others went as wealthy capitalists and exploited the locals for personal gain. By 1945 millions of Japanese were residing across the vast expanse of Asia. Even the coastal cities of Siberia saw Japanese communities with thousands of residents.

Ultimately, all this territorial expansion and human dispersal were closely linked with Japan's effort at capital accumulation through the exploitation of colonized and occupied territories. Resource-poor Japan needed to secure territories rich in resources in order to have a successful capitalism. Such colonial exploitation followed the pattern long established by Western empires. Japan, however, confronted Western empires in the competition for resources and soundly lost in World War II. This was the second clash between the Japanese and Western civilizations.

After the defeat of World War II, all Japanese who were in Asia (North, East, or Southeast) or the Pacific—both those in military service and civilians—were supposed to have been repatriated as part of the terms of surrender. As a result, some six million Japanese returned to Japan from all over Asia, including, of course, the former colonies of Sakhalin, Korea, and Taiwan, as well as the Trustee territories in the Pacific. But what is not adequately known is that not all expatriate Japanese returned. For varied and complex reasons, unknown numbers of them—thousands, at least, or perhaps tens of thousands—stayed behind. The so-called orphaned Japanese in China, who were left behind by parents fleeing China, have been widely publicized. But less known are servicemen in Thailand, the Malay Peninsula, and

Indonesia who fled from their troops and remained behind, unwilling or unable to rejoin them after surrender. More than one thousand soldiers in Indonesia and more than seven hundred in Vietnam are said to have remained, many of whom participated in independence movements and played significant roles as military experts. In Vietnam these Japanese were named "New Vietnamese," along with minorities in Vietnam, and thus gained a legal status in society.[10]

In the Philippines, some civilian Japanese were not allowed to be repatriated for a variety of reasons; others were repatriated but found life in Japan intolerable and returned to the Philippines. Many of these Japanese Filipinos had to go into hiding or change their names after the war in order to escape retaliation from local Filipinos for their mistreatment of the local people. Even now most Japanese Filipinos suffer from extreme economic deprivation. The Japanese government extended little help to them until recently. The government has now begun to take a more positive attitude toward the problem by recognizing their Japanese citizenship and granting the benefits they deserve.[11]

The Third Initiative for Globalization

After the war, Japan's globalization resumed. Between the first and second initiatives some 230 years had elapsed, during which traces of Japanese settlements overseas had been all but obliterated, affording no continuity between initiatives. Thus the second initiative had to start totally anew. This was not the case with the third initiative. For one thing, a large number of Nikkei had remained overseas, not only in North and South America, but also in Asia, though in much smaller numbers. For another, the break between the second and third waves of globalization was brief. The repatriation of overseas Japanese began immediately after the war's end in 1945, but it did not end until several years later. In the meantime, Japanese dispersion was already starting anew in the early 1950s. Thus, recognizing the continuity between the second and third initiatives is important in understanding the dispersion of the Japanese in the third period.

By 1994, 699,895 Japanese citizens were living abroad on either a long-term or permanent basis, an increase of 201 percent since 1969. This figure does not include those who lost or gave up Japanese citizenship in order to become naturalized citizens of the countries in which they resided. Nor does it include the approximately two million descendants of immigrants in North and South America and elsewhere who are foreign citizens.[12] These Japanese residents abroad can be categorized into several different types, as described below.

Postwar Emigrants

Japanese dispersal after World War II began in 1952 in the form of a resumed emigration program to Brazil—a program sponsored by the Japanese government—that had been interrupted in the war years.

The Japanese economy was devastated by the war, and Japan could ill afford to feed its population, especially when millions returned from abroad and burdened the already weakened economy. The government figured that it needed to rid itself of excessive population. Emigration was a quick-fix answer to this serious problem. The Foreign Ministry announced a series of emigration plans to cope with the nation's serious population problem. The 1958 plan, for example, provided for the emigration of 101,000 Japanese in five years. Before that, in 1956, the first group of government–sponsored emigrants had left for the Dominican Republic. What awaited them was nothing short of total disaster.[13]

In 1973 the *Nippon Maru* took the last group of emigrants to South America and the emigration program officially ended. This postwar emigration resulted in the formation of communities separate from their prewar counterparts for a number of reasons. When Japanese began to arrive in the United States after the war, especially on the West Coast, where large concentrations of Nikkei could be found, the same phenomenon was observed. One reason for the separation was that the newcomers were relatively young—in their twenties and thirties—when they migrated. Those of a similar age in North and South America from the prewar period were Nisei who were more comfortable speaking English, Portuguese, or Spanish than Japanese and whose identity was definitely more American or Latin than Japanese. These communication and cultural barriers created a social gulf between the two groups. Yet the Issei, with whom newcomers could converse in Japanese, were much older, sometimes their parents' age, and had gone through hardships totally unknown to the newcomers, having lived through abject poverty and having gone through war experiences. This made it difficult to establish a common frame of mind or a ready and deep bond. Thus postwar immigrants tended to form their own communities, though they definitely maintained close relationships with prewar Nikkei communities.

Whether considering the prewar or postwar emigration program, we must note the callousness with which the Japanese government handled it. The saying "*imin wa kimin*" ("emigrants are abandoned people") is very apt here. In both the late Meiji and early postwar periods Japan was suffering from a population increase that could not be supported, especially in rural areas. The government's primary task was to rid itself of excessive population; this being the case, it did not matter much what happened to the Japanese after they left Japan. As a result, government officials hardly investigated the destinations where emigrants were to settle and cared little whether these destinations promised resources emigrants needed to survive, let alone improve their living conditions. Emigration companies that sprang up to exploit the opportunity made blatantly false promises. This collaboration of the government with emigration companies took place for the emigration programs to South America before and after the war, and for those to Manchuria during the war. The Japanese government should be held squarely responsible for its callous neglect of its own citizens.

In the 1970s, by which time Japan had achieved an initial degree of affluence, the Ministry of Foreign Affairs began a program of encouraging the resettlement of elders overseas, especially in the Third World, with the claim that retired Japanese should be able to live comfortably with their pensions because of the difference in the cost of living. This program was criticized from its inception by those who said that the government was trying to rid itself of its welfare burden by exporting economically useless and medically costly elder citizens. Critics called it a modern-day *uba-suteyama*, the legendary mountain where old men and women were abandoned to die. How elderly Japanese were expected to solve obvious problems such as learning a foreign language, let alone adjust to an unfamiliar culture, would not have entered the minds of the officials designing the program. This program, needless to say, folded within a few years.

War Brides

Other Japanese also began to move to and live in foreign countries after the war, though not as "immigrants" in the conventional sense. One such group was composed of the so-called war brides. This phenomenon was associated with the relative poverty and economic deprivation among the Japanese in the postwar years. Many women who, out of desperation, worked on and around military bases came into contact with servicemen and ended up marrying them. Some had unrealistic dreams of obtaining economic security and a better lifestyle in their husbands' countries, only to be rudely awakened by unexpected problems, such as the inevitable culture shock, the husband's low socioeconomic status, having to learn a new language, and learning to live with the husband's kin. These Japanese women were scattered throughout the United States, as most of them married Americans and followed their husbands wherever they returned to settle, rather than moving into areas of high concentration of Nikkei, or people of Japanese descent. This aggravated the problem of adaptation in the United States, since the women could not take advantage of an existing Nikkei community for help. Of course, those who married Australians and others whose homelands had no Nikkei population to speak of suffered the same fate.

Recently these war brides have organized themselves into an international group, and they now hold periodic conventions.[14] Thus after forty or fifty years they still maintain an identity as war brides and think of themselves as a distinct category of Nikkei.

International Marriage

Somewhat later, from the 1960s on, and more earnestly since the 1970s, a different category of Japanese women began to marry foreigners. As in the case of war brides, the so-called international marriages have been mostly between Japanese women and Caucasian men, though opposite cases have always been known and are on the increase, and increasing numbers of Japanese women are now marrying non-Caucasian, especially Asian, men. It is interesting to note that Japanese men tend to marry Asian rather than Caucasian women, though of course opposite cases are also known here.

These women of international marriage, like war brides, almost invariably follow their husbands to their countries, unless the husband holds a job in Japan. Thus most of them are scattered across North America, Europe, and elsewhere. Except for those living in Japan, they do not form a sociological group, as they do not have ways of contacting or communicating with one another, though the current electronic age may well change all of this.

The marriage of Japanese men to Asian—that is, non-Japanese Asian—women may well represent Japan's Orientalizing attitude, whereby Japan adopts a superior and condescending attitude toward the rest of Asia. This view of Asian women as inferior is akin to the view that Orientalist Caucasian men have toward Japanese women, that is, Asian women are looked upon as inferior and willing to serve Japanese men. Asian women are similarly seen by Japanese men as more attractive as wives than Japanese women.

Multinational Businesspeople and Their Families

Japan's postwar exportation of industrial products and capital investment overseas began in earnest in the 1960s. By now Japan's direct investment can be seen in more than one hundred countries, and the total amount is second only to that of the United States. As of 1995, 17,015 Japanese enterprises operated throughout the world as separate legal entities. Of these 7,643 were in Asia, 4,086 in North America, and 3,407 in Europe. These enterprises the world over employed 2,867,959 local hires and 50,657 expatriate businesspeople sent from Japan, generally known as *chuzaiin*.[15]

The scattering of these business expatriates and their families over the world constitutes by far the most important—for Japan's economy, at any rate—of the various types of postwar Japanese dispersals. By now there are a number of Japanese communities abroad with several thousand residents or more that are composed primarily of business expats and their families, plus other Japanese who either service the business expats' community or are hangers-on in them, as described below. Such communities can be found in Beijing, Taipei, Seoul, Hong Kong, Bangkok, Singapore, Sydney, Los Angeles, San Francisco, New York, London, Paris, and Düsseldorf. Japanese food stores, Japanese restaurants (some complete with karaoke facilities), bars, nightclubs, Japanese schools, Japanese bookstores, Japanese travel agencies, Japanese real estate agencies, and Japanese beauty parlors, for example, provide services needed by businessmen dispatched from Japan and their families, while also serving those in these services. The major characteristics of such communities are that the Japanese language is the exclusive mode of communication and that the community is organized on the basis of Japanese cultural values.[16]

The "Service" Community

As the expatriate communities began to grow, Japanese began to establish businesses that cater to the expat communities, be they travel agencies, restaurants, beauty parlors, food stores, bookstores, or gift shops. These businesses were needed by the expat communities because many members, notably the family members of businessmen, spoke little of the local language, especially in non-English-speaking countries, and trusted Japanese more than locals for no better reason than their prejudice. The larger the expat community, the more extensive the service businesses are. The Los Angeles expat community is complete with Japanese real estate agents, attorneys, physicians, employment agencies, used car dealers, and even car repair garages where Japanese is spoken regularly.

At the same time, we should note that business expats and their families, on the one hand, and those servicing them on the other, again constitute separate communities. One might think that both are Japanese from Japan and thus should constitute one and the same community. However, the reality is that these two categories of Japanese have vastly different careers, work patterns, lifestyles, and even worldviews. First of all, expats have been sent from their home offices in Japan and are expected to return home in a finite numbers of years, usually three to five, whereas most of those servicing them have no definite plans to return. Many of those in the "service" community have permanent residency status (known as having a "green card" in the United States). Because business expats plan to return to Japan eventually, they send their children to the local Japanese school, if there is one, or they try to provide an education equivalent to the curriculum in Japan so that the children can re-enroll in Japanese schools or will be prepared to take the entrance examination to high school in Japan. The Japanese school becomes a hub of activities for the expat community. Those in service businesses, on the other hand, having no definite plans to return, mostly send their children to local schools. Their lives revolve around a totally different educational environment.

Although space does not allow for much elaboration, other globalizing countries, such as the United States, Great Britain, Germany, and France, follow roughly the same pattern. Many of the so-called international schools are actually taught in English, following curricula adopted in one or another English-speaking country. Alliance Française, an institution for the education of expatriate French, among others, is located in most parts of the world where a large concentration of French population is found, and Germans have a similar institution. The expat population of a given country, whether Japanese, American, French, or German, tends to form its own community. Thus economic globalization may send people far afield, but those sent abroad do not necessarily become adapted to the local scene or become cosmopolitanized in the sense that Hannerz defines the term.[17] This is not to say that some of the expats do not develop close relationships with members of the local population and with expats from other lands; indeed, many do. But there is a danger in assuming that this is the general trend simply because "the world" is globalizing or because economic globalization spells cosmopolitanization of participants in the globalizing process. We need to differentiate between economic and institutional globalization on the one hand, and adaptations participants make in this economic and institutional process on the other.

Those Who Have Forsaken Japan

Since the 1970s a new breed of Japanese has been leaving Japan in increasing numbers, though the 1960s had already seen their predecessors. As Ishitoya says, these Japanese do not leave Japan because they are poor, or because they want to strike it rich abroad.[18] If they wanted to make money, they could have done it much more easily in Japan than where they are now. These Japanese have left Japan for a number of reasons. One is dissatisfaction with their situations in Japan. For women, gender discrimination in work, whether in employment or in independent business, is clearly a major reason. Some become aware of the problem while still in school, even before they start their first jobs; others become quickly disillusioned with the lack of opportunities for women. Also, Japanese society is especially unkind to marginal individuals, such as divorced women and Korean residents. For men, frustration with not being able to realize their potential and dissatisfaction with the excessive demands placed on them at work are important factors in their decisions to resign from their jobs and leave Japan. Salarymen and scholars have left Japan for these reasons. Another common pattern is for business expats to become so enamored with their assigned countries that they decide to stay there and resign from the company. They either start their own business there, such as a Japanese import-export business, using the networks and contacts they cultivated before resigning, or they become a "local hire" of a Japanese company. In spite of a considerable reduction in pay and benefits, they choose a life abroad over being sent back to Japan. These Japanese are at least content with their current situation; most of them are extremely happy that they left Japan and with the work they are doing now. It is these Japanese who fill a great deal of the rank and file of the service community.

Another group of Japanese now living abroad left the country without any strong motive to establish a life overseas. They left Japan because they were curious about exotic places, or because they were bored with life in Japan. With this group, it is important to stress their adventurous spirit, their willingness to face the unknown and take risks. A generation ago such souls were rare. Those were the days when Japanese tended to travel in the comfort and security of groups, in organized tours easily identified by the group flag carried by the tour guide. The economy of group travel notwithstanding, the spirit of independence required of individual travel was lacking in most Japanese in those days. But more recently, young Japanese traveling alone are a common sight. It is these independent-minded youths who, while abroad, find something irresistibly attractive about a place and end up staying there. This "something" may well be a romantic partner, but more likely it is a job or a profession, plus the social and cultural amenities that they find suitable to them.

Whatever the motivation for leaving Japan to live abroad, for this group of Japanese who have left the country since the 1970s, there is no question that they are riding the tide of Japan's economic success. It is only because of the strong yen that they can save up enough funds, even by working part-time, to travel abroad and stay there long enough to establish themselves.

Conclusion

In historicizing Japan's globalization in terms of the dispersion of its population, we have defined three major periods. In the first two periods the initiative for dispersion was disrupted and a new effort had to be made to reinitiate the process. The first period of dispersal was preceded by a century of exploration and piracy along the Chinese coast, and trading mainly with China in the fifteenth and sixteenth centuries, but trading with Southeast Asia began in earnest after the Jesuits brought guns to Tanegashima in 1543. From that time on, through the early seventeenth century, Japanese moved southward and their settlements dotted the Southeast Asian landscape. This ethnoscape, à la Appadurai, was a result of Japan's mercantile effort at capital accumulation, at which merchants were extremely successful.[19]

But the economic initiative of the merchants was ineffectual before the political power of the Tokugawa shogunate, and their efforts came to naught when shogunate edicts of the 1630s instituted seclusionary measures in order to avoid a clash of civilizations, one advancing with Christianity and the other defending itself with Buddhism and native Shinto.

Had this initiative not been disrupted by the edicts of the Tokugawa shogunate, what might have happened is a contrafactual question historians disdain from entertaining. Nonetheless, it is enticing to speculate about the consequences. Japan may well have become a colony or colonies of European powers, as the Tokugawa shogunate dreaded. On the other hand, Japanese merchants may have further expanded their activities from Southeast Asia into South Asia and even the Middle East. The Japanese ethnoscape correspondingly would have covered a good portion of coastal Asia. But this expansion had to be left to the next period of Japan's globalization, which did not come for more than two centuries.

By the time the second period of globalization started, due to its previous isolation Japan had lagged farther and farther behind in technological and military development. The second initiative for Japan's global expansion began with catching up with and emulating the Western model of globalization. Territorial expansion and human dispersion were crucial steps toward this goal, and that of obtaining resources for capital accumulation. Human dispersal had two motives. One was to solve problems of overpopulation. Excess population was to be drained off to other countries, notably to North and South America and to colonized and occupied parts of Asia. The second motive was to establish Japanese ethnic foundations in colonies and occupied territories. By the end of World War II, more than six million Japanese were living outside Japan.

But this expansion again came to naught in 1945 as a result of the second civilizational clash between Japan and the West. Virtually all Japanese in Asia and the Pacific had to be repatriated, and Japan's human dispersal had to begin anew after the war, with the notable exceptions of North and South America.

In addition to those Nikkei who had remained from before the war, mostly in North and South America, but also throughout Asia, we recognize seven types of dispersal in this period. More or less chronologically, they are 1) war brides, 2) emigrants to South and North America, 3) those involved in international marriages, 4) multinational business expatriates and their families, 5) those who provide a service infrastructure for the business expat community, and, finally, 6) those who have more or less abandoned Japan out of discontent with their situations there.

Thus one may recognize several types of Nikkei communities abroad in a particular locale. In North America one finds the largest number of different types of communities, except that postwar immigrants are much fewer there than in South America. Europe also has most of these types, but not the pre-war and postwar immigrant Nikkei communities. South America has more pre- and postwar immigrants than any other region but relatively few of the other types. Asia has a few Nikkei from before the war, although their numbers are declining, but it has no postwar immigrants from Japan in the traditional sense, very few war brides, and relatively few Nikkei of international marriage, though their numbers are growing. On the other hand, the expat community and the "service" community are thriving there.

What does the future hold? In spite of the current economic slump, the Japanese economy is likely to at least maintain itself in the near future, and to continue to expand in the long-range future. Given this prognosis, it is safe to say that Japanese business expat communities are here to stay, and, if anything, are likely to develop in areas where we do not currently find them in large sizes, such as China, South Asia, and the Middle East. Along with them, service communities are likely to develop as well. A growing number of Japanese are likely to abandon Japan, given the slow pace with which Japan is reforming its social structure to accommodate women, individualists, and marginal populations. Also on the increase will be the dropout population.

Notes

In addition to being part of the International Nikkei Research Project of the Japanese American National Museum, Los Angeles, this research was also funded by the Institute for Cultural and Human Research, Kyoto Bunkyo University, Japanese Ministry of Education (Project nos. 10041094 and 08041003), the Ito Foundation, and the Ito Foundation USA. Their generous support is gratefully acknowledged. I also wish to thank all the interviewees in the Hong Kong, Bangkok, Los Angeles, and San Francisco areas for providing valuable personal data so willingly. My thanks are also due Ms. Mari Honda for working on many iterations of the manuscript.

1. See, for example, Immanuel Wallerstein, *The Modern World System: Capitalist Agriculture and the Origins of the European World-Economy in the Sixteenth Century* (New York: Academic Press, 1974).

2. See Michihiro Ishihara, *Wako* (Tokyo: Yoshikawa Kobunkan, 1964).

3. See Samuel Huntington, *The Clash of Civilizations: Remaking of World Order* (New York: Simon & Schuster, 1996).

4. Toshihiko Konno and Yasuo Fujisaki, *Iminshi [I] Nanbei hen* (Tokyo: Shinsensha, 1994), 360–61.

5. See Shun Ohno, *Kanko Kosu de nai Fuiripinrekishi to genzai Nihon to no kankeishi* (Tokyo: Kobunken, 1997), 281–82.

6. See Toshihiko Konno and Yasuo Fujisaki, *Iminshi [II] Ajia Oseania hen* (Tokyo: Shinsensha, 1996), 43–164; and Shun Ohno, *Hapon-Fuiripin Nikkeijin no nagai sengo* (Tokyo: Daisan Shokan, 1991) and *Kanko Kosu*.

7. Konno and Fujisaki, *Iminshi [II]*, 26–29, 193–97.

8. Tomoko Yamazaki, *Sandakan Brothel No. 8* (Armonk, N.Y.: Sharpe, 1999).

9. Konno and Fujisaki, *Iminshi [II]*, 26.

10. Motoo Furuta, "Shokuminchi to Dainiji Sekai Taisen," in Daisaburo Yui and Motoo Furuta, *Sekai no rekishi*, vol. 28: *Dainiji Sekai Taisen kara Bei-So tairitsu e* (Tokyo: Chuo Koronsha, 1998), 124–90.

11. See Ohno, *Hapon-Fuiripin*, 314–18.

12. Japan Somucho, Gyosei Kansatsukyoku, ed., *Zaikai Hojin no anzen-fukushi no genjo to kadai* (Tokyo: Ministry of Finance Printing Bureau, 1995), 5.

13. Konno and Fujisaki, *Imin-shi [I]*, 284–332.

14. See Hiroshi Aoki, "Nikkei kokusai kekkon koryu sekai taikai," *Kaigai iju* 576 (1997): 7.

15. See Shukan Toyo Keizai, ed., *Kaigai shinshutsu ikigyo soran Kunibetsu hen '96* (Tokyo: Toyo Keizai Shinposha, 1996).

16. Harumi Befu and Nancy Stalker, "Globalization of Japan: Cosmopolitanization or Spread of the Japanese Village?" in Harumi Befu, ed., *Japan Engaging the World: A Century of International Encounter* (*Japan Studies* [Teikyo Loretto Heights University] 1:1 [1996]: 101–20).

17. Ulf Hannerz, "Cosmopolitans and Locals in World Culture," *Theory, Culture and Society* 7:2–3 (1990): 237–51.

18. Shigeru Ishitoya, *Nihon o suteta Nihonjin* (Tokyo: Soshisha, 1991), 9.

19. Arjun Appadurai, *Modernity at Large: Cultural Dimensions of Globalization* (Minneapolis: University of Minnesota Press, 1996), 29.

CHAPTER TWO

The Impact of Contemporary Globalization on Nikkei Identities

LANE RYO HIRABAYASHI

AKEMI KIKUMURA-YANO

JAMES A. HIRABAYASHI

In this chapter we will define the terms "Nikkei" and "Nikkei identities," and briefly examine the concept of community, since these constitute the primary focus of this anthology. We will also discuss our approach to studying the impact of globalization on Nikkei identities in more detail, and delineate five propositions in this regard.

Nikkei and Nikkei Community: Stipulative Definitions

From the beginning of the INRP project, we stipulated a number of basic definitions so that we would have a common framework for initiating and discussing our specific research projects.[1]

We defined "Nikkei" as a person or persons of Japanese descent, and their descendants, who emigrated from Japan and who created unique communities and lifestyles within the societies in which they now live. The concept also includes the *dekasegi*, or persons who returned temporarily to live and work in Japan, where they often had a separate identity from that of the larger Japanese population. "Nikkei" also potentially encompasses people of part-Japanese descent, to the extent that they retain an identity as a person of Japanese ancestry. Being Nikkei, in other words, has primarily, but not exclusively, to do with ethnic identity.[2]

We also stipulated from the beginning that "Nikkei community" refers to social networks and institutions set up by people of Japanese descent in their home nations in order to meet their varied needs as an ethnic group.[3] Nikkei community institutions often have a tangible territorial base, but they do not necessarily have to.

As we began to assess the INRP research papers after they were submitted in early 2000, we came to two conclusions. First, it seemed more appropriate to speak of Nikkei identities, in the plural. This is because even though Japanese living abroad might share a core identity as people of Japanese descent and as people who had created new lifestyles in overseas settings, there were clearly variations having to do with prefectural background, the type of destination (urban or rural), the dynamics of community formation (weak to strong), gender, and so forth.[4] Second, the research papers revolved around one of two opposing themes with regard to Nikkei identities. About half of the INRP scholars focused on the basic maintenance and reproduction of these identities at the end of the millennium. The rest of the INRP scholars, however, focused on a range of new developments among people of Japanese descent in the Americas, arguing to one extent or another that it wasn't clear whether the term "Nikkei" could really encompass these new experiences.

In order to highlight and respond to this division, we decided to organize the chapters into two major sections representing continuities in Nikkei identities (what we are calling "conjunctions") as opposed to disjunctions, which have to do with the fragmentation of Nikkei identities. Moreover, we decided that an interesting way to assess what is actually going on, as well as why and how, would be to take the debates generated by the International Nikkei Research Project and position them vis-à-vis current theories of globalization.

Globalization and Its Impacts

As stated previously, our primary goal in *New Worlds, New Lives* is to inquire if, how, and why globalization has impacted the evolution of Nikkei identities. In order to ask such questions, we need to determine what globalization is, and to conjecture how it might affect cultural identities generally, as well as Nikkei identities in particular.

Although some scholars argue that global phenomena are not new, it is generally accepted that contemporary globalization—or "all those processes by which the peoples of the world are incorporated into a single society"—is much more pervasive than ever before.[5] In a comprehensive assessment of the topic, the political scientist David Held and his colleagues posit that the term "globalization" is, "a process (or set of processes) which embodies a transformation in the spatial organization of social relations and transactions—assessed in terms of their extensity, intensity, velocity and impact—generating transcontinental or interregional flows and networks of activity, interaction, and the exercise of power."[6] In this sense, Held and other theorists of contemporary globalization such as Anthony Giddens propose that globalization has multiple dimensions in terms of finance and capital flows, technologies of communication and transportation, political relations, and cultural manifestations.[7]

Cohen and Kennedy usefully identify six characteristic features of globalization, which are worth listing here. Contemporary globalization entails 1) the marked compression of time and space, 2) increasing cultural interactions, 3) common problems, such as environmental pollution, 4) extensive interconnections and interdependencies, 5) transnational organizations, and 6) global social movements (which for Cohen and Kennedy include diasporas as well as international indigenous organizations). Moreover, as Cohen and Kennedy point out, "All the dimensions of globalization—economic, technological, political, social and cultural—appear to be coming together at the same time, each reinforcing and magnifying the impact of the others."[8]

For our purposes here, we propose that many of these dimensions of globalization are a direct or indirect result of the fundamental expansion of capitalism and capital to a qualitatively new level.[9] As Gary Teeple emphasizes, "Globalism is that stage in the development of capitalism in which corporations have superceded their former political embodiment, the nation state, and asserted themselves in strictly corporate form at the global level within a supra-national framework."[10] In this sense, contemporary globalization—the preconditions of which date to the 1970s—entails "the unfolding resolution of the contradiction between ever expanding capital [versus] national political and social formations."[11]

Beyond this, for social analysts who focus on its cultural impacts, globalization engenders globalism, a qualitatively different awareness that prioritizes the world as a whole.[12] In terms of the impact of globalization, in this regard, McGrew highlights "those processes, operating on a global scale, which cut across national boundaries, integrating and connecting communities and organizations in new time-space combinations, making the world in reality and in experience more connected.... These new temporal and spatial features ... are among the most significant aspects of globalization affecting cultural identities."[13] In the same light Giddens notes that, while globalization processes are inconsistent and uneven, globalization is said to produce a unification of sociocultural orientations that tend to break down national political and economic boundaries.[14]

More specifically, Crook et al. propose that globalization has an impact on identities because new, pervasive forms of global capitalism have two consequences.[15] At one level, due to increasing levels of control, centralization, and commodification, global capitalism leads to hyper-rationalization.

At the same time, the requirements of global production entail increasing levels of specialization, complexity, and thus differentiation. Because these processes are occurring across the world, irrespective of national boundaries, Crook and his associates note that the contradiction between monocentrism and hyper-differentiation serves to disassemble locally, regionally, and nationally based forms of organization. The impact on local forms of production, family, religions, political parties, and the state is that these institutions become increasingly separated from their traditional, often territorially circumscribed, functions.[16]

Stuart Hall on Globalization and Cultural Identities

Social theorist and critic Stuart Hall has adopted this general framework and has extended it with great insight, commenting on its implications for the realm of what he calls "cultural identities."[17] We draw from Hall's synthesis because it is relevant to our concerns here; it can also be utilized to develop propositions that can be operationalized and assessed as follows.

In the case of national and ethnic identities, Hall proposes that globalization can either intensify or erode them. Erosion occurs as per our previous discussion of differentiation or fragmentation. The "old bottles" of nationality and cultural identity basically can no longer contain all of the "new wines" of identity, so to speak, that are being generated. As for intensification, Hall argues that the same dynamics of differentiation and fragmentation can produce such strong feelings of resentment and resistance that they actually end up reinforcing traditional national or ethnic identities.

If globalization can reinforce or erode modern identities, Hall emphasizes that it can also be the source of new identities. Hall further proposes that when we try to conceptualize the cultural impact that economic globalization has, we must consider three possible outcomes: the development of global consciousness, the development of global market cultures, and the creation of "hybrid" identities.

Many authors cited in this chapter discuss the possible evolution of a truly global awareness. In this sense, globalism has a populist, democratic quality insofar as it appeals to a higher consciousness of one world, or the world as a whole. The implication is that such a perspective could have transformative political implications if millions of people started to think and act in this fashion (as we have already seen, in part, in regard to a global consciousness concerning environmental issues).[18]

On the downside, and as an extension of global levels of commodification, some theorists posit the development of a new global culture or cultures, but primarily in terms of consumer-driven markets. Here, specialized niches of consumers with a similar consciousness as determined by a similar set of interests and values evolve worldwide. One of the frequently cited examples along these lines is MTV, which profoundly influences the sale of albums, videos, concert tickets, clothes, and other consumer items. This has allowed artists such as Madonna to have an impact on youth culture on a global basis.[19]

Finally, Hall posits one additional outcome vis-à-vis globalization. It is possible, he notes, that globalization will produce brand-new "hybrid" identities that are transcultural in nature, being more than the sum of syncretic combinations simply made up of elements of older identities.[20] As we understand it, Hall is not talking about the "global" level here. Rather, he is suggesting that these new identities may also appear at a more localized level, but still go far beyond the traditional cultural identities involved in nationality or ethnicity per se.

Five Propositions About Globalization and Nikkei Identities in the Americas

Adapting Hall's approach to our own purposes, we advance the following propositions.[21] If globalization is having an impact on cultural identities, we should be able to examine a specific ethnic minority population, such as the Nikkei in the Americas. We should thus be able to find support for one of the following assertions about the impact of globalization on Nikkei identities and community formations.

First, we may find that globalization has had no visible impact on Nikkei individuals or identities. If this is indeed the case, then we should expect to find evidence that the reproduction of ethnic identities and ethnic communities has continued and continues as usual.

Second, we may find that globalization acts to intensify Nikkei identities and community formations. Here the standard forms are basically reproduced, but they are especially fixed and unchanging. It is their very lack of modification that makes them an act of defiance or resistance against a dominant power.

Third, globalization may erode Nikkei identities. In such a case we would also expect to find increasing levels of disorganization or fragmentation in Nikkei communities.

Fourth, economic globalization may result in a greater consciousness of and identification with the world as a whole. Thus people of Japanese descent may come to prioritize the integral connection between all people, in terms of issues and problems that impact everyone, equally. If this kind of situation prevailed, one would expect that Nikkei identities, as well as community formations and institutions that revolve around ethnic ties, would gradually fade away.

Fifth, following Hall, we might expect that a series of new "hybrid" identities emerge as globalization predominates. Again, as that happens, one would expect Nikkei identities to erode. These new identities would be characterized by new, creative configurations that do not directly mirror more traditional, or more fully global, identities. Again, one would expect ethnic community formations and their institutions to fragment, if not dissolve, since the latter are predicated upon the former.

Conclusion

In the previous chapter, Harumi Befu emphasized our need to examine the dynamics of the world system historically in order to understand the pattern of Japanese migration overseas. We fully agree with this point but also propose that contemporary theories of globalization—especially those theories that address how globalization impacts cultural identities—offer critical tools for assessing the evolving nature of Nikkei identities in the new millennium.

In this chapter, in order to respect and respond to INRP scholars' differing claims about Nikkei identities, we have had recourse to globalization theory as a useful tool for helping us to assess what is going on. We have outlined five propositions concerning how globalization might be expected to impact Nikkei identities in the Americas. Clearly, globalization theory does suggest that cultural identities will be impacted one way or another by the massive economic, technological, political, and sociocultural changes that have occurred since the 1970s.

Parts Two and Three of *New Worlds, New Lives* feature seventeen case studies. Since we, as organizers of the INRP team, gave participant researchers broad guidelines for examining Nikkei identities, we can assert that their topics and findings have not been unduly influenced by the framework introduced in this chapter. Therefore, we submit that the substantive cases presented in Parts Two and Three constitute a reasonable data base that was not overdetermined or biased in terms of theories concerning the impact of globalization on cultural identities.

On this basis, in Part Four we will draw from these case studies in order to assess the five propositions, as well as the possible future of Nikkei identities in the Americas and beyond.

Notes

1. These definitions were presented in two sets of materials distributed to participants at INRP meetings in the summers of 1998 and 1999. The 1999 documents were handed out in a large binder simply titled *INRP Assessment and Planning Meeting, June 24–25, 1999*, Los Angeles, California.

2. A useful discussion of the concept of "identity" is presented in the recent book by Richard Jenkins, *Rethinking Ethnicity: Arguments and Explorations* (Thousand Oaks, Calif.: Sage, 1997). In his first chapter, Jenkins identifies four key features of ethnicity that we have found useful for our work here. He posits that ethnicity 1) is about differentiation, 2) is a matter of both shared meaning and social interaction, 3) is not fixed, but rather is an evolving component of "the culture of which it is a component or the situations in which it is produced," and 4) is both individual and collective (pp. 1–15; 165–70).

In these terms Nikkei identity is a symbolic social construction negotiated by individuals and communities. It reflects a sense of affinity resulting from a shared set of historical experiences and common interests, as well as a shared lifestyle. At one level, Nikkei identity refers to individual identity and identification with an ethnic community, but at another level Nikkei identity is subsumed within a greater identity as a resident of a given home nation.

3. The INRP research framework also specified that Nikkei community was based on a common worldview, entailed culture building, and was always and by definition interactive with the host country. This was and is clearly a heuristic definition. The concept of "community" is an extremely slippery one. For a discussion of the use of the concept in Asian American studies, see Lane Ryo Hirabayashi, "Back to the Future: Re-framing Community-Based Research," *Amerasia Journal* 21 (1995): 103–18. For a list of some of the key Japanese American community studies, up through the early 1980s, see Lane Ryo Hirabayashi, *Asian American Community Studies: Selected References* (Chicago, Ill.: Council of Planning Librarians, 1982), Bibliography No. 94.

4. Harumi Befu's discussion in chapter 1 details such variation, through time and on a global basis.

5. M. Albrow, "Globalization, Knowledge and Society: An Introduction," in M. Albrow and E. King, eds., *Globalization, Knowledge and Society* (London: Sage, 1990), 9, as cited in Robin Cohen and Paul Kennedy, *Global Sociology* (New York: New York University Press, 2000), 24.

6. David Held, Anthony McGrew, David Globlatt, and Jonathan Perraton, *Global Transformations: Politics, Economics, and Culture* (Stanford, Calif.: Stanford University Press, 1999), 16. A useful companion piece, which presents excerpts from many key writings, is David Held and Anthony McGrew, eds., *The Global Transformations Reader: An Introduction to the Globalization Debate* (Cambridge: Polity Press, 2000).

7. In *A Runaway World* (New York: Routledge, 2000), Anthony Giddens offers a succinct overview of the concept and impact of globalization. Needless to say, some of the manifestations of globalization, such as transnational migration and linkages, date back many centuries as Befu, citing Wallerstein, points out. We acknowledge this, but agree with Giddens that the scope and the scale of globalization have changed, quantitatively and qualitatively, since the 1970s.

8. Cohen and Kennedy, *Global Sociology*, 24–34.

9. This is in accordance with our interpretation of Stuart Hall's views on the matter, as presented in two essays, "The Local and the Global: Globalization and Ethnicity," and "Old and New Identities, Old and New Ethnicities," both of which appear in Anthony D. King, ed., *Culture, Globalization and the World System: Contemporary Conditions for the Representation of Identity* (London: Macmillan, 1991), 19–39; 41–68. For the record, we acknowledge that Giddens and others believe that globalization is more than the sum of its economic dimensions; see "In Conversation" (Anthony Giddens and Will Hutton), in Will Hutton and Anthony Giddens, *Global Capitalism* (New York: New Press, 2000), 1–51. That is certainly true, but we find Hall's identification of capitalism as the material base of globalism both elegant and useful. Another useful resource that gathers a wide range of pieces documenting the impact of global capitalism on globalization is Frank J. Lechner and John Boli, eds., *The Globalization Reader* (Malden, Mass.: Blackwell, 2000).

10. Gary Teeple, "What is Globalization," in Stephen McBride and John Wiseman, *Globalization and Its Discontents* (New York: St. Martin's Press, 2000), 9–10; 21–22. This is another volume that situates economic dynamics at the foundation of contemporary globalism.

11. Ibid., 9.

12. Roland Robertson, *Globalization: Social Theory and Global Culture* (London: Sage, 1992).

13. As cited in Stuart Hall, "The Question of Cultural Identity," in Stuart Hall et al., *Modernity: An Introduction to Modern Societies* (Malden, Mass.: Blackwell, 1996), 619.

14. Anthony Giddens, *A Runaway World*. Similar arguments are presented in the anthology by Evelyn Hu-DeHart, ed., *Across the Pacific: Asian Americans and Globalization* (Philadelphia, Penn.: Temple University Press, 1999), 16; *passim*.

15. Stephen Crook, Jan Pakulski, and Malcolm Waters, *Postmodernization* (London: Sage, 1992).

16. Malcolm Waters, *Modern Sociological Theory* (Thousand Oaks, Calif.: Sage, 1994), 310–20. Our debt to Waters's commentary in this regard, which clearly identifies so-called "postmodernism" as a spin-off of globalization, deserves acknowledgment. For an interesting analysis of how globalization has had an impact on gender and family roles, see the chapter "Family," in Anthony Giddens, *Runaway World*.

17. Hall, "The Question of Cultural Identity," 618–29. As noted, our approach and the five propositions that follow owe a great deal to Hall's framework.

18. For examples of the impact of globalization and globalism on environmental issues, see "Toward a Sustainable Future: The Green Movement," in Cohen and Kennedy, *Global Sociology*, 321–39.

19. For a treatment along these lines with regard to the impact of mass media on youth culture and consumerism, see Jack Banks, *Monopoly Television: MTV's Quest to Control the Music* (Boulder, Colo.: Westview Press, 1996), especially chapter 5, "MTV and the Globalization of Popular Culture," 89–116. A general overview with pertinent examples is available in chapter 14, "Media and Communications," in Cohen and Kennedy, *Global Sociology*, 248–64.

20. For the concept of transculturation, see the classic work of the anthropologist Fernando Ortiz, *Cuban Counterpoint: Tobacco and Sugar* (Durham, N.C.: Duke Uni-

versity Press, 1995) (originally published in Spanish in 1947). Ortiz developed this concept to get at new cultural forms that go well beyond the domains of assimilation or syncretism in terms of the mutuality of influence.

21. Note that in these propositions we attend to community as an integral dimension of the reproduction and maintenance of Nikkei identities. This differentiates our approach from Hall's, and is largely a result of the substantive findings presented in the chapters that follow in Part Two regarding the centrality of community formations for Nikkei identities.

Conjunctions of Nikkei Identities

Introduction

LLOYD INUI

Part Two of *New Worlds, New Lives* foregrounds the themes of community formation and the politics of ethnic reproduction, especially as these have affected the maintenance of Nikkei identities. As the eight different chapters in this part indicate, this was a central theme that captured the attention of almost half of the INRP scholars. Four authors focused on the evolution and maintenance of Nikkei communities and identities. Of the four remaining authors, two focused on the topic of Japanese language and moral instruction in Nikkei communities in the Americas (North and South), and two focused on the topic of Nikkei in the political arena, locally and nationally.

This emphasis highlights what we are calling the conjunctions of Nikkei identities. In this sense, these eight chapters make it clear that Nikkei identities and communities are being reproduced into the new millennium, and that community formation itself is a key condition for said reproduction. In addition, the topics that the INRP scholars chose indicate that education (in terms of Japanese language and moral instruction) and ethnic political power grew out of the community base and, in turn, reinforced it. Thus, there is solid evidence that, given the context of a strong community formation, Nikkei identities are being reproduced in a similar fashion (and sometimes even in the same ways) as they have been in the past.

Part Two begins with the chapter "In Search of the Hyphen," by the historian Jeffrey Lesser. Lesser is concerned with the different strategies that Nikkei utilized in order to retain their ethnic heritage, even as they sought inroads into the mainstream society, as early as the 1930s. Taking a diachronic perspective, Lesser meticulously discusses the formulation and implications of 1) an initial "hyphenated" Japanese-Brazilian identity, 2) an ultra-Japanese identity, and 3) what he terms *"brasilidade,"* which is marked by the acceptance that Japanese immigrants and their progeny had evolved into true Brazilians. These transitions, however, were not smooth; rather, Lesser proposes that the identities of Japanese immigrants and their descendants clashed as each generation struggled in order to situate themselves at once with respect to Japan and to Brazil, their host society.

As Lesser notes, Brazilians of Japanese descent entered the political mainstream shortly after the end of World War II. Initially they were able to do so largely because of their concentration in certain states, such as São Paulo, or in local towns or districts. In recent decades, taking advantage of this "critical mass" has become no longer viable, and Japanese Brazilian candidates must appeal to the larger electorate in order to prevail. In a fascinating passage, Lesser argues that political aspirants may play up their Japanese heritage in order to inspire confidence in the electorate that they are more hard-working, frugal, and honest than Brazilian candidates from other ethnic backgrounds. Equally interesting, Lesser identifies a special Okinawan dynamic to all of this, given that Japanese Brazilians of Okinawan descent may claim that they are also closer to "real" Brazilians by background and temperament than non-Okinawan (*Naichi*) Japanese. We can see that "Nikkeiness" can take twists and turns in Latin America that the term itself would not allow us to predict.

In her chapter on LARA relief materials and the Nikkei, historian Masako Iino documents the now little-known relief efforts by people of Japanese descent in the Americas and Hawai'i. These people were deeply saddened by the destruction that the Allied victory visited upon prefectures like Tokyo, Hiroshima, and Okinawa, from whence many Japanese overseas could trace their roots.

As Iino makes clear, this sympathy and desire to help were not necessarily motivated by either agreement with the politics of the Japanese Empire or the plans and activities of the Japanese military throughout Asia. The sacrifices of the people of Japanese descent in the Americas and Hawai'i are intriguing precisely because they were being made by populations that had suffered their own wartime losses, including outright expropriation and imprisonment in some cases. In this situation, we must remember the profound risk that people of Japanese descent were assuming by "aiding the enemy," even though, by 1945, this enemy had been soundly defeated.

In an unknown number of cases informal aid was sent overseas by family members to help kin back in Japan. Iino also documents in detail the chronology of the relief efforts of organizations in the Americas that sought to provide aid to Japan immediately after the war. Readers will be surprised by the number of different groups, and by the size of the contributions raised during this difficult era.

In his study of Issei and Nisei identity formation in Peru, Raúl Araki begins by noting similarities between the arrival of Japanese in Peru and Hawaiʻi in terms of the early contract labor arrangements on plantations and the subsequent move to the cities. Araki tells us that by 1924 Japanese had settled in thirteen different provinces in Peru, although Lima was already the site of an important concentration of persons of Japanese descent. In addition, by the 1930s, the intragroup diversity of the Japanese immigrants and their children had increased based, in part, on rural versus urban locales, divergent economic pursuits, *mestizaje* (racial mixing), and political orientations. Under the United States' influence, both before and after the attack on Pearl Harbor, Peru pursued a policy of putting increasing restrictions on the Japanese Peruvian population, including "anti-alien" property laws and, in 1942, the deportation of more than two thousand Japanese nationals and second-generation Peruvians of Japanese descent.

As Araki describes it, Japanese Peruvians were intent on participating in Peruvian society. This was exemplified by the formation of "The Generation of '64," a group of progressive second-generation Japanese Peruvian students who advocated the advancement and integration of their generation in their home country.

Although outsiders might think that the situation of former Peruvian president Alberto Fujimori was a culmination of such aspirations, Araki indicates that this was not really the case. In point of fact, although the Japanese Peruvian community had fielded political candidates with some success, Fujimori was not well known in that community. At the same time, perhaps ironically, Fujimori's expertise with publicity meant that Japanese Peruvians were pushed as a group, by force of circumstance, into the national spotlight, whether they identified with Fujimori or not, and whether they liked it or not. Moreover, Fujimori himself freely used popular images and even stereotypes of Japan and the Japanese in order to underscore supposed features of his personal character, as well as his global connections.

In her chapter "The 'Labor Pains' of Forging a Nikkei Community," Kozy Amemiya focuses on the little-known history of people of Japanese descent in Bolivia. There were actually three different trajectories that must be considered in this regard. After delineating the first two cohorts of migrants, Amemiya focuses on the most recent group, the postwar immigrants and their descendants who live in the eastern lowlands of the Department of Santa Cruz. Arriving in Bolivia from Okinawa and other parts of Japan between the mid-1950s and the mid-1960s, these immigrants built two distinctive agricultural settlements, San Juan Yapacaní and the Colonia Okinawa.

Amemiya's ethnography captures these two communities during a moment of transition. She contrasts the older with the younger immigrants, finding that the older Issei in the provinces steadfastly retain their identities as Japanese. In part, this may be a result of the fact that Japan—under the auspices of the Japan International Cooperation Agency (JICA)—has given much in the way of aid and technical support to the farmers. In addition, there is the implication that Japanese immigrants see themselves as superior to the Bolivian masses, even while the former regard the latter in a generally positive light. In this fashion, hierarchies of racial formation in a given country must perforce take into account the position of an immigrant's country of origin as compared to that of the host society in the world system.

As Amemiya indicates, however, recent issues are causing intragroup dissension and division. She focuses on a number of different debates surrounding the centennial celebration of Japanese immigrants to Bolivia. She also discusses how the younger Issei and Nisei are pushing for a political voice within the larger Bolivian polity. This is a story that is still in progress, but as Amemiya observes, "What the Nisei do in coming years is the key to the future direction of the Nikkei community in the Santa Cruz region and, in fact, in all of Bolivia."

Historian Teruko Kumei offers a fascinating study of the development of Japanese language schools in the United States. What Kumei demonstrates, first, is that tensions between the United States and Japan, which were already growing in response to the curtailment of immigration rights and the treatment of Issei in the American west, had a decisive impact on the evolution of Japanese language schools' curriculum. Second, Kumei is concerned with documenting how Issei community leaders and parents debated the pros and cons of Americanization—even to the point of questioning whether there was any merit to having Japanese language schools to begin with. The importance of this fact is that the Japanese immigrants clearly understood the delicacy of the situation they were in, and their lively debates indicate that they were empowered: they were actively seeking the best strategies to acculturate to the larger society, even as they tried to pass the Japanese language and heritage along to their children.[1] Readers should also note how different the strategies of Nikkei in the United States were from, say, the orientation of post–World War II Issei and Nisei in contemporary Paraguay, as described by Emi Kasamatsu in chapter 8.

Very involved in the community herself, Kasamatsu has been a leader in the development of schools and curricula in her native Paraguay. In comparison to the Japanese in other Latin American countries, Japanese Paraguayans are a smaller, newer, community. Thus it was only in the 1980s that the education of second-generation children came to the forefront as a serious issue.

What is striking about Kasamatsu's chapter is that it suggests that the Japanese Paraguayans' experience reflects a strong Japanese influence and orientation. In fact, immigrants have generally retained their Japanese citizenship, and their children have dual citizenship. Almost all Nisei in Paraguay have been taught Japanese, and Japanese cultural traditions appear to be firmly in place. In some of Kasamatsu's other studies, she indicates that in the past the Japanese Paraguayans have exhibited an attitude of ethnocentrism with respect to the Paraguayans, indicating that Japanese Paraguayans feel they are culturally superior. On the other hand, for Kasamatsu the development of leadership training, by which the Paraguayan Nikkei youth can be encouraged and taught how to bring the best of their heritage to help solve pressing national problems, is a critical goal for the twenty-first century.

Amelia Morimoto's subject is the recent political experience of Japanese Peruvians. In her chapter "Peruvian Nikkei: A Sociopolitical Portrait," Morimoto presents an analysis based on two original censuses, one administered in 1989 and the other in 1998, just two years before Alberto Fujimori resigned from office.

Morimoto's data confirm the fundamental heterogeneity of the Japanese Peruvian population. A sector of this population, perhaps 60 percent, has either out-married, is assimilated into the larger Peruvian society, is not engaged with the Nikkei community, or feels actively disaffiliated from it. Morimoto's survey of Peruvian Japanese taps the opinions of those persons who more or less self-consciously identify as such. The 1989 census reveals the feelings of some five thousand persons of Japanese descent in response to questions about Peru, Japan, and the self-image of Japanese Peruvians. The 1998 census follows up on this with a sample of sixty, but focuses directly on the presidency of Alberto Fujimori and how Fujimori's reelection impacted Peruvians' perceptions of their compatriots of Japanese descent.

Again, what is striking about the 1998 data is the heterogeneity of the Japanese Peruvians' responses, which range from positive to negative, from passionate to indifferent. Still, while noting this heterogeneity in her conclusion, Morimoto finds that "the Nikkei, in significant percentages, maintain opinions and even a certain mindset distinct from the national population regarding specific national issues." Moreover, Morimoto found that, although generational differences are visible in her data, "there aren't such significant differences with respect to gender"—an interesting finding given Doris Moromisato Miasato's observations about Peruvian Japanese women in a subsequent chapter.

In the last chapter in Part Two, Lane Ryo Hirabayashi draws from Peter Eisinger's analysis of the evolution of ethnic political traditions in order to see if it sheds any light on people of Japanese descent in the Americas. Hirabayashi's approach is broadly comparative. He discusses three "positive" cases of empowerment—as found in a city (Gardena, California), a state (Hawai'i), and a country (Brazil)—and contrasts these to three "negative" cases at the city, state, and national levels, cases in which one might expect empowerment to occur but where it hasn't to date.

Hirabayashi's analysis is twofold. First, he identifies three different "pathways to power" that politicians of Japanese descent have followed. The politicians can be divided into the following groups: 1) those that rely upon a large and active base of Nikkei in their communities (as found in Gardena and in Hawai'i), 2) politicians who appeal to the public at large, even as they appeal to the ethnic constituency and take up their causes (as seen increasingly in Brazil and Hawai'i since the 1970s), and 3) the politicians of Japanese descent who have few ties to the community and who don't necessarily relate to its causes, but who are able to find popular support outside the ethnic group.

Hirabayashi also notes that the broad conditions posited by Eisinger, which are supposed to be correlated with the evolution of an ethnic political tradition, do not seem to be very applicable to people and populations of Japanese descent in the Americas, with the possible exception of Hawai'i. Hirabayashi believes that related questions might make an interesting research topic for future scholars: of what, exactly, is the unique ethnic political tradition of Japanese Americans in Hawai'i made up? And why is Hawai'i the only site that can boast important political careers for women of Japanese descent, such as Patsy Takemoto Mink, Jean Sadako King, and Patricia Saiki?

In conclusion, what is striking about these eight chapters is that—as much as they focus on different historical periods, differing conditions in Japan as the point of origin, and different destinations—they all feature the issue of community formation as a central theme. Certainly, there were Japanese immigrants who were not able to form communities, but the secondary literature is fairly clear on the point that these families and individuals tended to lose their distinctive identities as persons of Japanese descent within a generation or two.[2]

Nonetheless, both before and after World War II, where their numbers and degree of concentration were sufficient, the Issei have striven to build a range of community organizations.[3] These organizations became important vehicles for promoting common goals via cooperation and mutual aid, even as they provided an environment that was comfortable and enjoyable for immigrants and their children. Thus, the case studies presented by Jeffrey Lesser, Masako Iino, Raúl Araki, Kozy Amemiya, and Steven Masami Ropp

all testify to the importance of community in the maintenance and reproduction of Nikkei identities in the Americas, across time and through space.
And as almost all of the chapters in Part Two indicate, community formations have been a critical means for people of Japanese descent to seek empowerment for themselves, on their own terms, within any given home
country in the Americas. Whether we look at the chapters about education,
language, relief aid, or politics, this point is quite striking.

Notes

1. It is worth mentioning the case of Hawai'i here. Japanese Americans on the
Islands resisted the state's attempts to regulate Japanese language schools. The legal
battle went all the way to the Supreme Court, which ruled, in the 1927 decision regarding the Farrington v. Tokushige case, that the state government's actions were
unconstitutional (Richard Kosaki, personal communication).

2. In her detailed study of the state of the Japanese Peruvian community in 1989,
cited in chapter 9, Amelia Morimoto's survey revealed that some 40 percent of the
population of Japanese descent in Peru were in fact disaffiliated from the ethnic
community. This finding is supported by publications about Latin Americans of
Japanese descent in countries such as Brazil, Bolivia, and Cuba; see Christopher A.
Reichl, "Stages in the Historical Process of Ethnicity: The Japanese in Brazil, 1908–
1988," *Ethnohistory* 42 (Winter 1995): 52–56. Generally, it appears that assimilation
occurs in settings where persons of Japanese descent are isolated and in loose contact
with compatriots (and with Japan), and also where people of Japanese descent are
relatively well accepted.

3. Interested readers can refer to the companion volume to *New Worlds, New
Lives*, Akemi Kikumura-Yano, ed., *Encyclopedia of Japanese Descendants in the Americas: An Illustrated History of the Nikkei* (Walnut Creek, Calif.: AltaMira Press, 2002),
for histories of each of the major populations of Japanese descent in Latin America
and details about community formation and maintenance. A classic study along
these lines—and actually the first major study of a Japanese American community
on the U.S. mainland—that details the Issei's efforts in this regard is S. Frank Miya-
moto, *Social Solidarity Among the Japanese in Seattle* (Seattle: University of Washington, 1939).

CHAPTER THREE

In Search of the Hyphen

Nikkei and the Struggle over Brazilian National Identity

JEFFREY LESSER

> We, Brazilian descendants of Japanese, will testify in the future
> that we feel our hearts beating strongly, filled with love for the
> Brazilian pátria although our veins flow with Japanese blood.[1]
>
> Cassio Kenro Shimomoto's lead editorial
> in the first issue of *Gakusei*, 1935

> The Japanese colonists . . . are even whiter than the Portuguese
> [ones].
>
> Federal Deputy Acylino de Leão
> in a speech before the House[2]

> Who are we: Japanese or Brazilian?
>
> Lead editorial in the first issue of the
> magazine *Japão Aqui* (1997)[3]

This chapter analyzes the relationship between ethnicity, prejudice, and social integration by focusing on competing historical strategies used by Nikkei
in their attempts to gain political and social power in Brazil. I suggest that
the internal competition over the definition of terms like "Japanese," "Brazilian," and "Nikkei" was mirrored in majority society, creating a scenario in
which Nikkei embraced *both* an imagined uniform Brazilian nationality *and*
a series of new postmigratory ethnicities. These identities were multiple and
often contradictory, and the symbols available to draw upon and rework
were in constant flux. Over the course of the twentieth century, immigrants
and their descendants thus reformulated ethnic distinction to appropriate
Brazilian identity.

Japanese immigrants and their descendants created three flexible, competing, and intertwined public strategies in their struggle for Brazilian ethnicity: hyphenation, ultranationalism, and *brasilidade* (Brazilianness). Some
argued that all "japonês" were ethnically "white," proposing to render their

premigratory identities harmless in return for inclusion in the pantheon of traditionally desirable groups. A second group proposed that "whiteness" was not a necessary component of Brazilianness. Instead they promoted the idea that Brazil would improve by becoming more "Japanese," a term constructed to mean economically productive or supernationalist. These individuals sought to interpret class status as a marker of Brazilian identity, allowing ethnicity to be maintained even as its importance was dismissed. They also proposed that a presumed blind loyalty to the Emperor prior to migration would be turned into modern Brazilian nationalism, including absolute loyalty to the state. A third group of immigrants and their descendants seemed to reject all forms of inclusion by creating ultranationalist groups that, at least on the surface, sought to maintain political and cultural loyalty to Japan. The most famous of these, the Shindo Renmei, emerged in 1946, continued through the mid-1950s, claimed more than one hundred thousand members, and proposed that Japan had *won* World War II.

While many of the strategies I analyze were Brazil-specific, it would be erroneous to assert that some aspects of "Nikkeiness" did not cross formal state boundaries. Brazilian Nikkei, for example, used a form of post–World War II contributions to refugee relief in Japan as a means of local ethnic maintenance, just as Canadian Nikkei did via the Licensed Agencies for Relief in Asia (LARA). Furthermore, the diasporic sense of community found among Okinawans in Brazil can also be found elsewhere, notably in Hawai'i.[4] From a different perspective, the participation of Nikkei in explicitly ethnic politics in Brazil is mirrored in the United States.[5]

Competing Strategies

In mid-1908 the first 781 members of what would become the world's largest Japanese diaspora community arrived in Brazil as part of a much larger immigrant stream that began in the nineteenth century (see Table 3.1).[6] The Brazilian discourse on the newcomers was contradictory: it mixed a social fear of "Mongolization" with a desire to mirror Japan's economic and social development. This duality put Japanese immigrants in a unique position within Brazil's complicated racial schema in which a combination of class and color defined "race." Thus, even as Brazilian legislators prohibited federal subsidies for Asian immigrants in 1910, Japanese found themselves excluded "from the category of Asiatics" and thus formally placed in the highly desirable category.[7] Brazilian notions were reinforced by Japanese diplomats who eagerly promoted the notion that their subjects were "white."[8] Soon a "model minority" discourse (to use a contemporary concept) emerged that suggested that Japanese immigrants would lead Brazil to

TABLE 3.1

Immigrants Entering Brazil, 1872–1969, by Decade

	Portuguese	Italian	Spanish	German	Japanese	Other
1872–1879	55,027	45,467	3,392	14,325	—	58,126
1880–1889	104,690	277,124	30,066	18,901	—	17,841
1890–1899	219,353	690,365	164,293	17,084	—	107,232
1900–1909	195,586	221,394	113,232	13,848	861	77,486
1910–1919	318,481	138,168	181,651	25,902	27,432	123,819
1920–1929	301,915	106,835	81,931	75,801	58,284	221,881
1930–1939	102,743	22,170	12,746	27,497	99,222	68,390
1940–1949	45,604	15,819	4,702	6,807	2,828	38,325
1950–1959	241,579	91,931	94,693	16,643	33,593	104,629
1960–1969	74,129	12,414	28,397	5,659	25,092	51,896
TOTAL	1,659,107	1,621,687	715,103	222,467	247,312	869,625

SOURCE: Maria Stella Ferreira Levy, "O Papel da Migração Internacional na Evolução da População Brasileira (1872 a 1972)," Revista de Saúde Pública, supplement 8 (1974), 71–73.

economic and military power by recreating Japan's ostensible homogeneous society. As deputy Nestor Ascoli noted in a speech to Rio de Janeiro's Legislative Assembly, "the small and ugly Japanese recently sneered and did what he had to do, beating the tall and formidable Russian. The Japanese is now a better element of progress than the Russian and other European peoples." By harping on the idea that "intellectually the Japanese is frighteningly superior," Ascoli suggested that immigrants would help Brazil match the production levels of Japanese industry.[9]

From 1908 to 1923 about thirty thousand Japanese immigrants entered Brazil. In the decade beginning in 1924, however, the numbers exploded as more than 140,000 newcomers arrived, helping to create a Nikkei community that by the mid-1930s was well over half a million. Increasing visibility helped propel a "Campanha Anti-Nipônica" into the public sphere. Federal Deputy Fidélis Reis, a professor at the University of Minas Gerais who had led a movement to ban black immigrants, presented motions to the Congressional Commission on Agriculture in 1921 and 1923 that would limit new Asian entries because "the yellow cyst will remain in the national organism, unassimilable by blood, by language, by customs, by religion."[10] This powerful anti-Japanese sentiment was picked up by Miguel Couto, the president of the National Academy of Medicine, who rapidly became the most vocal proponent of the Campanha Anti-Nipônica, claiming that Japanese immigration was part of an expansionist plot to destroy the Brazilian nation.[11]

Since the debate over Japanese immigration was as much about assimilation as about production, the "pro" group had to marshal "scientific" evidence for the position that Japanese would rapidly be transformed into Brazilians. Japanese immigrant newspapers frequently printed statistics in their

Portuguese-language sections suggesting that of every one hundred marriages involving a Japanese immigrant, twenty-five were to Brazilians, usually women.[12] Such claims were ludicrous: a massive historical census of the almost four hundred thousand members of Brazil's Japanese community conducted in the late 1950s shows that exogamy among immigrants was rare. Between 1908 and 1942 the rate was less than 2 percent among immigrants and less than 6 percent among Nikkei. A smaller study, done in the early 1950s, reports that most marriages between Japanese and *caboclos* (rural Brazilians of mixed ancestry) "failed abjectly."[13]

Whatever the reality of intermarriage and Brazilian identity among immigrants, all those interested in continuing mass Japanese entry realized that the promotion of such ideas was critical. One tactic involved the proposition that Brazilian Indians and Japanese immigrants were of the same biological stock. If this assertion were accepted, Asians would be recognized as the progenitors of those who resided in the Amazon, making them more authentically Brazilian than most citizens.[14] The famed anthropologist Edgard Roquette-Pinto claimed that modern Japanese had emerged from the mixing of whites (Ainus), yellows (Mongols), and blacks (Indonesians), thus mirroring Brazil's "racial" development.[15] Bruno Lobo, whose ardent public support of Japanese immigrants garnered him the "Order of the Rising Sun" from the Japanese Empire, insisted that "Mongolian blood . . . incontestably exists in Brazil through the Indians and their descendants of mixed parentage," making Japanese and Brazilians "unique" (peculiar) in their lack of prejudice.[16] He even suggested that since the "Indian was similar to the Japanese" and since Indian/Portuguese mixing had created the "formidable Bandeirante Race," Japanese immigration would strengthen Brazilian society by creating a more original race in areas "abandoned by the European element."[17] An article in Rio's *Gazeta de Notícias* went even farther, claiming that "the Brazilian People already have a strong percentage of Mongol blood," a position repeated by Deputy Oliveira Botelho, who believed that "Our aborigines, of obvious Mongol origin . . . crossed with the Portuguese resulting in the *bandeirantes*."[18]

By suggesting that Japanese were Brazilians and vice-versa, those in favor of Japanese immigration were able to wrap the inherent racism of eugenics theory around itself. Such sentiments reached a wider public with the regular publication of photographs of "Brazilian" looking children who were, at least ostensibly, of Japanese and Brazilian or European parentage.[19] The pictures were almost always in books and pamphlets published with the financial support (both open and hidden) of Japanese cultural organizations, and were of a uniform type: white children produced by Japanese men married to white Brazilian women (or white European immigrant women). The symbolism of these photographs was both obvious and hidden. On the surface they gave the message that Japanese immigrants were an elite group, interested only in, and able to attract, those of high racial status in Brazil. Ironically, the photographs had a far different meaning from that based on the patrilineal Japanese perspective, according to which children born of Japanese fathers were considered genetically Japanese, irrespective of their physiognomy.

Brazilians who favored Japanese immigration may have honestly believed that science was on their side when they claimed a special relationship between Japanese and Brazilians. Japanese officials and immigration leaders, however, played with the discourse in ways that appear more strategic than heartfelt. When Japan's minister in Brazil visited Pará in the early 1920s he is reported to have frightened a Brazilian peasant when he confused him with an immigrant and struck up a conversation in Japanese.[20] Hachiro Fukuhara, a Japanese businessman who later founded a Japanese agricultural colony in the state of Pará, returned from an exploratory trip to the Amazon claiming that Brazil was "founded by Asiatics" because "the natives who live along the River Amazon look exactly like the Japanese. There is also a close resemblance between them in manners and customs . . . [and] a certain Chinese secretary in the German Embassy at Rio [has] made a careful study [of language] and concluded that these Indians descended from Mongols."[21]

Claims of a unique Japanese/Brazilian cultural affinity also emerged from interpretations of religiosity among immigrants. Here again, the Nikkei elite realized that religious practice was an important component of their public negotiation of Brazilian national identity.[22] Thus many in the Japanese diplomatic corps worked to make both immigrants and Nikkei into public Catholics.[23] In 1918 Ryoji Noda of the Japanese legation insisted that shrines and temples not be constructed in Brazil. In the 1930s a member of the Tenrikyo sect, which at the time was actively suppressed in Japan, was given permission to emigrate only after promising not to proselytize among immigrants. Kumao Takaoka, a scholar whose 1925 book on Brazil was widely read in Japan, suggested that all emigrants convert to Catholicism, and the 1.7 percent of Catholics among Japanese entries between 1908 and 1936 (a percentage significantly higher than the Catholic population in Japan) were featured prominently in articles and books.[24] An attempt to create cultural norms that could be taken as evidence of a special Japanese ability to become Brazilian can also be seen in sports. For example the *jogo do bicho*, a widely played but officially prohibited game of chance based on choosing animals to which numbers correspond, was one piece of evidence used to suggest the rapid transformation of Japanese immigrants into ultra-Brazilians. Whether Japanese immigrants won at the *jogo do bicho* more than anyone else is doubtful, but the newcomers' proficiency was legendary. One argument revolved around language, suggesting that the Brazilian saying "*O bicho leva so vício*" (the animal game leads only to addiction) had a special meaning for Japanese because the word "*vício*" (addiction) was pronounced by Japanese speakers as "*bicho*" (animal). The following story uses a similar convoluted logic:

> One day a Japanese immigrant, unsure on which animal he should place his bet, was eating a banana to which a grain of rice was stuck. The immigrant realized that the ideogram for "rice" could be decomposed into three parts, one of which represented the number eighty-eight. The number eighty-eight in the *jogo do bicho* represented a tiger, and the immigrant won handsomely with his bet.[25]

The story, of course, is not only about an immigrant striking it rich. Indeed, there is no reason for the banana in the story since it is the ideogram for rice that leads to the winning choice. Yet the placement of the stereotypical Brazilian fruit next to the quintessential Japanese food transforms the tale from one about gambling into one about the construction of a Japanese-Brazilian identity.

Taken together, these various manifestations (or assertions) of national identity sought to answer the very complex questions that immigrants, Nikkei, and members of majority society were asking in pre–World War II Brazil: How "Japanese" could or should a "Brazilian" be? How "Brazilian" could a "Japanese" be? Japanese immigrants and their descendants found an opportunity to provide one answer in mid-1932, when São Paulo began its "Constitutionalist Revolution" in support of delayed presidential elections.[26] Two young Japanese-Brazilians joined the unsuccessful opposition forces, becoming folk heroes among the Nikkei generation and important figures in the battle to define a Japanese-Brazilian ethnic space.

Cassio Kenro Shimomoto, who had arrived in Brazil as a baby, was a student at São Paulo's elite São Francisco Law School when he volunteered to fight along with the Brazilian-born José Yamashiro. Both were hailed for their decision after Shimomoto declared to a *Diário de S. Paulo* reporter that he was "before anything . . . a Brazilian."[27] Yamashiro's moment of fame came when a letter from his father published in the Japanese-language *Nippak Shinbun* was translated and sent to *O Estado de S. Paulo*. The elder Yamashiro played on the notion that Japan had a particularly nationalistic culture to suggest that Nikkei were uniquely Brazilian, thus naturally leading his son "as a Brazilian and Paulista, [to] obey the natural impulse to pick up arms to defend his State."[28] The message was clear: the best Brazilians were those whose loyalty was natural, and it was "Japanese blood" that insured this quality.

The positive publicity that stemmed from Nikkei participation in the 1932 revolt, however, was forgotten the following year when two unrelated issues came together during a period of relatively open political debate. The first was the establishment of a constitutional convention, charged with a producing what would become the Constitution of 1934, and the second was an increasing Japanese military presence in Manchuria. Debates about Japanese immigration thus became more public, as issues of imperialism, assimilation, and nationalism were conflated.

When it began to appear that the new constitution might place limits on Japanese entry, the Japanese government went on the offensive. Large advertisements in major newspapers promoted the high levels of production in Japanese colonies.[29] A family who had settled in the Recife area was extolled for making Brazil modern by setting up the Sorveteria Gemba, the first ice cream shop in northern Brazil.[30] The Japanese government also began publishing Portuguese-language books that asserted the "Brazilianness" of Japanese laborers. In the preface to *Aclimação dos Emigrantes Japoneses* (Acclimation of Japanese Emigrants), Guisuke Shiratori, the director of the semigovernmental Kaigai Kogyo Kabushiki Kaisha (Overseas Development Company) in Brazil, wrote, "I have the honor to direct the adaptation and nationalization of the Japanese emigrants . . . who are cultivating the land of this friendly and welcoming country that is Brazil and . . . are integrating themselves into your people, for themselves and for their children."[31]

The Constitution of 1934, passed in late April, did include an immigration amendment modeled on the U.S. National Origins Act of 1924. Although the amendment was designed to restrict Japanese immigration, U.S. diplomats understood that Japan's position as a buyer of many Brazilian agricultural products meant that the wording had to "cause as little offense as possible to Japan."[32] The new quota officially reduced Japanese entry to 3,500 a year, a marked drop from the 23,000 who entered in 1933.

From the halls of São Paulo's elite São Francisco Law School, with its progressive and anti-Vargas tradition, came the most sophisticated response to the Constitution of 1934. In 1935 law student and former soldier Cassio Kenro Shimomoto and a number of colleagues founded the Nipo-Brazilian Student League to promote the place of Nikkei within the "Brazilian race" via cultural, educational, and sporting events. The organization's name, with its explicit hyphen, emphasized that ethnicity and nationality were two separate yet connected items. José Yamashiro, another founder of the league, had a straightforward position on the subject: "Since we were here we had to act as Brazilians."[33] That those who had lived all or most of their lives in Brazil were or had become Brazilian was explained with regularity and care in the league's two newspapers, the Portuguese-language monthly *Gakusei* (Student), which had a circulation of about five hundred, and the more widely read Japanese-language *Gakuyu*, which appeared only occasionally but may have had a circulation of over two thousand. *Gakusei* remained in existence for about three years and became the first public expression of a hyphenated culture that was simultaneously Brazilian in nationality (including citizenship, language, and culture) and Japanese in terms of ethnicity (albeit from a collectively remembered rather than an actual Japan in many cases). It had a transliterated Japanese masthead and was written exclusively in Portuguese, suggesting an attempt to negotiate identity from both within and without. An editorial by Massaki Udihara noted that "We are a strange generation," whose problem was that "from our parents . . . we always received a bit of the East and in our schooling a bit of the West." The editors of *Gakusei* often echoed the discourse of the Brazilian elite, insisting that the mixing of Japanese and Brazilian cultures would "create a unique (Brazilian) mentality that condenses in itself the two." This new culture was denominated *dainissei* and was filled with people who were "more Brazilian than Japanese" and who believed "prompt assimilation" would help the country "whose nationality is still . . . in formation."[34]

The editors of *Gakusei* insisted that hyphenated ethnicity explained the kind of Brazilians that descendants of Japanese had become. The first issue's main editorial was entitled "What We Want" and was explicit in its position: "We Brazilians, children of Japanese . . . have the desire to . . . write in the beautiful language of Camões." Yet to embrace Luso-Brazilian culture did not mean accepting the nativism that had emerged from it, nor accepting "accusations that the Japanese form cysts, that they do not assimilate or adapt to Brazilian customs."[35] All the other issues of *Gakusei* contained articles in the same vein, arguing that "We are Brazilian in every way" while attacking intolerance. Yet the monthly was also an expression of the status quo. Articles on Freud and European music sat comfortably next to editorials that tried to energize Nikkei out of the sense of "resignation and indifference" with which they had responded to anti-Japanese rhetoric. Other columns expressed Nikkei ethnicity through plays on the Japanese and Portuguese languages.[36]

The intention of the Nipo-Brazilian Student League was broadly acculturative, but an examination of *Gakusei* suggests that interpretations of "acculturation" varied. Articles like the one lamenting the Nikkei who "prefer Brazilian customs and know almost nothing that is not superficial about the land of their parents" were common.[37] This collective, albeit limited, knowledge of Japan went hand in hand with a Brazilian education and the speaking of Portuguese as the language of social interaction in urban centers. Thus the advertisements in *Gakusei* show that Japanese-Brazilian businesses sought to reach Nikkei by marketing hyphenated ethnicity. The niche of the Nipo-

Brazilian Beauty School, for example, does not appear to have been in hair-styles as much as the context in which "beauty" was taught—"by Nikkei and for Nikkei." Many stores sold Japanese products that were used in "Nikkei" ways unrecognizable in Japan, over time creating an ethnic consumer market for the Brazilian-born with items divorced from their original cultural meanings. By the mid-1930s Nikkei households were distinguishable from both Japanese and non-Nikkei Brazilian ones by their use of symbols (paper lanterns, photographs of Japan, home temples) that in other contexts would not go together.[38]

Gakusei's exploration of Japanese-Brazilian identity ended in November 1937 with the imposition of the Estado Nôvo (New State) by Getúlio Vargas. The new regime, corporatist and authoritarian in nature, markedly changed the ways in which immigrant ethnicity would be treated in Brazil. Less than a month after the *auto-golpe* (since Vargas was already the president of Brazil, he in effect overthrew himself in order to impose the new state), Vargas banned all political parties, and the nationalist rhetoric that accompanied the decision mobilized nativist groups to viciously attack Japanese immigration.[39] Beginning in April 1938, new decrees sought to diminish foreign influence in Brazil, modifying the ways in which the Japanese and Nikkei communities operated. *Gakusei* now only printed community news, facts about Japanese and Brazilian history, and the occasional article complimenting Brazil for its hospitality. More important, the editors of *Gakusei* insisted that both immigrants and their children had been "Brazilianized."[40] In September 1938 *Gakusei* printed its last issue.

In 1939 Vargas initiated the "brasilidade" (Brazilianization) campaign. This state-driven homogenization program sought to protect Brazilian identity from the encroachment of ethnicity by eliminating distinctive elements of immigrant culture. New legislation controlled entry and prevented foreigners from congregating in residential communities. Decrees required that all schools be directed by native-born Brazilians and that all instruction be in Portuguese and include "Brazilian" topics. Non-Portuguese-language materials were prohibited, except by permission.[41] Nikkei had a different attitude than immigrants toward the brasilidade campaign. Although many newcomers contemplated a return to Japan (although they rarely remigrated), Nikkei wondered why their Brazilian citizenship was not a guarantee of recognition as a nonforeigner. In April 1939 the Nipo-Brazilian Student League elected a directorate comprised almost exclusively of Nikkei, including, for the first time, a number of women. One of the first decisions was to create *Transição* (Transition), an advertisement-filled magazine edited by the same group of students who had created *Gakusei*. *Transição*, like its predecessor, focused on hyphenated ethnicity. An editorial in the first issue explained:

We, Brazilian children of Japanese, are a transition. A transition between what was and what will be. A transition between the East and the West. . . . It is the understanding of our parents, the Japanese, by our brothers, the Brazilians, by a common language, Brazilian. The harmonization of two civilizations, apparently antagonistic. The fusion, in an ideal of mutual comprehension, of the qualities inherent in each. In the end, we are Brazilians conscious and proud of our land and that of our parents.[42]

Transição was targeted at both the government censors and the Nikkei community and painted Brazil as a heterogeneous society where eugenics proved that Japanese had become Brazilians.[43] Even so, *Transição* lasted only until 1941, when the Nipo-Brazilian Student League was declared illegal. In that same year a local official in rural São Paulo decided to enforce brasilidade measures to the letter and ended up arresting almost every Japanese resident of the town.[44] These new pressures on the immigrant and Nikkei communities were reinforced as Brazil moved toward the Allied camp after the attack on Pearl Harbor. The house arrest of Brazilian diplomats in Japan led to wild stories of "fifth column" activity in Japanese colonies.[45] The police were ordered to round up Japanese citizens and remove them from strategic locations, and the broadcast of weather reports was prohibited for fear they would be crucial to subversives.[46] Rio de Janeiro's *O Radical* screamed, "Important Japanese Official Is a Potato Planter in Brazil," while *A Notícia* claimed that a family of tomato farmers had a broadcast facility hidden on their farm.[47]

In March 1942 the Vargas regime ruptured diplomatic relations with Japan and began to attack Japan and the Japanese at every opportunity. The Department of Press and Propaganda (DIP), charged with spreading the regime's ideological and cultural directives, reported that a Nikkei informer had discovered a secret Japanese plan to occupy São Paulo with twenty-five thousand troops. The soldiers would be met by spies disguised as fishermen who had readied Japanese colonists to blow up strategic military sites near Santos and create a country in the Amazon called "New Japan."[48] Now Vargas had an excuse for compelling Japanese residents to move from areas defined as "strategic."[49] In Belém do Pará the entire Japanese community was sent hundreds of kilometers upriver to Tomé-Açu; in Recife the owners of the previously hailed Sorveteria Gemba fled the city on their own. In the town of Álvares Machado, some three hundred miles from the city of São Paulo, along the Sorocaba rail line, the Japanese cemetery founded in 1918 was closed.[50]

Although the supposed Japanese plot to invade Brazil never materialized, the social and ethnic tension created by the anti-Japanese attitudes led members of the Japanese and Nikkei communities to strike back against the public order by becoming increasingly "Japanese." Emperor worship, always strong among those educated in the first quarter of the century, soon began to replace ancestor worship as a form of identity preservation.[51] Those who did not actively show their loyalty to Japan were defined as "enemies," and the underground Japanese-language press was filled with denunciations of those judged to have lost their "right" to be "Japanese."[52] Wild rumors spread by Brazilians about Japanese were replicated by immigrants themselves. In Marília, a town with a population of some fifteen thousand Japanese and Nikkei, there was a widely believed report that a monster baby had predicted that Japan would win the war within a year.[53]

Social tension led to the emergence of a series of secret societies whose ultranationalism mixed with a desire to reinforce a space for Japanese-Brazilian identity. These movements would be confined to historical footnotes if they had not begun to expand enormously *after* it became clear that an Allied victory was assured. In May 1945, after the war in Europe ended, Brazil declared war on Japan so that the U.S. military could continue to use bases in the northeast.[54] This made Japanese immigrants the last "enemy aliens" in Brazil, and during this period of intense anti-Japanese propaganda the secret societies garnered their widest support. The idea of Japan's defeat had little resonance among immigrants and Brazilian-born rural dwellers educated in Japan or in Japanese-language schools in Brazil, where the curriculum was developed by Japan's Education Ministry. Furthermore, a ban on Japanese-language newspapers, and the poor circulation of Brazilian newspapers in rural areas, meant that factual information about the war was scarce. Newsreels of the surrender ceremonies, for example, were never seen by Japanese farmers who had no access to cinemas.[55] For many Japanese immigrants, the societies represented a counterattack on the way national identity was defined by demanding new spaces for Japanese-Brazilian ethnicity.

The most powerful of the secret societies was the Shindo Renmei (Way of the Subjects of the Emperor's League), whose leaders were retired Japanese army officers furious at Brazil for "becoming an enemy country." The group emerged after the Estado Nôvo was toppled in a 1945 coup and the subsequent period of wide-ranging political debates created openings for maximalist responses. The society's main goal, which became public in August 1945 following Japan's surrender, was to maintain a permanent Japanized space in Brazil through the preservation of language, culture, and religion among Nikkei and the reestablishment of Japanese schools.[56] What the Shindo Renmei did *not* promote was a return to Japan. Home was Brazil, and by December the Shindo Renmei claimed a membership of fifty thousand who believed that Japan had won the war.[57]

Critical to the growth of the Shindo Renmei was its monopoly on information since the ban on the Japanese-language press continued after Vargas's resignation. The group's circulars and secret newspapers were distributed from sixty-four district offices and found a willing audience among the many immigrants and Nikkei educated to believe in Japan's superiority and invincibility. Personal diaries with notations for August 15, 1945, collected by Susumu Miyao and José Yamashiro are filled with the absolute conviction that news of Japan's defeat was U.S. propaganda, a position repeated over and over in the Shindo Renmei's weekly mimeographed broadsheet.[58] Each Shindo Renmei document mixed fact and fiction: claims that General MacArthur had been imprisoned as a war criminal and that five major newspapers in Rio de Janeiro had been closed by the Vargas regime after reporting Japanese victory in the war were typical.[59] Just a week after Emperor Hirohito broadcast his surrender message over shortwave radio, the Shindo Renmei, playing on rumors already in circulation, released its own statement:

Emperor Hirohito has been forced to abdicate in favor of a regent because he accepted the conditions imposed by the Potsdam Declaration. The imperial combined fleet has been given the order for immediate action, and in a furious battle in Okinawan waters the Japanese navy and air force destroyed about four hundred Allied warships, thus deciding the course of the war. The Japanese employed for the first time their secret weapon, the "high frequency bomb." Only one of the bombs killed more than one hundred thousand American soldiers on Okinawa. [This led to the] "unconditional surrender of the Allies [and)] the landing of Japanese expeditionary forces in Siberia and the United States."[60]

By 1946 the Nikkei and immigrant communities were divided into two camps: the *kachigumi* (victorist) and the *makegumi* (defeatist), the latter calling themselves *esclarecidos* in Portuguese (clear-headed or enlightened).[61] These divisions were reinforced when some Shindo Renmei began to engage in extortion, although there is evidence that for most kachigumi the schemes were seen as donations to a cause rather than commercial transactions. By mid-1946 Shindo Renmei propaganda included altered photos of President Truman bowing to Emperor Hirohito, "press" reports of Japanese troops landing in San Francisco and marching toward New York, and notices that Getúlio Vargas would be signing surrender documents in Tokyo.[62] Soon thereafter a group of fanatical youth were recruited to assassinate both immigrants and Nikkei who spoke against the movement and thus against the place of Japanese in Brazil. The murders began in early March 1946 when five members of the *tokkotai* (the Shindo Renmei assassination squad) shot the director of the Bastos Cooperative, and continued the following month with the assassination of the former editor of *Nippak Shinbun*. Between March and September 1946 sixteen esclarecidos were assassinated, including the head of the Japanese Section of Sweden's Consulate General and a former army colonel who had headed the Cotia Agricultural Cooperative. Thirty other makegumi were seriously injured and hundreds received death threats bearing the Shindo Renmei's trademark skull and crossbones. Numerous silk, cotton, and mint farmers had their homes and fields destroyed.[63]

The killings resonated oddly among non-Nikkei Brazilians. Fears of Japanese militarism and ethnic solidarity were confirmed, but most incomprehensible was the attitude of tokkotai members who surrendered to authorities and then insisted that "Japan did not lose the war. As long as there is one Japanese on earth, even if he is the last, Japan will never surrender."[64] When a raid took place on Shindo Renmei headquarters in early 1946, piles of propaganda materials, a mimeograph machine used to produce the organization's weekly newspaper, and a list of 130,000 members were discovered.[65]

As the years passed a number of factors began to marginalize the kachigumi groups. Efforts to raise funds for Japanese war victims, without ever declaring winners and losers, created "sympathizer" or "hard-liner" groups (the terms were synonymous) that recognized defeat but, in a typical expression of minority group politics, took the position that a "family matter" should not be discussed with majority society.[66] Then, in early 1950, Japanese Olympic swimming champion Masanori Yusa arrived in Brazil with his team, the "Flying Fish." The group was welcomed with great emotion by the Japanese and Nikkei communities, and six thousand people greeted the team at Congonhas Airport in São Paulo. An exhibition match at the Pacaembu Stadium (a major *futebol* arena) was sold out and featured music by the State Military Police Band and the presence of the governor of São Paulo, Adhemar de Barros. During an interview, members of the Flying Fish expressed shock when presented with the idea that Japan had *won* the war. As a result the Shindo Renmei began a poster campaign claiming the swimmers were Koreans masquerading as Japanese.[67] Nikkei and Japanese alike were offended by the suggestion, and the Brazilian government's indictment of more than two thousand Shindo Renmei members in the middle of that year was greeted with relief. The immigrant and Nikkei communities now appeared to be unified, but this was not the case. Soon new divisions would appear as economic and social ascension brought new tensions.

Conclusion: Nikkeiness in Transition

The three strategies used by immigrants and Nikkei in creating their public Brazilian identities have had interesting ramifications. During the 1950s, just as Nikkei had established themselves in the middle and upper classes, a new wave of Japanese immigration began, following the U.S. occupation of Okinawa. Almost fifty-four thousand small landowners and farmers entered

Brazil between 1952 and 1988, some 43 percent following relatives who had migrated prior to the war.[68] Older Japanese residents were shocked by the new attitudes toward everything from the Emperor to sexual relations. The newcomers were equally aghast: they had trouble understanding old dialects filled with Japanized Portuguese words and wondered if earlier immigrants had become "Brasil-bokê" (made nuts by Brazil).[69]

As Japan returned to international power in the 1960s Brazilian Nikkei found themselves both hailed and rejected for their "biological success." An ugly joke that circulated widely among the São Paulo elite reflects this tension: "To get a place at the University of São Paulo, first you have to kill a Japanese." This kind of comment has created a sense among some Nikkei that they can become Brazilian only by changing their appearance, often via plastic surgery. High levels of interethnic marriage (almost 46 percent overall and over 60 percent in some regions of the country) are also a fact of life in the Nikkei community. From the Nikkei perspective majority pressure to stop "being Japanese" is intense, a point the anthropologist Koichi Mori makes in his discussion of exogamy.[70] Popular language focuses on physiognomy, and a recent issue of the political magazine *Momento Legislativo* headlined a story on Japanese-Brazilian relations "Slanty-Eyed Brazil" and made constant references to "the Brazilian Japan." This language is also used within the Nikkei community; an article in *Japão Aqui* (Japan Here), a glossy magazine with an initial circulation of about eighty thousand, used "Brazilian Japan" as the title for an article that combined the history of Japanese immigration with a sociological study of the Nikkei community.[71]

Strategies like intermarriage and plastic surgery have divided the Nikkei population. For the 340,000 "mestiços" in Brazil's population of more than 1.2 million of Japanese descent, the use of multiple identities is common. Many Nikkei *mestiços* reject their Japanese background in social situations yet embrace it in the economic sphere, where there is a belief that being "Japanese" provides an important advantage. For non-*mestiço* Nikkei the situation is somewhat different. They are viewed as "Japanese," which is one important reason that some 135,000 currently live and work in Japan (where they are called *dekassegui*), along with their 55,000 *mestiço* Nikkei and non-Nikkei spouses.[72] Since cultural identity is intimately tied to class status, higher wages in Japan play an important role in this migration (officially, almost two billion dollars was remitted by Brazilians living in Japan to Brazil in 1996, but the actual amount may be twice as high). Even so, oral histories given by *dekassegui*, most of whom work in factories although almost half are university educated, indicate that questions of identity are critical in making the decision to leave Brazil for Japan. A thirty-seven-year-old university professor who migrated in 1991 is typical. "In Brazil I am a stranger even though I like Brazil. I feel like I do not have Brazilian nationality and I feel like a gypsy. I wanted to make myself the perfect Brazilian but this is impossible. But here in Japan I also feel like a foreigner."[73] All Brazilians seem to agree on this point, and terms like "remigration" and "return" are often applied to Brazilians moving to Japan for the first time.

The question of how to maintain ethnic identity in a hesitant national culture is as present now as it was in the 1920s and 1930s. Pressure from majority society to become Brazilian is matched by an immigrant generation that complains that Sansei and Yonsei have become "too Brazilian." *Japão Aqui*, for example, includes a section on how to cook Japanese food in each issue. In the early 1980s the *Diário Nippak* newspaper began publishing a biweekly Portuguese-language supplement that sought to explore the history of Japanese immigration and "the duality of being Nipo-Brazilian." More recently *Japão Aqui* asked, as *Gakusei* did sixty years ago, "Who are we: Japanese or Brazilian?"[74] The Portuguese-language *Made in Japan* is produced in Tokyo for those "who understand Japan and Brazil," and a São Paulo weekly targeted toward teenagers and produced by the primarily Japanese-language *Diário Nippak* has articles about places for young Nikkei to meet. One nineteen-year-old interviewed at a Nikkei dance club stated, "Here [inside the club] we feel at home, we are all from the same nation."[75] These sentiments would undoubtedly be echoed by the many young Afro-Brazilians who have made Afro-dance clubs a rage throughout Brazil.

A search for "home" is not the only Nikkei reaction to the general Brazilian rejection of hyphenated identities. Another is the re-creation of "Japan" as a means for selling oneself as Brazilian. The old notion that Nikkei are "Japanese" (read "honest and hardworking") and thus better "Brazilians" than non-Nikkei "Brazilians" (read "corrupt and lazy") has found its way into popular culture through a television commercial for the state-owned petroleum company in which a grinning and bowing Nikkei sells "Brazilian" fuel to a group of hicks. The message is not subtle: Brazilian gas is good because it is "Japanese" and Brazilian country folk are in need of "Japanization" to become modern and stop retarding national growth. São Paulo's sanitation monopoly takes the same approach, proclaiming "Service so good you would think [the company] was founded by Japanese." Perhaps the most explicit representation of the idea that Brazil needs to become more "Japanese" can be seen in advertisements for the Bamerindus Banking Group, whose print advertisements for almost twenty years have included the phrase "[We] need more Brazilians like this Japanese."[76]

The popular acceptance of the idea that Japanese ethnicity improves Brazilian national identity should not be viewed as merely a call and response between majority society and a well-regarded minority group. For example,

Brazil's Nikkei community is marked by a clear divide between "Okinawan" and "Japanese," a division that is virtually imperceptible to majority society. Yet even this cleavage, and the lack of recognition of it, appears to have become a strategy for asserting Nikkeiness and Brazilianness. Nikkei politicians, a disproportionate number of Okinawan descent even though Okinawans constitute only 10 percent of Brazil's total Nikkei population, offer a striking example of this phenomenon.

In 1996 Koichi Mori, Michael Molasky, and I conducted oral histories with two of Brazil's most prominent Nikkei politicians, Luís Gushiken and Getúlio Hanashiro, both children of Okinawan immigrants. Gushiken is a three-time federal deputy (congressman) from the Workers' Party (PT), was a leader of the workers' movement during Brazil's military dictatorship, and was recently the campaign manager for Luís Ignacio Lula da Silva's unsuccessful presidential bid. Hanashiro, a sociologist, was exiled during the military dictatorship and has served as São Paulo's minister of transportation and minister of health. He is currently a member of the Brazilian Social Democratic Party (PSDB). The interviews showed a striking similarity between the ethnic discourse of the two, despite their clear ideological differences. First, both understood and took advantage of the positive image of Japanese that pervades Brazil. According to Gushiken and Hanashiro (who were interviewed separately), the majority focus on the "Japanese" virtues of hard work, honesty, frugality, and the high value placed on education derives in part from the success of Japanese immigrants in Brazil earlier this century, and in part from Japan's more recent emergence as a world economic power. Not surprisingly, Gushiken and Hanashiro (and their marketing strategists) have deftly deployed these images by marketing themselves as Brazilian candidates distinguished by their Japanese descent. Gushiken's political propaganda, for example, uses everything from a rising sun, to photographs with Japanese diplomats, to faux Japanese-style lettering to suggest that his ethnicity makes him a better Brazilian. Hanashiro recently created "Operation Rescue," which seeks to "save" unemployed Brazilian residents of Japan from the clutches of racist, uncaring foreigners (i.e., the Japanese).

Despite their willingness to use their Japanese ethnicity as a political strategy, both Gushiken and Hanashiro appeared to be somewhat uncomfortable with this tactic. Indeed, given that neither speaks Japanese nor Okinawan dialect, both emphasized their concern that they are referred to as "Japanese" rather than "Brazilian" or even "Nikkei." When asked directly about their identities as Okinawan-Brazilians rather than Japanese-Brazilians, both asserted a strong sense of difference from mainland Japanese immigrants. Thus, their ambivalence about marketing themselves as "Japanese" in the Brazilian political sphere is compounded by their own sense of difference as

Okinawans, a sense that remains essentially invisible to the majority. Indeed, Okinawanness was used by both Gushiken and Hanashiro, as well as other members of the Uchinanchu community, to explain Okinawan political success in Brazil. In a story that suggests a widely shared community discourse (given the number of times it was repeated by different people in different circumstances), Okinawan-Brazilians claim to have a special Brazilianness that "Japanese" cannot achieve. In this formulation, Okinawa and Brazil are constructed as similar "tropical" lands where people enjoy eating pork, enjoy alcohol and parties, and enjoy life. Implicit in the discussion is the notion that Japan is a place of staid people who only work. Shared Okinawan/Brazilian culture, so goes the argument, has been reinforced by the legacy of discrimination that Okinawans suffered at the hands of Japanese officials and immigrants. This discrimination led to a rejection of Japaneseness and an embracing of local culture, making Okinawan Nikkei more "Brazilian" than any other immigrant group, especially Japanese.[77] The struggle for the hyphen is far from over.

Notes

1. *Gakusei: Orgão da Liga Estudantina Nippo-Brasileira* (São Paulo) 1:1 (Oct. 1935).
2. Speech of Acylino de Leão, Sept. 18, 1935, Republica dos Estados Unidos do Brasil, *Annaes da Camara dos Deputados: Sessões de 16 a 24 de Setembro de 1935*, vol. 17 (Rio de Janeiro: Off. Grafica D' "A Noite," 1935), 432.
3. *Japão Aqui* 1:1 (Apr. 1997), 63.
4. Masako Iino, "LARA Relief Supplies and Nikkei," paper presented at the International Nikkei Research Project Assessment and Planning Meeting, June 25, 1999; Makoto Arakaki, personal communication, at International Nikkei Research Project Assessment and Planning Meeting, June 25, 1999.
5. Lane Ryo Hirabayashi, this volume, chapter 10.
6. Secretaria da Agricultura–Diretoria de Terras, Colonização e Immigração, June 30, 1908, file: Wilson, Sons and Co. Ltd., no. 121, pp. 3–7, Setor Manuscritos–Secretaria da Agricultura–Requerimentos Diversos, Ano-1908, Maço-38, Caixa-39, Ordem-7255, Arquivo do Estado de São Paulo.
7. Unsigned letter (Rio de Janeiro) to Ministers Komura and Uchida (Tokyo), Nov. 16, 1909, Japanese Ministry of Foreign Affairs, Tokyo, Japan, 1868–1945; Meiji-Taisho, microfilmed for the Library of Congress, 1949–51 (hereafter JMFA-MT) 38280 284/285/285a; Ryoji Noda, Provisional Minister Substitute in Brazil to Jutaro Komura (Minister of Foreign Affairs, Tokyo), Jan. 6, 1910, JMFA-MT 38280 326/327/327a, Arquivo do Centro de Estudos Nipo-Brasileiros, São Paulo.
8. *Correio da Manhã* (Rio de Janeiro), Nov. 30, 1908.
9. Republished as "Parecer apresentado á Assembléa Legislativa do Estado do Rio de Janeiro pelo Relator da Commissão de Justiça, Legislação e Instrucção Publica, e por esta Unanimente assignado, em 30 de Outubro de 1909, sobre o Contracto de Novembro de 1907 Firmado entre o Governo desse Estado e os Srs. Rio Midzuno e

Raphael Monteiro para a Fundação de Nucleos Coloniaes de Japoneses na Baixada Fluminense," in Nestor Ascoli, *A imigração japonesa para a Baixada do Estado do Rio de Janeiro* (Rio de Janeiro: Typ. Jornal do Commercio de Rodrigues e Co., 1910), 22.

10. Fidélis Reis, *Paiz a organizar* (Rio de Janeiro: A. Coelho Branco, 1931), 233–38. "Parecer apresentado á Commissão de Finanças da Camara dos Deputados em 4 de Julho de 1924 por S. exca. o Sr. Dr. Francisco Chaves de Oliveira Botelho, Deputado pelo Estado do Rio de Janeiro," *Diário do Congresso Nacional*, July 8, 1924; Letter of Clovis Bevilaqua to Fidélis Reis, Oct. 17, 1921, in Calvino Filho, ed., *Factos e Opiniões Sobre a immigração japonesa* (Rio de Janeiro: n.p., 1934), 44; Thomas E. Skidmore, *Black into White: Race and Nationality in Brazilian Thought* (New York: Oxford University Press, 1974), 195; R. Teixeira Mendes to Fidélis Reis, Aug. 15, 1921, in Bruno Lobo, *Japoneses no Japão-no Brasil* (Rio de Janeiro: Imprensa Nacional, 1926), 129–39.

11. *O jornal* (Rio de Janeiro), May 30, 1924; Oct. 26, 1924; Jan. 4, 1925; January 24, 1925. These editorials, along with other statements against Japanese immigration made by Couto, were collected by his son and published as Miguel Couto, *Seleção social: campanha antinipônica* (Rio de Janeiro: Irmãos Pongetti Editores, 1942).

12. *Nippak Shinbun* (São Paulo), Dec. 19, 1934.

13. Comissão de Recenseamento da Colônia Japonesa, *The Japanese Immigrant in Brazil*, 2 vols. (Tokyo: University of Tokyo Press, 1964), Statistical Tables (vol. 1), 356. The study shows that the majority of interethnic marriages were between Japanese men and non-Japanese women. James L. Tigner, *The Okinawans in Latin America*, Scientific Investigations in the Ryukyu Island (SIRI) Report #7 (Washington, D.C.: Pacific Science Board–National Research Council, Department of Army, 1954), 51. For a more recent comment on "ethnic" Japanese marriage see P. Pereira dos Reis, "A Miscigenação e a etnia brasileira," *Revista de história* 12:48 (Oct.–Dec. 1961), 334–36. For a fascinating discussion of the consequences of interethnic relationships see Hiroshi Saito, "O suicídio entre os imigrantes japoneses e seus descendentes," *Sociologia* 15:2 (May 1953), 120–21.

14. See, for example, the editorial in *O Brasil* (Rio de Janeiro), Apr. 26, 1924.

15. Edgard Roquette-Pinto, *Ensaios de antropologia brasiliana* [1933], 2nd ed. (São Paulo: Editora Nacional, 1978), 103.

16. Lobo, *Japoneses no Japão-no Brasil*, 151–52, 157.

17. Interview with Dr. Bruno Lobo, *Correio da Manhã* (Rio de Janeiro), Apr. 26, 1924. A more recent notion of Japanese immigrants as "bandeirantes" can be found in Agostinho Rodrigues Filho, *Bandeirantes do Oriente: drama íntimo dos japoneses no Brasil* (São Paulo: Emprêsa Editora Bandeirantes, 1949).

18. *Gazeta de notícias* (Rio de Janeiro), May 8, 1924. Oliveira Botelho, *A imigração japonesa; o parecer do illustre deputado Oliveira Botelho, apresentado em 8 de julho de 1925, a Comissão de Financas da Camara dos Deputados* (Rio de Janeiro: n.p., 1925), 35.

19. *Folha da Manhã* (São Paulo), July 5, 1934; Lobo, *Japoneses no Japão-no Brasil*, 159; Calvino Filho, ed., *Factos e opinões*, 17, 33, 97, 112; *Cruzamento da ethnia japonesa: hypothese de que o japonês não se cruza com outra ethnia* (São Paulo: Centro Nipponico de Cultura, 1934).

20. *Gazeta de notícias* (Rio de Janeiro), May 8, 1924; Interview with Dr. Bruno Lobo, *Correio da Manhã* (Rio de Janeiro), Apr. 26, 1924.

21. Hachiro Fukuhara, "Brazil Founded by Asiatics?" in *Japan Times and Mail*, June 26, 1927.

22. Constituição de 25 de março de 1824, I-Art. 5; Geraldo Fernandes, "A religião nas Constituicões Republicanas do Brasil," *Revista eclesiástica brasileira* 8:4 (Dec. 1948), 830–57; Jeffrey Lesser, *Welcoming the Undesirables: Brazil and the Jewish Question* (Berkeley: University of California Press, 1994), 56–57.

23. In Brazil it would be odd for a member of the first, or Issei, generation to refer to her- or himself as a "Nikkei." In the Brazilian context, the term "Nikkei" is used to mean "Japanese-Brazilian" (and also sometimes refers to Japanese Americans in the United States), as differentiated from Japanese immigrants to Brazil. For an expanded discussion, see Jeffrey Lesser, *Negotiating National Identity: Immigrants, Minorities and the Struggle for Ethnicity in Brazil* (Durham: Duke University Press, 1999), 125–27.

24. Takashi Maeyama, "O Imigrante e a religião: estudo de uma seita religiosa japonesa em São Paulo" (M.A. thesis, Fundação Escola de Sociologia e Política de São Paulo, 1967), 85–87; *DTCI: Boletim da directoria de terras, colonização e imigração* 1 (Oct. 1937), 38.

25. Tomoo Handa, *O imigrante japonês: história de sua vida no Brasil* (São Paulo: T. A. Queiroz, Centro de Estudos Nipo-Brasileiros, 1987), 185.

26. Hélio Silva, *1932: A Guerra Paulista* (Rio de Janeiro: Editora Civilização Brasileira, 1967); Thomas E. Skidmore, *Politics in Brazil, 1930–1964: An Experiment in Democracy* (New York: Oxford University Press, 1967), 17–19.

27. *Brasil e Japão: duas civilizações que se completam* (São Paulo: Empreza Graphica da "Revista dos Tribunaes," 1934), 238–40.

28. *O Estado de S. Paulo*, Sept. 19, 1932; José Yamashiro, *Trajetória de duas vidas: uma história de imigração e integração* (São Paulo: Aliança Cultural Brasil-Japão/Centro de Estudos Nipo-Brasileiros, 1996), 111–17.

29. *Folha da Manhã*, July 5, 1934; Mar. 28, 1935.

30. Rodriques Caldas, "O Estado de Minas Geraes e a immigração japonesa," published in the *Jornal do comércio* in December 1920 and reprinted in Nestor Ascoli, *A immigração japonesa para a Baixada do Estado do Rio de Janeiro*, 115–27.

31. Kaigai Kogyo Kabushiki Kaisha, *Aclimação dos emigrantes japoneses: Actividades da Kaigai Kogyo Kabushiki Kaisha do Brasil* (São Paulo: Kaigai Kogyo Kabushiki Kaisha, 1934), 3, 39.

32. Report of Joseph C. Grew (U.S. Embassy, Tokyo), Aug. 4, 1934, 739.94/2; John M. Cabot, Third Secretary, U.S. Embassy, Rio de Janeiro, to Secretary of State, May 31, 1934, 832.55/94, National Archives and Record Center, Washington, D.C.

33. Interview with José Yamashiro by author, Michael Molasky, and Koichi Mori, São Paulo, Dec. 12, 1995; John W. F. Dulles, *The São Paulo Law School and the Anti-Vargas Resistance (1938–1945)* (Austin: University of Texas Press, 1986), 26–30.

34. Interview with José Yamashiro by author, Michael Molasky, and Koichi Mori, São Paulo, Dec. 12, 1995; Risseli, "Os Dainiseis e a instrução primaria," *Gakusei* 2:11 (Oct. 1936) and 2:12 (Nov. 1936). See also *Gakusei* 1:4 (Mar. 1936).

35. *Gakusei* 1:1 (Oct. 1935).

36. *Gakusei* 1:3 (Feb. 1936); Rose Fukugawa, "Sob teu olhar," *Gakusei* 1:3 (Feb. 1936).

37. *Gakusei* 2:17 (Sept. 1937).

38. Koichi Mori, "Por Que os Brasileiros começaram a apreciar a culinária japonesa? As condições de aceitação da culinária japonesa na Cidade de São Paulo," unpublished paper (1997) used by permission of the author.

39. R. C. P., "Um Perigo para a nacionalidade:," *Mensario do "Jornal do commeri-cio"* 1:1 (Jan. 1938), 119–24.

40. *Gakusei* 3:22 (Apr. 1938).

41. Decree Law 479 (June 8, 1938), Art. 2, no. 1a; Decree Law 1,377 (June 27, 1938).

42. *Transição* 1:1 (June 1939), 5.

43. João Hirata, "A quem cabe engrandecer o Brasil," and Massaki Udihara, "Assimilação," *Transição* 1:1 (June 1939), 7–10.

44. Takashi Maeyama, "Ethnicity, Secret Societies, and Associations: The Japanese in Brazil," *Comparative Studies in Society and History* 21:4 (Apr. 1979), 589–610, 598; Y. Kumusaka and H. Saito, "Kachigumi: A Collective Delusion Among the Japanese and their Descendants in Brazil," *Canadian Psychiatric Association Journal* 15:2 (Apr. 1970), 167–75.

45. *Diário Carioca*, Mar. 8, 1942; Mario Botelho de Miranda, *Un Brasileiro no Japão em Guerra* (São Paulo: Companhia Editora Nacional, 1944), 265–66.

46. *O Globo*, Mar. 3, 1942; *New York Times*, Mar. 4, 1942.

47. *Diretrizes*, May 21, 1942; *O Radical*, Mar. 6, 1942; *A Notícia*, Mar. 11, 1942; *O Carioca*, Feb. 26, 1942; Samuel Wainer, *Minha razão de viver: memórias de um repórter* (Rio de Janeiro: Record, 1988).

48. *O Globo*, Mar. 21, 1942; *Correio da Manhã*, Mar. 22, 1942; *New York Times*, Mar. 22, 1942.

49. *Diário da noite*, Sept. 30, 1942.

50. Maria de Fátima Y. Asfora, "Colonos japoneses no Brejo Pernambuco: análise de uma trajetória (1956–1994)," paper presented at the IV Encontro Regional de Antropólogos do Norte e Nordeste (João Pessoa), May 28–31, 1995, 9; *Diário Nippak* (São Paulo), July 11, 1980, p. 1.

51. Christopher A. Reichl, "Stages in the Historical Process of Ethnicity: The Japanese in Brazil, 1908–1988," *Ethnohistory* 42:1 (Winter 1995), 31–62.

52. Maeyama, "Ethnicity, Secret Societies, and Associations," 594.

53. Handa, *O imigrante japonês*, 640. A broader analysis of the social meanings of rumor can be found in Patricia A. Turner, *I Heard It Through the Grapevine: Rumor in African-American Culture* (Berkeley: University of California Press, 1993).

54. *New York Times*, June 7, 1945. The Brazilian-U.S. military treaty stated that all bases would revert to Brazil six months after the end of the war.

55. Kumusaka and Saito, "Kachigumi: A Collective Delusion," 167–75.

56. Hekisui Yoshii, "Gokuchu kaikoroku" (Memories from Prison), 1948 manuscript cited in translation by Susumu Miyao and José Yamashiro, "A Comunidade nipônica no período da guerra," in Comissão de Elaboração da História dos 80 anos da Imigração Japonesa no Brasil, *Uma epopéia moderna: 80 anos da imigração japonesa no Brasil* (São Paulo: Editora Hucitec, 1992), 262. Translation of Shindo Renmei documents can be found in "Perigosa Atividade Nipônica em São Paulo," *Arquivos da polícia civil de São Paulo* 8:2 (1944), 567–71; Emilio Willems and Hiroshi Saito, "Shindo Renmei: um problema de aculturação," *Sociologia* 9 (1947), 143. Analysis of the Shindo Renmei and similar movements can be found in Takashi Maeyama, "Ethnicity, Secret Societies, and Associations," 589–610; Susumu Miyao and José Yamashiro, "A Comunidade Enfrenta um Caos sem Precedentes," in Comissão de Elaboração da história dos 80 anos da imigração japonesa no Brasil, *Uma Epopéia*

Moderna, 265–360; and James L. Tigner, "Shindo Remmei: Japanese Nationalism in Brazil," *Hispanic American Historical Review* 41:4 (Nov. 1961), 515–32.

57. See a translation of Shindo Renmei objectives and statutes in the report of João André Dias Paredes to Major Antonio Pereira Lira (State Police Chief, Paraná), Apr. 30, 1949, Secretaria de Estado de Segurança Pública, Departamento da Polícia Civil, Divisão de Segurança e Informações, No. 1971, Sociedade Terrorista Japonesa. Arquivo Público Paraná, Curitiba. Mário Botelho de Miranda, *Shindo Renmei: terrorismo e extorsão* (São Paulo: Edição Saraiva, 1948), 11; Tigner, "The Okinawans in Latin America," 42.

58. The only Japanese-language competition of the Shindo Renmei weekly was the Cotia Cooperative *Information Bulletin*, which rarely tackled political issues. Dráuzio Leme Padilha, *CAC: cooperativismo que deu certo* (São Paulo: Cooperativa Agrícola de Cotia, Cooperativa Central, 1989), 90.

59. The documents were found in a raid on Shindo Renmei headquarters in Santo André and published in translation in Herculano Neves, *O processo da "Shindo-Renmei" e demais associações secretas japonesas* (São Paulo: n.p., 1960), 288–90.

60. Reprinted in *Paulista Shinbun*, Apr. 29, 1947.

61. Handa, *O imigrante japonês*, 651–55.

62. *O Estado de S. Paulo*, Mar. 26, 1946; *Correio da Manhã*, Apr. 6, 1946; *A Noite* (Rio de Janeiro), Apr. 13, 1946. Other newspapers that regularly ran such stories, often on a daily basis for weeks in a row, were *Correio paulistano*, *Diario de São Paulo*, and *Folha da noite*. Neves, *O processo da "Shindo-Renmei,"* 97, 124.

63. *O Dia*, Apr. 6, 1946 and May 4, 1946; Miranda, *Shindo Renmei*, 160–61; Handa, *O imigrante japonês*, 660; Tigner, "The Okinawans in Latin America," 45.

64. Handa, *O imigrante japonês*, 673.

65. *Folha da Manhã*, Apr. 1946.

66. *Folha de Pinheiros*, "Perigos da imprensa japonesa no Brasil," July 9, 1949; *Burajiru jiho* (Notícias do Brasil), Apr. 5, 1949, translation in Secretaria da Segurança Pública do Estado de São Paulo–Departamento de Ordem Política e Social (DEOPS) #108981–Ordem Política/Shindo Remmey–Vol. 2, Arquivo do Estado de São Paulo; Pasquale Petrone, organizer, *Pinheiros: estudo geográfico de um bairro paulistano* (São Paulo: Editôra da Universidade de São Paulo, 1963), 67; Handa, *O imigrante japonês*, 687.

67. *Folha da Noite*, Mar. 21, 1950; Handa, *O imigrante japonês*, 746–52.

68. Between 1953 and 1959 more than thirty thousand new Japanese immigrants settled in Brazil, followed by another sixteen thousand in the next decade. Over 81 percent of all Japanese emigrants between 1952 and 1965 settled in Brazil. Moacyr Flores, "Japoneses no Rio Grande do Sul," *Vertias* 77 (1975), 65–98; Tetsuo Nakasumi and José Yamashiro, "O fim da era de imigração e a consolidação da nova colônia Nikkei," in Comissão de Elaboração da História dos 80 Anos da Imigração Japonesa no Brasil, *Uma epopéia moderna*, Table 2, 424; Harold D. Sims, "Japanese Postwar Migration to Brazil: An Analysis of the Data Presently Available," *International Migration Review* 6:3 (Fall 1972), 246–66.

69. Francisca Isabel Schurig Vieira, *O japonês na frente de expansão paulista: o processo de absorção do Japonês em Marília* (São Paulo: Pioneira, Ed. da Universidade de São Paulo, 1973), 83–89; Handa, *O imigrante japonês*, 715.

70. Centro de Estudos Nipo-Brasileiros, *Pesquisa da população de descendentes de japoneses residentes no Brasil, 1987–1988* (São Paulo: Centro de Estudos Nipo-Brasileiros, 1990); Gleice Carvalho, "Sutis Diferenças," *Japão Aqui* 1:2 (May 1997), 26–29; Koichi Mori, "Mundo dos brasileiros mestiços descendentes de japoneses," unpublished paper (1994) used by permission of the author.

71. *Momento Legislativo* 3:27 (Aug. 1993); *Japão Aqui* 1:1 (Apr. 1997), 11–15.

72. Centro de Estudos Nipo-Brasileiros, *Pesquisa da população*, Tables 2–1, 19, and 3–4, 43.

73. Masako Watanabe, ed., *Kyodo kenkyu dekasegi Nikkei burajirujin: shiryohen* (Group Study–Brazilian Dekaseguis), Vol. 2 (Tokyo: Akashi Shoten, 1995), 350–51. I would like to thank Professor Koichi Mori for translating the interviews in this volume for me.

74. "Imigrantes japoneses: na união, a sobrevivência," *Diário Nippak página um* (Sept. 19, 1980); "Criação x identidade x formação: Os descendentes e a literatura," *Diário Nippak página um* (July 12, 1980); *Japão Aqui* 1:3 (July 1997), 38–44; *Japão Aqui* 1:1 (Apr. 1997), 63.

75. Advertisement for *Made in Japan* in *Jornal Tudo Bem*, July 19, 1997; "Bailes agitam a noite da moçada Nikkei," *Revista Nippak jovem* 1:2 (Apr. 13, 1997), 28–34.

76. Advertisements for the Bamerindus Bank in *Veja*, 1975 and 1992.

77. Interview of Luís Gushiken by Jeffrey Lesser, Michael Molasky, and Koichi Mori, Dec. 8, 1995. Interview of Getúlio Hanashiro by Jeffrey Lesser, Michael Molasky, and Koichi Mori, Dec. 12, 1995.

CHAPTER FOUR

Licensed Agencies for Relief in Asia

Relief Materials and Nikkei Populations in the United States and Canada

MASAKO IINO

On August 15, 1945, Japan unconditionally surrendered to the United States, ending the war in the Pacific and World War II. In both the United States and Canada, many Issei recollect that they felt "happy" about the news that the war had ended, but that they "deplored" Japan's defeat. The progress of the Pacific war, beginning with the Japanese attack on Pearl Harbor, had significantly influenced their fates and must have been of utmost importance to the Nikkei population. They were naturally afraid that the outcome of the war would decide how they would be treated by the U.S. and Canadian governments, and Japan's defeat came as a severe blow to them. This war meant conflicting emotions for many Nikkei, as they wanted neither the countries where they resided nor Japan to lose the war.

Many Nikkei also suffered from the aftereffects of such experiences as forced removal from their home, internment, and the government's inquisitions concerning their loyalty. Some Issei recollect that during the resettlement period after their release from the camps, they "were forced to have even harsher experiences than during the relocation." To them, the end of the war meant starting from nothing, just as they had done when they migrated to the United States and Canada. In addition, because of Japan's defeat, they suffered various mental traumas such as "losing pride as Japanese," "collapse of the family," and "suffering from humiliation as second-class citizens."

Scholars argue that these mental traumas caused many within the Nikkei population, especially Nisei, to feel ashamed of being of Japanese origin, as if it were a crime. Nisei with such sentiments tried to distance themselves from anything that reminded them or made others realize that they were Nikkei.[1] Their ethnicity became a stigma attached to them because of their experience during the war. The late Amy Uno Ishii, who initiated the annual pilgrimage to the former War Relocation Authority camp at Manzanar in 1969 and tried to educate the general public by holding forums about the internment experience, compared the difficulty of sharing the experience of internment with the younger generation—Sansei—with sharing the experience of rape. She wrote, "Women, if they've ever been raped, don't go around talking about it. . . . 'I was a victim of rape,' or anything like that. This is exactly the kind of feeling that we as evacuees, victims of circumstances, had at the time of evacuation. Actually a lot of Nisei and Issei are ashamed that they have to own up to the fact that they were in a concentration camp."[2]

Many Nikkei who experienced internment by the U.S. or Canadian governments developed a very negative self-image and came to feel ashamed of their origins. In addition, many Nikkei, especially Nisei, were the victims of racism because of their Japanese origins, in spite of the fact they were American or Canadian citizens by birth. This sense of shame combined with racism directed against them caused many Nikkei to eliminate ties to Japan in order to survive in their adopted countries. Of course there were others who felt it necessary to do so because it was natural to support their own governments' policies since they were, after all, Americans and Canadians.

Some Nikkei, however, regarded the Japanese in Japan, devastated by their defeat, as "fellow Japanese," and tried to find a way to help them. They discovered that they could do so through an organization called Licensed Agencies for Relief in Asia (LARA), established by civilians in the United States. Twenty percent of the relief supplies sent to Japan by LARA were collected by Nikkei in North and South America, including not only Nikkei in the United States and Canada, but also those in Brazil and Argentina. Rather than eliminating their ties to Japan, these Nikkei reaffirmed them by becoming engaged in relief activities for defeated Japan.

This article examines, through an examination of LARA relief supplies, the experience and consciousness of Nikkei populations in the Western Hemisphere immediately after the Pacific war ended.

LARA Relief Supplies

Relief Supply Totals

When World War II ended Japan was completely devastated, as defeated countries always are. The majority of Japanese were experiencing difficulty securing food and clothing sufficient to survive. The Japanese called this aid

TABLE 4.1

LARA Relief Supplies Sent to Japan, 1946–1952

Type of supplies	Amount
Food (milk, crops, canned foods, oils, dried foods, syrup, etc.)	12,603 tons
Clothing (garments, underwear, blankets and linens, etc.)	2,928 tons
Medicine (vitamins, antibiotics, medical equipment, etc.)	75 tons
Shoes (for boys and girls, slippers, etc.)	331 tons
Soap (for bathing, laundry, medical use, etc.)	160 tons
Textiles (Pure wool, cotton materials, etc.)	149 tons
Cotton	222 tons
School products (stationery, leather materials, toys, etc.)	236 tons
TOTAL	16,704 tons
Goats	2,036
Milk cows	45

SOURCE: Ministry of Welfare, "LARA no seika" (The Results of LARA), June 1952.

"LARA relief supplies" or "LARA materials." Relief activities continued from November 1946 until 1952. According to the government record of the supplies it had received by May 1952 (Ministry of Welfare, "LARA no Seika" [The Results of LARA], June 1952), the supplies sent consisted of 16,704 tons of food, clothing, medicine, and other goods, not including livestock (see Table 4.1). The record claims that "if these supplies could be calculated in terms of the Japanese yen, the value of this aid would be far over forty billion yen."

According to the same record, "the first ship, the *Howard Stansbury*, entered Yokohama Port in November 1946 filled with LARA relief supplies." Seven months before, on April 1, the head of the Bureau of Social Policy of the Ministry of Welfare had sent "Request and Instructions Regarding Emergency Relief for Needy Citizens" to local Japanese social welfare agencies. It clearly indicated that the Japanese government felt it necessary to adopt more effective measures to assist the citizens reduced to below poverty levels. This document states in its introduction:

Reflecting the fact that the number of people who require relief is increasing daily, it is crucially important to see to it that these people should receive aid and their lives should be stabilized. The GHQ of the Allied Forces is also seriously concerned with this matter. Therefore, we request that the local social welfare agencies should further encourage relevant organizations to immediately take adequate relief measures with regard to the instructions given above and provide them with enough aid.

Ten pages of detailed instructions for relief operations then follow. Within these pages it is noted that it was regrettable that relief operations had not been "completely effective" because "the transfer of funds for the operation was significantly delayed." The government was "preparing to enact a set of new regulations for relief welfare by revising several existing regulations," but that process was also delayed. The instructions stated that the government expected to see "active initiative and oversight of relevant organizations" despite these difficult conditions. This indicates the ineffectiveness of governmental relief efforts in Japan, which were only a drop in the bucket.[3] It was at this time that information about LARA was reported to Japan.

The Role of the Japanese Government

The General Headquarters (GHQ) of the Allied Forces issued a memorandum to the Japanese government on August 1, 1946, clarifying Japan's responsibilities regarding LARA as follows:

1) The Japanese government, having been promised the receipt of such relief supplies, shall immediately prepare at the port for transfer of ownership, storage, and distribution of the relief supplies provided by civilian organization in the United States to aid needy people in Japan.

2) The Japanese government shall be solely responsible for the aid, from the port to the groups who would consume them, securing, transporting, allocating, and distributing the relief supplies. In discharging, transporting, and storing the relief supplies, sufficient police protection shall be supplied. The Japanese government shall be responsible to the GHQ of the Allied Forces for keeping the supplies from theft, breakage, and preventable damages.

3) The Japanese government must submit the general execution plan for distribution of the relief supplies on or before September 1, 1946.

Included in the memorandum was a detailed plan for accounting for, storing, distributing, and guarding the relief supplies. Records were to be included in monthly reports to the GHQ, which were also to include detailed information on "materials received, materials distributed, their receiving organizations, current inventory, and locations of undistributed materials."[4] In this way the Japanese government was made solely responsible for these arrangements, but rather than finding these duties troublesome, it must have been grateful for the aid.

According to the "Table of Limit on Aid to the Needy," issued by the Ministry of Welfare, the basic allowance of government aid per person varied according to the population of the area in which each lived. In the six major metropolitan areas, for example, the allowance was three yen per person (eight yen and forty sen for a five-member family); in towns and villages it was one yen and ninety sen per person (five yen and twenty sen for a five-member family). "LARA Kyuen Busshi ni Tsuite" (On the LARA Relief Supplies), published by the Bureau of Social Policy, the Ministry of Welfare

(January 1951), describes the distribution process as follows:

It was December 1946 when LARA relief supplies were delivered for the first time to infants, school-age children, and welfare institutions such as sanitariums and nursing homes. The areas in which the supplies were distributed were Tokyo, Kanagawa, Aichi, Kyoto, Osaka, Hyogo, Hiroshima, and Nagasaki prefectures, where the destruction during the war had been extreme. As there was a severe shortage of goods at the time, the receiving institutions were filled with joy and appreciation for such unexpected gifts as milk, sugar, candies, and clothing, which were rare then. It gave them a sense of recovery.[5]

Beginning in 1947, distribution areas were gradually expanded and the goods came to be "continually distributed to welfare institutions in all regions in Japan, according to the number of people that they sheltered." The temporary distribution of the relief supplies to the general population living in poverty and people other than those sheltered in welfare facilities started in December 1947, and in May 1948 the goods began to be distributed in national hospitals, sanitariums, and nursery schools throughout Japan.[6]

According to the above-mentioned "LARA no Seika," "the LARA relief supplies were impartially, accurately, swiftly, and effectively distributed from the Ministry of Welfare without cost to the recipients through prefectural offices to organizations and individuals all over Japan. Fourteen million, or some 15 percent of the total population, benefited from the relief supplies." A list of beneficiaries of LARA includes infants, schoolchildren, nursery schools, schools for the blind, dormitories for mothers and children, nursing homes, national sanitariums, health centers, hospitals, children in foster homes, leprosy hospitals, war victims, Japanese citizens returning from overseas colonies, widows, people at or below poverty level, school lunch programs, evening high school students, university students living in dormitories, and victims of natural disaster.[7]

Initially the receipt and distribution of LARA relief supplies was conducted according to instructions issued by the GHQ to the Japanese government. Beginning on April 1, 1950, however, the operation was governed according to a contract between representatives of LARA and the Japanese government. The contract states, "The Licensed Agencies for Relief in Asia will provide the needy with relief supplies, impartially, effectively, swiftly, and adequately, without cost to the recipients, regardless of nationality, religion, race, or political belief, to assist recovery of Japan." The representatives of LARA were G. Ernest Bott of the Church World Service, Esther B. Rhoads of the American Friends Service Committee, and Henry J. Felsecker of the Catholic War Relief Service. In addition, "authority figures from each field and the officials of the Ministry of Welfare" joined to form the LARA Central Committee, which consisted of twenty-two members. Its charge was "to evaluate the general direction and specific distribution plans for LARA supplies." The responsibilities of the Japanese government were, as before, "to be in charge of protection, transportation, allotment, and distribution of the materials, and to cover necessary expenses for these operations," from receipt of the goods to their delivery into the hands of aid recipients.

The value assigned to LARA aid thus received and distributed by the Japanese government is reflected in the statement below:

The LARA gift as a symbol of love of neighbor gave hope to the people in desperation and poverty, and they now live each day with hope and appreciation of the love of mankind that reaches beyond the national border shown by LARA. A number of meetings have been held to show recipients' appreciation for LARA in Tokyo, Kanagawa, Kyoto, Osaka, and other areas. At the diet, resolutions of appreciation for LARA were adopted three times. LARA supplies have been very useful for the social welfare and its management in Japan. Both materially and mentally, LARA makes great contributions toward the recovery of postwar Japan from total devastation. The Emperor and Empress are greatly interested in LARA supplies. Thus the entire nation expresses respect and appreciation for the kindness of LARA.[8]

LARA relief supplies saved many people who were suffering from despair and poverty "from hunger, cold, and illness, and gave them hope for tomorrow."[9]

Participating Organizations

Thirteen American religious, social welfare, and labor organizations participated in LARA. The major participants and their activities, according to the records of the Japanese government, are listed below. Other participants were Lutheran World Relief, Mennonite Central Committee, the AFL and CIO, Brethren Service Committee, Unitarian Science Committee, Christian Science Service Committee, Girl Scouts of the United States, Salvation Army, the YMCA, and the YWCA.

The Church World Service. This group, whose main office is in New York City, constitutes a federation of Protestant churches. It mainly sent clothes, food, and medicine to Japan through LARA. It contributed 55 to 60 percent of all LARA supplies. "Several thousand churches collect clothes, wash them, repair them, if necessary, and pack them to be sent. ... The entire process is based on the voluntary activities of church members."

The American Friends Service Committee. Its headquarters are in Philadelphia, with local offices in many cities, including New York, Seattle, Chicago, and San Francisco. Donations made to the local offices were sent to the headquarters, then to Japan. Its contribution to LARA supplies was 25 percent. The supplies included foods, clothes, textiles, and seeds.

The Catholic War Relief Service. Its headquarters are in New York City. It accepted donations such as medicine, chocolate, milk, and textiles through local churches and sent them to Japan. Its donations amounted to 10 percent of the total LARA supplies.

The Relationship Between Nikkei and LARA

People with good intentions in North and South America contacted one of these thirteen organizations and contributed relief supplies to it. LARA then sent them to devastated Japan. But what should be noted here is that 20 percent of all relief supplies were contributed by the Nikkei population in North and South America.[10] Immediately after the end of the war, "benevolent Americans and Canadians" started to send relief supplies, but they were exclusively interested in sending them to European countries. It was Nikkei who brought their attention to the situation in Japan; Nikkei started and promoted a system that enabled supplies to go to Japan.

Nikkei Relief Organizations

In 1952 the Ministry of Welfare requested that the Ministry of Foreign Affairs conduct an investigation. The detailed results were contained in "Report on Relief Organizations Established by the Fellow Japanese in North and South America."[11] According to the report there were thirty-six Nikkei relief organizations. Some had been established for social purposes but took this opportunity to participate in relief activities for Japan. Others were newly born with the express purpose of sending relief supplies to Japan. The following were the major organizations: Nihon Nanmin Kyusai Kai (Association for the Relief of Displaced People in Japan), Washington, D.C.; Cleveland Kokoku Nanmin Kyusai Kai (Cleveland Association for Relief of Displaced People in Japan); Nihon Kyusaki New York Iinkai (New York Japanese American Committee for Japanese Relief, Inc, which later became the Japanese American Association in New York); Nihon Nanmin Kyusai Kai (Association for the Relief of Displaced People in Japan), San Francisco; Chicago Nikkei Dantai Rengo Shusai Nihon Nanmin Iinkai (Chicago Committee for the Relief of Displaced People in Japan Sponsored by Nikkei Associations); Beikoku Seihokubu Nihon Nanmin Kyusaikai (U.S. Northwestern Association for Relief of Displaced People in Japan), Seattle; Ontario Nihon Kyusai Iinkai (Ontario Committee for Japanese Relief), Toronto; Nikkei Shimin Kyokai (Japanese Canadian Citizens Association), Toronto; LARA Nihon Nanmin Kyusai Iinkai (LARA Committee for Relief of Displaced People in Japan), Honolulu; Maui Nihon Nanmin Kyusai Iinkai (Maui Committee for Relief of Displaced People in Japan), Wailuku; Yuai Juji-Kai Hawaii Shibu (Friends Cross Association Hawai'i Branch), Honolulu; Sensai

Koji Kyusai Club (War Orphans Relief Club), Honolulu; Hawaii Doshikai (Hawai'i Comrade Association), Honolulu; Hakkokai, Honolulu; Brazil Sekijuji Konin Nihon Sensai Doho Kyusaikai (Brazil Association Officially Recognized by the Red Cross for Relief of Fellow Japanese in War Devastation), Rio de Janeiro; Okinawa Kyusai Kai (Okinawa Relief Association), Rio de Janeiro.

The Japanese government also recognized Nikkei organizations' efforts to send relief to Japan at an early stage. Its report in 1951 explains LARA as follows: "It is believed that more than one million members from thirteen organizations, including religious, social enterprise, and labor organizations, participate in LARA. Among them are Japanese citizens in North and South America, including Hawaii." Hawai'i's LARA Committee for Relief of Displaced People in Japan alone consigned $300,000 to the American Friends Service Committee. It reveals that "the Japanese organizations in Eastern Brazil sent textiles, clothing, futon cotton, sugar, and so on. The Japanese in Argentina sent assorted food packages, and smoked and canned meat. The Japanese in Peru, Chile, and Mexico sent blankets and other materials. They all worked through LARA."[12] It is obvious that the Japanese government recognized the contribution of the Nikkei population at this stage. The following cases show how some of the Nikkei contributions were made.

In New York

According to *New York Binran* (New York Bulletin), published by the Japanese American Association in New York (1948–49 fiscal year), nine Nikkei in New York, including Hachiro Yuasa, who later became president of the International Christian University, "issued a memorandum" to hold "a voluntary meeting" to begin setting up relief for Japan. It was the beginning of the relief effort in New York. The meeting took place on September 5, 1945, only three days after Japan's signing of the instrument of surrender on the battleship *Missouri*, officially ending the Pacific war. It is recorded that on September 14, "despite heavy rain," about forty Issei and Nisei responded to this appeal and gathered at a Methodist church to discuss the creation of a relief organization. However, these efforts did not immediately bear fruit. Although the war had ended, "the Issei were still foreigners from an enemy country," and were not even allowed to gather in public. Any monetary donations that were not channeled through the General Relief Committee in Washington, D.C., were not accepted by American banks. At this point, therefore, they only selected members to form a preliminary committee to "conduct research and investigation." Some insisted on collecting money immediately, but the chair of the preliminary committee, Hachiro Yuasa, issued a statement arguing that such efforts were premature.

Until today, it has been absolutely impossible to send goods and money to Japan. Even solicitation of nonrelief money and goods can be regarded as violation of the Regulation on Transaction with Enemy Countries. Following the instruction of the prosecutor-general, we made an inquiry to the Foreign Relief Control Agency, who replied that sooner or later we would be able to obtain permission. As of now, however, it would be unwise to solicit money or goods for relief of Japan. ... Although it is very frustrating for the Japanese in the United States, unfortunately, ... right now, there is no other way but for each of us to individually prepare for and store relief supplies.[13]

In this way, the preliminary Relief Preparation Committee stood by until official permission was issued.

The preliminary committee held a general meeting of "Fellow Japanese in the U.S.," where they proposed the establishment of the New York Japanese American Committee for Japan Relief. The proposal was accepted in the general meeting, and an office was opened. The committee was of a rather large scale, with a chair, vice-chair, secretary, treasurer, board of trustees, advisers, and people in public relations. Their names show that some of them were Issei and Nisei, and some non-Nikkei. In August, the committee was approved as a New York state corporate organization, making it possible to send relief supplies to Japan through LARA. In September, the organization formally started its relief activities and launched a fund-raising campaign. The record shows that they succeeded in raising $48,568.75 by the end of the year, including the $10,000 contributed by the New York Council of Churches.[14]

Toward the end of the year the committee, with the cooperation of the American Friends Service Committee in Philadelphia, started collecting contributions of clothing and other materials. In addition, the New York Entertainment Program to Help the Homeland was formed and put on a show in the city in March 1947, collecting more than $5,200. The following year a similar show earned $2,600. By then, sending relief packages to Japan using methods other than LARA was legally allowed, so the contributions the organization collected were smaller than in the first year of their campaign. The total value of relief supplies sent to Japan by the American Friends Service Committee reached $560,973 by September 1947. The total of cash contributions was $312,499, about 70 percent of which was given by the Nikkei population. It was reported that "in the fiscal year 1947, the New York Committee donated over 20 percent of the total monetary donation by the Nikkei population mentioned above."[15] Although the actual solicitation activities in New York began late—not until September 9, 1946, when the preliminary committee adopted the resolution for relief of displaced people in Japan—the effort was widely publicized by a Japanese newspaper in the Midwest. It read, "Stimulated by such news, Nikkei societies in many American cities established Japan relief committees one after another."[16]

In California

In California, where the Nikkei population was beginning to return from relocation camps, there was also a call to send relief supplies to Japan. Shortly after the meeting in New York, on October 24, 1945, a group of Nikkei in Los Angeles formed an organization called the "Southern California Relief Organization for Displaced People in Japan." In November 1945 in San Francisco a "Meeting to Discuss Relief for Homeland" was held, and the Association for Relief of Displaced People in Japan was formed in the following year. *Kikan Fukko Shi* (History of Returned People and Reestablishment), published by Nichi-Bei Times Publishing in San Francisco, relates how the Nikkei who had just returned from the relocation camps and were still struggling to establish themselves stood up to help Japanese in Japan:

It was immediately after the war in the Pacific when we were released from our isolated lives in relocation camps and returned to the cities on the West Coast. Every city was experiencing an extreme shortage of houses to rent. Nikkei people who returned could literally find no houses to live in. Some of them were lucky enough to rent a room in the whites' houses. Others had to sleep in single beds arranged in rows in basements or halls of so-called "hostels," newly prepared in churches. They were exactly like displaced people. News describing the situation in Japan was brought little by little by military people staying in Japan as the occupation army or by newspaper correspondents. They all depicted the desperate situation of poverty-stricken people in Japan immediately after Japan surrendered.

Other Nikkei who learned of the situation in Japan felt like this:

Although we experienced isolated lives in the camps, deprived of our freedom, we never experienced lack of food and clothes. War victims in our homeland, Japan, on the other hand, have lost their houses and are unable to obtain even bread, we hear. We, their blood relatives, cannot bear to see their difficulties. We gathered together and looked for ways to save them from such a situation. Then we started to discuss what we could do. Our desire to give a helping hand gradually grew.[17]

The purpose of the Association for Relief of Displaced People in Japan in San Francisco is expressed in its prospectus, written by Shichinosuke Asano, who eventually became secretary of the organization and was publisher of the Japanese-language newspaper *Nichi-Bei Times*. The association's founders had learned that "war victims in Japan did not have food to survive on, or clothing to keep themselves warm, nor even places to shelter themselves from wind and dew, and there was no knowing how many were on the verge of starvation as the severe winter approached." The San Francisco Nikkei "could not help taking pity on them." They "felt an urge to do something— they could not stay without taking any action" and organized themselves.

It was the Nikkei's "conscientious sense of moral obligation" to help the Japanese that moved them, as "they, reflecting upon their own situation, considered themselves rather fortunate that they had enough to eat and had something to spare for others." They wanted to help Japanese in Japan, "even if they had to share a meal with others and spare something from a small stipend." It is interesting to note that this activity was, for these Nikkei, a way of repaying the contributions they had received from Japan during their internment. The organization's prospectus says that the Nikkei "recollect how moved and touched [they] had been by such comfort articles as medicine, books, and toys, as well as soy sauce [and] miso, sent by their countrymen" and that they "recollect the warm kindness that Japanese people who were now destitute had shown" to Nikkei "whose food, clothing, and housing were secured." With such memories, they "could not help willingly sharing what [they] had with those living in poverty in Japan."[18]

In Chicago and Other Cities

In Chicago, where only two hundred Nikkei had lived before the war, the government set up a field office as part of their program to move the Nikkei out of the camps and resettle them in places other than California. According to the government policy a large number of Nikkei moved out of camps to Chicago, where the Nikkei population reached twenty thousand by the end of 1945. Although scattered voices to help Japan were raised among them, no action was begun because there was no central organization ready to mobilize relief efforts.

In October 1946, however, an organization called the Chicago Committee for the Relief of Displaced People in Japan Sponsored by Nikkei Associations was established. It was a joint effort of the JACL Chicago Chapter and representatives of sixteen existing associations, including six Christian churches, four Buddhist churches, the Catholic Young Men's Association, and the Young Women's Christian Association. According to the organization's statement of purpose, "Rescue displaced people of our homeland, and show our love to our fellow countrymen, with all our might, sharing their pains," they collected contributions. The record cites $13,090 as the value of contributions collected by the end of January 1947. The goods they collected were "carried to the storage of the Friends Service Committee, where Nikkei people were engaged, day after day, in packing them to be shipped to their homeland."[19]

In Utah, where some Nikkei were engaged in growing celery and tomatoes after being released from the camps, the Federation of Salt Lake City Churches for Relief of Displaced People in the Homeland was established immediately after the war. Representatives from three organizations—the Buddhist Society (Nakayama Faction), the Japanese Christian Church, and the Japanese Anglican Church—"asked each religious organization to send a few representatives to a meeting." This group became the Salt Lake City Federation of Churches. As its first project it established the Federation of Salt Lake City Churches for Relief of Displaced People in the Homeland. Each participating religious organization urged members to donate. In 1946 they raised $166.50, and in 1947 they shipped "105 large boxes" of old clothes to Japan. It is recorded that "regardless of the religion or beliefs, [the movement] tried to recruit all Nikkei with utmost sincerity," and the Nikkei in Utah moved beyond their religious boundaries and contributed to helping the Japanese. There are similar records indicating that in Denver, Colorado, and Seattle, Washington, there were also relief activities for the Japanese that included a variety of religious groups.[20]

According to the Record of Contribution from Nikkei Communities in the U.S., issued by the American Friends Service Committee in Philadelphia, as of April 1947 $5,781 of the total amount of $117,403.76 was sent from the Seabrook Farms in New Jersey. This was a place where many Japanese resettled after being released from relocation camps. It is surprising that such a significant amount of money was collected at a time when people were struggling to resettle in a new environment.

In Hawai'i

Since Hawai'i had a large Nikkei population, several relief organizations were formed there. The earliest and the largest was the LARA Committee for Relief of Displaced People in Japan, in Honolulu. It was established in November 1946 by Dr. Gilbert Bawls and others. Only one month after its establishment, between December 13 and 18, it shipped 9,363 pounds of goods, including clothes and milk, to Japan. The value of the shipment was $161,149.72. In 1948 it shipped 6,778 pounds of clothes, medicine, soy sauce, miso paste, shoes, and so on (worth $94,050.43). The Japanese record shows that a great quantity of relief supplies was received by LARA headquarters in Tokyo: in 1949, 3,249 pounds of clothes, shoes, and so on (worth $78,881), and in 1950, 3,777 pounds of clothes, shoes, kombu (seaweed), soy sauce, and so on (worth $89,923). It is interesting that materials indispensable for Japanese cooking, such as soy sauce, miso paste, and kombu, were sent to Japan from Hawai'i.

Responding to the activities by the committee in Honolulu, the LARA Committee for Relief of Displaced People in Japan, Maui Branch started its activities on Maui in December 1946. In January 1947 it was "strengthened and rearranged as a cooperative enterprise among Nikkei religious groups," and renamed the Maui Committee for Relief of Displaced People in Japan. The major groups active in the organization were Wailuku Jodo-In, Wailuku Honganji, and Wailuku Shingonshu Temple. It is reported that they shipped

1,810 boxes of relief supplies, estimated at 181,000 pounds, to Japan during the first six years after the war.

In Hawai'i, in addition to the organizations directed toward assisting displaced people in general, organizations with more specific purposes also actively promoted their own causes. The Friends Cross Association Hawai'i Branch, which attempted to assist wounded soldiers and the War Orphans Relief Club, which attempted to assist war orphans, are some examples.[21]

In Ontario, Canada

Relief activities for Japan were not confined to the United States but were seen also in Canada. Japanese Canadians, like Japanese Americans, were eventually released from "interior housing centers," the equivalent of American relocation camps. They moved to the east, inspired by the slogan "To the East of the Rockies," and Toronto, Ontario, was one of their major destinations. The Ontario Committee for Japanese Relief is an example of a relief organization in Toronto. The headquarters were in the United Church of Canada in Toronto, represented by the Reverend J. Larelle Smith. Relief activity was started under the leadership of Florence Bird, minister of the United Church, and Grace Tucker, minister of the Anglican Church, both of whom learned about devastation in Japan and contacted ministers working as missionaries among the Nikkei in Canada to discuss relief in Japan. On November 19, 1946, a meeting was held at which it was agreed that they would organize the Ontario Committee for Relief in Japan, with twelve committee members.

The committee activities lasted until 1948. During that period $20,000 and six million pounds of used clothes were sent to Japan through LARA. According to the Japanese government record, half of the contributions, in the form of both cash and used clothes, were from Nikkei in the area. The used clothes were washed, mended, and packed by volunteer Nikkei women. The committee was dissolved in 1948, when each of the five major churches in Canada started to be independently involved in relief activities. The Japanese Canadian Citizens Association (JCCA) then took over the job and collected contributions by visiting individual households. According to records, in 1949, the year after the association started its activities, they collected $5,364, with which they bought 13,200 pounds of powdered milk to be shipped to Japan. Activities were not confined to the Toronto area; in 1950 $3,818 of the $4,013 total contributions were from the JCCA in Alberta.[22]

In Brazil

In Brazil relief activities by the Nikkei started in the middle of 1946. Two factors evoked "a burning desire" among the Nikkei in Rio de Janeiro and

Saō Paulo to "send assistance from Brazil, in any way possible, for the recovery of [their] home country." One was that they had learned of the "devastating condition of the home country" through recovered communications between Brazil and Japan, and the other was that relief activities by Germans for Germany had started. It was difficult for the Nikkei to act independently, and they decided to seek official recognition by the Red Cross, following the German example. This connected them to LARA as the only association in Brazil officially recognized by the Red Cross for the relief of war victims in Japan. The activities of the Brazilian Nikkei included "collecting monetary donations, asking for contributions by putting on events such as bazaars, music concerts, dance parties, and lotteries, and by collecting used clothes, a job taken on mainly by women's groups." As a result, it is recorded that U.S.$300,000 of goods, including powdered milk, spaghetti, sugar, used clothes, cotton for futons, stationery, towels, flannel, and cotton textiles, were sent to LARA.[23]

An article in the *Paulista Newspaper Annals*, which was sent to the Japanese Ministry of Foreign Affairs with the report on relief organizations, reported the association's "historical dissolution" in 1950. To send aid to Japan was also to admit that Japan had really lost the war—a "historic" admission to some Japanese Brazilians. In addition to providing valuable assistance to Japan, the association's activities were significant as an attempt to make nonbelievers accept Japan's defeat as a fact. This recognition movement triggered hostility from the faction of nonbelievers. "It was not exaggerating to say that people were later distinguished by whether or not they accepted and participated in the relief activities." In the settlement, where the majority still did not recognize Japan's defeat, "participating in the relief activities became a source of strength and unity among the minority faction who recognized Japan's defeat." Also, the Brazilian Association was the largest of the Nikkei colonia organizations in forty years of Japanese immigration to Brazil. Considering that previously there had been no organizations to unify the Nikkei population in Brazil, this organization was of great importance, although it had a "very particular purpose of rescuing the home country."[24]

Conclusion: Ties to Japan

In addition to sending relief supplies through LARA, many Nikkei sent goods from the United States or Canada to friends and relatives in Japan. Many Issei women whom the author interviewed a few years ago recollected their own experiences of doing so. In the case of one woman in California, her relatives still show their appreciation to her, saying, "our children were raised by the powdered milk that [you], our 'aunt in America,' sent us."[25]

Another woman, engaged in farming while she was in Utah on temporary release from a camp in 1946, started to send packages to her relatives in Japan as soon as permission was issued. Although there were limitations on the size of the boxes that could be sent, she could "send relief supplies to the home country for the same cost as domestic postage." She explained, "I asked my children to get cardboard boxes thrown in the backyard of the market. They worked so diligently for me. As we, too, were short in sugar, we saved one spoonful of sugar for coffee or cocoa every morning, or for cooking, stored it in a bottle, and then sent the rest in matchboxes." She recollects that she decided to send one of her two monthly unemployment checks to three of her relatives in Japan, totaling $21, or $7 each sent to three families. It gave her pleasure to know her efforts were appreciated, and she proudly added that "each family sent letters of appreciation to 'the aunt in America.' "[26]

In addition to relief efforts of Nikkei through LARA and the mailing of individual packages, there were cases in which those stationed in Japan helped the Japanese. For example, a Hawai'i-born Nisei stationed in Sasebo as an intelligence agent immediately after the war came to know children in the neighborhood and found them "suffering from malnutrition and small for their ages." So, he recollects, "I gave them all the sweets and other stuff that I had." The children appreciated it and made efforts to "repay" him. A boy brought him a pearl he found at the shore. Another offered to get his mother to do his laundry. This kind of exchange lasted for the month he stayed in Sasebo. Before he left he gave this boy a winter blanket provided by the U.S. military, and later the boy showed him a pair of mittens that his mother had made out of the blanket.[27]

Another Hawai'i-born Nisei who also stayed in Japan as an intelligence agent visited his parents, who had returned from Hawai'i, and found that they "were living in a shabby house in extreme poverty." He tried to give his savings to his mother for their house to be repaired. His mother insisted that she could not accept such special treatment and suggested that "he utilize the money for the sake of all the people in Japan." Later, he was stationed in Maizuru, where he and his colleagues proceeded with a plan to plant cherry trees there. The reason, he explained, was that he could not forget how impressive the beautiful cherry blossoms in a burnt field were upon his first arrival in Japan. Fifty years later, the cherry trees are called "Aloha Trees" and are considered proof of friendship between Hawai'i and Japan.[28]

Although many Nikkei in the United States and Canada had felt ashamed and distanced themselves from anything Japanese, some were more concerned about the plight of the Japanese in Japan than with their own condition. These people came forward as members of the Nikkei community in order to help those they regarded as compatriots. They looked for ways to assist the Japanese and found that they could do so through LARA. It had only been a few years since those same Nikkei, many of whom were citizens of the United States and Canada, had been classified as enemy aliens, removed from their homes, and interned in relocation centers. There were even some Nisei who were willing to help Japanese in Japan, the country of their parents, even as others felt stigmatized by their ties to Japan. Some Nisei were included among the twenty members of the preliminary committee for the New York Japanese American Committee for Japanese Relief. Those who sent packages individually to relatives in Japan may have done so out of individual motivation, rather than as a collective effort on behalf of Japan. LARA activities, however, incorporated both individual motivation and compassion toward the Japanese as a whole. Naturally, the author does not mean to suggest that the only motivation for Nisei to participate in general relief activities was their personal ties to Japan. Clearly they could have chosen to give humanitarian aid to European people in order to avoid demonstrating their ties to Japan. The following statement may not be too much of an exaggeration: "The war in the Pacific brought Nikkei in North and South America immeasurable hardships. For those Nikkei, the starting point of the fifty years after World War II was to give helping hands to poverty-stricken people in their homeland over the Pacific, through LARA."[29]

Not enough studies have been done in this field. Although a record of the Japanese Ministry of Foreign Affairs states that activities in North America stimulated similar projects in South America, there is no documentation of the cooperation among Latin American Nikkei relief organizations. In addition, the relationship between relief activities in North and South America needs to be investigated in order to develop a more accurate picture of Nikkei activities globally. Finally, it would also be important to study the perceptions and activities of Nikkei assigned to work in Japan as intelligence personnel vis-à-vis relief efforts.

Notes

1. See, for example, Stephen S. Fugita and David J. O'Brien, *Japanese American Ethnicity: The Persistence of Community* (Seattle: University of Washington Press, 1991).

2. Arthur A. Hansen and Betty E. Mitson, eds., *Voices Long Silent: An Oral Inquiry into the Japanese American Evacuation* (Fullerton: Japanese American Project, California State University, Fullerton, Oral History Program, 1974), 4.

3. Ministry of Foreign Affairs, "GHQ ni taisuru shakai kyusai hokoku zasshu (1) shakai kyusai kankei" (1945–46).

4. Ministry of Foreign Affairs, "LARA (Ajia Kyusai Renmei) kankei zasshu" (1945–51).

5. Bureau of Social Policy, Ministry of Welfare, "LARA kyuen busshi ni tsuite (1951-nen 1-gatsu)" (Jan. 1951), 10.

6. Ibid., 11.

7. Ibid., 4.

8. Ibid., 12.

9. Ministry of Welfare, "LARA no seika" (1952), 7.

10. See Ministry of Welfare, "Commemorating LARA" (1952), cited in Kaigai Nikkei Shinbun Kyokai, ed., *Kikan kaigai Nikkeijin* (Nikkei people overseas) (Quarterly Journal) 36 (May 1995).

11. Ministry of Foreign Affairs, "Beishu kakkoku no zairyu doho ni yotte kessei sareta kyusai-dantai shirabe" (Report on relief organizations established by the fellow Japanese in North and South America) (1952).

12. Bureau of Social Policy, Ministry of Welfare, "LARA kyuen busshi ni tsuite" (Jan. 1951), 3.

13. New York Japanese Society, ed., *New York Binran* (New York Bulletin) (1948–49), 51–52. Cf. "Kokoku kyuen" (Relief for the homeland), *Hokubei Shinpo*, Dec. 8, 1945; "Nihon kyuen ni tsuite" (On relief of Japan), *Hokubei Shinpo*, Mar. 10, 1946.

14. *New York Binran* (New York bulletin) (1948–49), 53.

15. Ibid., 55.

16. Kaigai Nikkei Shinbun Kyokai, ed., *Kikan kaigai Nikkeijin*, 8.

17. "LARA kinenshi" (1952), cited in Kaigai Nikkei Shinbun Kyokai, ed., *Kikan kaigai Nikkeijin*, 10–11.

18. Ministry of Foreign Affairs, "LARA (Ajia Kyusai Renmei) kankei zasshu."

19. Ministry of Foreign Affairs, "Beishu Kakkoku."

20. Ibid.

21. Ibid.

22. Ibid.

23. Ibid.

24. Ibid.

25. From an interview of the author.

26. From an interview of the author.

27. Hawaii Nikkei History Editorial Board, comp., *Japanese Eyes American Heart: Personal Reflections of Hawaii's World War II Nisei Soldiers* (Honolulu: Tendai Educational Foundation, 1998), 184–85.

28. Ibid., 311–14.

29. Kaigai Nikkei Shinbun Kyokai, ed., *Kikan kaigai Nikkeijin*, 8.

CHAPTER FIVE

An Approach to the Formation of Nikkei Identity in Peru

Issei and Nisei

RAÚL ARAKI

Any observer first encountering the nucleus of the Nikkei community in Lima should be impressed by its apparent level of cohesion, organization, and institutional infrastructure, including schools, stadiums and social sport clubs, financial institutions, and newspapers. A cultural center is also part of a central association encompassing some fifty diverse community institutions.[1] Many of these institutions exhibit a clear identification with Japan and its culture. However, this is only a part of the immense mosaic formed by the population of Japanese origin in Peru—a population with a presence in a large part of the nation. For a part of this population, the conservation of Japanese customs is of limited importance.[2] In some respects the Japanese and their descendants are a fairly homogeneous group, but from the beginning of their immigration, intragroup differences based on regional origin and economic resources have been apparent.[3] These differences are magnified by differential socioeconomic trajectories and diverse strategies of adaptation, cultural mixing, and racial assimilation.

The growth of social and economic differences influences the ongoing conflict between the persistence of Japanese culture on the one hand, and assimilation into the new country's society on the other. In sum, the differences between sectors of the Peruvian Nikkei community are accentuated. At the same time, Nikkei are united by pride in their origins and the value they place on the pre-Hispanic cultures that have also marked them, just as the different regional cultures of Peru are reflected in their lives. Their self-esteem and sense of identity rest in part on pride in their Japanese origins.

Individual lives have followed various paths of development, but within a framework that includes shared historical experiences. These experiences include key events that, to a large extent, have determined the evolution and transformation of the Nikkei community and the ongoing process of the formation of a Nikkei identity in Peru. It is a history without public heroes: the real heroes are the grandparents whose sacrifices undergird each family and community. Our history begins with them.

Struggles, Strategies, and the Formation of the Nikkei Community

On April 3, 1899, the first group of Japanese immigrants arrived in Peru, having been contracted to work in the sugar plantations on the coast. Their arrival was followed by groups of immigrants who came in eighty-one trips up until 1923.[4] Prior to this period, a Peruvian presidential decree had authorized the immigration of Japanese workers to Peru in September 1898, and Morioka Imin Kaisha (Morioka Emigration Company) had received permission to include Peru in its area of emigration in October 1898.[5] The Japanese who came were motivated by the offer of better salaries than they earned in their own country. Many also arrived intending to return to Japan in a few years, after accumulating some savings. This explains, in part, the low numbers of women in these groups—less than 12 percent of the total—despite encouragement for married couples to immigrate.[6] When the Japanese immigrants arrived at the plantations, they found them to be based on colonial-style relationships, characterized by harsh methods of control and poor working conditions, in addition to outright violations of the contracts.[7] They began to look for ways to escape the plantations and find better-paying work. As a result of numerous claims of abuse, they went on strike, allying themselves with punished or fired workers, and many finally fled from the plantations. Immigrants began exchanging information about places where better working conditions or better salaries were to be found. Some even created small maps indicating which routes to follow so that the new immigrants could orient themselves.[8]

Soon, many began to move to urban areas, where they became street vendors or started businesses that required little initial capital, such as the sale of food or barbershops.[9] Some immigrants competed with the Chinese in establishing *tambos*, or plantation grocery stores. Others immigrated to the intermediary zones, or to the interior of the coast, where they rented small plots of land and cultivated cotton and vegetables.[10] Departure from the plantation, geographic mobility, and entry into entrepreneurial ventures of one kind or another happened rapidly and almost simultaneously. Even though there continued to be salaried Japanese working on the plantations until the middle of the 1930s, the majority of immigrants managed to change their situations within a short time.[11] In 1907, when the fourth wave of contracted immigrants arrived, twenty-five immigrant barbershops already existed in Lima, and the owners had formed the Hairstylists Association of Lima.[12]

A percentage of Japanese arriving between 1899 and 1923 ignored the contracts. Of these immigrants, many had been "called" (that is, invited to come) by friends and relatives already established in Peru.[13] Some immigrants, after reaching a certain level of economic affluence, requested brides from Japan through an arrangement based on the exchange of photographs (*shashin kekkon*).[14] In November 1923 contract immigration for the plantations was stopped, but immigration continued, fed by the practice of family reunification. Between 1924 and 1930, 7,933 new Japanese immigrants entered Peru. Generally, the new immigrants had decided to come as a result of being "called" by people from the same village, town, or prefecture. During the learning period of the new arrivals, which included achieving a minimal command of the new language, many provided inexpensive and reliable help that allowed other families to expand their businesses. Working within a paternalist and familiar environment, the established settlers facilitated bringing in wives from Japan for the young employees and provided them with the support necessary to help them establish themselves. Later, they assisted newcomers in opening up their own businesses; those who returned to Japan would also pass along their businesses to newcomers.[15] Affinity and solidarity among the immigrants coming from the same prefecture was very strong in the first decades of immigration. Takao, an eighty-one-year-old Nisei, gave us much information about the mutual aid exchanged by immigrants from Yamaguchi Ken, for example.

By 1924 Japanese had settled in thirteen provinces in Peru. Despite this apparent dispersion, Japanese tended to be concentrated in certain geographic areas, usually major cities with considerable commercial activity and important agricultural valleys close to commercial cities. Exhibiting a great capacity for organization, they created numerous associations as part of their strategy for growth and in their search for well-being. They formed numerous trade union associations based on their region of origin identities (*Kenjinkai*), and other associations based on their area of residence in Peru, where immigrants had been able to establish strong affiliations. The Japanese and their descendants put down deep roots in the places where they established themselves. Even today, those who were born or have lived outside Lima share a strong regional identity.[16] It can also be said that the immigrants established outside Lima developed deeper ties to the native population and have been involved in a steady process of cultural assimilation. Interracial marriages occurred more frequently in these settings as well. These Nikkei believe that this explains why village populations were less antagonistic than inhabitants of Lima during the years of the Second World War.

In time, Japanese immigrants began to increase the length of their stays. The Peruvian people became accustomed to seeing Nikkei in the urban landscape as they periodically visited their barbershops and began to accept the slight but progressive changes in the seasonings and ingredients used in preparing food in Japanese restaurants. On the plantations, Japanese grocery stores gradually became meeting places where workers gathered at the end of each day to chat and have a drink. The same thing happened in Japanese corner taverns in Lima and Callao. Many years after these first local ties had begun to develop, Degregori wrote the following with respect to the presidential elections of 1990:

Because of the vicissitude of the history of Peru, which Basadre would have called chance in history, Fujimori became the embodiment of the emerging dispossessed Cholos in his variable "Chinese" of the street corner. Because if anything was demonstrated by the election results, it was that, on the margin of how they perceive themselves within the ethnic stratification of the country, either from the Andes or from the coast, the Niseis and the Tusanes found themselves closer to the populist image than the Criolles in their snobbish ways.[17]

During this time, as they gradually managed to establish themselves in new geographic areas and expand their resources, the Nikkei became involved in the issues and problems of the country insofar as these affected their search for a place and recognition. In many of the interviews of Issei and the Nisei born before the 1930s, I find an exceptional understanding of the geography and history of Peru. Some individuals even had personal contacts with historical figures of the country during a time when the size of the cities and the number of inhabitants were considerably smaller.

Japanese immigrants regularly created central organizations whose goals were to protect the rights and well-being of the whole group. One of these, the Japanese Association (Nipponjin Kyokai), founded in 1912, led the initiative to create a newspaper for the community. In 1913, the first newspaper printed in Japanese in South America, the *Andes Jiho*, began circulating in Peru.[18] The immigrants' interest in the events and problems of the community in Peru and in Japan was always high. In 1911, a mimeographed newspaper called *Jiritsu* was circulated and read in the barbershops. In 1921 another printed paper, the *Nippi Shimpo*, appeared. Later, the *Perú Nichi Nichi* appeared, demonstrating the divergent concerns of one sector of the community. The three existing printed newspapers came together in 1929 under the name *Lima Nippo*.

Through their diplomatic representatives, the Japanese authorities always demonstrated great interest in the associations of the Nikkei community. In 1915, due to a series of internal differences within the Japanese Association, a group broke away and formed their own association, Peru Nipponjinkai. Socioeconomic differences were one of the factors that caused the split. This public antagonism worried the Japanese Consulate and, in 1917, the consulate sponsored the creation of the Central Japanese Society, dissolving the other two organizations.[19]

The economic activities of the members of the Nikkei community continued to expand, even though internal socioeconomic differences increased.[20] A plethora of different roads were taken, but all Nikkei were searching for a better life. Since their arrival, most immigrants had passed more than half of their lives in Peru, constantly struggling for recognition and a place for themselves. For these immigrants, the education of their children became a priority. In 1908, five years after the first group of women arrived, a Japanese school opened on the Santa Barbara plantation, sharing space with a Buddhist temple built one year before.

Wherever there was a significant concentration of Japanese, a school for their children was established. In addition, many who had the economic wherewithal sent their children to study in Japan, generally placing them in the homes of relatives. In Lima, in 1914, the newspaper *Andes Jiho* expressed anxiety about the problems caused by children being separated from their families and recommended the creation of a local school to decrease the number of children sent to study in Japan. Six years later, the Lima Nikko school was inaugurated.[21] The initial objective of Japanese immigrants, to live in Peru temporarily in search of a better life, was changing into a struggle to develop a strong next generation.

Ethnic Conflict: Strengthening Identity

Peru is a complex country in terms of society, culture, race, and class. It is highly stratified and full of contradictions, offering very different possibilities for access to power, wealth, and status. It is a mestizo country, where even today white people, or those with lighter skin, continue to enjoy more privileges. From the first years of the Republic until the 1930s, attempts to bring immigrants into the country had been an objective of every government. Initially, the intent was to bring European immigrants in to resolve the fundamental problem of scarcity of labor for agriculture, the harvesting of guano, and the construction of railroads.[22] However, despite the efforts and desires of Peruvian authorities, few European immigrants came. Actually, most workers came from Asia. Between 1849 and 1874 approximately one hundred thousand Chinese were brought into the country. The prejudice that built up against them preceded the Japanese immigration. An article directed against the economic activities of the Chinese and Japanese published in the newspaper *La Cronica* in 1918 exemplified racist attitudes of the time.[23]

During the 1930s, within the framework of the worldwide depression and the post-Leguiista crisis, unemployment in Peru, a new governmental orientation, and the power of certain political interests caused a series of demonstrations encouraging discrimination against the Japanese and their descendants.[24] The Nikkei population faced hostility due to their economic success. Moreover, one newspaper linked to the power elite began to spread false rumors about the Nikkei in order to distract people from the real national problems.

These efforts were relatively successful. The geographic concentration of Nikkei in certain areas and the unpopular militarism displayed by Japan encouraged acts of rejection and hostility, as well as the publication of opinions expressing xenophobic and racist attitudes toward all Japanese. It seemed that this anti-Japanese campaign was composed of several forces, including some with completely opposite interests. The government issued decrees that directly affected the Japanese, developed as a result of the demands of trade unions and Peruvian businessmen. The traditionally dominant groups in Peru took advantage of the situation to again promote their ideas about the need for "white European immigration." Forces supporting the opposition parties, with more populist and anti-imperialist ideology, believed that attacking the Japanese was a way of gaining sympathizers for their cause. In many of the attacks Japanese immigrants were blamed directly for Japanese military and economic expansion.

In 1934, the government of Peru ignored international reciprocity agreements with Japan. From 1934 to 1937 the daily newspaper *La Prensa* waged a campaign entitled "Japanese Infiltration." Akio Banno wrote a retort to this in the community paper *Lima Nippo*, which had little or no impact because it could only be read in Japanese. The Nikkei received threats from members of the local community venting their discontent with the national economic situation. Due to restrictions and anti-Japanese incidents, there was also discontent in the Japanese community. Japanese diplomatic representatives were criticized for their passivity. In the heart of the Central Japanese Society there was dissension, reflected in the resignations of directors. Japanese Peruvians from Okinawa split into two groups.[25]

On May 13, 1940, fliers were circulated inviting people to a demonstration against the Japanese and that also spread the rumor that the Japanese wanted to take over the country. In what is perhaps the most terrible memory for the Issei and Nisei residents of Lima and Callao, that demonstration degenerated into an attack against the Japanese and the plundering of Nikkei property.[26] More than five hundred people who had lost all their belongings took refuge in the Lima Nikko school. These events psychologically marked the immigrants and their families in that area. It is important to mention, however, that many Japanese and their families received support from and were defended by their neighbors and friends. Many Japanese families were saved from losing their belongings because their neighbors improvised defenses to impede the plundering of their homes and businesses.

On May 24, a violent earthquake hit Lima, which the populist adherents considered a divine punishment for the violence that had occurred in previous days. One immigrant tells us that "a family that lived next to my house and that had plundered the Japanese all night had to move out of the neighborhood after the earthquake. Everyone insulted them and blamed them. The earthquake was their fault. It was a punishment from God, they were told. In the end they had to leave and live some place else."[27] So an act of nature itself, combined with popular religious beliefs, managed to calm the aggression in the street. However, written articles against the Japanese continued to be published.

The United States had great influence over many successive Peruvian governments. With Japan's entrance into the Second World War, again the Japanese and their descendants suffered from serious aggressive acts. In 1941, after the attack on Pearl Harbor, the Peruvian banks froze the accounts of Japanese in the country. Later, the government confiscated businesses and closed Japanese schools. In the end, 2,118 Japanese and Nisei Peruvian citizens were deported. Some were taken to concentration camps in the United States. Some would later be used to exchange for prisoners.[28] This period marks the beginning of the lost years, also called "The Years of No Return," when the immigrants lost their dreams of returning to Japan to show off their success.

Many Japanese Peruvians had already decided to stay in Peru. We heard phrases that appeared to be excuses for prolonging their stay in Peru: "I like the weather [in Peru] and everything is here: ocean, sun, countryside. It's not too cold, and it's not too hot." "Children arrive and it is increasingly difficult to return to Japan." "I want to work a while longer and continue to save." "My children are Peruvian." The fact is that many had largely achieved the economic success necessary for their return, but they nevertheless stayed in Peru. As Morimoto remarks, "The roots, then, into their adopted country were deeper, and returning was only an ideal that allowed the Nikkei to generate and maintain a sense of self identity."[29]

The war years were definitely difficult for the Nikkei. They were years of austerity and fear. Many Issei lived in hiding for fear of being deported.

Leadership roles were progressively passed from the Issei to their children, the Nisei. The Issei, stripped of their savings and businesses, lost a large part of what they had achieved throughout their lives. These hard years forged the character of the Nisei. The possibility for them to lead comfortable and easy lives also vanished. The Nisei had to interrupt their studies, and they lost the freedom of movement and the freedom to gather for meetings. Many times they had to ingeniously improvise activities to bring in income to help maintain their families.

Beginning in the 1950s the majority of the Nisei studied in public schools, called Grandes Unidades Escolares (large school units), and many began attending universities. This reflected not only a change of place and educational trajectory for them but also a fundamental change in attitude. This is one of the reasons that the majority of the Nisei in Peru do not have a command of Japanese.[30] Since the late 1950s though, evidence has emerged to indicate the new generations' search for and reaffirmation of their identity. The Nisei have become involved in academic and cultural issues and have begun to develop an awareness of the need for greater participation in national life and, above all, the political arena.

An example of this newfound awareness is the appearance of an organization called "The Generation of '64," formed by a group of Nisei university students. This group gathered with progressive intellectuals of the time in the legendary Cafe Palermo, located in front of the University of San Marcos.[31] One of the founders of this group was Congressman Samuel Matsuda. During these years, a sense of normalcy returned to public life. Various traditional associations were reinstated, including those based on the Japanese prefecture of origin and on region of residency in Peru. New associations with academic, cultural, social, and sports orientations also appeared. Two of these associations were the Pacific Club and University Nisei Association of Peru. Beginning in these years, artists, painters, and erudite Nikkei intellectuals gained national and international recognition, becoming new and positive representatives of the community. The daily newspaper *Perú Shimpo*, founded in 1950, continuously increased the number of pages written in Spanish, decreasing those in Japanese. As one of its directors said, "We realized that our number of subscribers was decreasing and we needed to increase the information published in Spanish." The Peruvian Nikkei from the postwar generations on have had brilliant careers in the most diverse fields, including political, economic, professional, academic, social, cultural, and sports activities. Horie and Yanaguida write of this period:

After the Second World War, the Nisei began to form their own associations and take over important roles, at the same time maintaining themselves as persons of Japanese origin. The resulting balance between the two identities enriched the collectivity [Peruvian culture] in a diverse and complex manner. These diversities and complexities eventually produced a great number of professionals, including politicians, one of whom is the current president of Peru, Alberto Fujimori.[32]

It is clear, however, that the election of a Nisei as president of the Republic of Peru arouses contradictory feelings within the Nikkei community. On one hand, it disrupted the newly found tranquility of the Issei, and feelings of fear were reborn. Many remembered and feared breakouts of violence, as in 1940. "If he fails, we are all going to suffer. The people will blame us," said one Nisei. This anxiety is shared by the Issei and many Nisei from Lima, primarily the ones who suffered the vandalism of 1940. On the other hand, for many Fujimori's election symbolizes the people's recognition of the increasing importance and value of the Nikkei population. According to interviews that we have done, the Nikkei have at least three basic attitudes, from which we have created the following typology.

Some were against Fujimori's campaign because they remembered critical moments in their lives during the 1930s and 1940s. One small group even publicly gave their support to the candidate from FREDEMO, Mario Vargas Llosa,[33] although this group really was a minority. Many had some anxiety about Fujimori's campaign but did not publicly share their fears or display open opposition. I should also emphasize that Fujimori did not seek official support from Nikkei community organizations. As is the case for many postwar Nisei, Fujimori's individual and professional development had been accomplished outside the nucleus of the community. Inside this nucleus, he was virtually unknown.[34] Even though some members of the nucleus of the community did not support or vote for Fujimori, there was a general consensus to support him if he were elected. Some felt this way because Fujimori was a Nikkei, others because of his position on national issues.[35] It seems that the majority of Nikkei voted for Vargas Llosa's party, FREDEMO, although only a minority would support him publicly. One of the most frequently mentioned reasons was that Fujimori didn't show a clearly identifiable government program, nor did he have an experienced, organized team to support him.

Japanese Peruvians not tied to the Nikkei community had more individualized attitudes based on personal and political preferences that left the ethnic question completely out of consideration. For example, some Nikkei public university students responded that on April 8 they voted for leftist candidates. Some of the Nikkei interviewed who were from the northern coast of Peru and had developed an important regional identity affirmed that they voted for APRA, the political party with traditional roots in that area.

The election of 1990 had two rounds. The first was on April 8 and the second was on June 10. Between these dates, with only two candidates remaining, some of Vargas Llosa's supporters launched intense attacks against Fujimori to damage his credibility and image, including attacks related to his ethnicity. The sudden emergence of Alberto Fujimori into the highest level of Peruvian politics caused new outbreaks of racism, despite Vargas Llosa's public rejection of them. These manifestations of racism came primarily from the Creole population, many of them FREDEMO members or sympathizers. "Creole," as it is defined by Degregori,[36] refers especially to the upper- and middle-class white and light skinned mestizo, primarily of Spanish origin, but including other European immigrants who arrived at the end of the last century. This includes the Criollo popular sectors, especially those from Lima that share a series of codes of conduct with the Criollo power elite. Enrique Chirinos Soto, the official spokesman for FREDEMO, declared that "beyond the Constitution, a historical constitution exists, which wouldn't accept a first-generation Peruvian in the presidency of the Republic." He affirmed that while MVll (Mario Vargas Llosa) was Peruvian through and through and his native language was Spanish, Fujimori's native language was Japanese and his mother didn't speak Spanish.[37] His declarations were produced amidst a torrent of written and oral racist manifestations, during which even physical mistreatment of some Peruvian citizens of Chinese and Japanese origin occurred. Declarations of this kind ignored the multiethnic makeup of Peruvian society, including one of Peru's two largest distinctive, yet complimentary, contingents: the Quechua-Peruvians and the Hispanic-Peruvians. The mothers of most Peruvians didn't speak Spanish well, either. Fujimori, using this ethnic attack to his favor, won many votes by repeating the slogan "Little white ones on one side, and Chinitos and Cholitos [Chinese and Indians] on the other." Because of such remarks, Fujimori was also accused of promoting racism.

A number of factors made the election of Alberto Fujimori as president of the Republic possible.[38] Among them was the vote against the white traditional oligarchy, with which the parties on the right that formed part of Vargas Llosa's FREDEMO were associated. During an interview a street salesman of Andean origin said, "I am going to vote for Fujimori. It could suddenly go wrong for me, but I am giving myself that pleasure."

Another of the many factors was the acceptance of values attributed to the Nikkei community, like honor, work, and other virtues associated with modern Japan. Fujimori emphasized these values in his campaign theme, "Technology, honesty, and work." This acceptance was based on an ambiguous perception of the Nikkei by the *Chola* or indigenous population. On the one hand they related to these values and recognized many commonalities, like coming from humble origins, being the sons and daughters of migrants, having a strong work ethic, and being the target of discrimination. On the other hand, they continued to perceive the Nikkei as Chinese or *ponjaí* (jargon in Spanish for "Japan," spelled with syllables transposed); they associated them with the Asian Tigers of the Pacific Rim, and the more recent image of Japan as a highly technical country with great economic achievements.[39] The general electorate favored Fujimori because of his ties to an admired nation, because of public opinion in Peru, and because, with few exceptions, the Nisei don't ordinarily get involved in national politics.[40]

Conclusion

In the course of their hundred-year history in Peru, the Nikkei have followed a path of struggle and have developed many social, political, and economic strategies that have allowed them to improve their social position and become culturally integrated into the national society. During the first decades of immigration the importance of the *ken-jin* (persons from the same province) identity and the formation of a strong regional identity in Peru were critical. The relationships that established the Nikkei population as Peruvians, in their work and daily contacts, explain in part the position the group assumed in the popular imagination. The ethnic conflicts that were a result of economic and political competition and the discrimination they faced throughout their history, especially during the peak years from 1930 to 1940, only strengthened their identity as Nikkei.

Notes

1. The number of institutions was mentioned in the press release from the Peruvian Japanese Association of Peru on April 14, 1990, and in the daily newspaper *Hoy* (Lima) on May 5, 1990.

2. See Augusto Higa, "El rostro de los descendientes" (The face of the descendents), *Presa Nikkei*, special edition, Aug. 1993.

3. Jorge Nakamoto, "Discriminación y aislamiento: el caso de los japoneses y sus descendientes" (Discrimination and isolation: The case of the Japanese and their descendents), in Amelia Morimoto, ed., *First Seminar on Immigrant Populations* (Lima: National Council of Science and Technology, Volume II, 1988), 197.

4. The Japanese that arrived in the period of immigration under contract (1899–1923) came from at least forty-seven prefectures (*ken*) in Japan. From the year 1906, immigrants from Okinawa, considered a second-class minority by the Japanese, arrived. By 1923, 18,258 Japanese had arrived in Peru, the majority contracted to work on sugar plantations. Of the total, 2,145 were women and 226 were children. See Luis Ito and Ricardo Goya, *Inmigración japonesa al Perú, 75 aniversario* (Japanese immigration to Peru: 75th anniversary) (Lima: Editorial Perú Shimpo, 1974), section in Japanese; and Amelia Morimoto, *Los inmigrantes japoneses en el Perú* (The Japanese immigrants in Peru) (Lima: Seminar on Andean Studies, National Agrarian University, 1979).

5. Amelia Morimoto, *Los inmigrantes japoneses en el Perú*, 94. On the causes and background of this immigration, as well as the conditions of the contracts and the real work conditions, see Toraji Irie, "History of the Japanese Migration to Peru," *Hispanic American Historical Review*, trans. William Hime, 31:3 (Aug. 1951): 437–52; 31:4 (Nov. 1951): 648–64; and Amelia Morimoto, *Los inmigrantes japoneses en el Perú*.

6. Toraje Irie, "History of the Japanese Migration to Peru," 442–43. Mary Fukumoto, Bachelor's thesis in anthropology, "Migrantes japoneses y sus descendientes en el Perú" (Japanese migrants and their descendents in Peru), Major University of San Marcos, 84–85.

7. Jorge Nakamoto, "Discriminación y aislamiento," 183.

8. Amelia Morimoto, *Los inmigrantes japoneses en el Perú*, 47.

9. Irie mentions that up until December 1909, 414 immigrants returned to Japan, 242 emigrated to other countries, 481 died, and 5,155 remained in Peru. One of the causes of the high number of deaths was endemic illness on the plantations.

10. Jose Watanabe, in an excellent article, discusses savings, establishment of the first businesses, and the cultural mix. Jose Watanabe, "Laredo: donde los japoneses se hallaban" (Laredo: Where the Japanese found themselves), *Puente* 1:1 (Dec. 1980): 52–53.

11. See Jose Matos, *Yanaconaje y reforma agraria en el Perú* (Yanaconaje and agrarian reform in Peru) (Lima: Institute of Peruvian Studies, 1976).

12. Amelia Morimoto, *Los inmigrantes japoneses en el Perú*, 42. In documents from the Archive of Agrarian Code (1906–7), Morimoto found that the administrator of the San Nicolas plantation noted that within six to eight months after their arrival on the plantation, sixty percent of the workers escaped.

13. Toraji Irie, "History of the Japanese Migration to Peru," 663. Lucia Arakaki, Bachelor's thesis, "La educadora familiar y la situación del Nisei" (The family educator and the situation of the Nisei), Pontific Catholic University of Peru, Social School.

14. Luis Ito and Ricardo Goya, *Inmigración japonesa al Perú*, 35.

15. Taeko Akagui has written a paper on the influence in social and commercial activities of the personal networks formed through the "calling" of new immigrants originating from the same prefecture, highlighting the character of the *"ken-jin"* identity. "Formation of a personal network and the collective feelings of pertaining to the same prefecture in the case of those from Fukushima in Lima," in Toshio Yanaguida, comp., *Lima no Nikkeijin* (Tokyo: Meiseki Shoten, 1997).

16. In the literary works of Jose Watanabe and Nicolas Matayoshi we can see manifestations of this strong regional identity.

17. Carlos Degregori, "El aprendiz de brujo y el curandero chino: etnicidad, modernidad y ciudadanía" (The witch's apprentice and the Chinese healer: Ethnicity, modernity and citizenship), in *Elecciones 1990: demonios redentores en el nuevo Perú: una tragedia en dos vueltas* (Lima: Coleción Mínima, IEP, #22, 1991), 116.

18. Luis Ito and Ricardo Goya, *Inmigración japonesa al Perú*, 30.

19. Ibid., 30–31.

20. The *tanomoshi*, or rotating credit association, fulfilled an important role. Sentei Yaki, a native of Okinawa, introduced it in Peru.

21. Luis Ito and Ricardo Goya, *Inmigración japonesa al Perú*, 33.

22. Rogger Ravines, "Migración y colonización en el Perú: preámbulo necessario"

(Migration and colonization in Peru: Necessary preamble), *Boletín de Lima* 20, no. 114 (1998): 9–18.

23. *La Crónica*, Jan. 22, 1918, 2; Feb. 8, 1918, 12.

24. See Amelia Morimoto, *Los japoneses y sus descendientes en el Perú* (The Japanese and their descendants in Peru) (Lima: Editorial Fund of the Congress of Peru, 1999); C. Harvey Gardiner, *The Japanese and Peru, 1873–1973* (Albuquerque: University of New Mexico Press, 1975); and Jorge Nakamoto, "Discriminación y Aislamiento."

25. Luis Ito and Ricardo Goya, *Inmigración japonesa al Perú*, 38.

26. *El comercio*, May 14, 1940.

27. Interview with Michiko Hayashi (female, sixty-five years old), Dec. 14, 1998, in Lima.

28. Jorge Nakamoto, "Discriminación y aislamiento," 187.

29. Amelia Morimoto, *Los japoneses y sus descendientes en el Perú*, 148.

30. According to the census of 1989, in 48.78 percent of Nikkei homes no members use the Japanese language; see Amelia Morimoto, *Población de origen japones en el perú: perfil actual* (Population of Japanese origin in Peru: Current profile) (Lima: Commemorative Commission of the 90th Anniversary of Japanese Immigration to Peru, 1991). Among those that do speak Japanese, many do not have a command of the written language. However, there is an inventory of Japanese words used in daily life as a code among them. Through these words, values that are key symbols of identity are transmitted and understood. See Rumi Marimoto, "Ocha o café: un acercamiento al habla de los Nikkei" (Tea or coffee? An approach to Nikkei speech), *Anuario 92*, Nikkei Press (1992): 105–6.

31. See Guillermo Thorndike, *Los imperios del sol: una historia de los japoneses en el Perú* (The empires of the sun: A history of the Japanese in Peru) (Lima: Editorial Brasa, S.A., 1996).

32. Fukashi Horie and Toshio Yanaguida, "La transformación de la colectividad peruana japonesa después de la Guerra Mundial y el Presidente Fujimori" (Transformation of the Peruvian Japanese collectivity after the Second World War and President Fujimori), in Toshio Yanaguida, comp., *Lima no Nikkeijin* (Tokyo: Meiseki Shoten, 1997).

33. *El comercio*, Apr. 12, 1990; *Caretas* 1110 (May 28, 1990): 10–11; and *Oiga* 484 (May 28, 1990).

34. Interview with Gerardo Maruy in *Caretas* 1104 (Apr. 16, 1990): 28–31.

35. See Amelia Morimoto, *Los japoneses y sus descendientes en el Perú*, 222.

36. Carlos Degregori, "El aprendiz de brujo y el curandero chino," 89.

37. *Caretas* 1104 (Apr. 16, 1990); *Caretas* 1121 (Aug. 13, 1990); and *La republica*, Apr. 19, 1990, 4.

38. See Romeo Grompone, "Fujimori: razones y desconciertos" (Fujimori: Reasons and bewilderment), in *Elecciones 1990: demonios redentores en el nuevo Perú: una tragedia en dos vueltas* (Lima: Coleción Mínima, IEP, #22, 1991); Jose Maria Salcedo, *Tsunami Fujimori* (Lima: La Republica, 1990); *Caretas* 1103 (Apr. 19, 1990).

39. Between September and November of 1998, we conducted field interviews to collect popular images of the Nikkei in Peru. My colleague, Juan Rivera Andia of the Pontific Catholic University of Peru, collaborated in this fieldwork. We confirmed the ambiguous perception that the general population has about the Nikkei. They

consider us both Peruvian citizens and Asian foreigners at the same time. Many still have difficulty distinguishing between descendants of Chinese and Japanese. The most common stereotypes attributed to this group are that we are hard workers and maintain a closed group.

40. *Caretas* 1103 (Apr. 10, 1990): 24. Opinions of Alfredo Torres and Manuel Torrado.

CHAPTER SIX

The "Labor Pains" of Forging a Nikkei Community

A Study of the Santa Cruz Region in Bolivia

KOZY AMEMIYA

At the close of the twentieth century, Bolivia was undergoing positive economic and political changes—liberalization of state-owned industries, increase in foreign investment, and political reform for popular participation. The Department of Santa Cruz, the eastern lowland of Bolivia bordering Brazil, shows all the signs of continuing economic development, thanks to its rich agricultural production and natural gas. Its capital, Santa Cruz de la Sierra (referred to simply as Santa Cruz from here on), has become Bolivia's economic center and most affluent city, boasting the highest standard of living in the country. A stream of internal migrants flows into the Santa Cruz region from poorer parts of the country, where life is harder and future prospects bleak. At the same time, as the economy of the Santa Cruz region has become involved in world trade, it has also become susceptible to the ups and downs of the global economy. The decline in prices of farm products in the last few years has reduced the profits of Bolivian farmers, and stiff competition from surrounding countries threatens the viability of some Bolivian farm products.

Japanese immigrants and their progeny in the Santa Cruz region share in this mixture of prosperity and precariousness, confidence and concern, enthusiasm and caution. These conflicting elements surfaced in the tensions within their community in the face of the crisis in agriculture and on the occasion of the centennial celebration of Japanese immigration to Bolivia. Tensions between the generations—the Issei (who immigrated to Bolivia as adults) versus the junior Issei (who accompanied their parents or other relatives when young) and the Nisei (Bolivian-born second generation)—are the most prominent and prevalent.

As the younger generations move into leadership roles and are urged on by external factors that affect their lives, changes have become apparent in the ways in which people work, think of themselves, educate their children, and relate to other Bolivians. These changes are slowly reorienting the Japanese immigrant community away from reliance on Japan toward reliance on themselves as members of Bolivian society. Until recent years, the community had set itself apart, as if it were an oasis in the desert, sustained by springs of endowment in the form of Japanese governmental aid. Now it is consciously making itself an active participant in determining the future course of Bolivia. This reorientation is a sign of the maturity of the Japanese immigrant community as an integrated ethnic Japanese-Bolivian, that is, Nikkei, community. I am concerned with the process of such a reorientation. In order to document this reorientation, I will examine data collected in 1999 and compare it with data from 1996 and 1997.[1] The goal is to investigate how worldviews are shaped and explore how they may change and influence the direction of the Nikkei community in Bolivia.

The Nikkei in Bolivia

Bolivia's Nikkei are divided between three regions: the northern Amazon basin, old highland cities, and the Department of Santa Cruz. The northern Amazon basin has the largest number of individuals with Japanese surnames, with the largest concentrations in Riberalta and its surroundings (7,000), Trinidad (1,300), Guayaramerín (500), and Cobija (1,000).[2] They are the progeny of early Japanese immigrants and their Bolivian wives. These immigrants worked in the rubber industry of the Amazon region or engaged in commercial activities in the first few decades of the twentieth century. They and their descendants have been cut off from Japan and the rest of the Bolivian Nikkei for so long that they have not established a distinct Nikkei community. Japanese surnames alone have not helped most of them forge an awareness as Nikkei: only a handful of the affluent and those educated in Trinidad have developed a sense of such an identity. Most had paid little attention to their Japanese ancestry until they became aware that those with Japanese surnames could take advantage of special job opportunities in Japan in the late 1980s.[3]

As the rubber boom died down after World War I, many of the original Japanese immigrants left the Amazon region for the old cities of La Paz, Oruro, and Cochabamba. Engaged mostly in commerce, they joined the small Bolivian middle class. Those in La Paz, which is the political and cultural (and, until recently, economic) center of Bolivia, have functioned as a cultural bridge between Bolivia and Japan. However, as they are extremely few in number (eight hundred in La Paz, two hundred in the other cities) and confined to the realm of commerce, they have made little impact on Bolivian society.[4] Some from the postwar immigrant communities in the Santa Cruz region have joined the Nikkei community in La Paz, but the flow is not significant.[5]

The Nikkei in Santa Cruz are mostly postwar immigrants and their descendants. Postwar immigration in the Department of Santa Cruz took place from the mid-1950s through the 1960s and comprised two groups. One came from Okinawa and established Colonia Okinawa, northeast of Santa Cruz, and the other came from all over Japan and settled northwest of Santa Cruz, at San Juan de Yapacaní.[6] A total of 3,200 people immigrated to Colonia Okinawa and 1,600 to Colonia Japonesa San Juan de Yapacaní in the span of ten years. However, the population of these two *colonias*, or settlements, has dwindled. The majority have left the colonias as a result of extreme hardship and a series of crises, or in search of better economic opportunities and education for their children. Many moved to Santa Cruz, reemigrated to another South American country, or returned to Japan. As of 1999, the total Nikkei population in the Department of Santa Cruz was about 2,500: 820 in Colonia Okinawa, 800 in San Juan, and the rest in Santa Cruz.[7] There were also about 500 residents in Santa Cruz with Japanese surnames whose fathers or grandfathers migrated there from the northern Amazon region. Having blended into Bolivian society, these descendants of prewar immigrants have neither retained a self-identity nor established characteristics as Nikkei. They have no contact with the postwar immigrant community in Santa Cruz.[8]

The three groups of Nikkei in Bolivia are thus geographically and historically separated from one another. Of the three, the group in the Santa Cruz region is by far the most prominent. The Nikkei population in the Amazon basin is large but indistinguishable from ordinary Bolivians, and the old, established Nikkei community in La Paz is too small and its activities too narrow to make a mark in Bolivian society. In contrast, the community of Japanese immigrants and their offspring in Santa Cruz has grown as a dynamic ethnic group in Bolivian society. Not only are they already making significant contributions to the Bolivian economy and culture, but their contributions are recognized by Bolivians at all levels. Thus, they have established themselves as a distinct ethnic group in Bolivia. Currently, they are undergoing a transition of leadership from the immigrant Issei generation to the younger junior Issei and Nisei. This is where tensions have surfaced. How they resolve these tensions will affect the direction not only of their own community, but of all Nikkei communities in Bolivia as well.

How to Farm, How to Live

In 1999 the mood was gloomy in Colonia Okinawa (referred to simply as Okinawa from here on), reflecting a 180-degree turn from the utmost optimism of only a few years before. In 1996, when I first visited, the farmers were beaming with confidence about their large-scale farming and ranching and were very hopeful about their continuing progress. By then Okinawa had become famous for its large-scale production of soybeans. The acreage of cultivation was vast, the equipment gigantic, and the wealth conspicuous. Since 1997, however, a cascade of disasters has struck Okinawa. Floods brought crop damages three years in a row. The price of soybeans in the global market fell sharply due to worldwide overproduction. The domestic price of soybeans was once relatively immune to the fluctuation of world market prices, but now the futures market in Chicago affects the domestic price instantly.[9] Furthermore, the entire Santa Cruz region suffered from a serious drought. To make matters worse, powerful winds swept through the wheat fields in Okinawa on August 15, 1999, and destroyed the crop ready for harvest. Such an onslaught of disasters exposed some farmers' fragile economic foundations built on money borrowed at high interest rates.[10] Okinawa was then faced with a major crisis endangering its cooperative, CAICO (Cooperativa Agropecuaria Integral Colonias Okinawa), because almost half of the members were now unable to repay their huge debts, leaving CAICO holding bad loans.

The situation was not so critical in Colonia Japonesa San Juan de Yapacaní (referred to as San Juan from here on). Nor was its cooperative, CAISY (Cooperativa Agropecuaria Integral San Juan de Yapacaní), faced with such serious peril as CAICO, due to different crops and management policy. Okinawan farmers cultivate soybeans, wheat, sorghum, and sunflowers with huge machinery in a drier climate and richer soil than San Juan's. Farmers in San Juan, in contrast, faced with a clay-type soil and higher rainfall, tend to be successful in labor-intensive and smaller-scale operations, such as egg and fruit production. They also grow rice and produce higher priced items, such as macadamia nuts and top-quality papayas. However, some of the younger farmers expanded their acreage on borrowed money like their Okinawan counterparts and were worried about poor crops. Even farmers without debt cannot afford to relax due to the overall drop in agricultural prices, stiff competition from domestic and other South American producers, and declining productivity owing to the decreasing fertility of the soil.

Under these circumstances, criticisms about the way in which the younger generations practice agriculture have surfaced among the Issei. For many Issei, the junior Issei's and Nisei's expansion of land with borrowed money and their large-scale operations appear risky or even reckless. "Younger people kept borrowing money without clear plans for repayment and have ruined our good reputations," griped one Issei in San Juan. "Young people don't think twice about borrowing money and spending it on expensive new cars and big tractors. That's what is at the bottom of the current problems," echoed an elder in Okinawa.

For the Issei, debt symbolizes a threat to economic stability. The elder quoted above proudly proclaimed, "I've borrowed money only from JICA and never from banks."[11] From the viewpoint of the younger generations, such an attitude toward loans is too old-fashioned, or too Japanese, to be applied in Bolivia. One junior Issei in San Juan complained that all he heard from the Issei were criticisms about debt being "dangerous" and large-scale farming being "stupid." He protested, "I practically got sneered at by the Issei when I bought a lot of land eight years ago." He planned to use much of his considerable acreage as pasture. He noted that many Issei raised cattle on fifty-hectare lots, and pointed out, "You can't make money on cattle with such limited acreage. You need a lot of it for cows."

Underlying the tensions between the generations are their different life experiences and worldviews. The Issei had brought with them from Japan old-fashioned ethics that valued hard work with low risk and no debts and toiled hard alongside their Bolivian workers.[12] Those who have succeeded in farming in the colonias feel their hard work has been rewarded, thus reinforcing their belief in hard work, which they regard as one of the Japanese virtues. The junior Issei, growing up watching their parents sweat alongside their Bolivian workers and laborers in the field, became convinced that such a mode of agriculture is not for them. Instead, they observed, farmers have to behave like any Bolivian boss. One junior Issei in Okinawa, who changed the relationship with his employees when he took over the farm from his father, explained, "You must give orders to your workers, or else they will not look upon you as their *patron* [boss]." Another junior Issei in San Juan commented, "The fundamental part of agriculture is how well you get Bolivian employees to work." The Nisei cannot even imagine themselves doing the same work as their workers. They are, as one Issei declared, "born *patrones*."

The Issei's criticisms are not limited to how to practice agriculture, but are aimed more generally at how to live. Many of the retirees enjoy gateball (a game like croquet devised in Japan for senior citizens), but they did not even think about having fun during their productive years. The younger generations are different. They do not think that their lives should be all work. It is just as important for them to enjoy life. So the younger generations in Okinawa spend much time on golf, and in San Juan on fishing. This draws more complaints from the Issei, whose vocabulary does not include the phrase "enjoy life."

The generational conflict does not mean that each generation is unified in its views and attitudes. There are variations within each generation, and, more importantly, there is a clear difference between the junior Issei and the Nisei. One junior Issei in San Juan reflected, "Though I'm conscious of myself as different from the Nisei and have no longing for Japan, I'm sometimes conscious of myself as Japanese after all, particularly when I'm with Bolivians." Another junior Issei in Okinawa remarked, regarding the CAICO crisis, "We have inherited from the Issei the Japanese way of thinking and try to come up with a solution to help everybody. The Nisei are totally different from us. They are willing to cut off those who are going to fail. That's the big difference between us."

However, the older and younger generations are not as different as they appear on the surface. The younger generations who have worked in Japan as dekasegi prefer life in Bolivia because, as they remark, in Japan it is all work and no play. The Issei prefer living in Bolivia, too, for they see their lives in Bolivia as more comfortable than their counterparts' in Japan. The difference is that the Issei's worldview does not provide them with a language in which to express their desire straightforwardly, without a sense of shame.

The 1999 Okinawa farm crisis is a challenge for the younger generations, as the CAICO leadership is already in their hands. The president and general manager are junior Issei, and many on the board of directors are Nisei. A clear indicator that the leadership has shifted to the younger generations is that all CAICO meetings are conducted in Spanish. CAISY has been slower to change. Both its president and general manager are Issei, and CAISY meetings are still conducted in Japanese. However, there is no question that this will change in the near future.

What to Celebrate and How to Celebrate It

In 1899 ninety-one Japanese men crossed the border from Peru into Bolivia. They had fled harsh working conditions and sought better jobs in the Amazon region, where the rubber business was booming. A hundred years later, a grand ceremony in Santa Cruz celebrated the centennial of Japanese immigration to Bolivia. VIPs from both Bolivia and Japan were invited, including the Bolivian president and Princess Sayako from Japan's Imperial family. Following the ceremony, the Japanese princess visited San Juan and Okinawa, attending a grand reception at each colonia. Bolivian media not only covered the events, but before and during the celebration ran special reports on the Japanese immigrants' history and contributions to Bolivian society. The princess not only impressed the Issei with her modest demeanor, elegance, intelligence, and air of accessibility, but she was also enormously popular with the Bolivian press. Thus, the centennial provided both the Nikkei and the Japanese with an opportunity for good publicity. Consequently, the celebration was regarded a success in the Nikkei community to varying degrees.

The idea of celebrating Japanese immigration's centennial had been put forth in 1996 at a meeting of a coalition of Nikkei associations with the hope that the celebration would galvanize the community and unify the Nikkei groups.[13] However, it was also an event that brought tensions between competing interests and worldviews to the surface. There were disagreements about how to define the first Japanese immigrants in Bolivia, where to hold the celebration, how to proceed with the ceremony, and where to place the Nikkei community in Bolivian society. Some in the Santa Cruz region questioned the definition of the centennial itself. As far as they were concerned, the Japanese who crossed the border from Peru in 1899 were not the first Japanese immigrants in Bolivia but refugees. One Issei in San Juan argued, "those who came to Bolivia [in 1899] did not immigrate here. They ran away from harsh working conditions in Peru." In his opinion, which he indicated that quite a few members of his community shared, the first "true immigrants to Bolivia" were those who came from Japan in the 1910s. A Nisei in Santa Cruz echoed, "The first Japanese in Bolivia simply migrated from Peru in order to make money, not as formal immigrants."

The choice of Santa Cruz as the venue for the centennial ceremony also seemed inappropriate to many. The eightieth and the ninetieth anniversaries were celebrated in La Paz, where the Nikkei community had long been established and functioned as a bridge between Bolivia and Japan. The shift in venue from La Paz to Santa Cruz indicates the growing prominence of the Nikkei community in Santa Cruz. Nonetheless, it was not a logical choice for the centennial. Most Nikkei in the Santa Cruz region are postwar immigrants and their offspring, with little connection to the earlier immigrants. For them, immigration to Bolivia began less than a half century ago.[14] On the other hand, the leaders of the descendants of Japanese immigrants in Trinidad in the northern Amazon region thought that the centennial ceremony should have been held in the Department of Beni, where the earliest Japanese immigrants originally arrived and worked and where thousands of their descendants now lived. Yet, with neither political nor economic clout, nor a close association with the more prominent Nikkei groups in La Paz or Santa Cruz, these descendants are isolated and ignored by both the Japanese government and the more powerful segment of the Nikkei community.

Without a consensus on the basic points of the centennial celebration, raising funds for the ceremony was difficult. The problem did not surface in the colonias because the contribution assigned to them by the Centennial Committee was paid by the Associations of Bolivian-Japanese, the main portion of whose budget came from Japanese governmental aid. It was an entirely different matter in Santa Cruz, where the organization depended solely on individual contributions. Each household was required to contribute US$100, by no means a small amount of money in Bolivia.[15] That amount, however, entitled only one person per household to attend the ceremony. Due to limited seating and a limited budget, an additional sum for "cooperation" was required for a couple to be invited.[16] The high price of participation put off so many in Santa Cruz that the committee had difficulty soliciting contributions. An Issei who was in charge of collection observed, "I don't know whether people simply could not afford to pay both the assigned contribution and the voluntary cooperation money or whether they thought it was unnecessary to do so much. I myself take the latter position. Younger people were very explicit about it and would not put up extra money." He thought that part of the problem was that the reason for holding the centennial had never been sufficiently explained, a point that the younger generation's criticism of the centennial also stressed.

The Nisei criticisms also addressed the issue of how the centennial should have been celebrated. The ceremony was held at a grand hall in a brand-new deluxe hotel in Santa Cruz, which precluded the participation of most people. One Nisei vehemently criticized this aspect: "It was after all an event only for the haves. To be more precise, it was for the Japanese with money and was carried out primarily only among Japanese. I would have liked a celebration held in a big, open place like a stadium where anybody—Japanese and Bolivians, rich and poor—could have participated, like they did in Peru."[17]

In this vision of the centennial celebration, this Nisei projects an ethnic Japanese community in Bolivia into the future, where it is inclusive of all Bolivians. In contrast, the Issei and organizers of the centennial were looking back at the Japanese immigrant community in the past and at the same time affirming the current status of their community as an oasis in the larger Bolivian culture.

In spite of such disagreements, the celebration itself turned out well. The chair of the Centennial Committee commended even the Nisei group for having pitched in despite their opposition to its venue when it was feared that preparations might not be completed in time. He attributed the cooperation of the Nikkei to the "good Japanese characteristics that came to the surface." As a consequence, most people in retrospect think that the centennial celebration was a success.

The younger generations take a utilitarian view of the success, seeing it as generating good publicity and thus improving the image of the Japanese, and therefore themselves, in the eyes of Bolivians. One junior Issei described his views:

I think it was good that we did it. It taught Bolivians the history of Japanese immigrants. It was also good that the princess came. She became a link between Japan and Bolivia. Thanks to all this, the Bolivian president is going to Japan next year. Bolivian TV did reports for about a month before the celebration on Japanese aid. It taught Bolivians about Japanese aid. I have been heckled a couple of times before because I was a foreigner. Nobody will do that now.

The Issei, too, acknowledge the practical benefits of the publicity surrounding the centennial. One Issei in Santa Cruz admits, "The visit by an Imperial family member helped advertise the centennial of Japanese immigration and the Japanese community." To the Issei in both colonias and Santa Cruz, the visit by an Imperial family member had greater significance. It was tantamount to the long-awaited official recognition by Japan of their early struggles in Bolivia. There was no difference between reactions to the princess's visits in Okinawa and San Juan. The Issei women, in particular, traditionally kept in the background, were ecstatic. The president of the Federation of San Juan Women's Societies observed, "It meant for these women that the Imperial family acknowledged their struggles. That's the most significant thing for them. It made the Issei women very happy."

In general, the Nisei were more detached, as one of them in Okinawa remarked, "It was okay [to celebrate the centennial], I guess." He professed, "We weren't particularly interested in the Japanese princess because we are Bolivians. The Issei regarded her like a goddess. But for us, the Bolivian president is more significant." His self-identification as a Bolivian is neither ideological nor political. It is simply a matter of fact for him and his generation.[18]

Even some among the Issei were not entirely pleased with the presence of the princess, but for different reasons. So much time and effort were taken up by preparations for receiving her. Moreover, those who were involved were appalled by the tight security and rigid instructions from the Japanese government. One junior Issei who worked for the reception in Okinawa candidly professed, "I'd rather not have anyone from the Imperial family come again." His sentiment was shared even by some Issei in San Juan. One of the delegates from Trinidad laments that he was barred by a security guard from taking a photo of the princess. "It's against the open feeling of the eastern region," he complained, and he blamed the people from La Paz for the rigid procedure.

Such complaints did not dampen the overall good feelings about the centennial. And yet, the centennial failed to achieve what the organizers had hoped: to unify Nikkei groups into a stronger federation. It failed because the decision to celebrate the centennial in Santa Cruz was made, and preparations for it began, without a consensus as to 1) how Japanese immigration to Bolivia should be defined, 2) when immigration began, 3) why the centennial ceremony should be held in Santa Cruz, and 4) how it should proceed. Without consensus on such fundamental points, the plan for the centennial was received with cool detachment everywhere.

Rather than taking up these questions or considering the different views on Japanese immigration in Bolivia, the organizers simply imposed the celebration plan upon the entire Nikkei community, fueling resentment among various groups and alienating the younger generations even further. When the celebration was over and everyone deemed it a success, the Centennial Committee could have held an open forum to review the issues that had surfaced before and during the celebration. This would have allowed the dissenters to clarify their views, and perhaps they could have found common ground. Such a forum, for example, would have revealed that questions regarding the definition of Japanese immigration to Bolivia were common among not only the younger generations but also among some Issei, which in turn might have cleared away prejudices, at least to some degree, and clarified misgivings between generations and various regional groups. In failing to hold an open exchange of viewpoints, the federation missed an opportunity for bridging the gulf between generations, as well as between the urban and agrarian sectors of the Nikkei community. The centennial provided only a limited, short-lived success in unifying and stimulating the Nikkei community, and fell short of forging a sense of solidarity for the future. Thus, it left the goal of unifying the Nikkei in Bolivia still to be accomplished.

Moving into the Mainstream of Bolivia

Some Nikkei are considering a project that will have a longer-term and wider impact than the centennial celebration had, both inside and outside the Nikkei community. That is, they are interested in achieving active participation in the Bolivian political system. This is a remarkable change from only a few years ago. No one in the Nikkei community thinks that the Bolivian government is good enough as it is. Regarding the Bolivian government's incapability or unwillingness to provide what they believed it to be the government's responsibility to provide, the Issei have always turned to the Japanese government for aid, and have resorted to their idealized image of Japanese characteristics for moral sustenance.

The younger generations think they should abandon this reliance on Japan. As one Nisei puts it, "We should either take care of ourselves or negotiate with the Bolivian government first. It's only logical because we live in Bolivia. Yet the Issei still rely on the Japanese government for help. It's a disgrace." Not that the younger generations think the Bolivian government will take good care of its citizens. They share the Issei's view of the Bolivian government as corrupt. Unlike most Issei, however, they insist they should participate in changing the Bolivian government by sending their own representatives. Even some Issei now talk with great enthusiasm about supporting these political ambitions as their last contribution to the Nikkei community. Such a thing was unthinkable for most Issei when I first interviewed them in 1996.

This is not merely a phenomenon brought about by a transfer of leadership to younger generations. The Nikkei's enthusiasm for political participation corresponds to, reflects, and is encouraged by major political reform in Bolivia that went into effect in 1996. The reform, launched by then President Gonzalo Sanchez de Losada, urged by the IMF and the World Bank, was intended to decentralize the government and redistribute the national revenue according to the population size of a local administrative unit, thus aiming to eliminate the political machine. Enthusiastically embraced by Bolivians, the reform has stimulated the general populace to participate in politics and awakened the Nikkei community from a total indifference to Bolivian politics. The Nikkei's interest in entering the Bolivian mainstream also corresponds to the prospect that aid from Japan will shrink in the future. In fact, this trend has already begun.[19]

As political reform has brought more elected officials into local government bodies, some Nikkei are encouraged to make preparations for sending their representatives into all levels of government. Also, as each *cantón* (an administrative unit separate from the province) now has more control over its revenue, the idea of making the colonia as such a unit within the Bolivian political system enthused the younger generations anxious to integrate their communities into Bolivian society. Several junior Issei in Okinawa have taken the lead. First, in 1996 they succeeded in getting Katsuyoshi Taira elected mayor of Okinawa, then a section of Warnes Province. This was by no means a small achievement, considering that Bolivian residents already outnumbered Okinawans by five to one in Colonia Okinawa. Second, in 1998 these leading junior Issei succeeded in getting Okinawa formally recognized as a cantón, effective in 2000. San Juan is following suit.

In the face of the anticipated end of Japanese government aid, active participation in the Bolivian system was the right move for the colonia to protect its economic base. At first, however, the old guard of the immigrant community perceived instituting the colonia as an administrative unit within the Bolivian system as a threat to the colonia's "establishment," that is, the Japanese-Bolivian Associations. These associations are the administrative offices of the colonias, managing the aid money from the Japanese government, collecting dues from residents, running clinics and schools, and even managing a police force. They have been, in effect, the Japanese immigrants' government. Exclusive of Bolivians, the members took great comfort in the fact that these offices were uncontaminated by corrupt Bolivian politicians. In other words, the Japanese-Bolivian Associations have been cultural as well as economic institutions, and safe havens for the Issei.

However, those in the colonia establishment have come to realize that change was inevitable. They have begun to think about ways to save the association. Candid about his anxiety, the president of the Japanese-Bolivian Association in Okinawa conceded:

Frankly, I'm quite concerned [about Okinawa as an administrative unit in the Bolivian political system]. But we can't stop it because that's the direction the trend is going. We have held the leadership [in Okinawa] so far. They [Bolivians] don't have money, but they have numbers. [With so many of them in the colonia] they can push us away into a corner [if they so choose].[20]

Another Issei in the leadership concurred, "We have reached the age of change. We can't keep the colonia to ourselves forever. We have to work together with Bolivians from now on in the administration of our community." Most Issei now hold such a view, a marked difference in attitude from a few years ago.

Some junior Issei and Nisei in Santa Cruz are thinking a step further: they want to send representatives into the sphere of national politics. They believe it is time that the Nikkei stop being "good immigrants" and join forces as full-fledged Bolivian citizens. In this scheme, the Nikkei's reputation as "sincere, hardworking and honest" is no longer an asset. One leading junior Issei maintained, "the Nikkei are regarded like dolls, that is, loveable, neat, and do-nothing." He acknowledged that if the Nikkei as an ethnic community went into politics, they would be exposed to harsh criticisms, as some Issei worried. "Naturally, we will," he bluntly asserted. "Still, we must get involved. We shouldn't expect to be treated politely as guests forever."

Some Issei are equally enthusiastic about political participation. One of them in Santa Cruz implores the Nisei not to sit idly on the foundation the Issei worked hard to build, but to make efforts on behalf of their community in a different way from their parents by getting involved in Bolivian politics. He points out that various other ethnic groups are powerful because they send competent, assertive representatives into national politics, thus protecting their interests. In his view, the Nikkei tend to be too inhibited to develop political networks. Consequently, he asserted, "we will continue to work to serve the interests of the elite, no matter how large our shares might be in the egg and the soybean markets. We can't even control the prices of our own products." Another Issei in Okinawa shares this view: "We have achieved success in agriculture, but that is not enough. We must cultivate our representatives in Bolivian politics, because politics determines everything, including agriculture."

The purpose of getting into national politics is, as one junior Issei put it, to establish and implement a policy you believe in. Those with political aspiration have a remarkably long-term vision. They want to pursue the dissemination and improvement of primary education. Thirty percent of Bolivia's population, explained one of the most successful junior Issei, is illiterate, and the whites, who comprise only 20 percent of the population, hold all the power. He contends, "Bolivia cannot modernize itself unless the remaining 80 percent of its population can receive basic education." The spread of basic education will help raise the living standard of the majority, which will increase the buying power of the population and help reduce the disparity between rich and poor, and eventually help the Nikkei community. If he sounds overly idealistic, a shrewd Issei echoes that improving the education level of ordinary Bolivians is the key to Bolivia's progress. Those actively involved in preparing to send representatives into politics are small in number. However, they are no longer looked at with suspicion by fellow Nikkei because the Nikkei population as a whole now has a consciousness that they and their progeny are part of Bolivian society.[21]

As the Nikkei community looked inward, on the one hand, at the celebration of the centennial of their immigration to Bolivia, on the other hand they also began to reach outward to the larger Bolivian society through political participation. At the current stage, this project of sending representatives, if one can call it that, is just a bundle of enthusiasm and a phase where feelers are extended and plans quietly made. Potentially, however, these long-term plans could revitalize the Nikkei community and bring it further into the mainstream.

Where to Next?

A clear sign of an emerging Nikkei consciousness of being part of Bolivian society is a shift in emphasis in language education. Until a few years ago, education in the Japanese language was given primary importance in the colonias. Parents were most concerned about preserving Japanese culture and the connection with Japan, and they believed that teaching their children Japanese would be helpful on these fronts. Now, however, even the Issei have come to realize the importance of fluency in Spanish. One elder in Okinawa reflected, "It is time we selected as head of the Japanese-Bolivian Association someone who is more fluent in Spanish than in Japanese and who can converse with Bolivians without an interpreter." Another Issei emphasized the importance of cultivating a social network with Bolivians, for which, of course, fluency in Spanish is essential.

Most Issei in the colonias speak only limited, if any, Spanish and socialize with almost no Bolivians. They need translators when they do business with Bolivians. They eat mostly Japanese food and watch NHK programs on TV.[22] They identify themselves as Japanese and set themselves apart from Bolivians.[23] The urban Issei live among Bolivians and therefore are more confident speaking Spanish than their counterparts in the colonias. In contrast, most junior Issei speak much better Spanish than their parents, and have Bolivian friends, thanks to their education at schools outside the colonias, from secondary level and beyond.

As reform in the political system has unfolded, even the Issei have come to realize that their community is deeply entrenched in Bolivian society. Likewise, both Japanese teachers at elementary schools in the colonias and parents have come to think that Spanish education must be given top priority, even while maintaining that Japanese education preserves an important cultural asset. Although such a realization has not been fully translated into practice, it marks a notable shift in thinking from only a few years back. This change is a significant one because language is a key to acculturation.

Each generation has different life experiences, thus forging different worldviews. The Nikkei, therefore, are facing new challenges as the leadership shifts from the first to the next generation. On the one hand, these challenges are universal in the transformation of an immigrant to an ethnic community in a given society. On the other hand, they are magnified by specific conditions particular to Bolivia: the press for political reform, the domestic and world market to which the Nikkei community is intricately connected, the anticipated reduction in aid from the Japanese government, and Japan's own weakened economic condition. In spite of all the obstacles and tensions, the Nikkei community in the Santa Cruz region is optimistic about its future and is striving to make a difference in Bolivian society through politics as well as the economy.

However, postwar immigrants and their progeny in the Department of Santa Cruz are only part of Bolivia's social fabric. There is a gulf between the colonias and Santa Cruz, as well as the one between the Issei and younger generations that I discussed. The greatest gulf is between postwar and prewar immigrants and their descendants. In particular, those situated in Beni and Pando are living in a completely separate world from other Nikkei and have no contact whatsoever with the rest of the Nikkei community. Their process of acculturation in Bolivian society is entirely different from that of those in Santa Cruz. The Nikkei in the Santa Cruz region regard most of the descendants of prewar immigrants as "others." For example, an internationally renowned poet, Pedro Shimose, has emerged from among those "other" descendants. Yet none of the Nikkei in the Santa Cruz region have a sense of affinity with him or take pride in having a famous Nikkei-Bolivian poet from Riberalta. They often make negative references to the groups in the northern Amazon region such as, "we should not become like them." They are not interested in establishing a relationship with the northern groups, whom they consider "the same as uneducated Bolivians."

Perhaps it will take another generation to forge a sense of unity among all the Nikkei in Bolivia. Maybe the gulf will be too wide by then to be bridged. Or maybe Nikkeiness will not matter at all to the third or fourth generations. What the Nisei do in coming years is the key to the future direction of the Nikkei community in the Santa Cruz region and, in fact, in all of Bolivia.

Notes

I am indebted to all the people and organizations in Santa Cruz, Okinawa, San Juan de Yapacaní, Trinidad, and Riberalta that provided me with unlimited cooperation and bountiful help. Without their generosity, this study would not have been possible. I regret that they are too numerous to name here individually.

1. In 1996 I conducted survey research in Colonia Okinawa and Santa Cruz as well as forty-four in-depth interviews, primarily of the Issei. In 1997 I interviewed thirty individuals, most of whom were junior Issei in Santa Cruz, and also thirteen Issei who had reemigrated to Brazil from Bolivia.

2. Estimates by the Federación Nacional de Asociaciones Boliviano-Japonesas in the pamphlet of the centennial of Japanese immigration to Bolivia. Slightly different figures as of October 1997 are reported by the Centro Cultural Boliviano Japonés. There has never been a systematic census or study done about Nikkei in the Amazon basin.

3. This raises fundamental questions about the definition of Nikkei: what are the criteria, what importance should a surname bear in the definition of Nikkei (the immigrant's daughter carries no Japanese surname in the patrilineal system), and where does self-identification fit in?

4. These numbers are from the centennial pamphlet by the Federación Nacional de Asociaciones Boliviano-Japonesas.

5. Wakatsuki notes that the destination of the majority of urban migrants from San Juan is La Paz and that from Colonia Okinawa is Santa Cruz. See Yasuo Wakatsuki, *Hatten tojokoku e no iju no kenkyu: Boribia ni okeru Nihon imin* (A study of immigration to a developing country: Japanese immigrants in Bolivia) (Tokyo: Tamagawa Daigaku Shuppanbu, 1987), 14. However, the flow of Nikkei to La Paz from San Juan is much smaller than that to Santa Cruz from Colonia Okinawa.

·

6. See The Centennial Record Committee, ed., *Boribia ni ikiru: Nihonjin iju 100-shunenshi* (To live in Bolivia: A centennial of Japanese immigration) (Santa Cruz: Federación Nacional de Asociaciones Boliviano-Japonesas, 2000), 103–324; Colonia Okinawa Fortieth Anniversary Committee, *Uruma kara no tabidachi: Koronia Okinawa nyushoku 40-shunen kinenshi* (The history of the forty years of Colonia Okinawa) (Santa Cruz: Colonia Okinawa Fortieth Anniversary Committee, 1995), 55–126; Kozy Amemiya, "The Bolivian Connection," in Chalmers Johnson, ed., *Okinawa: Cold War Island* (San Diego, Calif.: Japan Policy Research Institute, 1999), 53–69; San Juan Fifteenth Anniversary Committee, ed., *San Juan 15-nenshi* (The history of the Colonia Japonesa San Juan de Yapacaní in its first fifteen years) (San Juan: San Juan Fifteenth Anniversary Committee, 1971); San Juan Japanese-Bolivian Association, *San Juan ijuchi 30-nenshi* (The thirty-year history of the Japanese immigration to San Juan de Yapacaní, Santa Cruz, Bolivia, 1955–1985) (San Juan: San Juan Japanese-Bolivian Association, 1986); Kunimoto Iyo, *Boribia no "Nihonjin mura"* ("Japanese village" in Bolivia) (Tokyo: Chuo Daigaku Shuppankai, 1989).

7. Okinawa's figure is as of February 1, 1999, reported by the Association of Bolivian Japanese in Okinawa. San Juan's is as of August 31, 1999, reported by the Association of Bolivian Japanese in San Juan. Unlike the associations of Bolivian Japanese at both colonias, the Japanese Social Center of Santa Cruz, which has a list of 120 households with 630 persons as its members in 1999, cannot count all Nikkei as members. A fraternity of the Nisei, called Fraternidad Fuji, has 52 households as its members, which accounts for approximately 200 persons.

8. By an estimate of the Centro Cultural Boliviano Japonés as of October 1997, presented by Nobutoshi Sato to the Japanese embassy in La Paz. Some of these descendants are listed as members of the Centro Social Japonés, but they neither pay the fee nor participate in any activity of the society. Per conversation with Kiyoshi Sakaguchi, 1999 president of Centro Social Japonés, on September 14, 1999.

9. Bumper crops in the United States and aggressive expansion of soybean production in Brazil and Paraguay pushed the price of soybeans down from US$225 per metric ton in 1997 to $180 in 1998 and down to $135 as of September 1999. This is more devastating than flood damages because soybeans comprise 80 percent of the income of the Cooperativa Agropecuaria Integral Colonias Okinawa (CAICO). CAICO exports 50 percent of their soybeans, to Peru and Colombia, and sells the remaining 50 percent on the domestic market. Per conversation with Tadashi Yamashiro, president of CAICO, on September 1, 1999.

10. CAICO lent its members money using bank loans at a 14 percent interest rate with an additional 2 percent. Most farmers used such loans to buy large equipment or expand their farming land.

11. JICA (Japan International Cooperation Agency) is an agency run by the Japanese Ministry of Foreign Affairs and is in charge of the bilateral grants portion of Japan's official development assistance (ODA). Its interest rate for loans to the Japanese immigrants is far lower than that of Bolivian banks.

12. My reference to Japan here includes Okinawa, to respect the viewpoint of Okinawan immigrants and their offspring, who regard Okinawa as only a region of Japan and reject the recent popular separatist thinking in Okinawa prefecture about Okinawans. Okinawan identity in Bolivia is an issue, but separate from the subject of this study.

13. In addition, a federation of Nikkei associations was established to unify all the Nikkei groups. Thus, the Asociación Boliviano-Japonesa Colonia Okinawa, the Asociación Boliviano-Japonesa San Juan de Yapacaní, the Centro Social Japonés (Santa Cruz), and the Sociedad Japonés de La Paz came together under the Federación Nacional de Asociaciones Boliviano-Japonesas. The federation's associate members were the Asociación de Descendientes Boliviano Japonés, the Centro Cultural Boliviano Japonesa de Riberalta, the Asociación Nikkei de Descendientes de Japonesas de Guayaramerín, the Asociación Boliviano Japonesa de Rurrenabaque, and the Asociación Nikkei de Cobija. See "1999 Borivia Nikkei Kyoukai Rengokai gaikyo," prepared by the Federation of Bolivian Nikkei Associations, March 1, 1999.

14. The prewar immigrants are better appreciated in Colonia Okinawa because they instigated the plan of postwar Okinawan immigration to Bolivia, proposed it to the Ryukyu government, and prepared the first Colonia Uruma for the new immigrants. For that reason, the postwar Okinawan immigrants feel obliged to the early immigrants, despite the fact that the first Japanese immigrants to Bolivia may indeed have been refugees from Peru rather than true immigrants.

15. Average schoolteachers do not earn much more than that per month. Most of them, unable to support their families, hold two jobs to make ends meet.

16. The Centennial Committee made the utmost effort to carry out the celebration within the budget of a half million U.S. dollars. Per interview with the committee's chair, Kenji Takeda, September 14, 1999.

17. Mr. Takeda cited the security issue, explaining that the Japanese embassy would not have allowed a ceremony involving a member of the Imperial family to be held at a stadium. Peru was supposedly allowed to do so because the Peruvian police were accustomed to dealing with guerrillas!

18. As an example of the process of Bolivianization of younger generations, I witnessed at a joint sports meet of all Okinawan groups on August 29, 1999, that children sang the Bolivian national anthem with vigor but remained silent while *Kimigayo* was being played on tape. Of course, they were taught the former at school.

19. As a clear sign of the direction of the Japanese government regarding aid to Nikkei communities, the Ministry of Foreign Affairs abolished the Bureau of Overseas Emigration in 1999. JICA closed its office for technical aid in San Juan in 1991 when it saw San Juan was able to support itself.

20. The president of the Japanese-Bolivian Association in Okinawa writes candidly in his memoir that he felt threatened by the establishment of Cantón Okinawa and that "it was not a small shock to me." See Kotei Gushiken, *Okinawa ijuchi: Boribia no daichi to tomoni* (Colonia Okinawa: my life with the great earth of Bolivia) (Naha, Okinawa: Okinawa Times, 1998), 305.

21. As of 1999, their role model for their political aspiration, if not a method of governing, was Alberto Fujimori, then president of Peru. He was extremely popular in Bolivia. Indeed, the most politically ambitious Bolivian Nikkei would have said in 1999 that it would be possible to see a Nikkei Bolivian president in their lifetime.

22. Broadcast of NHK programs simultaneous to their broadcast in Japan began in Okinawa in 1998 and in San Juan and Santa Cruz in 1999.

23. Unlike Okinawans in Okinawa prefecture, who emphasize being Okinawans first, Okinawans in Bolivia emphasize being Japanese first. The Okinawan Issei hold

on to a historically shaped and politically oriented identity and are eager to maintain a close connection with Okinawa prefecture. However, having left Okinawa before its reversion to Japanese sovereignty, and having been transplanted to a country where "Okinawan" is synonymous with "Japanese," they maintain that they are Japanese first and their Okinawan identity is a cultural one within the Japanese.

CHAPTER SEVEN

"The Twain Shall Meet" in the Nisei?

Japanese Language Education and U.S.–Japan Relations, 1900–1940

TERUKO KUMEI

In the spring of 1999 the Japan Broadcasting Company aired a program in the metropolitan Tokyo area on the educational problems of Vietnamese refugee families. A mother lamented her inability to communicate with her Japanese-speaking youngest daughter. The program also reported that in Yamato city, Kanagawa prefecture, where there are many diaspora families, in addition to conventional Japanese language classes, public schools had begun to teach the language and culture of the students' home countries.[1]

Immigrants are defined as people who move outside their national boundaries and settle in another country. Regardless of whether or not immigrants are able to form their own communities within their newly adopted country, ultimately they are subordinated to the existing community. Immigrants have no power to change the political, social, and cultural frameworks of the countries they settle in. On the contrary, they are subject to strong pressures from the new country to change themselves. Even though they made the decision to immigrate, immigrants develop a sense of crisis about their cultural and social identity as a result of immigration. The refugee mother mentioned above felt isolated because of the "Japanization" of her children. "Vietnam" was disappearing even at home. This melancholy must have been shared by many immigrants who came to the United States.

However, in this "country of immigrants," the United States, melancholy was also regarded as the price to be paid for other "blessings." Hector St. John de Crevecoeur insists in *Letters from an American Farmer* that, despite nostalgia for people he left at home, an immigrant "[left] behind him all his ancient prejudices and manners" to become a totally "new" man in the "broad lap of our great" America. He further insists that the Americans created in this way are "incorporated into one of the finest systems of population," unprecedented in world history. From this point of view, becoming an American should mean entering a life of good fortune. Therefore, in his view, immigrants should never feel any nostalgia for their home country.[2]

Does immigration bring happiness or estrangement to immigrants? As the case of the Vietnamese mother suggests, language is a key to understanding the issue. It is said that subordinates have no real voice. However, often they eloquently express their sentiments and opinions in their own native language, which the dominant society of the adopted country cannot and is not willing to understand. When immigrants have settled in new countries, facing pressure to choose between exclusion and assimilation, how have they tried to maintain their cultural identity, to attain self-realization, and to pass their values on to the next generation? I plan to examine this problem by focusing on Japanese immigrants in the United States and their efforts to maintain the language of their heritage. I also plan to investigate their transformation from self-identification as Japanese immigrants to self-identification as Nikkei in the United States who still maintain attachments to Japan.

The Education of Japanese Imperial Subjects Abroad

In 1902 the first Japanese grade school was established in the mainland United States. The following year similar schools were established in Seattle, San Francisco, and Sacramento. According to the U.S. census of 1900, there were only 2,990 Japanese in Seattle, 1,781 in San Francisco, and 336 in Sacramento.[3] Although the Japanese population was rapidly increasing, their communities were still struggling to survive. At that time, many Japanese immigrants were single males of working age, so there must have been few school-age children. In addition, in both California and Washington public schools were well established, so there was little concern that Japanese children would be left uneducated. (This was one difference between the situation in the United States and that in the Japanese immigrant colonias or settlements in Brazil, where children would have been left uneducated if the Japanese communities did not provide education.) The fact that they nonetheless established Japanese schools shows their zeal for Japanese education. But we have to remember that Japanese communities accepted public education and established their own parochial schools.

Many of these schools were initially called Japanese grade schools.[4] We should not overlook that these schools were established in order to maintain a form of Japanese nationalistic education in the United States. It was expected that children would assimilate to the school environment once they started school. Naturally, if they went to public schools, they would grow up to become members of U.S. society. On September 21, 1909, the *Ohfu Nippo* (Sacramento daily news) insisted on the need to establish Japanese schools in order to counter the Americanization of children. It warned, "However competent in English, if one is ignorant of Japan, he will be regarded as handicapped by the Japanese." In fact, Zaibei Nihonjinkai (Japanese Association of America), an umbrella organization of Japanese associations within the jurisdiction of the consulate general of San Francisco, observed: "grade schools ... provide Japanese curricula and education ... and try to cultivate nationalistic perspective among children."[5]

Despite an increasing anti-Japanese atmosphere, according to the "Report on the Education of Japanese Children" in 1913, among twenty-five schools in the jurisdiction of the consulate general of San Francisco, approximately half had a policy of providing supplementary Japanese language education, while the other half had one of maintaining a nationalistic education based on the spirit of *Kyoiku Chokugo* (the Imperial Rescript on Education).[6] According to the report, Japanese grade schools considered Golden Gate Institute in San Francisco an exemplary model. Its school regulations explained that the school had been established to "educate children of Japanese compatriots in the United States." It had a kindergarten division, a preparatory division to provide an English-language education for children planning to attend public schools, and a supplementary division to provide a "Japanese language and literature" education for children attending public schools. School holidays included regular American holidays and Japanese holidays such as New Year's Day, National Foundation Day, and the Emperor's birthday. School sessions followed the Japanese system, starting on April 1 and ending March 31.[7] According to an article in the *Ohfu Nippo*, which described the graduation ceremony of another school, it seems that the schools followed Japanese tradition, with pupils singing the Japanese national anthem and reciting the Imperial Rescript on Education.[8] Judging from these primary materials, many schools must have conducted some form of Japanese nationalistic education, which drew attacks from anti-Japanese activists. At the same time, however, it was natural that Japanese immigrants tried to maintain the Japanese educational system until the 1910s because their population included many Japanese-born children, although the number of U.S.-born children was rapidly increasing. Legally speaking, even those who were born in the United States were Japanese nationals.[9]

To Become Citizens Valuable to the United States

The mounting momentum of the Americanization movement made it difficult for Japanese communities to pursue nationalistic education. In April 1912, the Japanese Association of America held an educators' conference and invited thirty-four representatives of Japanese schools in California. They discussed "purposes and principle of education for Japanese children in America" and set themselves the task "to inspire the spirit of permanent settlement among children in America and help them contribute to this land." Although they admitted the priority of U.S. public school education, they insisted on "supplementary instruction in the Japanese language and Japanese national situation," reflecting "the spirit of the Imperial Rescript on Education." According to them, "it should cultivate the good qualities of the Japanese and American spirits."[10] The avowed goals were based on an early decision of the Japanese Association. However, the fact that there was a need to encourage "permanent settlement" even with regard to U.S.-born citizens (Nisei) suggests a persistent *dekasegi* mentality among the first-generation immigrants (Issei). It reveals that immigrant parents and educators still lacked solid awareness that the Nisei were U.S. citizens. Thus, they wanted the Nisei to be educated as Americans in U.S. public schools and as Japanese in Japanese schools.

Here lay an underlying contradiction. On the one hand, educators accepted the U.S. educational system as the first priority, but, on the other hand, they insisted on the Japanese spirit as embodying superior values. In addition, judging from such a phrase as "the Japanese children in America," it is reasonable to believe that they were unconsciously continuing an education for Japanese nationals. Having said that, the Japanese teachers who wrote the recommendation thought it possible to maintain Japanese qualities and become good U.S. citizens at the same time, implying that it was desirable not to lose Japanese qualities. This duality would be considered today a multicultural educational policy. However, in order to determine whether or not being Japanese and American simultaneously would be praiseworthy in the United States, they should have taken other political factors into consideration. Despite the difficult political environment existing at that time, they still could not refrain from wanting to keep their Japanese values. This demonstrates how difficult it is to go beyond cultural boundaries.

Among the nine representatives who expressed what they considered most important, five mentioned the Imperial Rescript on Education and four mentioned the friendship between Japan and the United States or the harmony of Eastern and Western civilizations. However, even among those who valued the Imperial Rescript on Education, Keitetsu Kudo of Ohfu Japanese School and Mitsunari Ichimura of Fresno Japanese School clarified that it should be interpreted "broadly." As Japanese educators they could not have protested publicly against the Imperial Rescript on Education. However, they felt it would be problematic to teach Japanese children who would settle permanently in the United States unconditional loyalty to the Emperor and love for Japan. As a solution, they avoided referring to the issue of loyalty to the Emperor and focused on more general moral issues. In this fashion, they tried to let the two sets of values coexist. During the Teachers Association Conference in 1913, the school officials acknowledged that Japanese textbooks that met Japan's national standard were not adequate to teach Japanese children in the United States, and they decided to develop their own Japanese readers.[11]

However, there was no significant progress in development of textbooks in northern California. But on May 29, 1918, the Central Japanese Association of southern California adopted a resolution to "promptly complete the development of the textbooks for Japanese children in America" by appointing a special committee, financed by Japanese associations located in the Pacific states. The board submitted the resolution to the Fifth Pacific Coast Japanese Association Deliberative Council.[12] Shiro Fujioka, a representative of the Central Japanese Association of Southern California, explained the proposal at the council: "For the independence and future development of Yamato [Japanese] people, it is crucially important to provide children with Japanese language education along with American compulsory education so that they have a clear understanding about the Japanese Empire and have a general knowledge of its history and geography." Concerned that foreign language education might be banned as a result of the Americanization movement in the United States, he insisted that it was imperative to develop a new textbook: "We have no choice other than developing the textbook based on the principle of genuine ethnic self-reliance and future development." The task of textbook development was assigned to the Education Research Committee. In 1919, during the Sixth Deliberative Council, however, it was decided that "each regional Japanese Association could develop its own textbooks to reflect local needs," instead of developing uniform textbooks.[13]

During the sixth conference, the Deliberative Council, except for Canada, adopted a resolution to "make a best effort to encourage Americanization among compatriots, to meet the current situation in America." To this end, they selected several activity goals:

1. Abolish female labor in the fields [revised so as to improve labor conditions].

2. Reform education system [dropped as a matter of the Educational Research Committee].

3. Advise unemployed delinquents to work.
4. Do not send American-born children to Japan [later deleted as too interfering].
6. Master English [unanimously approved].
7. Discourage return of immigrants and the practice of sending remittances to Japan [amended to promote permanent settlement and local investment].
8. Encourage punctuality.

Such goals suggest that "Americanization" was a countermeasure to the West Coast anti-Japanese movement. Tsuneji Chino, a representative of the Central Japanese Association, explained, "Americanization does not mean to become an American but to prove that we are of a good and gentle race capable of adopting external [American] customs." His statements mean that in terms of spirit and nationality, Japanese immigrants could remain Japanese and still become good residents of the United States. Parenthetically, an editorial in the *Rafu Shimpo*, a Japanese language newspaper in Los Angeles, explained on August 21, 1921, that Americanization meant to act in "accord with American spirit," and that American spirit meant "democratic ideology" and a "spirit of independence and self-governance." In other words, the Japanese could be Americanized if they understood the spirit of democracy and acted upon it, regardless of their nationality.

Even at this stage, however, they called their children "American-born." It took "outside pressure" to modify that to the concept of U.S. citizenship.[14] The next year, in 1920, there was a special conference at which members of the council—concerned with the fact that Congressman Albert Johnson had submitted a bill to amend the Fourteenth Amendment of the Constitution, which proposed to deprive of citizenship the children of aliens "ineligible to citizenship"—discussed the protection of the citizenship of American-born children. Kiichi Kanzaki, of the Japanese Association of America, insisted on the need to educate parents to perform their "duty of providing their children with a decent education so they could become good citizens." The Japanese Association of Oregon requested that the council adopt a resolution to "abolish Japanese language schools, and to use the facilities for English language schools or for home education, in order to carry out Americanization thoroughly for the better future for children of Japanese immigrants." Their representative, Toyoji Abe, raised the criticism that Americanization and maintenance of "the national [Japanese] language school" were "utterly contradictory" and "totally against the tide of the times." He then asserted, "the abolition was primarily the result of concern about the future of fellow Japanese." Chuzaburo Ito of the United Northwestern Japanese Association insisted that Americanization and Japanese language education were compatible and that Japanese in the United States must know Japanese in order to achieve their mission of cultivating friendship between the United States and Japan.

At the seventh regular conference, in 1920, the resolution was discussed again. Concerned that Japanese schoolchildren might become segregated from the other schoolchildren, Abe expressed his opinion that, "as parents, it is unbearable to place our children in shadow." However, many thought that it would be difficult to execute so drastic a plan as eliminating all Japanese schools. In the end, the resolution was amended. The new priority was to "reform the curriculum and organization of national [Japanese] language schools so as to make them in accord with the spirit of Americanism in order to provide a better future to the children of compatriots in the United States." Regarding the "protection of the citizenship of American-born children," the following recommendations were adopted:

1. Avoid disputes over nationality issues of American-born children,
2. Encourage establishment of citizens' associations in each region. Guide the children to become good citizens,
3. Make efforts to get parents to become aware of their duty to educate their children to become good American citizens, and
4. Adopt countermeasures to the movement for amending the American Constitution to deprive Japanese immigrants' children of citizenship.

The council continued discussing to what extent rescindment of Japanese nationality could be facilitated in the next few years. It was December 1923 when the council submitted its formal request to the Japanese government, and the amendment of nationality law was passed in 1924.[15]

Regarding the textbook problem, following the resolution made during the sixth conference, the United Northwestern Japanese Association developed its own textbooks. In 1921, they published an eight-volume textbook. A total of six thousand textbooks were printed, at a total cost 6,565 yen.[16] On the other hand, textbook development in California was delayed, and the revisions had not been completed before the promulgation of the California Private School Law of 1921. The sixteen volumes of California textbooks, edited to "conform to the new law and yet at the same time be adapted to the minds of the American-born Japanese," were approved by the California State Board of Education in 1923 and published in 1924. Their main object was "to impart" Japanese language skills. Materials were mainly selected from U.S. textbooks and "supplemented by adaptations from various readers in Japan."[17]

Ken Ishikawa, who in 1922 conducted a year of research on Japanese language schools in California, was doubtful about the Americanization of Japanese language education brought about by pressure from the outside. Ishikawa charged that with the educational goals of Japanese language schools they made the schools to be a tool for the Americanization movement. He went on to say, "How could anybody with common sense possibly accept the notion of establishing Japanese language schools in order to promote Americanization?" In fact, as Ishikawa pointed out, as long as children attended a public school, they would speak English and learn about American culture. If Americanization were the goal, the Japanese language school would not be necessary.[18]

However, from the viewpoint of promoting the "development of good citizens," Japanese language schools would not necessarily be useless. In addition, some Japanese language schools, such as Sakura Gakuen, functioned as boarding schools, as parents shifted around among labor camps. Children otherwise might have been left alone. These schools took in such children, fostered them on behalf of their parents, and sent them to U.S. public schools. A Japanese grade school, Japanese School of Stockton, responded to a query in Ishikawa's questionnaire: "The pupils of our boarding school are praised by teachers of public schools because they are always on time and present in classrooms. They are also clean and bathe regularly." Guadalupe Boarding School responded that it was established so that parents would have an alternative to sending their children to Japan to be cared for. Even non-boarding schools still "took in" pupils in the form of offering "classes" after public school classes were over for the day. So one function of Japanese language schools was similar to that of today's after-school activities programs. In fact, of the twenty-three schools Ishikawa investigated, seventeen provided reinforcement to family discipline and proper manners, twenty aimed at facilitating communication between parents and children, and seventeen referred to enhancing the future of children. Ishikawa interpreted the situation as follows: "Today, school is no longer a national educational institution but a mere extension of family education."[19] However, Japanese language schools must have been necessary, even as "an extension of family education," where immigrants were not able to establish a fully functional family life.

Ishikawa also conducted an investigation of knowledge and ethics among the pupils of Watsonville Gakuen.[20] He asked twenty-six pupils between the ages of ten and sixteen to name "good Japanese persons." Half of the pupils could not name anyone accurately. Some even named fictional people or people closely associated with themselves. The most frequently cited names were Masashige Kusunoki (five pupils), Maresuke Nogi (three pupils), and Masatsura Kusunoki (three pupils). Considering that the children were allowed to name more than one person, the number of responses was very small. On the other hand, pupils were able to list a larger number of "good American persons": Washington (twenty-four pupils), Lincoln (eighteen pupils), and Franklin (thirteen pupils) were the three most cited people. On the other hand, pupils in Tokyo asked to name "ideal persons" cited such names as Washington, Nightingale, and Christ. Ishikawa concluded that the pupils in Tokyo demonstrated a stronger Western influence than the pupils in Watsonville did a Japanese influence.

For one of the ethical question on the survey, pupils were asked "what do you think 'good' is?" Among pupils younger than nine years of age in Watsonville, thirty-three referred to self-oriented ethics (honesty), thirteen referred to family-oriented ethics (obligation to parents, obedience to mothers), and twenty-two referred to society-oriented ethics (kindness, getting along with friends, obedience to teachers). Among those older than ten years of age, forty-two referred to self-oriented ethics (honesty, righteousness), six referred to family-oriented ethics (obedience to parents), thirty-six referred to society-oriented ethics (kindness, helping others, etiquette), and one referred to nation-oriented ethics (love of homeland). The same questions were asked of 107 pupils in Tokyo. When the results are compared, both groups selected the same factors in self-oriented ethics. In family-oriented ethics, in both Japan and the United States obligation to parents ranked high. However, in other categories Watsonville pupils recorded a smaller number of responses. In addition, no pupils in Watsonville listed "respect ancestors" or "getting along with siblings," and the percentage of pupils who referred to loyalty to the nation was also very low. Ishikawa concluded that the pupils in Watsonville lacked a Japanese sense of family values. In the category of society-oriented ethics, Watsonville pupils referred to individually oriented ethics such as "kindness" and "to help others," while Tokyo pupils were more publicly oriented, giving responses such as "public interest," "collaboration and cooperation," and "respect public morality." Ishikawa interpreted the latter answers as reflecting a sense of ethics oriented toward the abstract organization called society, which was typically Japanese. The implication was, then, that Watsonville pupils were not Japanese in spirit. Ishikawa concluded that even with education at a Japanese language school, "Nikkei citizens" would not lose morality as U.S. citizens. Ishikawa insisted that education at Japanese language schools was not conducted to Japanize Nikkei citizens. He was concerned, however, that Americans did not understand the real nature of the Japanese language schools.[21]

The educational goals of Japanese language schools were highlighted to provide counter-evidence against the anti-Japanese arguments. Therefore, the *Rafu Shimpo* hoped that the current misunderstandings would be resolved once the California Private School Law came into effect and the actual curriculum aims of the Japanese language schools were uncovered.[22] Although concerned about the future of the Ozawa naturalization test case, on April 23, 1921, the same newspaper editor presented an optimistic view of the future of Nikkei American citizens: "At least we should make our children

become great American citizens. ... If our children can obtain a good education, have great integrity and are talented, then even when they are facing racial discrimination, there will be no doubt that they can become very successful as compared to the children of other ethnic groups."

In this way, Japanese immigrant parents firmly believed that even if there
was racial discrimination, in the United States, where people were fundamentally judged in terms of their abilities, Nikkei American citizens should
be able to realize the dreams their immigrant parents once pursued and were
denied, as long as they obtained a good education. This conviction was supported by sentiment regarding the ideals of justice, humanity, and fraternity,
which they believed foundations of the American spirit, and by their trust in
U.S. society.

Foundation for World Peace

However, the situation was not necessarily as people had hoped. If it were
not for the decisions reached by the U.S. Supreme Court in 1923 and 1927,
Japanese language schools in California would all have disappeared. The
Japanese Association of America called the decade between 1917, when the
Americanization movement in Japanese language schools started, and 1927
the "Era of Sufferings." Thanks to the Constitutional guarantees, the "almost
closed Japanese language schools were revitalized" and regained momentum
up to the "golden age" of the 1930s. At least that is how the association interpreted the situation.[23] Actually, however, the Supreme Court decision allowed Japanese language schools to exist, but did not guarantee their prosperity. The prosperity of the 1930s was brought on by the fact that many
Nisei reached school age and the Japanese culture was reevaluated at that
time.

The Japanese culture was reevaluated partly because Japan became recognized as a great power. Japanese immigrants were proud of Japan's international prestige. On the other hand, in the United States they were still facing
discrimination. The proud immigrant parents were concerned that prejudice
and discrimination would have a negative influence on their children. The
Nichibei Shimbun published two articles on October 20 and 21, 1927, titled
"The Second Generation and their Japanese Language Education from the
Ethnic Viewpoint." In these articles, author Toshiaki Yonezawa warned, "it
was natural for the Nisei who lack self-esteem to become intimidated and in-
active, or sink down into the depth of depravation" as a result of discrimination. He insisted on the importance of nurturing a "sense of mission" and
"ethnic pride" among the Nisei through Japanese language education, in order to help them to overcome their inferiority complex. The *Nichibei Shim-*

bun also warned in an op-ed article of June 17, 1930, that the Nisei accepted the superiority of "Caucasians" and had developed a "servile" attitude. According to the newspaper, people with higher education had a stronger tendency toward reacting in this way.

The Pacific State Consuls' Conference also seriously discussed this problem. During the third conference in 1928, Morizo Ida, consul general of San Francisco, criticized the Nisei for turning into "spiritual half-breeds" who could be neither full-fledged Japanese nor Americans, due to insufficient education at home and in Japanese schools. He insisted on the importance of establishing good Japanese schools and adequate youth organizations. Responding to this opinion, Suemasa Okamoto, secretary of the Japanese embassy in the United States, pointed out that the Nisei were U.S. citizens, even though many of them held Japanese nationality, and insisted that it would be important for Japan to cooperate with the United States. However, Kojiro Inoue, consul of Portland, doubted, considering the political movement to deprive the Nisei of citizenship and the difficult employment situation facing them, that American society would take any serious measures for their education. He suggested that the Nisei were not acknowledged fully as U.S. citizens, saying, "The Nisei are Americans only in terms of the nationality law." He further warned that unless the Nisei became good citizens, deprivation of their citizenship—a measure that would diminish Japan's national prestige— might indeed result; therefore, "whether the Japanese American will succeed or fail is a problem for the Japanese race as a whole." Yoshitaka Hanawa, deputy consul of Seattle, agreed on this point, indicating that the Nisei lacked self-esteem because of the discrimination that their parents were facing. He insisted on the necessity of teaching them the "true value" of Japan and its culture in order to nurture human dignity among them. In conclusion, they agreed:

Since the future of the Japanese in America depends on the so-called Nisei, there is no doubt about the importance of their education. At the same time, however, they are in the special situation of being American citizens and of the Japanese race simultaneously. ... Taking these special conditions into account when educating and guiding the second generation, it is important not to deal with the issue only on the Japanese side. As long as they are American citizens, we should try to get the American society to cooperate with us in order to achieve our goal of nurturing the Nisei to be good American citizens.[24]

Regarding Japanese language schools, they observed realistically that as long as the Issei existed, it would be difficult to abolish them completely, but that they would eventually disappear. However, since it did not look particularly "harmful" to the U.S.–Japan relationship at this point, the consuls decided to leave them as they were with cautions not to exacerbate anti-Japanese sentiment. Obviously, the decision was greatly influenced by the political situation and by U.S. public opinion. The consuls were not indifferent to the educational issues of the Nisei. However, they could not give support to the continuation of Japanese language schools in the United States.[25]

Teachers at Japanese language schools also started to reevaluate the importance of going beyond simple language education and teaching Japanese morals. During the second U.S.–Canada Japanese Teachers' Conference in the summer of 1930, Masato Yamazaki of the Tacoma Japanese Language School reported that after careful deliberation, the Tacoma school had decided to add *shushin* (Japanese national ethics based on Confucianism) classes to their curriculum to teach values such as "obligation to the parents."[26] This was partly in response to requests from parents. Careful deliberation was probably required because they were concerned that Americans might once again misunderstand the intent of such classes. Kenzo Ogasawara at Mountain View Japanese Language School reported that lately people had been more supportive of shushin classes due to the increase in delinquent behavior among the Nisei, and that some schools were actually using the Japanese textbook as a way of teaching discipline. He also acknowledged the delicacy of the problem.[27] Both teachers and parents believed that shushin classes would be the most effective means of cultivating pride in their origin and morality among the Nisei. At the same time, they were aware of the danger of directly importing shushin class from Japan, which placed primary importance on loyalty to the Emperor and filial piety. Even so, they expected that if the lessons were used carefully, they could help the Nisei to conquer their inferiority complex. Japanese immigrants could not stop the discrimination and prejudice practiced against them in U.S. society. The only thing they could do was to teach the Nisei about the greatness and the glory of their origin in hopes of giving these young people a sense of pride, even if it was based on the glory of modern Japan's increasing military power.

However, Japanese education was also necessary purely as language education. According to the Nikkei census within the jurisdiction of the Los Angeles consulate in 1935, among the 25,000 Nisei, excluding those who were pupils (13,000), under school age (4,000), and females remaining at home (4,000), approximately 4,000 were deemed of employable age. Of these 3,500 were estimated to be employed, with the remaining 500 unemployed. Of the 3,500, 2,300 were in the produce business at one level or another, and another 700 were involved in agriculture or gardening. The number of those in professional occupations such as physician, dentist, lawyer, and journalist was very small. In each of these categories there were ten people or fewer, and most of them were earning a living within Japanese immigrant communities.[28] If the Nisei could not advance within U.S. society, then knowledge of the Japanese language was indispensable. The United Northwestern Japanese Association once conducted a census among fifty-two males and females in the job market. One of the questions asked was how important fluency in the Japanese language was to finding a job. Almost all (96 percent) answered that they felt that it was difficult for them to find a job because they did not have a full command of Japanese. All but three (94 percent) believed that not knowing Japanese at all would hamper prospects for employment. On the employers' side, out of thirty-six respondents, thirty-five answered that they would only hire those who were proficient in both English and Japanese. The remaining one would hire those regardless of their proficiency in Japanese.[29]

However, enthusiasm for acquiring the Japanese language did not necessarily enhance loyalty to Japan. The Japanese had come to the United States in pursuit of opportunities for success, but they never detached themselves from Japan completely. It must have been the same for the Nisei. Merely attending Japanese schools or going to Japan to study did not cause the Nisei to abandon their attachment to U.S. society. Rather, learning the Japanese language was a further means for them to become productive U.S. citizens. Takashi Suzuki, principal of Golden Gate Institute, wrote in a Japanese educational magazine that "children of the Yamato people lived in the United States as citizens of the most civilized nation of the world," and that they were outstanding in terms of schoolwork and behavior. He emphasized the importance of the Japanese language school, describing it as "the only educational organization to pass the Japanese culture that the Yamato people owns to the Nisei and to educate the great Nikkei citizens who hold the best qualities of both Japanese and American societies, and who would lay the foundation for good U.S.–Japan relations or even for world peace."[30] His words show how proud teachers were that, thanks to Japanese language schools, the Nisei did not become delinquents but undauntedly overcame obstacles to become loyal U.S. citizens.

Thus, the Issei believed that through the Nisei the greatness of Japanese culture would be introduced to U.S. society, which would result in a good relationship between the United States and Japan. Then, "a harmonious union of Americanization with what Japan stands for is greater than Americanism alone," as a Japanese girl in Seattle wrote, inspired by the last lines of Kipling's "Ballad of East and West":

> There is neither East nor West,
> Border nor Breed nor Birth
> When two strong men stand face and face
> Though they come from the ends of the Earth.[31]

Such an attitude might have contributed to the realization of a truly multicultural society if the U.S.–Japan relationship had been a harmonious one. However, expectations for the Nisei did not end with the contributions they might make to U.S. society. They were expected to play a more political role, as well. As U.S.–Japan relations deteriorated, and the Nisei were reaching the age to become more socially active, the expectations placed upon them also increased. The expectation, especially from Japan's side, was that the Nisei, who were proficient in both Japanese and English, would work to resolve the "misunderstandings" that the Americans held about Japan. In other words, the Nisei were expected to be spokespersons for Japan. This notion that producing good Nikkei American citizens would lead to good U.S.–Japan relations or even world peace made the Nisei's position delicate in view of the deterioration of U.S.–Japan relations.

Nevertheless, the Nisei and Japanese immigrants were by no means used as tools by the Japanese government. The Nisei and their parents, and even Japanese consuls, definitely saw the Nisei as U.S. citizens. Seattle consul Sato stated, "Even if anything should happen between Japan and America, if the immigrants are determined to live and die in America, we have to trust in the fairness of America." He continued that even if a war broke out between Japan and the United States, as long as residents obeyed American laws, no matter what their nationality might be, "they would be treated as American people unless the president orders otherwise." He further advised that Japanese immigrants as well as Nikkei citizens take pro-American measures. Responding to his advice, the United Northwestern Japanese Association adopted a resolution: "Although the current situation is deteriorating ... we urge Japanese immigrants to be good American residents as the parents of Nikkei citizens."[32] It was not only Japanese immigrants in Washington State who were determined to stay and be loyal to U.S. society. In fact, even after the war broke out, the immigrants continued to be good residents.

Despite their efforts, however, they were collectively sent to concentration camps.

Notes

1. Metropolitan network of Apr. 28, 1999. According to the Bureau of Education of Yamato City there are 270 foreign students. Teachers of the students' mother tongues were invited to the supplementary Japanese classes. Since several languages are involved, only one or two classes for each language are given per month. Information obtained by phone on Aug. 23, 1999.

2. J. Hector St. John de Crevecoeur, *Letters from an American Farmer* [1782] (New York: E. P. Dutton, 1957), 39.

3. House of Representatives, *Japanese Immigration Hearings before the Committee*

on Immigration and Naturalization, House of Representatives 66th Congress [1920] (New York: Arno Press, 1978), 1202; Zaibei Nihonjinkai (Japanese Association of America), *Zaibei Nihonjin shi* (History of Japanese in America) (San Francisco: Zaibei Nihonjinkai, 1940), 588. The Japanese Association of America was originally an umbrella organization of Japanese associations under the jurisdiction of the Japanese consulate general in San Francisco for California, Nevada, Utah, Colorado, and Arizona. With the creation of a new Japanese consulate in Los Angeles, the Nanka Chuo Nihonjinkai (Central Japanese Association of Southern California) was formed in 1915, which took over local associations in Southern California, Arizona, and New Mexico. Local associations in Oregon, Idaho, and Wyoming formed the Ohshu Nihonjinkai (Japanese Association of Oregon) in 1911, and those in Washington and Montana founded the Seihokubu Renraku Nihonjinkai (United Northwestern Japanese Association) in Seattle in 1913.

4. Later, in California most of those schools were called *nihongo gakuen* (Japanese language schools), while in the state of Washington many were called *kokugo gakko* (national language schools). Diplomatic Record Office of Ministry of Foreign Affairs of Japan (hereafter cited as DRO) 3-10-2-1. Kazuo Ito, *Nakagawa Yoriaki no sokuseki* (Biography of Yoriaki Nakagawa) (Seattle: Nakagawa Kimiyo, 1972), 68–71. English names of those Japanese schools are from the translation in Hokka Nihongo Gakuen Kyokai (Japanese Language School Association of North California), ed., *Beikoku Kashu Nihongo Gakuen enkakushi* (History of Japanese language schools in California) (San Francisco: Hokka Nihongo Gakuen Kyokai, 1930), 211–234. Hereafter cited as *Enkakushi*.

5. Zaibei Nihonjinkai, *Zaibei Nihonjinkai kaiho: zairyumin no genjo* (Bulletin of the Japanese Association of America: Japanese in America today) (San Francisco: Zaibei Nihonjinkai, Oct. 1909), 55.

6. The English translation by the Department of Education reads:

Know ye, Our subjects:
Our Imperial Ancestors have founded Our Empire on a basis broad and everlasting and have deeply and firmly implanted virtue; Our subjects ever united in loyalty and filial piety have from generation to generation illustrated the beauty thereof. This is the glory of the fundamental character of Our Empire, and herein also lies the source of Our education. Ye, Our subjects, be filial to your parents, affectionate to your brothers and sisters; as husbands and wives be harmonious, as friends true; bear yourselves in modesty and moderation; extend your benevolence to all; pursue learning and cultivate arts, and thereby develop intellectual faculties and perfect moral powers; furthermore advance public good and promote common interests; always respect the Constitution and observe the laws; should emergency arise, offer yourselves courageously to the State; and thus guard and maintain the prosperity of Our Imperial Throne coeval with heaven and earth. So shall ye not only be Our good and faithful subjects, but render illustrious the best traditions of your forefathers.
The Way here set forth is indeed the teaching bequeathed by Our Imperial Ancestors, to be observed alike by Their Descendants and the subject, infallible for all ages and true in all places. It is Our wish to lay it to heart in all reverence, in common with you, our subjects, that we may all thus attain to the same virtue.

Hide Sato, ed., *Zoku gendaishi shiryo 8 Kyoiku 1 Goshinei to Kyoiku Chokugo* (Education 1: The portrait of Emperor and the Imperial Rescript on Education: Documents of modern history, 2nd series 8) (Tokyo: Misuzu Shobo, 1994), Appendix 465.

7. From the data in DRO 3-10-2-10. Letter from Ujiro Oyama, San Francisco acting general consul, to Nobuaki Makino, minister of foreign affairs, on Apr. 7, 1913. There was only one school that expressed an educational policy based on Buddhism, but there were many schools, such as Sacramento Japanese School, that did not refer to Buddhism as educational policy but belonged to Buddhist temples.

8. *Ohfu Nippo*, Mar. 18, 1917, and Apr. 4, 1918.

9. According to the report of Kihachi Abe, acting consul in Seattle, among seventy-eight pupils at Seattle National Language School, forty-four were American-born and thirty-four were Japanese-born. Reported in the letter to Jutaro Komura, Minister of Foreign Affairs, on May 2, 1911. DRO 3-10-2-1. According to the *Nichibei Shimbun* (Japanese American news), May 31, 1920, Golden Gate Institute enrolled 207 children, of whom 187 (89 percent) were American-born. The ratio of American-born children was even higher at the kindergarten; only one out of thirty-six was born in Japan.

10. *Enkakushi*, 24–40.

11. Ibid., 45.

12. Shiro Fujioka, *Beikoku Chuo Nihonjinkai shi* (History of the Central Japanese Association of America) (Los Angeles: Beikoku Chuo Nihonjinkai, 1940), 59. At the Teachers Association Conference on June 8, the following were decided (ibid., 60):

> 1. Regarding the education of Japanese children in America, the priority will be given to the American system over Japanese. The Japanese school will teach only the language. Considering the social situation, it is necessary to reemphasize this point.
>
> 2. If there are children in a Japanese school who are not attending an American public school, direct them to attend.
>
> 3. If there are some expressions that are against the Americanism in Japanese textbooks, interpret them broadly.
>
> 4. To develop new textbooks to match Americanism.
>
> 5. To establish a special committee for Americanization.

13. Information regarding the minutes of the Conference of the Pacific Coast Japanese Association Deliberative Council was obtained from UCLA, JARP collection.

14. The term *Nikkei shimin* (Nikkei citizen) was used in "Research on Occupation of Nikkei Citizens" during the tenth conference of the Deliberative Council in 1923. It seems the term Nikkei began to be used around the time when citizens associations began to be formed. *Rafu Shimpo* used the term *Nisshu Beijin* (Americans of Japanese race) on Aug. 11, 1920. More detailed research should be done on the origin and spread of the term Nikkei.

15. On efforts to amend Japanese nationality laws, see Teruko Kumei, "'Uchina-ru Teki': Nikkei Amerikajin to Niju Kokuseki Mondai" ("Enemies within": Japanese Americans and the dual nationality problem), in Imin Kenkyukai et al., eds., *Senso to Nihonjin* (War and Japanese) (Tokyo: Tohrin Shorin, 1997), 52–67.

16. Beikoku Seihokubu Renraku Nihonjinkai (United Northwestern Japanese

Association of America), *Ji Taisho junen kugatsu tsuitachi itaru juichinen nigatu niju-hachinichi: kaimu oyobi kaikei hokoku* (Transaction and financial report from Sept. 1, 1921, to Feb. 28, 1922).

17. Editors were Kohei Shimano and Zenji Yoshinaga of the Central Japanese Association and Isoji Nakajima, Yoshizo Sano, and Takashi Suzuki of the Japanese Association of America. *Nihonjinkai kaiho* (Bulletin of Japanese Association of America), July 15, 1921; Tamezo Takimoto, *Nihongo Gakuen ni kansuru hokokusho* (Report on the Japanese language schools), DRO 382-339-1-8.

18. Ken Ishikawa, "Beikoku Kashu Nihongo gakko ni kansuru kenkyu" (A study on Japanese language schools in California), *Kyoikukai* (Education world) (Apr. 1923), 17. This is the first of the three articles; the others were published in May and June 1923.

19. Documents in the archives of the Sakura Gakuen. Also "Kashu Nihongo Ga-kuen kaizo shiryoshu" (Documents on reformation of language schools in Califor-nia) in Seitaro Sawayanagi Collections at Seijo University in Tokyo. There were sev-enty pupils boarded at Fresno Japanese School. Ishikawa, "Beikoku Kashu Nihongo gakko ni kansuru kenkyu," 22

20. For analysis of the investigation, see Ishikawa's second and third articles. For the sake of comparison, he asked a friend to conduct the same research on pupils in Tokyo.

21. Ishikawa used the term *Nikkei shimin* (Nikkei citizen). Quote was taken from the previously mentioned article (May 1923), 60.

22. Op-ed in *Rafu Shimpo*, Apr. 29, 1921.

23. Zaibei Nihonjinkai, *Zaibei Nihonjin shi*, 477, 482.

24. DRO M2301-1.

25. This policy of assigning higher priority to the condition of the receiving countries had been discussed at the Pacific Coast Consul's Conference in 1922 and 1924. It was also expressed in Gaimusho (Ministry of Foreign Affairs), *Dai 60kai Teikoku Gikai Setumei Shiryo* (Explanation materials for the 60th Imperial Diet), in DRO. On the educational policies of the ministries of education and foreign affairs for the overseas Japanese children, see Masaru Kojima et al., *"Zaigai shitei" kyoiku no kiteiyoin to ibunkakan kyoiku ni kansuru kenkyu* (A study on the educational deter-minants to the "overseas Japanese children" and intercultural education), Report to the Grant-in-Aid for Scientific Research, Japan Society for Promotion of Science, Mar. 2000.

26. Beikoku Seihokubu Renraku Nihonjin Kai (United Northwestern Japanese Association), *Showa gonen hachigatsu juhachinichi dainikai Geika Nihongo gakko kyo-iku kondankai* (U.S.–Canada Japanese Teachers' Conference on Aug. 18, 1930), mimeograph.

27. *Nichibei Shimbun*, Jan. 1, 1929.

28. Gaimusho Americakyoku (Bureau on American Affairs in Ministry of For-eign Affairs), *Hokubei Nikkei shimin gaiyo* (General conditions of Nikkei citizens in North America) (1936), 81–83, DRO.

29. Beikoku Seihokubu Renraku Nihonjinkai (United Northwestern Japanese Association), *Ji Taisho juninen sangatsu tsuitachi itaru taisho jusannen nigatsu niju-kunichi: kaimu oyobi kaikei hokoku* (Transaction and financial report from Mar. 1, 1923, to Feb. 29, 1924), 126–28.

30. Takashi Suzuki, "Zaibei Nikkei Nisei to sono yushusei" (Nisei in the United States and their excellence), *Teikoku kyoiku* (Imperial Education) (Dec. 1938), 69–75.

31. This is what a young U.S. pupil dreamed in 1921. Thelma Shizu Okajima, "True Kiplingism," *Great Northern Daily News*, Jan. 1921, 73–74.

32. Beikoku Seihokubu Renraku Nihonjinkai (United Northwestern Japanese Association), *Showa jurokunen teiki kyogikai hachigatsu tsuitachi gijiroku* (Minutes of regular council meeting, Aug. 1, 1941).

CHAPTER EIGHT

The Nikkei's Education in the Japanese Language in Paraguay

The Japanese Educational System and Its Influence on the Colonies

EMI KASAMATSU

> You can speak any language
> But don't forget your *kokoro* [spirit]
> The soul of your race.
>
> A Japanese proverb

Young and adult Nikkei in Paraguay are considered to be among the most accomplished speakers of Japanese on the continent, and to live in a way that most closely reflects their ancestors' lifestyle and customs. This fact led me to conduct this research to discover why generations of Paraguayan Nikkei have been able to preserve the Japanese language, with its capacity for the expression of deep human emotion, and how they could retain so much of their Japanese culture in spite of being surrounded by non-Japanese influences.

For many Japanese living in Paraguay, the Japanese language is still the main language used at home. Successive generations have not greatly altered this orientation. However, for the Nikkei who live in the capital or other large cities, integration into the larger society commonly occurs, and later generations have substantially modified their sense of the importance of using the Japanese language. Nevertheless, keeping Japanese a living language for future generations is an ongoing concern among the Issei and Nisei. What are the characteristics of the Nikkei in Paraguay that got us interested in the use and preservation of this language?

The history of Japanese immigration to Paraguay dates back to 1936, but the majority of Japanese arrived after World War II. The arrival of the Japanese in Paraguay is recent, in relation to other countries with a one-hundred-year history of immigration from Japan. For this reason the Issei in Paraguay still exert a very strong influence, preserving Japanese culture and organizational structure, in no small part because of their day-to-day use of Japanese.

"*Issei no yona Nisei*" is the term used for the Nisei in Paraguay. In some instances their identity is closer to the Japanese, due to family influence as well as the fact that Japan is a world power. Paraguay's deteriorating national ethos causes many Nikkei to identify with and feel closer to their ancestors' country of origin. The Nikkei's physical attributes also allow them to be recognized as having Japanese origins.

For these and other reasons, this investigation is being done to consider such issues. I propose that, in the long run, learning the Japanese language will be very beneficial to the Nikkei. However, as the Nikkei become more integrated into Paraguayan society, we will find it less important to learn to speak Japanese. Related issues include: What do we, as Nikkei, expect from Japan and from Paraguay? And, given our situation, what do we wish to contribute?

The Japanese Education System and
Its Influence on the Colonies

Toward the end of World War I, Japan was viewed and accepted as a nation building a "modern state" according to Western precepts. I wish to point out that this acceptance was based solely on physical aspects and was not in any sense spiritual.[1] In Japan, such changing attitudes led to the notion of *wakon yosai*, the combination of Japanese spirit and Western efficiency.[2] The idea of taking the country toward modernization and, at the same time, westernization, is known as "democracy of the Taisho" (from Emperor Yoshihito). Some educators of that time, influenced by this reform movement, with its democratic ideas and socialist trends, passed it along to their students.[3] But by then, the Japanese people, visualizing the future, had ascertained that the only way to succeed would be to provide an excellent standard of education, one that would enable the Japanese to compete with the more advanced Western technologies.

The creation of the Educational Reform Council was imperative. This advisory entity of the Japanese Education Ministry was needed to define the directives for Japanese education. The receptiveness toward Western ways, occurring since the Meiji era, was based on the concept of wakon yosai. But it was convenient for the Educational Reform Council to exclude the "yosai," which refers to "occidental efficiency," to avoid corruption, and also to give their reform purpose.[4] Thus, the council determined that education needed to be based more on the concept of a "national politics and a Japanese spirit," founded upon the basic trilogy: Shintoism, education, and government. In this way, elementary education would rely on people having had the same consistent instruction, which would incorporate the moral principles of the Japanese Empire.[5]

After World War II, American influence on education was widespread. The "six-three-three-four" system was adopted. Elementary education consisted of six years followed by three years of middle school learning; these nine years were mandatory for all. It was optional to continue with three more years of secondary education and four years of college. According to the Basic Law of Education of 1947, the purpose of education was to form self-confident citizens as peaceful constituents of a democratic nation and to develop a society respectful of human values. Within this framework, Reischauer states that Japan has become a country with one of the highest educational levels in the world.[6]

The Beginnings of Japanese Education in Paraguay, 1936–54

The first group of Japanese immigrants arrived in Paraguay in 1936, a time when education in Japan was still centered on the Empire. As part of the migratory program, that same year the Japanese government sent Professor Shozaburo Fujisawa to set up a Japanese language school for the growing Japanese colony. The idea was that the children—even those far from their native country—would be able to acquire an education based on discipline and good judgment. It would teach them to be stoical and restrained in adversity, and at the same time inculcate optimism and continued confidence in the colony. Above all, parents wanted their children always to keep in mind the invincible fighting spirit—*yamato damashi*—that characterizes the Japanese people.[7]

The presence of a schoolmaster was essential to the immigrants since education was considered a vital part of human development, especially during childhood. The precarious physical state of the first school building did not impede the teaching of the Japanese language. Later on, the first Japanese school built in the country was constructed on a plot of three hectares of land. It was named La Colmena Elementary School of the Japanese Language by PARATAKU, the colonizing company of Paraguay.

In 1940, student enrollment had reached 131, and students ranged from first through sixth graders. The number of teachers had grown to three in order to meet student needs. The teachers taught five hours a day in Japanese. The rest of the day was spent following the country's teaching curriculum in Spanish, as dictated by the local Ministry of Education.

Once the system of teaching in both languages was established, Paraguayan natives started helping the Japanese teachers with local education.

However, Japan's entry into World War II in 1941 put a stop to any hopes for normal integration.[8] The Japanese had to close all their schools and recall their own teachers. Given the circumstances, in March of 1942 the Parents' Association of this Japanese school decided to give up the property and all its furnishings as a goodwill gesture. This gesture was also a reflection of the fact that the government of Paraguay never humiliated any Japanese immigrant during this time.

With Professor Fujisawa gone, those in the Japanese colony of La Colmena tried to remain respectful of both countries' positions. They quietly organized reading and learning time in individual homes, using what few materials they had to keep the Japanese language alive.

In 1946, the parents of Paraguayan Nisei as well as children born in Japan were anxious to have a Japanese language school reinstated. So, secretly, more formalized schools, including Yazawa Gakuen, Takahashi Gakuen, and the Rinkan Gakko of the Moriya family, started springing up in private homes.

Teaching Methods before the War

Children six to seven years old were admitted to study and finish the first and second grades during the school year from March to November. Classes went from 7 A.M. to 11:30 A.M. Subjects studied included Japanese, math, drawing, writing, arts and crafts, singing, and physical education. After completing the first and second grades students transferred to the local Paraguayan school, where they started over with the first grade. But this time they were taught in accordance with the Paraguayan Education Ministry's requirements.

At this stage, beginning at approximately eight years old and continuing throughout the six-year elementary cycle, students took Japanese language classes during summer vacation periods, which lasted from the beginning of December to the end of February. Other activities of the Japanese school year included writing contests, drawing contests, sports events (*undokai*), and day trips during which manners, discipline, and courtesy were taught in the Japanese tradition. Professor Naka Yazawa was very strict about the students' behavior and, above all, about the practice of *enryo*, or deferring to one's elders and "betters." This rigid form of discipline helped Paraguayan Nikkei learn how to fit into society, both at home and among Paraguayans, developing their social skills in a suitable and traditional way.

At first schools used learning materials brought from Japan; later they incorporated other materials edited or copied by parents for the children's use. Families also shared among themselves the few books that each had brought from Japan. This created a sort of circulating library with books protected by homemade covers and treated with the utmost care so they would not deteriorate. Therefore, a lot of young people became used to reading classic Japanese works, as well as foreign books in translation, rewritten for children in the Japanese language.

In addition, some mothers would extract dyes from flowers to create colored paper. Others would draw animals native to other environments and depict unfamiliar scenes to show the existence of creatures and landscapes that were not observable in the surrounding community.

In this way Japanese education, expectations about behavior, and cultural observances such as New Year, Obon, undokai, and baseball games exclusively for the Japanese were deeply rooted in the children's experience. The parents' firm determination that their children should speak proper Japanese and the mandatory use of the language at home kept it alive for many decades, and in some homes, even up to the present.

Japanese Education after World War II

According to Reischauer, after World War II the educational system in Japan was restructured as a consequence of the American Occupation to be less elitist and match the international models being used and developed at the time. For this to take place, the Educational Administration had to become more fully centralized and the educational system had to undergo reform; this entailed "required curriculum" revisions, Japanese language reforms, and the adoption of romaji (Roman letters) as a teaching tool.

In March of 1947, the basis for the Law of Education was declared as follows:

Having established a Japanese Constitution, we have demonstrated our determination to contribute to world peace and humanity's well-being, by building a democratic and refined Nation. We hold individual dignity in high esteem and we strive to form people who love life and peace. We would like Education to help create a general culture that will enrich the individual as well as extend throughout all of Japan. By way of this law, and in accordance with the spirit of Japan's Constitution, we decree the clarification of the purpose of education and the establishment of an educational foundation for the new Japan.[9]

It was in this manner that the postwar Japanese educational system was transmitted to the immigrants that started arriving in Paraguay in 1955, and who settled in the southeastern and northeastern regions, in colonies near the districts of Itapua (Chaves, Fram, La Paz, Santa Rosa, Fuji, Pirapó), Amambay, and Alto Paraná. These new arrivals experienced a new way of teaching and a curriculum based on current needs. Such reform also reached the Japanese school in La Colmena.

The Status of Japanese Education in the New Colonies

As we know, one of the first acts of the Japanese in settling the colonies was to create an institution capable of teaching their children the Japanese language. At first, due to lack of a specific site, these schools were run from immigrants' homes or storerooms. Most of the time there were no benches or chairs where students could sit and write. However, Professor Midori Maruyama, who was a child at the time, remembers fondly how their teacher entertained them with paper theater games, and how they ran around amid recently cut tree trunks. Already by 1958, the Fuji colony had established a large school site as a result of parental efforts. This site also housed the elementary educational program of the local educational ministry, hiring Paraguayan teachers to carry out instruction there.[10]

Residents of other colonies, such as Santa Rosa, together with the immigrants from Kochi prefecture, built a school in 1957. Then, with the consent of the Paraguayan Ministry of Education and Culture, they expanded the school to include Paraguayan educational classes. They also hired a Paraguayan teacher in 1958. In the 1970s, the governor of Kochi donated about seven hundred of the actual textbooks used in schools in Japan. Thanks to him it was possible to teach three hours a day of Japanese in school, all the way up to the fifth grade. In 1969, the school's first graduation ceremony was held.[11] With the opening in 1956 of the Company for the Development of Japanese Immigration—a Japanese state agency for the development and settlement of Japanese immigrants—many projects came into being. One example was the establishment, in 1960, of widespread elementary education for the Japanese children of the colonies. In 1965, this agency built some concrete school structures, a house for the principal, and a boarding school for students. They even provided a school bus.

In 1953, the Amambay colony, located in northeastern Paraguay, was the first one in which immigrants became tenant farmers of coffee plantations. In spite of the scarcity of provisions from the contracting company, the colony's inhabitants were more concerned about their children's education than they were about the scarcity of supplies. In 1958, Otoshiro Kuroda arrived in Paraguay as a special emissary of the Japanese embassy in Paraguay.[12] He visited the Amambay site, became interested in the educational welfare of the children in that forsaken community, and provided much support for it.

In 1961, the year after the Pirapó colony was founded, it opened its first Japanese language school. Having initially taught in Japan, Professor Mizumoto taught there with great dedication for thirteen years. Because the majority of the area's residents were tied to agriculture, most conversation (about 90 percent) centered around agricultural themes. So both teachers

TABLE 8.1

Japanese Language Elementary Schools in Paraguay, 1981

School name	Location	Number of teachers	Number of students	Class hours
Central de Chaves	Chaves	2	32	43
Fuji	Fram	4	45	61
La Paz	Fram	3	58	45
Santa Rosa	Fram	5	62	56
Acacaraya	Alto Paraná	4	71	50
Pirapó Central	Alto Paraná	5	74	62
Pirapó Central 2	Alto Paraná	3	60	66
Fujimi	Alto Paraná	3	52	57
Yguazú	Yguazú	4	117	132
La Colmena	La Colmena	2	99	140
Amambay	Pedro J. Caballero	4	163	175
Ciudad del Este	Ciudad del Este	1	16	100
Encarnación	Encarnación	2	66	200
Asunción	Asunción	2	76	220
Saniku Gakuen	Asunción	2	60	
Japanese School	Asunción	3	21	
TOTAL		49	1,072	

SOURCE: *Miotsukushi*, Aug. 1981, 12.

TABLE 8.2

Japanese Language Secondary Schools (both Junior High and High Schools) in Paraguay, 1981

School name	Location	Number of teachers	Number of students	Class hours
Fram	Fram	2	34	150
Pirapó	Alto Paraná	3	53	50
Yguazú	Yguazú	3	39	138
Amambay	Amambay	1	44	76
Ciudad del Este	Ciudad del Este	1	3	100
Encarnación	Encarnación	1	17	104
Asunción	Asunción		13	
TOTAL		11	203	

SOURCE: *Miotsukushi*, Aug. 1981, 12.

and volunteers from the Japan International Cooperation Agency (hereafter, JICA) had to relate their teaching to that field.[13] This, in turn, led to the development of a friendly scholastic environment.

Yguazú, located approximately 286 kilometers from the capital city, was one of the last colonies established in Paraguay, and 1963 marked the establishment of its Japanese language school. In 1965, the Partnership for the Development of Education was created. In 1967, the Japanese government built and equipped a school providing both elementary and secondary education. In addition, a bus was provided to transport students. The prefecture of Iwate contributed to the effort by sending teacher trainers of Japanese.

Thanks to all the efforts of parents, educators, and the Japanese institutions that shared their successes and failures, the "teaching-learning" system of the Japanese language was perfected. By 1981, Paraguay already had sixteen Japanese language schools with a total enrollment of 1,200 students (see Tables 8.1 and 8.2).[14]

Some Issei Parent Concerns

In several countries, the 1980s brought about a renewed interest in learning Japanese among Nikkei and non-Nikkei. This interest was due to the boom in Japan's economy, as well as Japan's growing importance in the world scene.[15] On the other hand, modern means of communication made possible closer contact between countries, as well as access to electronically transmitted material. Consequently, several concerns arose with regard to the Nikkei. Professor Sato, president of the Japanese Teachers' Association in Paraguay, raised the following questions with both teaching staff and parents:

Is the knowledge of both languages really so important and necessary?
Is the Japanese language a necessary tool for the future?
Why should the Nisei study Japanese?
The unanimous consensus was that the Nisei needed to learn Japanese no matter what.[16]

Another comment sometimes voiced in the community was that even if the students graduated from a college in Asunción, the capital city, their integration into the workforce as professionals would be difficult to achieve. Therefore, it would be better for them to learn Japanese and then get a scholarship to study in Japan.

The Height of Japanese Education in Paraguay

Interest in Japanese education peaked around 1986. There had been an increase from sixteen to twenty-four schools nationwide, with eleven *chugaku* (junior high schools), and two *koko* (high schools). At that time, there were 72 teachers and 1,219 students, of whom 915 were elementary school students and 304 were high school students. The Amambay colony had the largest number of students.[17]

The learning level of the students, however, was thought to be lagging behind that of Japan by two full grade levels. However, if we compare the level of knowledge of Japanese among Paraguayan Nikkei to that of Nikkei in other Pan-American countries, we find it quite high. Seventy-five percent of the Nikkei in Paraguay were studying Japanese. In proportion to the population, the number of both teachers and schools was higher than in other Pan-American countries.

Educators coming from Japan would often comment about the similarity between the everyday conversation of children in Japan and that of the children in Paraguay, such has been the level of commitment to the learning of Japanese and the preservation of Japanese cultural values. Ambassador Nakasone once said that learning the language contributes to the preservation of the Japanese spirit and to human interactions between oneself and nature—both important Japanese characteristics.

According to Sekai Nishino, former director of the JICA in Asunción, the fact that Japan became a world power can be attributed to education. Most of Japan's surface (80 percent) is made up of mountains and hills, and it has a scarcity of natural resources, so the country and its families rely on the people's education. His theory is that education is related to the search for a better way of life, and thus parents work hard to provide a good education for their children. Education is not only what is learned at school; it also entails the molding of a human being. The impact of human caring and upbringing at home is so strong that "the knowledge parents impart is equal to that of one hundred schoolteachers."

> Thus, education is:
> teaching by saying it,
> showing by doing it,
> making them learn by practicing it,
> praising what is done.[18]

Japanese Governmental Support of
Japanese Education in Paraguay

From 1987 up to the present, the effectiveness of instruction in the Japanese language has been evaluated via *Nihongo Noryoku Shiken*, which is basically an assessment of comprehension and writing skills. The Japan Foundation sponsors the assessment, working through the Japanese embassy in Paraguay. The organization sends test materials from Japan, which are then sent back to Japan after being administered. This evaluation has had a considerable impact on both students and teachers. It has encouraged improvements in both expression and comprehension of the language. The results of the evaluation are published by the appropriate organizations. Students who reach the second level—*nikyu*—have a good chance of obtaining a scholarship to Japan. They are ranked from *ikkyu* to *yonkyu* (first to fourth level).

Several students in the Japanese Paraguayan community have reached the first level.

There is also an annual speech contest (*benrontaikai*). The Japan Foundation subsidizes some of its expenses and provided prizes when the competition first started. The contest takes place each year in Asunción, with nationwide participation. Recently the JICA generously supplied prizes of a trip to Japan for both the winner and the runner-up.

In addition, the Japan Foundation supports Japanese language schools in Asunción, La Colmena, Amambay, Ciudad del Este, and Encarnación, as well as the Saniku Gakuen school in Asunción. They do this by paying teacher salaries and supplying texts and educational materials

Other schools in the colonies are organized under the auspices of the Japanese International Cooperation Agency. These schools are located in the Chaves, La Paz, Pirapó and Yguazú colonies. The schools in all these colonies receive the same subsidies from the JICA, including aid that allows the construction of school buildings.

The Japan Foundation offers scholarships to local teachers of Japanese by way of the Nihongo Kenshukai at the Nihongo Center. Scholarships fall into three categories: 1) *Choki*, a nine-month scholarship for Nikkei teachers, 2) *Tanki*, a two-month scholarship for Nikkei with at least two years of teaching experience, and 3) a one-month scholarship for Issei teachers.[19] In 1999, Professor Norma Tornadu, a Paraguayan teacher from the Centro Paraguayo Japonés, won a scholarship, in spite of the fact that she was not Nikkei. Since 1979, the JICA has also sent forty Nikkei teachers to Japan for training.[20]

Organizational Structure of Japanese Education

The administration of the Japanese Language School consisted of the president of the Japanese Association of Asunción, the principal, and the teachers. The course of study was divided into preschool, first to sixth grade (elementary school), four years of study corresponding to junior high, and two years plus high school. The school year ran from March to November, and students attended school every weekday for two to three hours (in morning and afternoon sessions) and on Saturday for six hours, with homework given for the entire week.

Professor Teruko Okamoto, an expert on Japanese education in Paraguay, stated, "One can observe a higher level of learning in those students who attend school only once a week and come to school prepared, with all their homework done correctly. The Saturday group devotes the entire day exclusively to studying. This present-day form of correspondence course has achieved fairly good results."

Students at every grade level attend school every day Monday through Friday. Their goal is to learn to communicate in Japanese, to better understand Japanese culture, and to develop as human beings that are able to get along in society. From March to December, more time is devoted to comprehensive reading classes and being in contact with other schools, stressing the use of Japanese conversation and interpretation. Also, once a week students have music classes, physical education, sports events, arts and crafts, and field trips. Once a year they participate in a writing contest (*sakubun*) in order to qualify for a nationwide competition.[21] The winner gets to go to Japan for a one-month stay.

Professor Okamoto notes that within Paraguay one can see a marked difference in the learning levels between students living in the colonies and larger cities, including Asunción. The former speak Japanese quite well but are deficient in Spanish. The latter, on the contrary, express themselves better in Spanish than in Japanese. As we have seen, these differences are the result of the cultural environment as well as social and parental influence.

Given the above conditions, students in the former group can be taught using traditional teaching methods used in schools in Japan, as put forth by the University of Tamagawa in Japan. Students in the latter group, particularly those who know little Japanese or who use Spanish on a daily basis, need to be taught Japanese as a second language. This requires very different teaching methods. Students whose parents went to Japan on scholarships also fall into this category. These parents want their children to be educated in the traditional Japanese way, even though the children don't know the language. The Shinjuku Nihongo Gakko offers a curriculum geared to foreigners, including Spanish-speaking Japanese. Their way of teaching would probably be best suited for most future Japanese language education in Paraguay.

As new generations emerge and a growing interest in Japanese education is expressed by non-Nikkei, it will become necessary to modify the Nihongo teaching methods to fit the situation now prevailing in Paraguay. In order to do this, six principals have been selected to form the Kyozai Kaihatsu Iinkai (Committee for the Development of Teaching Materials). Led by Professor Sayoko Shimaji, an expert in the field, this group has put together a series of bilingual textbooks. These materials were to be published at the end of December 1999.[22]

Organizations Supporting the Study of the Japanese Language

The seven-member group Nihongo Kyoiku Kenkyu Kyokai (Association for the Study of Japanese Language Education) does research on Japanese language education in Paraguay. It meets twice a year to discuss advances and analyze problems relating to Japanese education in Paraguay.

TABLE 8.3

Countries Represented at 1999 Meeting of the Japanese International Cooperation Agency Training Course for Teachers of Japanese in Latin America

Country	Number of participants	Number of schools	Number of Nikkei teachers	Number of students
Brazil	7	113		
Mexico	2	40		860
Canada	4	40		
Peru	3	16	75	3,500
Paraguay	6	11	77	1,119
Colombia	1			
Bolivia	4	8		
Argentina	3	32		
Dominican Republic	2	8	25	141

SOURCE: *Miotsukushi*, Dec. 1998, 12.

Each year the Japanese International Cooperation Agency offers a two-week training course for teachers of Japanese residing in different Latin American countries. Renowned educators in the field are sent from Japanese universities to impart their knowledge. They concentrate on child development and demonstrate strategies for improving listening, speaking, and writing skills. They also work on drawing up a suitable curriculum for the entire Pan-American continent.

The last such meeting took place in January 1999, in Asunción (see Table 8.3). The theme was "Strategies for Integrating Nikkei into International Society in the Next Millennium." Speakers addressed various topics, including the need to promote the field of Nikkei teaching; student self-motivation for learning Japanese and integrating more successfully into Japanese culture; evaluating the appropriateness of learning materials used in each country; having a curriculum accessible to all; and recommending the study of Japanese as a second language.[23]

Who Studies the Japanese Language in 2000?

Japanese is studied in 115 countries (besides Japan) around the world and involves more than 2,102,013 students and some 27,611 teachers. These numbers don't include those who study and teach via television and radio programs, or those who study privately. The majority of these Japanese language students reside in China, Korea, the United States, and Australia. In terms of percentages, approximately 65 percent of the students are in Eastern Asia, 16 percent in Oceania, 6 percent in the United States, 6 percent in Southeast Asia, 6 percent in Europe, and 1 percent in South America.[24]

TABLE 8.4
Descent of Elementary and High School Students in Japanese Language Schools in Paraguay, 2000

School city	Nikkei (number of students)	Half Nikkei (number of students)	Non-Nikkei (number of students)	Total (number of students)
Asunción	90	34	2	127
Amambay	50	21	17	98
Yguazu	95	18	35	148
Ciudad del Este	26	12	1	39
Encarnación	30	17	4	51
Capitan Bado	11	5	37	53
Chaves	12	10		22
Sanikugakuen	50	19	17	86
Pirapó	157	15	3	175
La Colmena	22	21	13	56
La Paz	73	13	2	88
TOTAL	616	187	131	943

SOURCE: *Miotsukushi*, 1999, 22

It is interesting to note that in Paraguay children of half-Japanese descent, and even those of non-Japanese descent, attend the Japanese language schools (see Table 8.4). This is something that the Japanese Paraguayan community finds very encouraging.

In addition to the above schools, there is also a Japanese language class offered at the Paraguayan-Japanese Center for the Development of Human Resources. Those in attendance are almost all non-Nikkei.

Conclusions

As we have seen, the teaching of the Japanese language has steadily developed since the first Japanese colonies were established in Paraguay. Parental efforts, the dedication of selfless teachers, and the constant support of the Japanese government all contributed to the impetus in Paraguay. As recently as the 1980s, most of the Nikkei (both children and adults) spoke Japanese. In fact, many of them spoke Japanese better than they spoke Spanish.

However, with the passing of time, scholastic texts brought directly from Japan are becoming outdated. Up until a few years ago, these materials were still considered adequate. In Paraguay, changes are occurring in the emerging Nikkei generations. The elementary and high school Nikkei are slowly reaching the Sansei (third generation) and Yonsei (fourth generation) levels. Persons of mixed racial backgrounds are drifting away from their Japanese ancestry as well. The need to overhaul the curriculum in order to better serve these new generations has become urgent.

The new generations abound with an increased number of school-age children. Professor Naoko Yamagami completed a survey and found that in the larger cities, only 9 percent of children entering schools have a knowledge of Japanese. In the colonies, the number rises to 40 percent. She also found that many of the Nikkei parents, although they know Japanese themselves, still choose to speak Spanish with their families because it will allow their children a more effective integration into Paraguayan society. They consider Spanish to be the "mother tongue" and Japanese to be a second language.

With the regional and global economic expansion taking place as we enter the new millennium, the Nikkei have to rethink their relationship to the Japanese language. It would seem beneficial for them to strive for a degree of bilingualism, from generalized to elite. For Nikkei, the preservation of the Japanese language or the learning of it, in any form, continues to be a worthwhile venture.

Notes

1. Michio Morishima, *Porqué ha triunfado Japón* (Barcelona: Editorial Crítica, 1984), 74.

2. Ibid.,73.

3. Makoto Aso and Ikuo Amano, *Education and Japanese Modernization* (Tokyo: Japan Times Edition, 1983), 53.

4. Ibid., 55–57. The Educational Reform Council was established as an advisory board to the Education Ministry in 1935, with the mission of developing the direction in which Japanese education should proceed.

5. Ibid., 53–55.

6. Edwin Reischauer, *The Japanese: The Story of a Nation* (Cambridge, Mass.: Harvard University Press, 1979, ninth ed.), 170.

7. Emi Kasamatsu, *La presencia japonesa en el Paraguay* (Asunción: Biblioteca de Estudios Paraguayos, Universidad Católica, 1997), 146. For the early immigrants of La Colmena, *yamato damashii*, or the Japanese spirit, helped them conquer the initial difficulties of settlement.

8. Paraguay sided with the Allied cause and declared war on Japan, an act that was purely symbolic.

9. Aso and Amano, *Education and Japanese Modernization*, 62–67.

10. *Miotsukushi,* Aug. 1981, 6.

11. *Miotsukushi,* Aug. 1981, in Introduction by Shintoku Miyazaki, p. 5.

12. The Japanese legation, to which Mr. Otoshiro Kuroda was attached, is the equivalent of the present-day Japanese embassy.

13. JICA is a branch of the Japanese government that handles foreign aid, among other matters.

14. *Miotsukushi,* Aug. 1981, 12.

15. Kaname Saruya, "Nihongo kyoiku no ikuseika ni tsuite no hokokushi" (Japanese Association for Study Abroad, 1989), 15.

16. *Miotsukushi,* June 1986, 1.

17. According to Teruko Okamoto, former head of the Japanese Language School of Asunción and past president of the Japanese Women's Association of Paraguay (personal communication).

18. *Miotsukushi*, 1998, 6.

19. Interview with Teruko Okamoto, Aug. 1999.

20. Interview with Naoko Yamagami, Sept. 1999.

21. Ibid.

22. According to Yuji Eida, head of Saniku Gakuen and the past president of the Japanese Language Study Center (personal communication).

23. Interview with Chuzaburo Murakami, December 2000.

24. The survey report was published in Japan Foundation, International Japanese Language Center, Survey Report on Japanese Language Education Abroad (Tokyo: 1998), 7.

CHAPTER NINE

Peruvian Nikkei

A Sociopolitical Portrait

AMELIA MORIMOTO

The postwar Japanese population of Peru has entered a period of diversification of its activities and internal socioeconomic differentiation. This process has been accompanied by the mixing of races and assimilation into other local cultures, to the point that heterogeneity is one of the most significant changes of those recorded in recent decades.[1]

Prewar Japanese cultural expressions persist only as remnants in certain cases, like Japanese rituals in funerary ceremonies and the use of Japanese words in the domestic sphere, for example. Other Japanese cultural expressions, on the other hand, appear intermixed with local cultures, as is recognized with the so-called "Nikkei food." Studies of these and other cultural characteristics lead to the conclusion that the Nikkei—from a racial and cultural viewpoint—would be assimilated by local cultures in the near future.

The question underlying the current study is whether there exist certain features peculiar to this Nikkei population beyond those immediately visible and measurable. This study is centered on those aspects of collective thought related to group identity. I study three stages by means of surveys and interviews focusing on national and political topics. The first stage is the year 1989, the second is the election of 1990, when the candidacy of Alberto Fujimori was announced, and the third is 1998, during Fujimori's second term of office.

The initial, exploratory stage of the study was carried out in 1989 via a survey to which more than five thousand persons of Japanese origin from throughout Peru responded. The survey was focused on ideals and statements about national issues. The conclusions reached from this stage are that Peruvians of Japanese descent or origin identified fundamentally with their country of birth and that they proposed original ethical solutions to the national crisis of that time.

With respect to the second stage studied, 1990, there is a heterogeneous range of opinions about the somewhat controversial candidacy of a person of the same origin as those surveyed. However, differences of opinion gave way to a united front when it was a matter of national importance, such as the presidential election. Also, the Nikkei were in agreement with respect to their rights as citizens, even when a sector of the population was reluctant to accept collective responsibility for the highest political office of the land when that office was assumed by a person of Japanese descent. Questions about the electoral experience expose the dynamics of national identity and of group or ethnic identity, one or the other prevailing in each of the distinct situations posited by the interviews.

The election and government of a president of Japanese origin for two consecutive terms has not changed the Nikkei population's daily expectations, or opinions and attitudes toward national issues. Rather, these are viewed from within the heterogeneous range of attitudes held by the Peruvian population in general. Nevertheless, in the third period studied, 1998, the views of a relatively high percentage of Japanese descendants differ from the national majority public opinion with regard to the issue of reelection. With respect to this issue, 40 percent of the sample supports Fujimori's reelection at a time when such an opinion is not so commonly held among the electorate as a whole, as reported for November of that year.

The results of this study, carried out during the period 1989–98, are presented in the following sections. Each will include details about the methodology employed and summaries of the results, with analysis and the general conclusions presented at the end.

Nikkei Opinions in 1989

During the elections of 1990 a well-known Peruvian politician, contrasting Fujimori's decision to run for president with the attitudes and opinions of other persons of Japanese descent, declared to a local newspaper that, unlike Fujimori, the Nikkei were concerned only about their own affairs. Such a comment was an expression of the stereotyping of persons of Japanese origin that had persisted since World War II. This attitude may be explained by the fact that in the arena of politics persons of Japanese descent had not achieved the success they had in other spheres of national activity, such as business, sports, and culture. Rather, descendants of the Japanese seemed in general reluctant to enter politics. Nonetheless, my 1989 survey reveals that the Nikkei as a group had solid ideas and opinions about Peru, as well as a global consciousness, with Japan and the United States being the objects of greatest admiration and attraction. Interest in politics, therefore, was not foreign to them.

In the political context of the time the survey was carried out, the progressive and liberal ideals expressed in the responses were not part of dominant trends in Peruvian political thought. The latter tended strongly toward a populist and socialist view on the one hand, while on the other, the Shining Path and the Tupac Amaru Movement had become a focus of attention with the spread of their terrorist actions throughout Peru. Peru at that time was a victim both of the consequences of the highest inflation it had experienced in its history and of terrorism, and in addition was faced with the demoralization and uncertainty spread by numerous cases of government corruption that were denounced by the press and national opposition groups. Those years saw the beginning of the massive emigration of Peruvians to other countries, including that of the Nikkei to Japan, in search of work and better economic conditions. The general attitudes of Peruvian society at that time are also reflected in the responses of the Nikkei. Some of their answers reflect desperation in the face of a growing crisis, but others reflect hope for change.

The survey consisted of five open-ended questions, one of which included an additional question for the purpose of explaining or clarifying the answer.[2] The questions were: 1) What country is ideal for you? Why? 2) What is your opinion of Japan? 3) What is your opinion of the Nikkei? 4) What is your opinion of Peru? 5) What changes would you propose for Peru? The survey was statistically processed by coding the thousands of answers in order to quantify them. The answers were also processed according to the generation of each respondent.[3]

There were forty-seven different responses or choices for "ideal country," including three negatives or nonanswers. Primarily because of linguistic affinity, these included ten Spanish-speaking countries besides Peru. The favorites were Spain, Argentina, Mexico, Chile, Venezuela, Paraguay, Cuba, and Uruguay. Japan was the "ideal country," chosen by 40 percent of the respondents from all the generations combined. It was also the first choice of each individual generation. In total, the United States occupied second place as "ideal country," named by 20.70 percent; and Peru was in third place with 17.71 percent. However, the order varied among the generations: among the Issei and Nisei, Peru took second place with 26.37 percent and 21.61 percent respectively, while the United States came in third with 12 percent and 17.75 percent. Among the Sansei and Yonsei, the order was reversed: the United

144 / AMELIA MORIMOTO

States occupied second place with 23.77 percent and 26.53 percent respectively, while Peru came in third with 13 percent and 12.24 percent.

In response to the question "What makes a country 'ideal' for the Nikkei?" economic reasons comprised 36.81 percent of choices. Development, industrialization, modernity, technological advances, stability, well-being, high standard of living, and opportunities for work were significant reasons for this choice. Other essential criteria in the selection of an "ideal country" were linked to the cultural and moral quality of the country and the characteristics of its inhabitants. Scientific, technological, and educational progress were also attractive, as well as social security and attention to the youngest and oldest sectors of the population.

Political stability and a well-run, well-organized country were also given as reasons, as well as linguistic affinity, the ability to communicate, physical beauty, and natural landscapes. Still, in spite of all the qualities of the other admired locations, more than 8 percent of answers made reference to the attractions of their own country (Peru), which motivated their choice. More than 7 percent of answers mentioned that the "ideal country" does not exist, or that it is necessary to build it through one's own efforts.[4]

For 43.82 percent of those interviewed, Japan was attractive and admired for its moral and cultural values such as discipline, the work ethic, nationalism, mutual respect, good citizenship, and social solidarity. Japan was described as a great nation, a great country, respectable, exemplary, fantastic, interesting, admirable, excellent, the best, incredible, and a country of great culture, one that preserves its traditions. The Japanese people were considered vigorous, progressive, brave, accustomed to war, and strong and having a great future.

A persistent image of Japan across all generations of Nikkei was that of the postwar era: "Japan reemerged after the war, thanks to the efforts of its people, from the ashes of destruction, like the Phoenix." Second, Japan was admired for its economic achievements, its level of development, industrialization, and modernity, and for the economic well-being of its people; third, for its scientific, technological, and educational accomplishments; and fourth, for its pacifist political stance internationally and its support of underdeveloped countries like Peru and also of the Nikkei.

Alongside this positive image of Japan, 8 percent of answers mentioned negative aspects, some of them contradicting other responses. The primary negative response was linked to the pace of living and industrialization, for example, that "life is very agitated, the work is hard, there is great competition and perfectionism, and a high social cost to progress." Concerning the Japanese people, and contrary to other responses, opinions were expressed that "the people are mechanized and metallic, cold; there is no human warmth or family life." Also criticized were Japan's discrimination against foreigners, Nikkei, and women.[5]

In terms of self-image, the Nikkei in general have a positive concept of self. More than 50 percent of answers were favorable and related both to individual qualities and to characteristics of the group. The Nikkei described themselves as "studious, hard-working, disciplined, respectable, serious, good examples"; also, "dynamic, happy, optimistic, self-sacrificing, altruistic, generous, good, kind, respectful, sincere, honest." With respect to their intellectual qualities they described themselves as intelligent, competent, and skillful. Also noted was their ability to overcome obstacles and achieve their goals.

As a group, they recognized their "unity, homogeneity, solidarity, and integration into their country"; and equally their efforts to preserve their "ancestral values, traditions and culture." Generational differences were noted: "Young people are more open, positive, and liberal than their parents, and the Sansei are more enthusiastic and have progressed more." Compared to the Japanese, the Nikkei are warmer and friendlier, among the best on the continent. In contrast, they mentioned negative characteristics, such as a lack of unity and communication, lack of progress in integrating with the rest of the country, and the loss of ancestral and cultural values. They also criticized Nikkei traditionalism, and other negative characteristics were mentioned, such as the lack of self-identity, isolation, and timidity. They described their prejudice, racism, egotism, vanity, superficiality, materialism, lack of manners, overprotectiveness, insecurity, instability, and weakness. In summary, 24 percent of answers relating to the Nikkei were negative.[6]

Nineteen eighty-nine was an especially critical year for Peru, and therefore it is not surprising that more than 61 percent of opinions having to do with Peru are negative. Thirty-one percent of answers made special reference to the national crisis in all its manifestations: economic, political, social, and moral. More than 16 percent drew attention to governmental responsibility for this situation, 7 percent attributed these problems to structural and historical reasons, and nearly 14 percent noted the idiosyncratic nature of the Peruvian people as the cause.

On the other hand, 17 percent of answers mentioned the country's positive characteristics, such as its natural resources, natural beauty, great history and culture, and the hospitality of its people. Similarly, 13 percent of answers expressed hope for change and mentioned work, learning, and maturity as conditions for achieving it. Around 3 percent declared their identification with Peru, the land of their birth.[7]

In terms of desired change, 37 percent of all respondents' ideas for change mentioned the country's political-administrative order, from changing or replacing the government to concrete alterations in internal politics and international relations. Such ideas as decentralizing and regionalizing the system were mentioned with regard to the administration. Also suggested were concrete measures, such as reducing bureaucracy, changing the system of taxation, and altering the law and the constitution.

The second greatest number of suggestions had to do with education, culture, and morals. Principal ideas were improving education, changing people's idiosyncratic behavior, and fighting corruption. In third place were ideas for the economy, from general ones such as development, industrialization, and improving technology to individual behavioral changes to realize greater productivity. Concrete suggestions had to do with support for depressed sectors such as farming, fishing, and mining, developing natural resources, creating more job opportunities, developing businesses, and reestablishing international economic relations. Three percent of answers related to social concerns such as better nutrition, health, safety, childcare, providing for youth and the aged, birth control, control of migration to Lima, and control of immigration.

Outstanding among these proposals was the idea of the necessity of Nikkei participation in leading the country and the surprising suggestion that "a Japanese should be president of Peru." In contrast with this notion was an opposing one, that it was important to remember the country's past and model one's values on the ancient Incan empire.[8]

The Early 1990s and Their Impact on the Nikkei

In Peru, 1990 began with a widespread crisis carried over from the past, but it also brought expectations for change owing to the elections planned for the first half of the year. For the community of Japanese origin, it was a year of turbulence due to two unexpected situations. On the one hand, the emigration of persons of Japanese descent to Japan in search of work and better pay—named the *dekasegi* phenomenon—had begun the year before in a massive wave. On the other hand, among the many candidates for president of Peru, there was one of Japanese origin who became the rival of the candidate favored by national surveys. After the primaries, two candidates were left. The Nisei, Alberto Fujimori, was ultimately elected president.

During the elections and in the months intervening, the Japanese community was enveloped in a storm of aggressive and hostile actions carried out by the supporters of Fujimori's rival, while at the same time Nikkei found themselves the object of unexpected gestures of support from the Nisei candidate's non-Nikkei followers. In the absence of a true political support group for Fujimori, the Japanese community became a center of attention, its opinions and attitudes gaining in importance, especially with the press. Although for a time the Japanese community did not appear to favor Fujimori's candidacy, during that two-month period between the primary and the final election, approximately one hundred Nikkei were interviewed. The opinions of these interviewees reveal as much of a heterogeneity of attitudes as they reveal multiple dimensions of Nikkei self-identity.

The 1990 elections themselves and their results were invaluable in illustrating the social dynamic in Peru, especially in Lima, as well as in considering the performance of the winning candidate and many other factors discussed in numerous subsequent analyses. The election experiences also verified that exclusion and discrimination had been used as political tools in the past, and that a wider definition of democracy was possible in our country.

Of the sixty Nikkei interviewed during April and May of 1990, 48 percent were male and 52 percent female, with ages ranging from twenty-three to sixty years old. The interviewees were randomly selected.

Drawing from our content analysis of the content of the interviews, we can conclude, first, that during the 1990 elections the Japanese community was quite heterogeneous in its opinions and attitudes about the national campaign for president.[9] Second, we can conclude that the experience of having a candidate and later a president-elect with their own ethnic background elicited conflicting opinions and attitudes and caused both rejection and reproach from other segments of the national population.[10] Third, the experience brought to light other issues possibly not evident other than through interviews. Concerns related to values, thoughts, and feelings were expressed in the responses. The heterogeneity of responses tended to shift toward homogeneity when interviewees perceived a need for a united country in the event of Fujimori being elected president. That is, initially opinions differed about the candidate and Nikkei's identification with him, but they united with the imminence of the final elections and in consideration of the critical situation in Peru.[11] Fourth, the greater part of the community of Japanese descent recognized their rights as citizens, although a segment of it was reluctant to accept the risk of a Nikkei's candidacy for the highest office of the land.[12]

Answers to indirect questions about the candidacy of Fujimori were more often related to national or general issues than ethnicity. In questions pertaining directly to the candidacy, the greater part of answers related to common ethnic origins. This makes evident the dynamic of national identity and group or ethnic identity within the Japanese-origin population, given that either national or group/ethnic identity can prevail in different situations. Finally, both identities blended or unified at a time when the Nikkei could relate to contenders in terms of ethnicity, as personified in the form of a candidate of the same origin as themselves.[13]

In sum, the 1990s surprised the Japanese community with the success of a candidate of their ethnic origins, not to mention his election as president for two consecutive terms. The responsibilities and expectations of the majority of the Nikkei community, as well as those of the country, have not changed, and day-to-day attitudes and opinions blend together within the heterogeneity of Peruvian citizenry as a whole.

Findings of the 1998 Survey

Between October and November of 1998, sixty interviews were conducted with several sets of questions. Some of the answers, those concerning President Fujimori's current administration, are shown in this section. The preoccupation with "national concerns" prevails in certain situations in which "ethnic concerns" are also implicated. Nonetheless, both national and collective ethnic interests continue appearing in a dynamic way, depending upon the situation, and in both fashions—parallel and mixed. The survey-interview was administered to men and women of Japanese descent between the ages of eighteen and sixty-five. They were persons who have frequent contact with and are a part of institutions within or pertaining to the Japanese Peruvian community.

According to the results obtained, in general, the viewpoints of the Nikkei don't differ from those of the rest of the local citizenry. In only two out of sixty interviews was a reference made to an issue concerning only the Nikkei. Opinions about the current government were divided, with 46.57 percent approving of the government and in favor of a third term for Fujimori. The remaining 53.42 percent were critical, recognizing the achievements of the administration while at the same time referring to those aspects of it with which they did not agree. There were some other marked characteristics of the results. First, the Nikkei did not respond homogeneously. Second, with regard to national issues, the answers of the Nikkei don't differ from those of the Peruvian population in general. However, the Nikkei's opinions about an issue of national concern do differ in one area. According to national surveys from the months in which these interviews were conducted, the majority of the public would not support a third term for President Fujimori, but a relatively high percentage of Nikkei did support his reelection. A portion of the interviews follows:[14]

He's done a lot of good things. What I don't like is his authoritarianism, but in general I recognize that he's done a lot of good things. (male, 18–25 years of age)

Up until now it's seemed like a good administration. I think that Fujimori is the only president who's had the strength to face many problems that we've had for a long time. It's a very good government, although many people have quickly forgotten the inflation we had before, the danger of terrorism, etc. We've gained many things. There are still problems, but we shouldn't criticize. A lot has been said about the reelection, human rights, etc., but in spite of everything a lot of good has been achieved. Personally, in spite of how good he's been, I'd like to see Fujimori retired because according to history those who have spent a lot of time in government end up getting burned, so to speak. It might be a good idea for him to retire and finish his administration on a good note. (male, 18–25 years of age)

I believe he's done a very good job. He's solved … he's solving three big problems, mainly terrorism, the problem of inflation, and what happened a short time ago with Ecuador, and my personal opinion is that I want him to carry on with the job. I would support another term. I believe another term would be fifteen years of continuity, the same course of action, and in fifteen more years another generation will be practically coming of age. They'll have their own distinctive government, having been educated in the schools that he's created. I believe they'll have their own, different ideas. (male, 26–35 years of age)

It's a bit difficult to answer. Certain things have gotten better, and that's because of the way Fujimori has governed, but there are other areas where he's made the same mistakes, or maybe that's just part of who we are, part of Peruvian society, and to change it would take twenty, thirty years … or more. But in general, compared with other administrations I've lived through, it's been better than previous administrations. (male, 26–35 years of age)

Overall, his work has been creditable. (male, 26–35 years of age)

I think that all these years he's done honorable work. I don't know if he's accepted, but the important thing is that he's worked honestly and with clear goals. (male, 36–45 years of age)

There are many positive things about him. Above all in economic issues, in the free market. Shall we say that things are more pragmatic now? But nevertheless, he still makes a lot of mistakes, especially political ones. (male, 36–45 years of age)

He has his good side: he's conquered terrorism, he's stopped hyperinflation. I think he should govern for another term. Of course this is against the constitution, but since there isn't going to be a referendum he could run and he could better the country. It has gotten much better; let's hope that it continues. (male, 46–55 years of age)

I think he does a lot of good things, although there are still a lot of problems. I believe that the social cost of his policies is very high, don't you think? His policies are very harsh, but I think he's doing a good job. (female, 18–25 years of age)

I think he's reached his limit; he should step down. He's done a good job—why deny it?—but it's time for him to leave. (female, 18–25 years of age)

I think he does what he can. He's failed in some things but he's doing what he can. The only problem is they're always dragging in the Japanese. [In what sense?] Any mistake he makes, it's because of his race. We all take the blame. (female, 36–45 years of age)

I think he's good. But in social issues I think he needs to give the poorer classes more support. If there isn't enough work, that's a problem. (female, 36–45 years of age)

It seems to me that Fujimori has done a lot of good things for Peru and also that he plans to keep on doing them, but the problem I see is the economy. There's a lot of unemployment, low pay, and when morale is low everywhere because you're not getting enough to eat, that's a problem, isn't it? It reminds me of a government, a book I read about China. It said that the Chinese people say when rice is getting low in the pot it's because there should be a new government ... and now I don't know how far this Chinese saying applies to Peru, but I don't think there's an ideal candidate. For me it's still Fujimori. (female, 46–55 years of age)

I think he's done a lot. He's doing an excellent job, and as Nikkei we should be proud. I think he's improved Peru's image, both in Peru and abroad. (female, over 55 years of age)

It's a good government, but he shouldn't try for reelection. (female, over 55 years of age)

I think reelection is getting more and more distant. Well, right now the best candidate would be Andrade [the current mayor of Lima] as far as Lima goes, but at the national level, I don't know. If we don't see another candidate with the same economic policies, yes, I do think he should run again. (female, 36–45 years of age)

I don't see him in a third term. (female, 36–45 years of age)

I think he'll be reelected ... in spite of the crisis. (female, 46–55 years of age)

With all the steps he's taken up to now, he's got the wind at his back, as they say, doesn't he? Instead of going backward we're going forward. It's very different from how it used to be. [Do you think he'll make a third term?] It depends on the popular vote. [Do you think the people will support him?] It isn't certain. But he would have my vote. [You're saying that if he ran, you would vote for him?] Of course. (female, over 55 years of age)

I think he should carry on. [Why?] Well, just think! What happens if another Alan Garcia wins and destroys us again? Some people think that he shouldn't continue, but in my opinion, he should stay for another term. (female, 46–55 years of age)

The first term was good; the second one, bad. (female, 36–45 years of age)

Since he won in 1990 he has managed to overcome a series of high-priority problems like violence and economic instability. From a very personal point of view, it seems he's lost his bearings, that is, structural growth to assure sustained economic growth and also to assure social change, the fight against poverty. I think those government interests linked to the reelection are making him lose his bearings, his orientation, his perspective on what should be done. In my personal opinion, I think that the government, through the president, should concentrate on governing for the years he has left and not think about reelection. (male, 36–45 years of age)

The first administration was good—I greatly hoped that the country would move forward—the second administration, discouraging. (male, 36–45 years of age)

In fact he does have a good economic team, but in the field of politics he's left a lot to be desired, especially because of the Referendum that 70 percent wanted because of legal problems. But the process was stopped, cut off, so that the referendum wouldn't be carried out. This is terrible because if the people want something, why say no. And aside from the conflict, if Fujimori could be reelected, others should have been allowed to express their opinion, it should have been carried out. But in the field of economics, he's on the road to good things; he's got a good economic team. (male, 18–25 years of age)

On one hand he's improved things, and on the other, no. For example, terrorism: things are more peaceful now but there's a lot of poverty. And also, jobs and the economy, in those areas we're not doing so well. (male, over 55 years of age)

In my opinion I think that he ought to end his term. Another group should run, not a party, but there should be another leader, because it's not good for the power to be centralized in just one person. I think in the two years he has left he'll continue the same way as now, I don't think he'll improve much, because the situation right now is very difficult, next year will be very difficult. I think it's time for him to finish up his term. He'll finish in 2000 and then we'll have a change, right? (female, 18–25 years of age)

Well, it's time they elected a new president. I think the people tired of his authoritarianism. The economic situation in general hasn't improved; it's worse, especially for small or medium-sized businesses. There wouldn't appear to be any freedom of expression. (female, 26–35 years of age)

I really don't know, his term is almost up, he should make way for another team. We need new ideas and ways of facing problems since with all these years there's also the possibility that with all the power he now has it could become (if it hasn't already) a dictatorship in disguise. It seems to me it's time for him to go. (female, 26–35 years of age)

Well, the way the situation is now I don't think people will vote for Fujimori. But I do believe that one more term would be good for us. Although at times it is like what Chile went through with Pinochet, which was not a democratic government, and look: they want to sentence him to now for what he did in his time. I think that we are not prepared to face another period of privations. We Peruvians are something of a wild card. We're unpredictable, we're always looking out for our own interests, even if the country goes to the dogs, and that's the problem. He should finish stabilizing things, but since the municipal elections have already taken place ... [You don't think there will be a third term?] I don't think he'll achieve that, because the people feel very hard hit, but it's also true that there aren't any other candidates, either, right? I think that Fujimori will have to step carefully because Peru is a very changeable country. Today we say no and tomorrow we say yes; there is nothing very coherent in this. What I do believe is that Fujimori hasn't shaped the cultural side of the country, tried to vary ways of thinking. In these ten years he could have tried to do something to form our character, but nothing has been done. He's given priority to economic affairs. (female, 36–45 years of age)

Provided that he concentrates on completing the foundation for the state reforms and the other pending reforms, I think he'll finish his term as one of the best administrations, but if he insists on reelection, I believe everything will become more and more distorted and above all the people will become more and more polarized. It's increasing right now just because of his inadequate political management and his prioritization of the reelection question, on top of the great needs the country has. (female, 36–45 years of age)

I think he'll finish this term and that will be the end of it. There's a lot of poverty, and no work. (female, over 55 years of age)

General Conclusions

1. This study, completed over a period of nearly a decade, reveals that the Nikkei in Peru are not only continually and daily informed of political affairs and national problems, but also have very concrete opinions about these. The Peruvian Nikkei, as a group, firmly identify with Peru. Its problems and potentials, and its future, are part of their concerns. To sum up, their judgments, opinions, and visions for the present, past, and future of their country are based mainly on ethics and how their own collective contribution could potentially be made on that basis.

2. The three different time periods studied show a heterogeneity of opinions on national affairs.

3. Within this heterogeneity there are certain collective responses peculiar to the group; that is, the Nikkei, in significant percentages, maintain opinions and even a certain mindset distinct from the national population regarding specific national issues.

4. The preoccupation with "national concerns" prevails in certain situations related to "ethnic concerns," while the interests or privileges of the group are sacrificed. Nonetheless, both national and collective ethnic interests continue to be presented in a dynamic way dependent upon the situation, both in parallel and combined fashions.

5. There are differences of opinions and differences in thinking with respect to generational and age variables. However, there aren't such significant differences with respect to gender.

6. Even though there is also an identification with two "ideal countries" as models of development (Japan and the United States), the Peruvian Nikkei are not only strongly identified with their own country, but also seem to be in sync with the main trends of Peruvian thinking as a whole.

Notes

1. This was one of the main conclusions of the Nikkei national census study, carried out in 1989, and whose results were published in Amelia Morimoto, *Población de origen japonés en el Perú: perfil actual* (Lima: Comisión Conmemorativa del 90 Aniversario de la Inmigración Japonesa al Perú, 1991). The primary data for this 217-page study were collected from more than five thousand Japanese Peruvian respondents above the age of eighteen, selected at random from all over the country.

2. In the survey, the gender of the interviewee, his or her generation, and the date were also stated. The survey was anonymous and was answered individually by one or more members of families included in the 1989 census of the Nikkei community in Peru. The eligible age to complete the survey was eighteen years of age (the age of official majority in Peru) and up; the survey respondents included persons eighty years of age and older.

3. The total number responding to the survey, individually and voluntarily, was 5,121. According to the general census of Japanese-origin population for that year (1989), those eighteen years of age and older totaled 29,371; that is to say, the survey covered 17.43 percent of that segment of the population. The nature of the sample by generation was as follows: 106 Issei, 2,396 Nisei, 2,551 Sansei, and 68 Yonsei. The percentages with respect to the total number interviewed are 2.06 percent, 46.78 percent, 49.81 percent, and 1.32 percent respectively. According to the general census, the Issei population comprised 5.06 percent of the total Nikkei population (2,311 persons); the Nisei, 33.26 percent (15,183); the Sansei, 47.82 percent (21,827); and the Yonsei, 13.5 percent (6,165).

4. There was some variation in these arguments among the generations. For the Issei, the primary motives were economic (35.26 percent). Peru, with all its problems, distinct national characteristics, and possibilities was their second choice (16.17 percent). A country's cultural and moral values were also important (15.43 percent), as well as the characteristics of its inhabitants, the physical environment, and technological and educational progress. Political stability and organization were among the least important. More than 3 percent chose Japan because it was the country of their forebears. Among the Nisei, the main reason for choosing a country as "ideal" was economic (30.1 percent), followed by the country's moral and cultural values. Peru, with its problems and opportunities, took third place and Japan fourth. Political stability and a well-run and well-organized public administration were also attractive; linguistic affinity and the characteristics of the inhabitants followed. Among the Sansei and Yonsei the primary choice was very much influenced by economic conditions—40 percent and 38.75 percent in each case. For the Sansei political considerations took second place, followed by technological and educational advances, national cultural and moral values, the physical environment, and the people. The Yonsei chose economic conditions, followed by moral and cultural characteristics. Peru was chosen by 11 percent of the respondents. Technological and educational considerations, politics, and the environment followed. More than 2 percent chose Japan because it was the country of their forebears.

5. Classified by generation, the Issei, Nisei, and Sansei felt greatest admiration for Japan's cultural and moral values, followed by economic conditions, technological

and educational advances, natural beauty, and political organization. The greatest attractions for the Yonsei were Japan's economic achievements, followed by cultural, moral, technological, and political characteristics. For the Issei, 12 percent of answers were related to the negative aspects already mentioned; among the Nisei almost 7 percent of all comments were also negative, and among the Sansei and Yonsei, 9 percent and 2 percent were negative respectively.

6. It was noteworthy that more than 11 percent gave a distinct definition to the term Nikkei. More than 4 percent referred to their racial mix, their identity as a different group. In addition, they use the term, implicitly or explicitly, to refer to the descendants of the Issei (the first-generation immigrants) or as synonymous with Nisei (second generation) or Sansei (third generation). Some answers referred to religion as one of their diverse institutions. Almost 8 percent of answers pointed out the responsibilities and the gratitude of the Nikkei, including their obligation to preserve the ancestral culture, their parents' toils, their duty to those younger, and the achievements of the group. Other answers were related to the current situation of the Nikkei—above all their exodus from the country, their economic status in Peru, and the discrimination they suffered in Japan.

7. By generation, 50 percent of the Issei's answers were negative and 39.6 percent were positive, expressing hope and identification with Peru. Fifty-nine percent of the Nisei's answers were negative and 35.6 percent positive; other answers related to their expectations and responsibility. Seventy percent of the Sansei's answers and nearly 63 percent of the Yonsei's were negative, while 27 percent and 30 percent of their answers, respectively, were positive and hopeful.

8. By generation, 40 percent of the proposals of the Issei tended toward education, values, and morals, 34 percent toward the political, 14.8 percent toward the economy, and 1 percent toward social concerns. Political structure was the most important issue for the Nisei and Sansei, comprising 40 percent and 36 percent, respectively; for both generations changes in education, morals, and values took second place with 25 percent and 27 percent, respectively. Economics took third place with 19.96 and 21 percent; and social concerns, fourth place. In decreasing order, concerns for the Yonsei were education, politics, economics, and social issues. A considerable proportion of each generation inclined toward fundamental national change. Other significant but rare ideas reflected the anguish, insecurity, uneasiness, and demoralization of the times, such as "civil war," "dissolution of the country," or the "colonization of the country." It was even suggested that it would be impossible for Peru to change.

9. Notes 10, 11 and 12 show the different kinds of responses given by the Nikkei interviewed.

10. The following are excerpts from interviews with Nikkei that show how attitudes Peruvians have toward the Nikkei vary in middle-, high-, and low-class neighborhoods in Lima. Question: "After the results of the first election were made known, did you perceive any change in the attitudes about you or behavior toward you by those with whom you work or study, or in the treatment you receive in your neighborhood or in the streets, etc.?" Among the answers were the comments: "I haven't noticed any change, people's behavior to me is still the same. They don't treat me any differently, because you can't really tell that I'm of Japanese origin." "Nothing's happened to me because I'm always around other Nikkei." "There haven't been

any problems because the people I deal with are usually middle- or upper-class, and they're educated." "Personally, no, because I don't go to public places where people might treat me badly." "Barranco [a neighborhood] is a very special place where we all know each other, and I haven't noticed any change." "In nice neighborhoods they look at you with a certain distrust, and you can feel the chill. They ask whom we voted for. They look at us differently now, as if they didn't like us; they're unfriendly. They look down on us. Before they didn't even notice if we walked by; now every time we go down the street everyone turns around and looks at us or laughs at us. They yell 'Fujimori' at us, in Miraflores, Camino Real, San Isidro. In those places you feel rejected, they want to humiliate you, you feel them recoil from you with thinly disguised racism." "On the bus and in the street they say the president of Peru is going to be Chinese or Japanese. They reject Fujimori because of his ancestry, they say that he isn't Peruvian or that he's second generation, and so they consider him a foreigner and think that he's not capable of running the government. They talk about him in a racist way." "They don't call me by name any more, they say, 'Hello, Fujimori!' They make fun of me, too, saying, 'You've made it now; what would you like to be minister of?'" "It's somewhat annoying, because as soon as they see that you're of oriental descent, they say you voted for him." "We were driving by Fredemo in Javier Prado Street, and there were a lot of people in the street, so we had to go slowly, and I had to honk the horn and they began yelling, 'Fujimori, you Chinese, go back to Japan!'" "At the university the professors call on us and ask us, 'What do you think of Fujimori?' and immediately they begin to tell us how they disagree with him." "They say that if Fujimori wins he'll favor us, but that's not true; we're all Peruvian and Fujimori won't have any favorites in our community." "A customer told me that I was hoping that Fujimori would become president so that I could raise my prices. Right there in the market there are people insulting us." "Those who know that the majority didn't vote for Fujimori say that it's too bad he doesn't look more Nisei, because we're all going to be sorry." "The Nikkei individual is seen by 95 percent of the population as just another Peruvian, as if he were an Indian, black, or of mixed race. Suddenly, there's 5 percent that is prejudiced, people who have nothing better to do than brag that they're white, and usually they're poor whites." "They tell me, 'that Chinese guy thinks he's good enough to be president!' And I say, 'we all come from somewhere else. Your family's Italian, theirs is Jewish. That has nothing to do with it.'" "The insults come from people in Miraflores, San Isidro. ... The most educated are the most ignorant, and the most ignorant are the most educated; it's a contradiction. They should change their negative attitude." "They've congratulated me. People who voted for Fujimori are more sympathetic to us, they praise us. They're very pleased with us because we're Japanese." "If native Peruvians want to win your favor, they say: 'I voted for Fujimori,' thinking that you'll do them a favor tomorrow, because they think he's our candidate." "I'm in contact with the native Peruvian customers, those of Andean origin. I've noticed a certain satisfaction when they deal with me, they really think Fujimori's going to change Peru." "Some people look at me as if I were going to be minister or advisor to the ministry where I work." "They don't use my last name anymore, they call me Fujimori. But they treat you with affection and respect; they're not trying to insult you." "In Magdalena everybody agrees with Fujimori. It's fine with the street vendors. They're for Fujimori; they say they'll vote for him again." "I live in Rimac. Everybody knows us and they haven't bothered us." "I live in a middle-class neighborhood and I haven't had any problems, because most of them are for Fujimori. They know the Japanese are honest and hardworking." "In Chancay, Huaral, where I live, the Nikkei are well thought of by the upper classes and by the lower classes as well; in general they accept us." "Taxi drivers ask you, 'who are you voting for?' They're all pro-Fujimori. They think Fujimori is the hardworking, respected person the country needs. One taxi driver told me, 'You're morally obligated to support your countryman. If he becomes president, you have to support him. If he doesn't, you'll be singled out as cowards for not having backed him.'" "The people at work, from the supervisors down, spoke to me positively of Fujimori, with great happiness, as if he represented those forgotten. The great majority of the people identify with him."

11. The next examples show the complexity of responses. Question: "If the candidate, Alberto Fujimori, was elected president of Peru, what would you think?" "I don't think it would be a good idea for Fujimori to be elected, because he doesn't have a plan for government. ... He doesn't present any alternatives or agenda in answer to the expectations Peruvians have. I am deeply worried because he isn't prepared to govern the country." "If he were elected, it would be the first time in the history of Peru that the people would really govern." "He doesn't listen to sound advice. His lack of political knowledge and his ingenuousness could cause him to make mistakes that would continue to drag the country down. At this time I believe that it would be very difficult for any candidate to adequately carry the burden of government. If he wins, I don't think it will turn out well because the country's situation is a difficult one. To improve things will take ten to fifteen years. From the few ideas I've heard from Fujimori, I don't think things would improve very quickly." "Fujimori would be the best person right now to put forward the concept of making Peru something like Taiwan, because he has the charisma, intelligence, and very strong leadership. He will be able to do this without a parliamentary majority, because he's not interested in the political point of view." "I see a high risk in his team. He's focused on other parties' techniques, including those of FREDEMO, the ministers. The problem will be trying to make the technical compatible with the political. It's a bit difficult, but he'll resolve it pragmatically, everyone where they belong. Politically he won't have any problems, but technically, yes." "The fear of the Nikkei community is that he will not perform well and then all that our grandparents worked for will go for nothing. We've been here for ninety-one years, but the image we've created will be erased." "It would be a great sensation for the country and the world because for the first time, someone of Japanese descent would be governing the country. It will revolutionize everything that's happened in politics, not only in Peru but also on an international level, because it's the first time we've seen such a phenomenon. Mr. Fujimori is going to make history; he has a lot of merit." "If Fujimori wins we're going to close the store and I'll look for work abroad, because we're going to have a lot of problems here." "What are we going to do? If the majority elects him we have to respect that. If the majority is mistaken, that's their right. The majority rules, and we're in a democratic country." "We have to unite, we have to help him. The objective is not just Fujimori but Peru. I hope everyone gives him a hand. I think we should support him no matter what."

12. The following responses of the Nikkei address the issue of citizen rights. Question: "What do you think of the participation of a Peruvian of Japanese origin

in the country's political process?" "One shouldn't make distinctions based on sex, race, or religion in politics." "We Nikkei were born in Peru. We are Peruvians of Japanese descent and as such we have the right to participate in our country's politics on any level or hold any political office." "Children born in Peru of foreigners have this right of participation in the political process of our country, because their ideas are different from their parents'." "The Nikkei should be involved in politics because as Peruvians, we are responsible for solving the country's problems, difficulties, and failures." "I am a member of a political party and I am involved in the political life of the neighborhood I live in." "I don't see any problem. It doesn't seem remarkable that a Peruvian of oriental descent should be a candidate for the presidency." "A Japanese individual can't govern Peru; a Peruvian of native origin should be president." "I don't agree that a Nikkei should participate in the country's political process or be presidential candidate right now, because the current situation is a difficult one. There's a lot of violence and poverty. I don't believe that the candidate [Fujimori] can solve these problems." "A third- or fourth-generation Nikkei perhaps could occupy the office of president." "I feel flattered, it would be extraordinary, it's the biggest thing we've attained, it's an achievement, it's setting an example, it would be something to be proud of because we are descended from the Japanese. For my parents' sake I would be very proud that a Nikkei has succeeded in running for president."

13. A selection of responses shows the dynamics mentioned: Question: "Do you feel you have something in common with Fujimori?" "Physical characteristics, we're Nikkei, elongated eyes, our last names, our Japanese heritage, we're Peruvians descended from Japanese, our ancestors, our origin, our families, our heritage. Many of us are from [the prefecture of] Kumamoto." "Like everyone of Japanese origin he's really a perfectionist." "When you see someone else who's Nikkei you believe, feel, or think that the other Nikkei believes, feels, and thinks like you do. He represents honor, technology, and work; those things are important to me, and I agree with his motto. The Nikkei are very analytical, thoughtful, and calm, these are things common to all Japanese. Sentimentally, I can't deny that I feel something in common." "I have rather a lot in common with him, racially and professionally. He's an educator and so am I." "He comports himself sometimes unlike one of the community. In his reactions you can see that he's very politicized or that he knows how to act. You don't think of someone in the community responding that way to interviews, with a sly smile." "I felt a certain sympathy when he was on the Board of Regents and there was a problem at my university. I identify with him because I'm a university student and he was president of the Universidad Nacional Agraria." "Ideas about renovation and modernization, but they have to be realistic. Modernization in Peru has to begin from the bottom, and that's what I think Fujimori wants to do. His desire for change for the better in Peru, for progress, for national unity. He speaks of helping the poor, and I feel that way also." "I observe him and I see that he's very sharp, and above all very analytical. He doesn't lose his head; he can be very cold-blooded, and that's very important." "Nothing, happily, nothing at all; we have nothing in common. Definitely not." Question: "Leaving aside the question of who you voted for, what do you believe should be the attitude of the Nikkei community if Fujimori is elected president?" All of the responses mentioned the word "support," accompanied by both ethnic and national or general arguments. The following are

some of these: "We should support him in every possible way, because he can't govern alone. We must collaborate, personal interests aside, as we have always done, honestly, working together eagerly." "We should support him however we can because he's a citizen of Peru like any other. We should support him because the image he reflects is the Nikkei image." "No matter who wins, all Nikkei and all Peruvians must support the president; the country is at stake. We must do it for our country, because we are Peruvians." "We should support whoever wins, it doesn't matter who, just so that he puts an end to 50 percent of the problems we now have." "Although I'm not on Fujimori's side, we must think of Peru, support the work of whoever wins. We can't turn our backs on the president of Peru."

14. These interviews were conducted in Lima, where more than 84 percent of the Japanese Peruvian population resided. The sample was selected with attention toward representing the larger population in terms of age, gender, and neighborhood (as an index of socioeconomic standing). Here readers should note that we relied on community-based organizations in order to contact respondents, but not all Japanese Peruvians participate in such organizations. A previous study indicated that only 32 percent of the population participated in community-based organizations on a regular basis; concomitantly, the majority of Japanese Peruvians don't participate, or even have relationships with other ethnic compatriots. Because of this situation, we initially interviewed one hundred individuals in 1990, and then interviewed another sixty people in 1998. In any case, we feel confident that the responses allow us to see what the main ideas would be in the national debates of 1999 and 2000 in the context of the Peruvian national elections and their consequences.

CHAPTER TEN

Pathways to Power

Comparative Perspectives on the Emergence of Nikkei Ethnic Political Traditions

LANE RYO HIRABAYASHI

In her capacity as a community leader, Emi Kasamatsu has delineated an ambitious program for national development that features the contributions of Paraguayan Nikkei.[1] Given the instability that has characterized political life in Paraguay of late, Kasamatsu proposes that Paraguayan Nikkei youth, in particular, can and should draw from their ethnic heritage in order to provide a new standard of political leadership as the nation enters the twenty-first century.[2]

From the standpoint of the larger International Nikkei Research Project, Kasamatsu's proposal immediately brings two questions to mind. One is substantive. What lessons can we glean from cases in which Nikkei in the Americas have actually gained access to formal political power? In order to deal effectively with this question, however, we also need a method. Is there an approach that would allow us to compare and analyze Nikkei political trajectories in the Americas, given that these span a range of countries, time periods, and political systems?

Although the comparative study of Nikkei involvement in the political systems of their "host" societies is still in its infancy, I have always been fascinated by the few select cases on the record that seem to exemplify political empowerment. By "empowerment," I refer primarily to the attainment of formal political office via an electoral process in a two- or multiparty polity. Since Nikkei are typically minorities, in both a numerical and sociocultural sense, such cases attract attention because they suggest higher levels of self-determination than one would ordinarily expect, as well as the ability to impact processes and policies in the larger society.

With regard to Nikkei in the Americas, three cases stand out in the extant literature. Although each of these cases involves Nisei, or second-generation Japanese Americans, each represents a distinct level of analysis.

At the local level, in Gardena, California, Japanese Americans living in a multiethnic city were able to elect a Nisei to two successive terms as city councilman and one as city mayor. By the early 1980s, four out of six elected city officials were Nisei.[3]

The state of Hawai'i is well known for its high levels of Asian American political representation. As early as 1917 there were already 179 registered Nisei voters. By 1930, two Nisei Republicans and one Democrat had won office.[4] The percentage of Nisei within the overall electorate was also on the rise over the first three decades of the twentieth century. Constituting only 3.5 percent of Hawai'i's voters in 1922, by 1936 Nisei made up almost 25 percent of the voting population. This was the foundation of the "phenomenal" postwar political achievement that put Nisei into office at every level of the state government and bureaucracy.[5]

In terms of nations, an outstanding case of formal political empowerment of Nikkei can be seen in Brazil. Although initially Japanese immigrants were not involved in Brazilian politics, a new orientation emerged after World War II. In 1948, a watershed event occurred when a Nisei ran for and won a seat on the São Paulo city council. In the decades that followed, Brazilian Nikkei became involved in virtually every level of government. As of the late 1980s, there were "three Japanese Brazilians serving in the national Congress ... [and many] other Nikkei held offices at the state and municipal level."[6]

Although these cases represent a very small (and admittedly atypical) sample, they are a place to begin. Furthermore, there are tools that we can use to study these and other cases comparatively, in order to understand the various "paths to empowerment" that Nikkei in general, and Nisei in particular, have followed to achievement in the Americas. As I will explain below, the procedure that I have in mind entails some assumptions and compromises. However, the rewards are worthwhile: the ability to begin to develop a more systematic understanding of how, where, and when people of Japanese descent in the Americas (and beyond) have attained a measure of formal political power within a larger multiethnic and multicultural society, as well as an understanding of what kind of "price" political empowerment may entail for people of Japanese descent.

Conceptual Framework

A basic framework that can be used to facilitate the comparative analysis of what I am calling Nikkei electoral "paths to power" is presented in an article by University of Wisconsin political scientist Peter K. Eisinger.[7] In this study, Eisinger focuses primarily on what he calls the evolution of an ethnic political tradition—or EPT—among six American "ethnic" populations: four European American groups (Germans, Italians, Poles, and Irish); one religious group (Jews); and one group of color (African Americans). After studying the political trajectories of each of these groups, Eisinger noticed that they display differential manifestations of, as well as different degrees of, political adaptation vis-à-vis the dominant society.

Eisinger proposes that a range of variables be considered to determine why EPTs vary so markedly from one American ethnic group to another. Although some scholars have focused on differences based on the immigrant generation's country of origin, Eisinger suggests that conditions and experiences in the United States are more formative of EPTs and notes that strong ties to the "home country" operate to discourage the development of an EPT.

Generally speaking, dramatic instances of interethnic conflict in the United States are associated with a self-conscious definition and delineation of ethnic group boundaries, as well as a strong EPT. Eisinger denies that EPTs are solely or even primarily a matter of economic disadvantage. Rather, a strong EPT is a result of 1) economic adjustments, including the ability of a population to supersede, but not forget, historical experiences of "group trauma," 2) the consolidation of collective resources, especially those revolving around community "defense" organizations, as well as ethnic leaders who can effectively promote group issues and needs, and 3) a period of initial political consolidation vis-à-vis the mainstream polity. Since Eisinger proposes that each of these three broad conditions needs to be taken into account when evaluating the evolution and strength of an EPT, I would like to describe each condition in a bit more detail below, and specify how Eisinger indicates that they can be operationalized and measured.

The variable "economic adjustment," which Eisinger also identifies as "Stage I" in a diachronic process, is fairly straightforward. Here, he notes that all immigrant groups in the United States must acculturate and compete as best they can, often starting out on the bottom rung of the economic ladder. Economic adjustment must occur to the point that the ethnic group stabilizes, since either too much wealth or too much poverty can impede the development of a coherent EPT.

In addition, and very importantly, Eisinger postulates that when an ethnic

162 / LANE RYO HIRABAYASHI

population experiences a sustained period of "group trauma" that results in "intense collective suffering" during the Stage I period of initial adaptation, this is closely correlated with high levels of in-group solidarity, strong group boundaries, and the evolution and presence of a strong EPT.[8]

The second condition Eisinger highlights occurs in Stage II, and has to do with the capacity of an ethnic group to develop a set of corporately oriented resources, organizations, and leaders. These are all utilized by the group to assert and enact its varied collective interests. Economic stability thus lies at the base of such resources in that members must be willing to give money, goods, and time as a kind of working capital for community development. Institutionally, the presence of businesses, churches, schools, special interest groups, sociocultural and mutual aid organizations, the press, and so on are all indices of what Eisinger calls "community building." Leaders may be drawn from any or all sectors of the community base, but what is key is that both leaders and community organizations be able to clearly, even aggressively, assert their issues, priorities, and needs, and get these needs acknowledged and met by the dominant society.

As a third condition, Eisinger specifies that there has to be a Stage III period of initial political consolidation such that members of the ethnic group recognize their common destiny and goals, and make addressing these a collective priority. Eisinger proposes that a sign that this has been accomplished is that a given ethnic group has enough experience and resources to pursue entry into the mainstream political system of the larger society.

The Comparative Analysis of Qualitative Case Studies

A few general comments on methodology are appropriate at this juncture. As I implied early on, a case study approach to this topic is necessary, if only because there are so few examples of Nikkei political empowerment on the record that a statistical (i.e., variable-oriented) analysis would be inappropriate. Nonetheless, it is important to identify an approach that will help systematize the qualitative comparison of Nikkei electoral empowerment, given that the available cases represent different levels in the hierarchy of sociopolitical integration.

Although John Stuart Mill's book *A System of Logic* was published more than 150 years ago, "Mill's methods," as they are known, are still a staple in "critical thinking" textbooks that present elements of informal logic, as well as books on social science methods. This is because Mill offers a set of qualitative experimental methods that allow researchers to explore the power of causal claims revolving around independent variables that are correlated with a given outcome.[9]

One of these methods is known as "the joint method of agreement and difference," or, alternatively, "the indirect method of difference." The approach here is to compare instances in which a phenomenon or event of interest occurs with a set of closely related instances in which the phenomenon or event does not occur.[10] Hypothetically, the careful selection and juxtaposition of cases should result in a data set that allows the researcher to identify the key independent variable: the one that is present in every case in which the outcome of interest appears, and absent in every case in which it fails to appear. How could this method be applied to the topic at hand?

We would begin by specifying that what Eisinger calls "the evolution of an ethnic political tradition," in any form or manifestation, is the outcome of interest. Following Eisinger, we could hypothesize that the emergence of Nikkei political empowerment—at least in terms of the manifestations identified in the preceding section—requires the concomitant presence of the three broad conditions discussed earlier: 1) social trauma, followed by a period of economic stabilization, 2) community building, and 3) political consolidation. Within Eisinger's framework, each of these conditions is necessary, and thus the absence of any one would impede the development of a viable EPT. By pairing cases at the same relative level of analysis, in which the outcome of interest is present in one but absent in the other, I propose that an approximation of the "indirect method of difference" can be achieved. Toward this end, I'll present six different case studies, three that are generally "positive" and three that are "weak" to "negative."[11] To keep the length of the chapter reasonable, my discussion of cases will be perfunctory, although I'll cite references so that my claims can be cross-checked if desired.

Six Synoptic Case Studies

First let's examine the three salient case studies in which the outcome of interest does occur.

The City of Gardena, California

As suggested above, the case of Nikkei political empowerment in Gardena entails, at almost every level, each of the conditions Eisinger identifies. Before the war, Gardena, just outside Los Angeles proper, was a prosperous farming area. During the 1950s, Gardena became the site of a comfortable commuter/bedroom community, basically a middle-class suburb of Los Angeles, filled with new, single family, two-car garage homes that appealed to upwardly mobile Nisei who had recently started families.

A number of studies have documented the plethora of community-based organizations that sprang up in the area during the 1970s.[12] Many of these were social service–oriented, targeting youth, the elderly, veterans, and so on. Just as many promoted aspects of Japanese language, culture, arts, religion, and sports. Thus, while Japanese Americans in Gardena had a strong orientation toward autonomy and retention of ethnic heritage, they also had a strong orientation toward achievement in the larger society in terms of education, occupation, income, and representation in the political arena.

Nikkei political inroads in Gardena were first made in the early 1960s, after the bulk of the population could be said to have recovered from the losses of mass incarceration during the war. A Nisei veteran, Toshi Hirade, is reputed to be the first Nikkei to run for city office, although he was not elected. That honor goes to Nisei veteran Ken Nakaoka, who ran successfully for city council in 1966 and again in 1970. Nakaoka then was elected mayor in 1972, making him one of very few Japanese Americans who can claim this honor. By 1980, four out of six elected city officials were Nisei as well. Throughout the 1980s, Japanese Americans were recognized as a dominant political force in Gardena, although there is evidence that the "power block" that actually ran things was based on a coalition between European and Japanese Americans.[13]

What is notable, in terms of Eisinger's conditions, is that elected officials of Japanese descent, Democrats and Republicans alike, appear to have initiated their campaigns after sustained periods of local community involvement and service in both mainstream and ethnic-specific group organizations. To cite one example, Masani "Mas" Fukai was elected to the Gardena city council for six consecutive terms (1974–94), for a total of twenty-four years of continual service. Born in Gardena, Mas Fukai was incarcerated along with his family at the Gila River camp in southern Arizona. Fukai then served in the U.S. Army, attaining the rank of corporal.[14] After succeeding in two different careers—first running an automobile repair business and then working as an insurance salesman—Fukai decided to run for city council and initiated his political career. Fukai won a reputation as a hard-working politician and became prominent because of his long-term involvement in numerous community-based and -oriented services, especially on behalf of youth.[15]

Despite repeated success at the local level, only a few Nikkei in Gardena have been able to gain higher level offices. The most important figure in this arena is Paul Bannai, a Nisei, a veteran, a realtor, and a Republican, who parlayed his position as a member of the city's planning commission (1969), and later city council (1972), into a state assembly seat. He was initially appointed in 1973 to the 53rd Assembly District, an office that he held via election for a number of subsequent terms.[16]

The State of Hawai'i

For prewar Issei and Nisei living in Hawai'i, as for Nikkei throughout the Americas, the road to economic stability was long and hard. Initially recruited as plantation laborers, Issei worked and sacrificed to build a wide range of community groups and institutions.[17] Popular leaders like the Reverend Takie Okumura and Fred Kinzaburo Makino soon emerged with strong, albeit contrasting, visions of winning acceptance for Issei and Nisei alike.[18]

Periods of crisis had confronted the Nikkei population well before the war, especially with major strikes over plantation wages and conditions, first in 1909 throughout Oahu, and again, in concert with Filipino plantation laborers, in 1920.[19] The attack on Pearl Harbor heralded a period of serious stress and strain for Nikkei in Hawai'i. Although they were not subjected to incarceration en masse, they were subjected to suspicion, accusations, and restrictions (including curfews), especially during the first years after America's entry into the war.[20]

The definitive rise of Nikkei political empowerment in Hawai'i featured a historically rooted coalition of powerful new forces that came together after the war.[21] On one hand, there were the Nikkei labor organizers and plantation employees who had been increasingly successful in asserting their demands for better wages and working conditions on the plantations. On the other, there were the Americans of Japanese Ancestry (AJA) veterans, who returned to civilian life with dreams of furthering their education and breaking into the mainstream. These two sectors coalesced under the leadership of Democratic party movers and shakers like John A. Burns (who had won the AJA's backing by defending their loyalty to America during World War II), and Daniel Inouye. By 1954, Democrats were able to overturn Republican control over the islands.

Although inroads had been made since the end of World War II, by 1954 "Democrats captured more than two-thirds of the territorial house and nearly two-thirds of the Senate. Nearly half of the seats were held by AJA [as Nikkei in Hawai'i prefer to be called] candidates."[22] These victories were not a fluke, either, as they continued in subsequent decades. By the 1971–72 term, over fifty percent of Hawai'i's House of Representatives was still made up of Japanese Americans, the majority of them Nisei. In 1974, George R. Ariyoshi was elected governor of Hawai'i. Twice reelected, Ariyoshi was the first Japanese American, the first Nisei, and indeed the first person of color to become the governor of an American state.[23]

The state of Hawai'i is also notable because its Democratic revolution paved the way for AJA women to enter formal politics.[24] As Professors Moromisato Miasato and Kobayashi both emphasize in their chapters, many formal aspects of Nikkei community, including politics, are subject to gendered roles and rules. Thus, it is likely that gender has made it much more difficult for Nikkei women to obtain mentoring as well as opportunities for careers having to do with politics, but the state of Hawai'i provides an intriguing variation worthy of sustained attention.[25]

Perhaps the most notable case from Hawai'i is the career of Congresswoman Patsy Takemoto Mink. A Nisei born in Maui, Mink studied both in Hawai'i and on the U.S. mainland, including at the University of Chicago Law School.[26] Returning to Hawai'i, she set up her own law office, as no established firm would hire her, and she began to get involved in Democratic Party politics. A tireless organizer, Mink developed a great deal of experience and expertise during the 1950s. In 1956 she started her political career by successfully running for a seat in the state house.[27] Two years later, she won a seat in the Senate. After serving two terms in the Senate, Mink successfully ran for Congress in 1964. A progressive Democrat, currently back in office, Mink has been at the forefront of legislative projects involving women's rights, the pacifist movement (especially against the war in Southeast Asia), and education. Along the way, Mink served as role model and mentor for a part-Nikkei woman who became a prominent political figure in her own right: Jean Sadako King.[28]

Brazil

Nikkei empowerment in Brazil bears an interesting resemblance to that in Gardena and Hawai'i. This is especially true of São Paulo, the premier city in Brazil, a country where there has historically been a concentration of persons of Japanese descent—where, in fact, the largest overall number of Nikkei in any country in the Americas can be found.[29]

Before the war, Issei who came to Brazil typically found their livelihood in agriculture or small business. They were a favored immigrant group, but in point of fact, they often kept their distance from the larger Brazilian society. Initially, there was not a great deal of interest in Brazilian politics because of the Issei's orientation toward their homeland, but also because many Japanese immigrants saw themselves as apart from, and perhaps even superior to, the Brazilians in their immediate milieu.[30] This attitude, however, was brought into question by members of the Nikkei colony who began to enter the Brazilian academic system before World War II, and also by Nisei, who, after all, had been born, raised, and educated in Brazil.[31]

As is well known, the war was a period of tremendous crisis for Nikkei in Brazil. Among other pressures, Nikkei themselves split into two groups—those who favored Japan, and those who supported the United States and the Allies—causing the community to turn upon itself.[32] These intragroup divisions only gradually disappeared during the decade after Japan's surrender in 1945.

Immediately after the war, according to Celia Sakurai, there were enough Nikkei concerned about accommodation to elect a city councilperson of Japanese descent in São Paulo (and this was accomplished on the basis of a primarily Japanese Brazilian constituency). This opened the door for a whole new set of Nikkei politicians, who pitched their campaigns to their ethnic compatriots. If they were elected, Nikkei politicians would repay support by doling out favors and other forms of patronage to their constituents. Still, according to Sakurai, as well as Shiotani and Yamashita, as little as three decades later Japanese Brazilian politicians were no longer able to do this; they had to find acceptance and backing from a wider set of constituents in order to succeed.[33]

It is notable here that there have been Japanese Brazilian politicians who have worked with non-Nikkei constituencies in order to gain access to power. According to historian Jeffrey Lesser, labor leader and politician Luiz Gushiken has not garnered much in the way of support from his Brazilian ethnic compatriots because he is "a member of a well-known Okinawan (i.e., non-Japanese) family."[34] Nonetheless, in a fascinating turn of events, Gushiken has recently used popular Brazilian characterizations of Japanese to his own advantage. Since, as Lesser points out, "Japaneseness" has become a vernacular metaphor for "honest" and "hardworking" in contemporary Brazil, Gushiken has used a wide range of Japanese symbols in his campaign literature to appropriate these stereotypes into his political persona.[35] Moreover, Lesser suggests that Japanese Brazilians of Okinawan descent are able to deploy their ethnicity in a dual fashion, maintaining, at one and the same time, that their Okinawanness makes them more Brazilian than Naichi Japanese, and more "Japanese" than (i.e., superior to) other Brazilians.[36]

Three Cases of "Weak" Levels of Empowerment

In the paragraphs below, I present contrasting examples of "negative," or "weak," cases of empowerment. I have selected one for each of the levels of analysis above, with the intent of imposing some control in examining Eisinger's conditions and stages.

The City of San Francisco

There is little doubt that San Francisco's Japanese American population suffered its share of "group trauma" during the early twentieth century, in the process of establishing a modicum of economic stability. It is equally the case that San Francisco has seen as many community-based organizations as

Gardena, and that the political representatives who emerged were skillful and articulate in their efforts to see that the needs of the community as a whole be recognized and met.[37]

Although the Japanese American population of San Francisco has some very polished and able representatives, Nikkei entry into the city's corridors of power has been very slow indeed. Prior to the last decade of the twentieth century, no Japanese American had ever been elected mayor, let alone a member of the San Francisco Board of Supervisors. In the 1990s, Michael Yaki, who is of part-Japanese descent, become a member of the Board of Supervisors, joining two other Asian Americans (Mabel Teng and Leland Yee), who had already been seated. Yaki was originally appointed by then-mayor Willie Brown, but he subsequently campaigned for his position during the 1998 election. So perhaps this is an indication that things may be changing.[38]

The State of California

The historical trajectory of Japanese Americans in this state indicates that it basically fulfills the conditions Eisinger specifies in Stage I and Stage II of his framework. It is more difficult to determine if Nikkei in California have actually been able to achieve major inroads to higher levels of political power, other than by appointment.

Although Los Angeles, San Jose, and San Francisco have significant concentrations of Japanese American residents, it would be hard to argue that any notable candidates from these cities have gained electoral power by affiliating themselves with the ethnic community and its issues.[39] On the contrary, if we examine the trajectories of California's successful Japanese American politicians, apart from Paul Bannai, my sense is that they have been able to succeed primarily by appealing to a far broader constituency than their Japanese American or even Asian American compatriots. Take the case of Norman Mineta, who was elected mayor of San Jose before successfully running for Congress in 1974. Since only 2.5 percent of his district was of Asian (let alone Japanese) descent, it is clear that Mineta couldn't have campaigned on a set of "ethnic" issues alone and won.[40]

Yet another trajectory is exemplified by the case of the late senator Samuel I. Hayakawa. Hayakawa was the first and only person of Japanese descent to become a full professor at San Francisco State College before the late 1950s. A tenured faculty member and renowned semanticist, Hayakawa rose to prominence as a strong-willed college president willing to quell student rebellion on campus.[41] Hayakawa subsequently ran for the U.S. Senate, with scant support from Japanese Americans or any other community of color. In fact, Hayakawa became famous for attacking the Japanese American community. Even local and national leaders of fairly "status quo" community organizations such as the Japanese American Citizens League clashed with Hayakawa.[42] He found his backing among conservative, rich, European American Republicans. What is more, in city-level elections in Gardena, the majority of Japanese Americans voted for John Tunney, Hayakawa's Democratic opponent in this contest, rather than their "ethnic" compatriot.[43]

Mexico

Labor migration from Japan to Mexico, in small numbers, goes back to the late nineteenth century. Although many of the ventures that brought the Issei failed, some Japanese stayed behind, eventually intermarried, and put down roots. Subsequently, between 1901 and 1907, a peak period of "contract immigration" brought approximately 8,706 more Japanese who were assigned work at different jobs throughout Mexico.[44]

Mexico's response to these laborers differed from that of the United States in one very important respect. Immigrant Japanese could naturalize after a period of five years in Mexico. It is possible that, facing increasing levels of institutional racism in the United States in the early twentieth century, some Nikkei even decided to cross the border and begin farming in northern Mexico. Despite certain privileges, over the course of Mexican history Nikkei have been periodically persecuted. For example, they were subject to attack during the Mexican Revolution, especially in the northern states. By 1920, the population had declined to little over two thousand persons.[45]

Nevertheless, between 1921 and 1940, many of the Nikkei who remained were able to establish themselves economically. This has been characterized as a period of upward mobility for Mexican Nikkei, who began to gain a foothold in the independent farming and business sector economy. Intermarriage was not uncommon, and one scholar states that by the end of the 1930s, "their assimilation into Mexican society on the local levels was well underway."[46]

Mexico severed diplomatic relations with Japan after the attack on Pearl Harbor. Initial restrictions were set into place, but soon after, with some exceptions, any of the approximately 4,700 Japanese immigrants who were too close to the coast or to the U.S.–Mexican border were required to report to Mexico City or Guadalajara. Although they were not incarcerated, Watanabe makes it very clear that Nikkei in Mexico had "a very hard time ... filled with trying experiences."[47] By 1945, prewar demographic patterns had been totally disrupted, and Mexico City and Guadalajara emerged as the primary points of Nikkei concentration in the country.[48]

After intragroup divisions exacerbated by the war died down, Mexican Nikkei were dispersed throughout Mexico City, but their networks revolved around two formal community organizations—the Japanese Mexican Association and the Mexican Japanese Academy, an educational institution—and a range of groups such as *kenjin-kai* (prefectural associations) and various "mutual aid" organizations. Watanabe indicates that, while the Mexican Nikkei as a whole have moved into middle- to upper-middle-class levels, they remain ignored, insofar as their "population has been small enough not to arouse much attention."[49]

By the early 1980s, the Mexican Nikkei community understood the importance of political representation, but faced some barriers. Candidates could not run for election unless both parents were Mexican, which left Issei and Nisei out of the political picture. After citing the relatively tiny numbers of Mexican Nikkei, Watanabe implies that other Mexicans would not react favorably to an explicitly Japanese Mexican candidate. She cites the case of Guillermo Hori, who gained prominence in politics as the vice-minister of labor. Watanabe writes, "People like him have no affiliation with the Nikkei community, and are said to even consciously avoid contact. Because of the strong nationalistic sentiments prevailing in Mexico, it is to the advantage of people like Hori to identify themselves as one hundred percent Mexican."[50] For the most part, Nikkei in Mexico are not subject to overt prejudice. "Yet, when the Nikkei try to break into established Mexican political, financial and social circles, strong discrimination is experienced on the basis of ethnic and racial differences, thus preventing the inclusion of Nikkei in these networks."[51]

In sum, by the 1980s, while Mexican Nikkei might have liked to see community members seek political office, both for the purpose of self-defense and self-protection, their overall numbers and proportions were too small. In any case "race relations" still appeared to be too delicate to make political salience on the part of Mexican Nikkei advisable.

Interpretations: The Three Pathways to Political Power

My analysis of the cases we've examined here is that Eisinger's stages and conditions appear to be relevant to the three "strong" cases, but not to be very influential in accounting for why Nikkei in the Americas have or have not been able to gain access to power. Additionally, I propose that we are looking at not one, but at least three fairly distinctive "pathways to power."

The first pathway, which is manifest in the electoral victories in Gardena, Hawai'i, and (to a lesser extent) Brazil, does appear to depend upon economic and community consolidation for making inroads into political party structures and local elected positions. However, "aggressive assertion of the ethnic group's rights" is only marked in the case of Hawai'i. Even here, the most obvious manifestations of militancy were the AJAs directly involved in prewar strikes against the plantations and the postwar victories of the ILWU. The rest of the cases indicate that Nikkei are able to gain access to formal power without violence or even marked protest. In other words, this is not a "necessary" condition, at least in terms of Nikkei in the Americas.

Above and beyond Eisinger's conditions, these cases indicate that a basic demographic precondition of "critical mass" (that is, not so much "numbers" but rather overall percentage) must be met for political empowerment to occur.[52] This makes sense in that in electoral systems with two or more parties, where "majority rules," overall percentage does make a difference. Thus, it would seem that for Nikkei to develop a viable ethnic political tradition, they have to have a strong demographic base—on the order of 20 percent or more—whether we are talking about the city, state, or national level. In other words, Eisinger may be right in asserting that numbers, either absolute or as a relative percentage of the population, have had little to do with the evolution of an EPT among the ethnic groups he studied, but numbers do appear to have been influential for Nikkei in the Americas.

Moreover, the dynamics of this "pathway to power" in two of the cases cited above include important conditions that Eisinger's framework does not identify or discuss. In Gardena—and this appears to be the case in Hawai'i, too, especially after the war—the initial breakthrough into mainstream electoral politics seems to have been tied to, if not based on, the ability of Nisei to highlight their "service to the country," as highly honored veterans of World War II. As far as I can determine, this record of military service was essential for Nisei to gain mainstream legitimacy and initial access to electoral power. A second feature that appears both in Hawai'i and Gardena is that there was some indication that Nikkei were willing to cross party lines to support ethnic compatriots running for office.[53] Such practices may be the reason that criticisms of a so-called Nikkei voting block have arisen in both Gardena and Hawai'i.[54] Research carried out in the 1980s indicates that this may be a transitional phase that occurs in the initial stages of formal electoral empowerment of the Nikkei.

Now, if we looked at only the "strong" or "positive" cases, we might be left with an impression of the sole importance of "critical mass." However, examination of the "weak" cases indicates that there are at least two additional pathways to political power that do not revolve strictly around overall numbers.

A second pathway to power is apparent in the case studies of San Francisco and California (and, reportedly, more recently in Brazil, as well). Again, in these situations there was economic and ethnic community consolidation, but little impact was realized for most of the twentieth century in terms of formal electoral empowerment. Only a handful of Nikkei politicians—including the Nisei Floyd Mori, Robert Matsui, Norman Mineta, and most recently Sansei Michael Yaki of San Francisco—gained broad recognition as viable candidates and officeholders. As in the "strong" cases described above, there are large Nikkei populations in the city and state, but their relative percentage is low, and this appears to have hurt their ability to gain access to mainstream political parties and offices. In terms of 1990 U.S. Census Bureau estimates, it is worth remembering that while California had almost 313,000 persons of Japanese descent within its borders—which represented approximately 37 percent of all persons of Japanese descent in the United States—Japanese Americans made up only slightly more than 1 percent of the total state population. By contrast, AJAs in Hawai'i—247,486 strong in 1990—made up over 22 percent of the state.[55]

In fact, no other state had even 1 percent Nikkei in 1990, with the state of Washington coming closest at .7 percent, and the rest ranging from .4 percent down to .03 percent in Mississippi. Given these figures, it is understandable why Japanese American political candidates outside Hawai'i must appeal to broad constituencies in order to win elected offices. The same equation is likely to hold for most cases in the Americas except, perhaps, at the local level of a city or district where there are many Nikkei constituents, or a smaller number of especially influential Nikkei.

A third distinct pathway to power involves a situation in which there is an independent candidate who happens to be of Japanese descent, but who is not linked to the larger Nikkei community. In some cases, like that represented by S. I. Hayakawa, there was no ethnic base to begin with, and nothing was done to build or mobilize one when he was in office, as he preferred to emphasize his view that "total assimilation" was the most constructive strategy for people of Japanese descent. Some Mexican and Brazilian Nikkei politicians appear to be similarly detached from their ethnic compatriots, although the primary reason in each case I've treated here differs. Guillermo Hori apparently feels that he can't afford to be labeled as anything except a "Mexican." Luis Gushiken has had little support from the larger Brazilian Nikkei community, and yet has appropriated popular stereotypes of Japanese in order to bolster his own image.

Having briefly considered the question of Nikkei paths to political power, it remains to be determined whether people of Japanese descent overseas have developed an actual ethnic political tradition. My sense is that, among Nikkei in the Americas, the strongest EPT appears in Hawai'i. The demographic mix that makes up the contemporary state of Hawai'i, the use of pidgin, the achievements of the 442nd/100th, and the coalition politics that put an end to Republican dominance all suggest a rich backdrop for the evolution of a distinctive AJA political style and mystique. We may need additional research on this topic, especially by ethnic "insiders," to get the qualitative data needed to determine whether or not Eisinger's operationalization of an EPT is valid in this instance. In any case, three characteristics of a Nikkei ethnic political tradition as exemplified in the case of Hawai'i seem to be: 1) a communal/cooperative orientation, 2) increasingly since the 1970s, an orientation toward consensus, 3) building broader multicultural ties and coalitions since, even in a setting like Hawai'i, AJAs cannot hope to win political offices completely on their own.

At the same time, the AJA case in Hawai'i, as well as the cases in California and Brazil, suggest that, in point of fact, the integration of Nikkei in the Americas has been a critical dimension of their ability to attain political power at the local, state, and national levels. If true, this is ironic because it embodies a dilemma. If Nikkei have to integrate aggressively into the dominant society in order to get access to higher levels of decision and policy making, will any ties to the ethnic community, or even remnants of an ethnic sensibility, be left? This might not prove to be too overwhelming a challenge for Nisei politicians, but what of the Sansei, Yonsei, or Gosei generations?

Conclusion

My conclusion is simply that Nikkei in the Americas, including Japanese Americans, cannot be said to have avoided formal politics for historical or cultural reasons. Rather, occasions in which Nikkei have reached a level of critical mass that would allow them to play a significant role in open elections have been very few indeed. Beyond this, it is clear that intragroup heterogeneity, resulting from various times of arrival and different socioeconomic trajectories and political orientations, have made solidarity among Nikkei in any given country difficult.

Thus, in terms of the cases and approach adopted here, Eisinger's stages and conditions do not appear to be efficacious for understanding political empowerment (let alone an EPT) among Nikkei populations in the Americas. Eisinger's conditions are neither "necessary" nor "sufficient," singly or in any combination. Empowerment and an EPT do not seem to appear among Nikkei without them making up a large proportion of the overall population—that is, 20 percent or more—at whatever level in the hierarchy of sociopolitical integration we happen to be considering. If and when this precondition is met, Eisinger's conditions bear consideration. I have also identified two additional pathways to power that do not depend upon "critical mass." Whether either of these pathways will lead toward other manifestations of a Nikkei EPT, or actually entail further Nikkei integration into the larger society, is a question that we will have to wait to have fully answered.

The relevance of these findings for the program proposed by Professor Kasamatsu is as follows. It seems clear that Nikkei youth who enter politics in Paraguay cannot expect to achieve formal political empowerment through mobilizing only their ethnic compatriots. Instead, the pathway followed by Nisei politicians in California seems to offer a middle road between those we have surveyed in a country like Brazil, where Nikkei numbers and percentages are relatively high and "Japaneseness" is seen as virtue, and Mexico, where politicians of Japanese descent have literally had to deny their ethnicity in order to succeed within the larger society. Since the national polity in Paraguay is quite different from that found at a state level in California, perhaps the most appropriate recommendation is that Nikkei youth in Latin America study various cases of political empowerment, since they alone are in the best position to creatively appropriate what has been accomplished elsewhere with an eye toward their own situation, resources, and needs.

A final point has to do with formal political empowerment and gender. Without a doubt, formal politics in both North and South America has been a domain monopolized by Nikkei men. As the chapters by Professors Kobayashi and Moromisato remind us, as we enter the twenty-first century, we need to ask ourselves: Why have women in the Nikkei communities not been encouraged or trained to assume roles as leaders too? Is there something more that we can or should be doing in order to remedy this situation? In this sense, Hawai'i, which has produced a number of women who have played significant roles in electoral politics, is a case for other Nikkei in the Americas to ponder.

Notes

I would like to acknowledge, first and foremost, Dr. Akemi Kikumura-Yano, director of the INRP, for inviting me to join as a participant researcher, and later as senior editor of this anthology. I would like to thank Akemi, Satomi Takeda, INRP project coordinator, and Dr. Masayo Ohara, INRP research specialist, for their assistance and support. I'd also like to express my appreciation to Irene Hirano, her staff, and to the members of the Japanese American National Museum for initiating this path-breaking research project. Finally, I would like to acknowledge the help of the INRP researchers and team members for providing information and resources that I have drawn from in writing this paper. As always, conversations with Evelyn Hu-DeHart have been helpful, as have communications from Malcolm Collier, Timothy P. Fong, and Kenji Taguma.

1. Emi Kasamatsu, "The New Perspective of the Paraguayan Nikkei: A Challenge for the Upcoming Millennium," unpublished paper.

2. Kasamatsu's concerns are widely reflective of concerns among Nikkei throughout Latin America. This was evident at the X COPANI (tenth Convención Panamericano Nikkei) meetings, held in Santiago, Chile, in July 1999, especially in

the oral summary of the discussions and resolutions of the "Youth Convention" afternoon plenary session on Friday, July 30.

3. For background on the contemporary Japanese American community in Gardena, see Kaoru Oguri Kendis, *A Matter of Comfort: Ethnic Maintenance and Ethnic Style Among Third Generation Japanese Americans* (New York: AMS Press, 1989), and Lane Ryo Hirabayashi, "Community Lost? Notes on Contemporary Japanese American Community in Gardena, California," in *Asians in America: A Reader*, Malcolm Collier, ed. (Dubuque, Iowa: Kendall-Hunt, 1993), 169–83.

4. See Bill Hosokawa, *Nisei: The Quiet American* (Niwot: University of Colorado Press, 1992; rev. ed.), 457–72.

5. Ibid., 460.

6. Ryan Shiotani, and Karen Tei Yamashita, "Japanese Brazilian Immigration," *Rafu Shimpo*, Dec. 1989.

7. Peter K. Eisinger, "Ethnic Conflict, Community-Building, and the Emergence of Ethnic Political Traditions in the United States," in *Urban Ethnic Conflict: A Comparative Perspective*, Susan E. Clarke and Jeffrey L. Obler, eds. (North Carolina: Institute for Research in the Social Sciences, Comparative Urban Studies, Monograph No. 3, 1976), 1–34. All subsequent quotes from Eisinger are drawn from this publication.

8. For additional commentary concerning the relationship between "group trauma" and intragroup social and political solidarity see Marc Howard Ross, "Culture and Identity in Comparative Political Analysis," in *Comparative Politics: Rationality, Culture, and Structure*, Mark Irving Lichback and Alan S. Zuckerman, eds. (Cambridge: Cambridge University Press, 1997), 42–80.

9. My understanding of Mill's methods, including their weaknesses, is largely indebted to Charles C. Ragin, *The Comparative Method: Moving Beyond Qualitative and Quantitative Strategies* (Berkeley: University of California Press, 1987).

10. For an example of how Mill's methods have been applied to the differential analysis of Nikkei community formation, see Harumi Befu, "Contrastive Acculturation of California Japanese: Comparative Approach to the Study of Japanese Immigrants," *Human Organization* 24, no. 3 (1965): 209–16.

11. I admit from the beginning that this is a totally "opportunistic" sample. Still, I propose that the effort is of utility and interest, even while I acknowledge that a much larger sample, encompassing much more variation (which might even allow for the randomized selection of cases), would greatly improve the analysis.

12. See Oguri Kendis, *A Matter of Comfort*. Also, the entry on "Gardena" in *Japanese American History: An A-to-Z Reference from 1868 to the Present*, Brian Niiya, ed. (New York: Facts on File, 1993), 144–45, lists relevant publications.

13. Data on a key election in Gardena presented by Akira Mori indicates that Mas Fukai had support from both Japanese and European American voters. *Political Participation of Asian Americans: Problems and Strategies*, Yung-Hwan Jo, ed. (Chicago: Pacific/Asian American Mental Health Resource Center, 1980).

14. These data are cited in an official "City of Gardena" brochure on elected city officials, which was made available to me at the Gardena Public Library (copy in the author's possession).

15. Details about Mas Fukai's community service are presented in an article in *Gardena Valley News*, Nov. 2, 1975.

16. Paul Bannai's biography and career have frequently been covered in the local newspapers; see, for example, *Gardena Valley News*, July 4, 1976, Nov. 7, 1976, and Dec. 1, 1979.

17. See Franklin Odo and Kazuko S. Sinoto, *A Pictorial History of the Japanese in Hawaii, 1885–1924* (Honolulu: Bishop Museum Press, 1985).

18. Harry H. L. Kitano, "Japanese Americans on the Road to Dissent," in *Seasons of Rebellion*, Joe Boskin and R. Rosenstone, eds. (New York: Holt, Rinehart, and Winston, 1972).

19. Ronald Takaki, *Pau Hana: Plantation Life and Labor in Hawaii, 1835–1920* (Honolulu: University of Hawai'i Press, 1983).

20. Gary Y. Okihiro, *Cane Fires: The Anti-Japanese Movement in Hawaii, 1865–1945* (Philadelphia, Penn.: Temple University Press, 1991).

21. Roland Kotani, *The Japanese in Hawaii: A Century of Struggle* (Honolulu: Hochi, 1985).

22. George Cooper and Gavin Daws, *Land and Power in Hawaii* (Honolulu: University of Hawai'i Press, 1985), 42–43; passim.

23. Ibid., chapter 12, "One Man's Career: George Ariyoshi," 392–409. Also see Ariyoshi's autobiography, *With Obligation to All* (Honolulu: Ariyoshi Foundation, 1997).

24. I could find no published information on Japanese American women in politics outside the state of Hawai'i, although I am sure that there are other cases worth mentioning. Thus, I agree with the point made by Professor Audrey Kobayashi during INRP meetings in 1999: in studying Nikkei, we must attend to how gender biases influence the shape of available databases.

25. This point is extensively and effectively illustrated by Doris Moromisato Miasato, this volume, chapter 11.

26. See Patsy Sumie Saiki, *Japanese Women in Hawaii: The First 100 Years* (Honolulu: Kisaku, 1985), 130–34.

27. See "Mink, Patsy Takemoto," in *Japanese American History*, Brian Niiya, ed., 233–34.

28. Saiki, *Japanese Women in Hawaii*, 119–25, contains a short biography of Jean Sadako King.

29. In his research note, "Nikkei in the Western Hemisphere," *Amerasia Journal* 15, no. 2 (1989), Yuji Ichioka cites an informed estimate of 1.1 million Japanese Brazilians in 1989, p. 177.

30. Shiotani and Yamashita, "Japanese Brazilian Immigration."

31. Celia Sakurai, "A Fase Romantica Da Politica: Os Primeiros Deputados Nikkeis No Brazil," in *Imigracão e Politica em São Paulo*, Boris Fausto et al., eds. (São Paulo: Editora Sumare; Editora da UFSCar, 1950), 144–47. I am very grateful to Professor Jeffrey Lesser for bringing Sakurai's research to my attention.

32. See "Kachigumi," in *Japanese American History*, Brian Niiya, ed., 194. Niiya indicates that this kind of phenomenon was found not only in Brazil, but also in a number of Nikkei communities.

33. The most detailed information available, in terms of listing specific names and campaigns, is presented by Sakurai in "A Fase Romantica Da Politica."

34. See Jeffrey Lesser, this volume, chapter 3.

35. Ibid.

36. Ibid.

37. Surprisingly little has been published about San Francisco's Japantown, let alone the city's population of Japanese descent. Two pieces are Suzie Okazaki, *Nihonmachi: A Story of San Francisco Japantown* (San Francisco: SKO Studios, 1985), and Harry H. L. Kitano, "Housing of Japanese-Americans in the San Francisco Bay Area," in *Studies in Housing and Minority Groups*, Nathan Glazer and Davis McEntire, eds. (Berkeley: University of California Press, 1960), 178–97.

38. I'd like to thank Malcolm Collier, Timothy P. Fong, and Kenji Tagumi for their insights on the San Francisco Board of Supervisors in general, and Michael Yaki in particular.

39. By the 1980s, however, Nikkei had not acted as an "ethnic voting block" anywhere, even in Hawai'i. See Michael Hass, "Comparing Paradigms of Ethnic Politics in the United States: The Case of Hawaii," *Western Political Quarterly* 40, no. 4 (1987): 647–72.

40. These data were culled from *Political Participation of Asian Americans: Problems and Strategies*, Yung-Hwan Jo, ed.

41. See the biographical information on Hayakawa in Dikran Karagueuzian, *Blow It Up! The Black Student Revolt at San Francisco State College and the Emergence of Dr. Hayakawa* (Boston: Gambit, 1971), 149–65. Karagueuzian, incidentally, is a Syrian of Armenian descent, and was the editor of the S.F. State campus newspaper, the *Gator*, during the strike.

42. See the entry, "Hayakawa, Samuel Ichiye," in *Japanese American History*, Brian Niiya, ed., 158–59. The accompanying bibliography lists various works where readers can consult Hayakawa's views, as well as some of the critiques issued by Japanese and Asian Americans.

43. An article that offers both statistics and analysis in terms of the Tunney-Hayakawa contest appeared in the *Gardena Valley News*, Nov. 7, 1976, 1.

44. Chizuko Watanabe, *The Japanese Immigrant Community in Mexico: Its History and Present* (M.A. thesis, California State University, Los Angeles, 1983).

45. Ibid.

46. Ibid., 57; 188–89.

47. Ibid., 91.

48. Ibid., 108. This trend continues today. For example, in 1980, out of a total of 12,545 Nikkei in Mexico, 7,016 lived in the Federal District, while another 760 lived in Guadalajara. In other words, 56 percent of all Mexican Nikkei lived in the capital, and almost 62 percent lived in one of the two cities.

49. Ibid.

50. Ibid., 110

51. Ibid., 175.

52. "Critical mass" refers to both demographic and ecological conditions, such that overall numbers and relative percentage of a given ethnic group result in a dynamic transformation of that group's sociocultural system. See Claude S. Fischer, "Toward a Subcultural Theory of Urbanism," *American Journal of Sociology* 80 (1975): 1319–41; and Claude S. Fischer, *The Urban Experience* (New York: Harcourt and Brace, 1970).

53. Professor Akemi Kikumura-Yano points out that, early on, it was common for AJAs to cross party lines in order to support and vote for ethnic compatriots (personal communication, 1999).

54. See the discussion of the presence of a Japanese American voting block in Gardena in Akira Kubota, "Japanese Americans in Local Politics: The Case of Gardena," in Y. H. Jo, ed., *Political Participation of Asian Americans: Problems and Strategies* (Chicago: Pan-Asian American Mental Health Research Consortium), 30–37.

55. These figures, and the ones listed in the paragraph immediately below, are from an unpublished manuscript, "1990 U.S. Census Analysis," by the Japanese American National Museum, Marketing Committee, n.d. Copy in the author's possession.

PART THREE

Disjunctions of Nikkei Identities

Introduction

RICHARD KOSAKI

The following essays by nine INRP scholars identify and discuss three broad sources of disjunction—conditions that appear to block or impede the reproduction of ethnic identities and communities. According to these scholars, disjunction first has to do with patriarchy, and with gendered hierarchies within Nikkei families and communities. A second disjunction was produced by the *dekasegi* phenomenon, in which first-, second-, and third-generation Latin Americans of Japanese descent returned to Japan in the 1980s and 1990s in order to seek employment and better salaries. Another set of disjunctions has largely to do with new kinds of consciousness among people of Japanese descent that constitute a response to new issues and new kinds of linkages. Two significant populations along these lines are persons who out-marry and their families. Another is the Uchinanchu, or Okinawans, in global diaspora.

As we will see in the chapters in this section, there is evidence that these disjunctions have created tension for people of Japanese descent who live outside Japan. On the other hand, it is not clear whether these disjunctions will result in permanent splits between self-identified Nikkei and others of Japanese descent who believe that they must prioritize more immediate concerns.[1]

The issue of gender inside Nikkei communities is taken up by Doris Moromisato Miasato. In her chapter "I Woman, I Man, I Nikkei," Moromisato begins by asking why the history and experiences of Peruvian Nikkei women have been erased from the official record, despite the many contributions and achievements of women. Drawing from a set of original interviews with first-, second-, and third-generation women, Moromisato demonstrates that Japanese Peruvian women have been subject to norms and expectations revolving around the familial and domestic sphere, even as they have generally been shut out of leadership positions in many of the major community-based organizations.

Taking a decidedly feminist perspective, Moromisato also observes that the younger women—those of the third and fourth generations born since the 1960s—appear to avoid Japanese Peruvian community organizations. Taking this as a new and significant development, Moromisato asks, is this phenomenon a sign of women's rejection of the patriarchal setup and operation of the Japanese Peruvian family and community? Or is the phenomenon merely a reflection of the younger women's educational and career aspirations, given the fact that the larger society is the best place for them to fulfill these aspirations?

In this sense, we note that there is really no contradiction between her analysis and Amelia Morimoto's in chapter 9 because Moromisato is focusing on gender and power dynamics related to gender *within* Japanese Peruvian families and community organizations. Moromisato's intriguing analysis demonstrates the application of feminist perspectives to the study of Nikkei identities in order to allow us "to understand the complex structure that leads to the construction of hierarchies, privileges, and subordination."

In chapter 12, Audrey Kobayashi discusses contemporary Japanese migration to Canada. Kobayashi indicates that there is a higher percentage of Japanese women immigrants in Canada who are single or married to non-Japanese men than in any other country in the world. Perhaps one of the most interesting aspects of Kobayashi's interviews is that she is able to demonstrate the gendered dimensions of Japanese out-migration. In the late twentieth century, a significant proportion of Japanese immigrant women have chosen to settle in Canada, even though it is clear that the new setting is very challenging—linguistically and otherwise—and sometimes overwhelming for them. The women express how profoundly migration impacts their interpersonal and family lives. Nevertheless, as Kobayashi's interviews make clear, Canada provides a setting where Japanese immigrant women have room to renegotiate what Nazli Kibria has called "the patriarchal bargain."[2] In her conclusion, citing parallels between her chapter and that of Doris Moromisato Miasato, Kobayashi also emphasizes how far Canadian Nikkei have to go in terms of understanding this dimension of family and community, especially in terms of supporting new Japanese immigrant women with services and programs.

In chapter 13, Naomi Hoki Moniz focuses on Brazil and the construction of ethnicity in relation to national identity. She does so, however, in terms of a sustained analysis of the Japanese Brazilian film director and auteur Tizuka Yamazaki. Treating Yamazaki's major feature films, Moniz describes how each challenges the European and patriarchal bases of Brazilian national identity. By introducing immigrants, non-European women, workers, protesters, and even Brazilian dekasegi guest workers as the major subjects of her films, Yamazaki opens new vantage points on critical questions: who is Brazilian, and whose experiences need to be counted in formulating new constructions of national identity?

Integral to Moniz's analysis is the supposition that Yamazaki's own evolving consciousness is the director's guide to the selection and treatment of cinematic themes. Moniz echoes and complements Jeffrey Lesser in suggesting that, whether we consider politics or cinema, Brazilian Japanese have sought their place in Brazil as Brazilians and, in the process, have been able to fashion a larger vision of national identity worthy of consideration by all.

The subsequent subsection deals with the dekasegi phenomenon, which dates back at least to the Meiji era.[3] Traditionally a dekasegi was a person who was compelled to leave his or her home village and go somewhere else to seek a better job. There is a fascinating literature about the roots of this internal migration in Japan. The scholarship on both internal migration and dekasegi migration overseas, to sites like Hawai'i, the U.S. mainland, and Latin America, has primarily been carried out using Japanese-language sources.[4] Here, however, our emphasis is on the fact that contemporary dekasegi migration back to Japan is distinctive, although readers are invited to remember that the term describing such movement goes back at least 140 years.[5]

In the subsection that deals with the dekasegi phenomenon, readers will find three chapters that treat this theme. First, Edson Mori points out that Latin American countries have been experiencing high rates of inflation and underemployment since the 1970s—precisely the same time that the economy in Japan was starting to experience unprecedented growth. The boom (or "bubble") economy in Japan generated a tremendous interest in returning to make a good living on the part of second- and third-generation Latin Americans of Japanese ancestry. Thus, during the past two decades the world has seen a significant pattern of return migration on the part of Brazilian, Peruvian, and other Latin American dekasegi of Japanese descent.

The many conditions and constraints that surround the return migration of Brazilian dekasegi, which also hamper their ability to adapt effectively in Japan, give cause for concern. Clearly, by soliciting Brazilians of Japanese descent in preference to other foreign laborers, the Japanese acquire labor for menial and dangerous jobs that they themselves would hesitate to perform. Although work visas have been easy enough for Brazilian Japanese dekasegi to obtain, Japanese have not always treated such workers favorably, or even fairly. Moreover, it has become a point of some frustration that, even though they are of Japanese descent, and even though they have lived and worked long enough in Japan to have had children born and educated there, Japanese Brazilians are given little opportunity to obtain naturalization in Japan. Some authorities speculate that, should they decide to stay permanently, colonies of Japanese Brazilians may evolve in Japan that parallel other foreign populations, including Chinese and Korean, who can only get access to Japanese citizenship through a long and arduous process, even after decades of permanent residence.

Masato Ninomiya offers a focused case study that illustrates some of these charges, and examines the challenges facing dekasegi parents who seek to educate their Brazilian Japanese children in Japan. To begin with, until the recent past, dekasegi parents were faced with the fact that their children had to enroll in and adapt to Japanese schools. Their children were exposed to pressures that interfered with their education, given that conformity, and not diversity or difference, is the hallmark of the Japanese educational system. Moreover, given that most dekasegi initially planned to return to Latin America, there was always the issue of how to keep their children up to speed in terms of language, history, culture, and so forth, knowledge that they were missing by virtue of having been out of their natal country.

In recent years, dekasegi parents have supported the creation of special language and cultural schools that their children can attend after their regular day of instruction. Although these schools seem to parallel the Japanese language schools developed by the Issei on the U.S. mainland (as described in Part Two by Teruko Kumei), the schools for the dekasegi's children are different insofar as their parents still contemplate returning to Latin America once they have saved enough money.

In chapter 16, Marcelo Higa focuses on the emigration of Japanese Argentines to Japan. The characteristics in this case, however, are markedly different from those described by either Mori or Ninomiya. First, Japanese emigration to Argentina occurred relatively late and was smaller than the flow of people to either Brazil or Peru. Labor contracting was also not as significant. Second, out of the current population of close to fifty thousand, a surprisingly large percentage of immigrants, including prewar immigrants, came from the prefecture of Okinawa. Third, there was little negative impact on the Japanese Argentine population during World War II as compared to, say, what many Japanese Peruvians suffered.

Higa outlines the legalities of return migration to Japan during the 1980s very nicely, supplementing Mori's account with additional details about how Nikkei status was deployed in order to control the entry of foreign workers.

He also questions the applicability of the term "dekasegi" to the Japanese Argentine experience, considering that the compression of time and space, and the concomitant evolution of transnational networks, renders the old polarities between the points of origin and destination moot. Higa also sketches the relationship between the Japanese Argentine and other sojourners and immigrants of Japanese descent from Latin American countries in Japan. His account should give us pause, not only because he discusses the ways that nationality as a Peruvian, Brazilian, etc., impacts Nikkeiness; he also emphasizes that the differences between Okinawans (Uchinanchu) and mainland Japanese (Naichi), and between Latin American Nikkei and the so-called *chicha* (or dekasegi posing as persons of Japanese descent), make for fascinating new complexities to the experiences of being a sojourner, or new immigrant, in Japan.

Finally, it is critical to highlight Higa's analysis of the use of the term "Nikkei." Higa's thesis is that we should eschew an essentialized definition of this concept. Given its heterogeneous manifestations, there is little use in trying to look for a set of unchanging qualities or characteristics, even though the term assumes a common historical experience, which Higa interprets as a linkage to previous Japanese ancestors. Rather, Higa argues that the salience of the term "Nikkei" has precisely to do with its ambiguity, which permits it in certain circumstances to supersede national and traditional classifications and to recover links pertaining to blood connections. At the same time, Higa proposes that there is no core to the term and its utilization is, more than anything else, strategic.

The final subsection of Part Three focuses on newly emerging identities. Taking a decidedly comparative approach, Steven Masami Ropp examines the historical formation of the Japanese American and Japanese Peruvian experiences. His innovative thesis is that, while a racial formation perspective is useful for understanding Japanese Americans, this is because they are a relatively small minority population, living within a society and a state that is dominated by a Euro-American majority. Such an approach is not as viable in Peru, where a small, largely Euro-Peruvian elite dominate a large indigenous and mestizo population. Japanese Peruvians are thus sandwiched between the two groups and, as is noted in a number of chapters, they have always been viewed with some suspicion by the elite, who have periodic fears that Japanese Peruvians might lead, aid, or otherwise side with the disenfranchised masses. In any case, Ropp argues that being Nikkei in Peru is not a matter of "race" per se but rather a pragmatic ethnic network of potential opportunities.

In sum, Ropp's chapter attends to intragroup diversity. Ropp addresses, for example, the significance of the differences between Naichi and Uchinanchu, which are important, given that some 50 percent of Japanese Peruvians are of the latter background. Ropp also raises the issue of differences between Japanese Peruvians from Lima, the capital city, and those from the towns and communities in the hinterlands or jungles.

Another important dimension of Ropp's chapter has to do with his questions about the future. Drawing from his first-hand experience with the 1998 "Ties that Bind" conference—a conference dedicated to exploring the themes of identity, community, and diversity—Ropp invites us to consider whether there is in fact enough similarity between the diverse people of Japanese descent domestically, let alone internationally, to think of them all as Nikkei. The proposals in this regard advanced at the "Ties that Bind" conference will make up an ongoing part of any discussion or debate well into the new millennium.

Makoto Arakaki's chapter about the Uchinanchu diaspora presents one of *New Worlds, New Lives'* most explicit rationales for the need to adopt a global framework in order to get a handle on the evolving dynamics and dimensions of today's manifestations of Nikkei identities. Focusing specifically on the ties between the Okinawan American community in Hawai'i and in the prefecture of Okinawa, Arakaki demonstrates that Uchinanchu identity has become essentially decentered and diasporic in nature. Arakaki argues, in other words, that instead of gradually transforming themselves into Okinawan Americans, assimilated Americans, or even Okinawans proper, something else is going on. Uchinanchu certainly relate to their home province and seek ties to it, but at the same time they have broader notions of being related to other Uchinanchu in diaspora. In this light, Arakaki describes the first Worldwide Uchinanchu Festival, which drew some three thousand overseas Okinawans back to Okinawa for a plethora of cultural, social, and political workshops.

In terms of managing the differences between being "Okinawan," "Japanese American," and "American," Arakaki observes that each generation decides to highlight one or another of these identities. Earlier generations were more sensitive to the differences between the Uchinanchu and the Naichi. The second-generation Uchinanchu who lived through the crucible of World War II tended to emphasize their common Americanness through patriotic discourse and service. Interestingly enough, the third- and fourth-generation Uchinanchu came of age in the spirit of multiculturalism of the 1980s. This context allowed them to reinscribe their identities in terms of the "Uchinanchu spirit," a new representation of ethnic identity, according to Arakaki, that entailed a conscious rejection of the negative stereotypes of Okinawans. In effect, Arakaki asks us to acknowledge a revitalized sense of Uchinanchu ethnicity that can be seen in terms of sustained contact with the home prefecture, contact with other Uchinanchu in diaspora, and contact with "local culture," as found in Hawai'i.

Yasuko I. Takezawa's contribution featuring a Kobe case study complements the other chapters in this subsection, even as Takezawa's findings indicate that a dual outcome was produced in response to the Great Hanshin-Awaji Earthquake in Kobe in 1990. On the one hand, ties between overseas Latin Americans of Japanese descent in the Kobe area were intensified, on both the intranational and pan–Latin American levels. On the other hand, as Takezawa's careful ethnographic research indicates, the crisis created a context in which new levels of identification and mutual aid, which were only scant before, emerged in response to this terrible natural disaster.

As a result, Takezawa proposes that a new social formation having to do with the emergence of consciousness about a *tabunka kyosei*, or multicultural existence, came into being. In other words, a completely new vision of social relations and society emerged. In terms of this last point, Takezawa, like Higa, questions whether the term "Nikkei" wouldn't, in fact, gloss over many new experiences, thus clouding the emergence of new perspectives on being of Japanese descent in overseas settings, which are significantly different from what we ordinarily ascribe to the term "Nikkei," if not unique. In sum, this is yet another piece of evidence that the boundaries of what is "Nikkei" and what is not are shifting in ways that may not be easy to discern.

In conclusion, the chapters presented in Part Three compel us to make two final points. They indicate quite clearly that the minimal context for any viable analysis of contemporary Nikkei identities must involve a triadic perspective. In other words, three elements must be examined as pertinent variables in determining how and why Nikkei identities have taken the shape they have taken: 1) Japan, as the point of origin, 2) any given nation in the Americas, as a point of destination, and 3) the Nikkei community or communities in any given area, including Japan. The need to apply a triadic perspective is because these nine chapters effectively capture Nikkei identities— their fluid, negotiated, and continually evolving nature. We will return to this point in more depth in chapter 20, the conclusion to *New Worlds, New Lives.*

Clearly, the chapters in this section of *New Worlds, New Lives* are also of relevance and importance because they delineate a number of topics that beg for systematic investigation. In particular, Audrey Kobayashi's analysis of the dynamics of Nikkei intermarriages in Canada, Marcelo Higa's observations concerning the different stereotypes attributed to the dekasegi, and Makoto Arakaki's emphasis on the differences between the Hawai'i and mainland

U.S. Nikkei, including the position of the Uchinanchu within those populations, are not only path-breaking, but they also attune us to the fact that the
next big step will be to design and carry out rigorous comparative research
that encompasses the Americas, and eventually the global ecumene.

Notes

1. To anticipate some points raised in chapter 20, the conclusion to this volume,
we acknowledge that these are all themes that have been treated in the extant literature. The INRP project and *New Worlds, New Lives* differ from these, however, in
that we treat these emerging identities *together*, and in terms of how each has been
affected by processes of globalization.

2. Nazli Kibria, *Family Tightrope: The Changing Lives of Vietnamese Americans*
(Princeton, N.J.: Princeton University Press, 1993).

3. Yuji Ichioka, *The Issei: The World of the First Generation Japanese Immigrants,
1885–1924* (New York: Free Press, 1988).

4. Two pioneers in the use of Japanese-language sources to study the early history of the Issei have been the historians Yasuo Sakata and Yuji Ichioka. For Yasuo
Sakata see his *Fading Footsteps of the Issei* (Los Angeles: Asian American Studies Center, UCLA, and the Japanese American National Museum, 1992); also "'American
Immigration Statistics' and 'Japanese Immigrants' during the Latter Half of the
Nineteenth Century: Unreliable Reports" [in Japanese], *Kurisutokyo shakai mondai
kenkyu* 38 (Mar. 1990). For Yuji Ichioka, see his *A Buried Past: An Annotated Bibliography of the Japanese American Research Project Collection* (Berkeley: University of
California Press, 1974). The JARP Collection, held at UCLA, is one of the largest collections in the United States of primary materials in Japanese that can be used to
study the Issei experience.

5. See Harumi Befu, this volume, chapter 1.

CHAPTER ELEVEN

I Woman, I Man, I Nikkei

Symbolic Construction of Femininity and Masculinity in the Japanese Community of Peru

DORIS MOROMISATO MIASATO

Until now, discourses about the historic experience of Japanese immigration to Peru have had a uniformly epic and grandiloquent tone that has hidden the richness and heterogeneity of its individual voices. It is appropriate now to lower this tone and to consider from an intimate symbolic and cultural perspective the deeply rooted nature of these underlying identities.

Material included in this chapter has its origins in questions that have concerned me for more than three decades. If women are fundamental actors in the Nikkei world, organizing daily life and major events of the community, why are they devalued in terms of our collective memory? Why are they omitted from historical texts as well as discussions about power? Why, after a hundred years, do they continue to lag behind in the arena of political involvement? Why do they remain in a marginal role? Is endogamy—that is, marrying within the Peruvian Nikkei community—taught as a sort of ethnic mission? Is discomfort with masculine and feminine stereotypes the reason why many Nikkei, both men and women, choose to live outside their community's boundaries?

Throughout the years I have searched for answers, observing carefully the ways in which the roles and interrelationships of power have been distributed throughout private and public spheres within the Nikkei community. Following the proposal of Benedict Anderson, that "communities should not be distinguished by their falseness or legitimacy but for the way they are imagined,"[1] I have ventured to search for these imaginings. In addition to intensely analyzing readings, interviews, conversations and letters, and organizing and participating in conferences and workshops with young people, I have never avoided autobiographical reflection as a means of finding answers.[2] That I have chosen this approach is due to my own situation: I am a Nikkei woman interested and involved in the search for harmonious, mutually supportive lifestyles within my community.

The main focus of my research concerns power—who has it and on what basis is it held, as well as the access, distribution, and exercise of that power in an ethnic community. Even after a century of Japanese immigration to Peru, the political imbalance between men and women continues to produce conflicts and resistance within the community, in both private and public spheres. One of the consequences is a significant lack of recognition of women. This lack of recognition is rooted in the symbolic construction of feminine and masculine identities, since power, like other categories, contains generic elements that incorporate values based on physical differences. In this chapter I will use the gender perspective as a tool that can be effectively utilized to deconstruct the Nikkei identity, allowing us to understand the complex structure that leads to the construction of hierarchies, privileges, and subordinations, and the inclusion or exclusion of individuals within the borders of their ethnic communities.[3]

Identity from a Gender Perspective

Culture, as defined by Clifford Geertz, "is a pattern of meanings in historically transmitted symbols, a system of concepts inherited and expressed in a symbolic way through which human beings communicate, reproduce and develop their knowledge about and towards life." From this viewpoint, we understand that the persistence of a Nikkei identity has been due to affinity and complicity with a symbolic world constructed collectively and voluntarily.

The symbolic construction of femininity and masculinity has also fed the creation of this identity. Power is exercised from those generic constructions because, as Joan Scott states, gender is "the primary field from which or by which power is articulated." Gender, as Scott explains, is the knowledge that gives meanings to bodily differences; and each culture constructs its own generic identities from those differences. This process is present in the construction of Nikkei identity and, when taken together with other variables such as class and generation, is a powerful factor supporting inequality. The reconstruction of a historical process and the analysis of the Nikkei identity from a gender perspective is innovative and creative; it also provides the basis for a better understanding of some aspects of the community that have been largely unrecognized. The following analysis will allow us to become aware of underlying patterns in order to determine whether a common historical experience has created a common symbolic world for men and women. An intersubjective view, which highlights how men and women see themselves and each other, enriches this analysis. The results will allow us to measure existing power relations in public and domestic spheres, and will also highlight conflict, forms of resistance, rebelliousness, and discomfort. We may even be able to understand more fully why rates of out-marriage have been on the rise in recent times.

In the Nikkei community values, beliefs, and meanings about what is feminine and masculine are constructions that derive both from the culture of origin, Japan, and from the collective response of Japanese immigrants and their descendants to their country of residence, Peru. In order to understand this process of gender definition, it is necessary to research a century of symbolic constructions that have emerged and been put into practice by men and women living together inside the Nikkei community within Peruvian society. It is necessary to perform a deep analysis of attitudes and dichotomies, such as feminine/masculine, and to think about the construction of identity in these specific terms.

This chapter is an initial statement of an ongoing and much broader analysis that regards the construction of identity and power relations from a gender perspective through a quantitative and qualitative analysis of images and textual narratives, as well as through interviews of men and women of different generations in the Peruvian Nikkei community. The emphasis placed on aspects such as marital relations and maternity is due to the particular objectives of the present research. This does not imply that these are the only forms of existing relationships, nor the only ways of living an identity.

Construction of Femininity in Peruvian Nikkei Women

The research presented here is based on the current situation observed in the Peruvian Nikkei community. At the present time, its younger generations show a trend towards exogamy—that is, marrying outside the ethnic community. Already by 1989, the census reported that one-third of all marriages involving at least one Nikkei were mixed marriages, involving a spouse of part-Nikkei ancestry or a non-Nikkei person.[4] Furthermore, almost none of the women born after 1960 participate in women's organizations because they consider them to be domestic and gender segregationist, and thus as working against their search for meaningful integration and professional involvement in Peruvian society. At this time, women's leadership in Peruvian Japanese institutions—such as *kenjinkai* (mutual aid associations based on prefectural background in Japan, led primarily by men), *fujinkai* (women's committees within the kenjinkai), *sonjinkai* (associations representing Japanese villages), youth centers, clubs, schools, cooperatives, foundations, and mass media, among others—is nonexistent.

These three phenomena are going to influence profoundly the destiny of the ethnic community. It is important, then, to know why they occur. Is it because of explicit or implicit choices about the need to integrate into Peruvian culture? Or are out-marriage and integration into the mainstream a rejection of established patriarchal hierarchies within the Nikkei Peruvian community? We are confronting realities that, because of their comparatively recent development, generate contradictions within the symbolic sphere and become threatening for the future of a group whose continuity is basically sustained through reproduction and motherhood.

If we take into account that the overall social dynamics of Peruvian Japanese are almost the same as they were a hundred years ago, based on the existence of an institutional core—that is, the Peruvian Japanese associations throughout Peru, around which other organizational forms mentioned above operate—we may ask what has changed. My understanding is that Nikkei women are the ones who are changing; or, more precisely, it is the feminine world and its manifestations, among both men and women, that now challenges the public and private organization of the Nikkei universe.

As Norma Fuller states, it is very important to understand the process of the construction of gender identity, because in it each person learns what it is to be a man or woman, how to assume the proper roles and attitudes, and to recognize or self-censor her/himself according to such generic patterns.[5] Identifying this process allows one to see how women perceive themselves and what place in the world they believe to be their own. Therefore, issues such as endogamy (marrying inside one's group), exogamy, and other forms of inclusion/exclusion are related to the way that the notions of femininity and masculinity have been constructed.

Nikkei Women: Model to Be Assembled

According to the census of 1989, the Nikkei community consisted of 45,644 people: 49 percent (22,485) were men and 51 percent (23,127) were women. Of the women, the generations broke down into 5.5 percent Issei (or first generation), 35 percent Nisei (second), 47 percent Sansei (third), 13 percent Yonsei (fourth), and 0.3 percent Gosei (fifth). In terms of marital status, 13,381, or 58 percent, were single women, 7,432 were married, 1,752 were widowed, 132 lived with a male partner, 294 were separated, and 61 divorced. The professions where women were represented included teachers and other educators, public accountants, chemist-pharmacists, administrators, biologists, economists, social workers, physicians, psychologists, and pediatricians.

Considering that the majority of Nikkei households are middle class, I chose to compare and contrast the different generations as the basis for this research. I also utilized a phenomenological approach in order to guarantee the endogenous character of this research, as well as to preclude distancing ourselves from the feelings of Nikkei men and women. As proposed by Lévi-Strauss, the information we acquired was based on subject-subject relationships, not subject-object, and our conclusions were partly drawn from those dialogues. We chose not to use surveys because that method does not facilitate dialogue. The analysis of personal narratives through interviews allowed us to approach the self-perceptions of each person interviewed. Interviews were based on an open-ended list of topics that stimulated the reconstruction of generic stereotypes, thus fulfilling our objective: that the subjects narrate their ideas, memories, feelings, values, and beliefs with the aim of allowing the interviewer to hear their voice, thus helping to develop the articulation and recovery of a collective memory. As Anthony Giddens says, when persons narrate their biographies, not only stating the facts but also what led up to certain choices, they give coherence and continuity to their lives; that is, at the same time that they are reconstructing a biography, they are articulating an identity as well.

Eighty-eight people living in Lima, where more than 80 percent of the Nikkei population of Peru lives, were interviewed. They were asked for their name, age, generation, place of origin in Japan, occupation, marital status, nationality of their spouse, and number of children. Obviously, more attention was placed on the feminine population, including single women, married women (Nikkei marriages and out-marriages), widows, divorced women, housewives, employees, traders, professionals, *dekasegi* (or women workers in Japan), artists, activists and nonactivists in Nikkei institutions, directors, and even women working for the Peruvian government.

Work and Motherhood: Submissiveness as Femininity

I took life histories from nineteen Issei women born between 1904 and 1918. All of them married Japanese men, and the majority of them did so by family arrangement. When they spoke about their intense days of work, during which they worked as hard as their husbands, they remarked that it was the husband who was the head and representative of the family, even if the woman had control of the money. The more numerous their children and grandchildren, the better they felt, and they wished that the Japanese customs they had brought with them would not be lost.

These declarations confirm a historical fact: the immigration of this co-hort of Japanese women was inspired not by economics but by marital bonds. The first 108 women who arrived in Peru in 1903 illustrate this point.[6] Dr. Fukumoto Sato notes that the arrival of Japanese immigrant women in the early decades of the twentieth century was a response to the problems of early Japanese bachelors: "Considering that the scarcity of women led to evil, and observing that married couples were more stable and worked better, the administrators of the plantations made arrangements with the immigration companies to allow the arrival of married men exclusively."[7] The desire to bring in women to marry immigrant men is more evident still during the pe-riod 1924–41, when men might pick their "picture brides" after seeing a photograph sent from Japan, in *shashin kekkon*, or "marriages through pic-tures." However, the marital status of these Issei women did not make adap-tation to a foreign country less difficult. On the contrary, it was worse. As soon as they landed, women had to work like any other immigrant, but they were also required to fulfill their domestic obligations as spouses, mothers, and workers, which meant taking on a double or triple workload. In addition to these tasks, they had to continue to maintain their Japanese culture within the foreign setting of Peru. Along with their search for social integration into a new society, Issei women preserved the customs and values of their home-land, and in this way guaranteed that the Japanese culture would not be dis-solved within Peruvian society. So, in the anonymity of everyday life, immi-grant women constructed the symbolic world of the Nikkei community.[8]

It is interesting to note that in the early years of Nikkei migration to Peru, between 1899 and 1909, a mere 230 women sustained that symbolic universe. This speaks to the powerful ability of these women. Their perfect dedication helped the Japanese community to become the most numerous and eco-nomically successful foreign group in the country. By 1940 Japanese ran 60 percent of the trade, 25 percent of the agriculture and 6 percent of the in-dustry in Peru. By 1978 there were 4,998 men and 5,650 immigrant women.[9] In spite of the great capacity shown by these women, however, they did not have access to public (as opposed to domestic) spheres. They did not partici-pate as leaders in the ethnic community, nor in *tanomoshi* (rotating credit associations), which meant not having access to financial credit and having less social status within the community.

In the case of immigrants from the prefecture of Okinawa, where the majority of Nikkei in Peru come from, there is a curious fact that allows us to see how Japanese codes were transported to Peru through immigrant men and women from the prefecture of Okinawa. When we reviewed immigra-tion documents, we found that the names of women were related to species of flora or fauna, elements of nature, or domestic or work devices.[10] For example, there were women named Kame (turtle), Ushi (ox), Tsuru (crane), Ume (plum tree), Matsu (pine), Hana (flower), Oto (sound), Nabe (pot) and Kama (sickle). By contrast, men had names written in kanji (or Chinese characters), and their meanings—greatness, honor, happiness, or splendor— were related to an abstract world associated with hierarchy and power.

In Okinawa, a male child's ideogram was selected according to sounds and mathematical calculations, because it was more than a name; it represented the aspirations placed on the child and the symbolism of his lineage. Women's names did not reflect lofty abstractions, but rather concrete and earthly realities close to daily life. Women, in fact, did not have the right to a kanji, which indicates that their destiny was to construct and preserve the collective symbols of gender identity. Perhaps this example of gender-coded customs helps to explains why it took until 1978, almost seventy years, for Japanese Peruvian women to create their own organization, the Okinawan Women's Association. Even then, the group was formed against the wishes of men who had their own organization (naturally, with a prominently male orientation) since 1909.

Nisei Spouses and Mothers: The "Complement" as Femininity

The Nisei generation embodies a link between Japanese and Peruvian cultures. Maybe this is the reason why they are more conflicted than the other generations, as they had to remain within the ethnic boundaries representing Japanese values and customs without losing consciousness of their Peruvian identity. In my understanding, the Nisei generally remained within the sociocultural limits of the ethnic community because, outside this frame of reference, there were few alternatives. Or, if there were alternatives, they were typically unstable because of the characteristics of Peruvian society.[11] In the case of women, although they were already Peruvians by birth, were full citizens, and could participate in the feminist accomplishments of the twentieth century, their de facto situation within the Peruvian Japanese community was very different. They were not considered individuals protected by law. Rather, they were judged according to rigid patriarchal codes that kept them in a kind of legal subjugation, making it impossible for them to act autonomously. This was manifested in a stance of total submissiveness and obedience on the part of Nisei women themselves. Those who dared to protest or to deny the validity of this authority were marginalized in the family and the community. Economic control was in the hands of men, which meant that they also controlled female autonomy. Women could only have access to a kind of relative privilege if they attained the status of spouse, as being a daughter had no value in patrimonial terms. It was evident that the production of male heirs and the continuation of family lineage was promoted, protected, and even rewarded. For example, property was inherited not through the father but through the husband. Single women were the responsibility of their brothers, as if they were in a situation of permanent disability. There was written material that transmitted these beliefs and taught women to behave with submissiveness, including the teaching of the three famous forms of obedience: to the father, to the husband, and to the sons.[12] But Japanese women lacked control not only of the assets of the earthly world, but also of the spiritual, because they were discriminated against in terms of participating in religious services. In the Okinawa community, to keep a *butsudan*, or family shrine, and thus preserve the spirits of family ancestors is even now a role reserved for males. Education was also a man's privilege. In any case, as women were relegated to the domestic sphere, there was no sense in investing in their education, as there was no possibility of recovering the investment. The women who could overcome this worldview and manage to attain the status of professionals typically had feminine accomplices within their homes to support them.

In the interviews of nineteen second-generation or Nisei women born between 1920 and 1957, the ones who were married, single, or widowed lived according to Japanese customs and traditions. They worked part-time and participated in feminine Nikkei institutions such as *fujinkai* and *fujinbu* (the women's section of the sonjinkai). Almost all the women who were separated or divorced worked full-time and did not participate in the Nikkei community.

Those married to persons of part-Japanese descent or to non-Nikkei men said that their engagement provoked initial resistance or even rejection on the part of their families. Once married, however, this resistance ended and the women said that they did not continue to experience discrimination by the family or by society. They also stated that in the beginning it was uncomfortable to adapt to non-Nikkei customs, but in the end all of them "Japanized" their spouses. Those that were mothers hoped their children would participate in the Nikkei community; in parallel interviews with the children, however, we found that they felt more comfortable with Peruvians and mixed groups.

Although Nisei women did not show resentment, they said that they took care not to replicate the gender discrimination they had suffered with their daughters. Although all of them remarked on their fathers' stability and capacity for work, recalling their fathers with respect and veneration, the women also had a negative view of them having to do with lack of initiative, inertia. In contrast, these women looked for partners with a much more active and dynamic masculine image. In spite of this, the majority confess that their spouse mirrored their father. Many Nisei women thought about relating to men of other races, but said that they ended up marrying a Nikkei because they were not used to associating with other groups, and comfort (i.e., similar customs and lifestyle) was an important factor in their decision. Only some of them showed interest in Nikkei institutions, because they did not believe that the future of their daughters and sons lay in that direction.

Sansei: Between Conservatism and Autonomy

Sansei (third-generation Nikkei) women born after 1960 have what I call a "key mission," one that differs from that of their compatriots born before that date. My perception of this chronological differentiation is shared by the Paraguayan researcher Emi Kasamatsu, who observed the same characteristic in her country.[13]

The 1960s were a special decade for Latin America. In the framework of the triumph of the Cuban revolution and the death of Che Guevara, nationalist winds were blowing over the continent. Latin America had previously been submerged in regional oligarchies and cultural dependency on the Northern Hemisphere. In the case of Peru, the military dictatorship of General Velasco instituted a radical project in a new attempt to rebuild the Peruvian nation. Velasco, for example, made education more uniform, imposed Quechua as the official language, redistributed land through agrarian reform, and nationalized the extraction of natural resources and the media. At that time television entered the home market, producing what Giddens calls "the penetration of the abstract systems," in which information is no longer based on daily life or tradition but on science and technology, and in turn shapes the construction of identities. Above all, these developments influenced the Nikkei children who were born in the 1960s, fostering a strong identification with the shared goals and visions of the progressive nation-state.

The twenty-five women of this Sansei generation interviewed, who were born between 1964 and 1983, presented urban characteristics as well as patterns and habits generalized throughout Peruvian society. Their personal histories showed a fusion of Japanese values and customs inherited from their ancestors with lifestyles that are particular to the non-Nikkei surroundings in which they were developing (school, university, workplace, and social circles). Likewise, they showed a greater capacity for ethnic and social mobility than their Issei or Nisei ancestors.

In almost all cases, their Nisei mothers exercised decision-making authority and were the economic pillars of the household. However, the public figure was the father. For this reason, Sansei women criticized their mothers for their lack of ambition and unwillingness to exercise that domestic energy in public spheres, as well as for being too conservative and too willing to be dependent on their husbands.[14] For reasons of security and psychological comfort, Sansei women preferred to establish a family with a Nikkei man, but they felt physically more attracted to non-Nikkei men because they considered them to be more joyful and dynamic. To them, Nikkei men were fearful and overly conscious of rejection. One of them even expressed the wish to find herself a "Nikkei *criollo*," or a Nikkei who has assimilated "typically" Peruvian attitudes. None of these women was afraid of establishing a family with other races; that was not a matter of "shame" nor a "reproachable act" for their families or society. They said they were ready to assume the risks implied in leaving the Nikkei community and adapting to other customs. They even thought that a non-Nikkei man would understand their personal aspirations better than Nikkei men, whom they considered to be male chauvinists, and whom they feared would ask them to leave their studies or work to devote themselves solely to taking care of their children. This threat to their future aspirations weighed upon them.

For Sansei women, to become a professional is the most important thing in their lives, because this will allow them economic independence and "to become somebody in the eyes of society." They express a symbiosis between private and public characteristics when they declare that their domestic and maternal attributes, which they assume to be essentially feminine, become virtues at work, manifesting themselves as order, responsibility, sacrifice, and total commitment. They feel themselves to be participants in the achievements of women at a global level and assume that they have the same citizenship as men in a democracy. Therefore, they are more conscious of their rights and are better informed than their mothers regarding Peruvian legislation affecting their property rights.

Very few of them participate in the activities of the Nikkei community, and those who do so do it for work-related or educational reasons. They respect Nikkei feminine organizations but do not want to participate because they believe they are intended to serve elderly women. They like the solidarity among Nikkei but are bothered by hermetic racial attitudes and the fact that so much importance is given to racial background. All of them declare, "We are in Peru." However, they also believe that Japanese customs should be maintained, as they consider them better than Peruvian customs. They assume the female search for pleasure and sexual liberation is a natural fact. Those who came from fragmented Nikkei homes did not deny this fact. If they were reserved about it, it was due to consideration for their mothers, who, they maintained, are weaker and could not confront the social consequences with the same ease as they themselves could.

Nikkei Masculine Identity and Public Spheres

The construction of masculine identity, like feminine, requires an exhaustive and deep analysis. On this occasion, I can only consider it in relation to its articulation with the feminine universe. As an illustration, this paper will focus briefly on the construction of such identity and the notion of masculinity in public spheres of influence.

I interviewed twenty-five Nikkei men. They had the same generational mix and diversity as the groups of women I spoke to. Issei and Nisei men expressed the view that their personal fulfillment was the result of having built a family. In the narratives of both generations, the idea of power was associated with moral authority over the family gained through protecting and providing for its economic well-being and the education of the children. Young, single Nisei men did not feel comfortable with the responsibilities they would have to assume in the future and were reticent about continuing with traditional religious rites. They prefer marrying Nikkei women because they consider them to be "more faithful wives" and "more responsible mothers" than Peruvian women.

In order to analyze gender equity in public spheres, a total of twelve years of annual assemblies of representatives of the Peruvian Japanese Association (PJA) were reviewed, since this is the organization most representative of the Nikkei community in Peru. In summary, women were limited to activities considered traditionally feminine: culture, art (dance, music, drawing, ikebana, origami, painting, sculpture), health, and education (teaching the Japanese language). Throughout this period only three papers from the women's organization mentioned above—the Okinawan Women's Association—were presented (in 1989, 1995, and 1997). The final agreements in the plenary sessions referred to women only with respect to marriage and maternity. By contrast, the greatest concern revolved around the incorporation of youth, especially young men, into the PJA. Women did not participate in leadership positions either in Lima or the provinces. The boards of directors were overwhelmingly composed of men. In the case of Lima, in 1997 the board included forty-two men and eight women. The following year there were thirty-seven men and eight women. Between 1960 and 2000 only one woman was president of the association.

At present, there is a conflict in Nikkei public life relating to the gender issue. A sector of the community proposes that, in order to balance women's participation, kenjinkai and sonjinkai must have a mixed composition and include both men and women. Concomitantly, organizations solely for women should be disbanded. However, women who are active reject this measure because they are afraid of losing the limited space for autonomy and decision making they possess within their own institutions. From the figures mentioned above, one can see that this fear is valid and well founded: if such a fusion took place, women would run the risk of being crushed by masculine hegemony.

It is curious to confirm that the masculine structure itself generates its own critical points of conflict and turns against itself to the point of provoking disruption. Men's organizations set up parallel but subsidiary groups for women—women's committees, or associations, within the larger organization—in an attempt to define and delimit the idea of feminine participation, intending to later exclude or freeze these activities and save themselves from feminine contamination. Today, these same women's organizations are autonomous and their control is the responsibility of the women themselves. This is provoking uneasiness in the public domain because masculine institutions still cannot accept the idea of an autonomous female leadership nor the sharing of public spheres of influence with women. It should not be surprising that, facing this desolate political panorama at present, women tend to become involved in Peruvian organizations rather than Nikkei institutions.

Peruvian Nikkei Gender Identities

Gender identity is a cultural construction based on sexual differentiation: masculine characteristics for men and feminine for women. At present, new proposals, such as those of Judith Butler, are modifying such notions.[15] Gender identity, as Norma Fuller mentions, legitimates power relationships in a community.[16] Naturally, Fuller's studies on feminine and masculine identities among the Peruvian middle class have been of particular value in helping to deconstruct Nikkei identity from a gender perspective.[17]

It is evident that the construction of femininity and masculinity have been of major importance in a century of symbolic building of the Nikkei identity, to the extent that it identified for each woman and man who she/he was, where she/he came from, what her/his place in the world was, what her/his limitations and boundaries were, and how she/he must relate to and behave toward others within and outside the Nikkei community. Through the analysis of texts and interviews in which people defined themselves and their experiences, we can see how, after a hundred years, an interesting hybridism has developed within the notion of femininity and masculinity brought by immigrants from Japan and eventually fused with the mestizo culture of Peru.

In the case of men, patriarchal codes inherited from Japan have mingled with characteristics of the Iberian American machismo.[18] Women, for their part, have fused the transmitted model of Japanese women with the western Marian Catholic model, as modified more recently by contemporary codes of postmodern individualism and consumerism. The result of this fusion is revealed in women's attitudes about the family, marriage, maternity, work, education, sexual ethics, and honor, attitudes that are different from those of their Peruvian female peers.

In addition, as for Peruvian women, attitudes about femininity and masculinity have changed from one generation to the next. However, some special characteristics stand out. The basic concept of what it means to be a woman is shared among Issei, Nisei, and Sansei, but each generation has defined it in terms of a different context. Thus, differences do not rest on values or beliefs per se, but rather on expectations about "life's projects" and on attitudes regarding experiences such as sexuality, maternity, work, and the importance of Nikkei organizations. For Japanese immigrants, the concept of femininity rests on ideas of submission, sacrifice, moral strength, and maternity, all associated with the ideology of gender-specific cultural duties. For them, femininity implies cleanliness and robust health rather than fragility. In their daughters, the rigid Japanese codes were reinforced by Catholic ideology, producing a Marian model (entailing strength, love, moral superiority, and a spirit of sacrifice) aspired to with greater devotion than by their Peruvian peers. The strength of this model is demonstrated in terms of the notions of sexual-affective complementarity vis-à-vis their men, as well as the role of motherhood in their lives. The codes of feminine beauty were taken from western stereotypes as part of the process of adopting Peruvian standards. Both Issei and Nisei women had control over the domestic world and inheritance, but at a discursive and symbolic level did not exercise real power. On the other hand, for Sansei women, expectations for autonomy and economic independence are basic to their thinking and facilitate the idea of integration into non-Nikkei spheres. Working outside the home and becoming professionals are key ways for Sansei women, unlike their Peruvian peers, to integrate with Peruvian society in general.

Issei and Nisei women are characterized by a lack of autonomy and sexual repression. Although they were never limited entirely to domestic spheres, they did not have access to public spheres since, symbolically, the public world was perceived to be masculine territory. Sansei women, for their part, give the public sphere great significance in their lives. For this reason, they are less resistant to identifying themselves with masculine values, and may assume ambiguous or masculine characteristics in order to enter those spheres of power. It is interesting to verify that notions such as approval, rejection, and guilt are no longer taken into account in the construction of feminine identity among the Sansei generation.

Threats to the Borders: Considering Ethnic Purity
from a Gender Perspective

Alternative orientations in the Peruvian Nikkei community, such as conformity/continuity versus dissent/change and in-marriage versus out-marriage, became problematic analytic issues as I developed the present study. Although the research carried out by Mary Douglas does not have a gender perspective per se, it was helpful in my efforts to understand such complicated issues.[19] What follows is a brief and tentative overview of these issues from a gender perspective.

The construction of an ethnic community is based on the principle of continuity, and thus conservation of the status quo. Power articulates a form of order, with concomitant restrictions, which is sustained through common agreement about the nature of the symbolic world, supposedly constructed by and for the benefit of all its members. Such authority designates the boundaries of the community, dictates the inclusion or exclusion of participants within their various spheres, and prescribes a morality that designates what can be seen as a threat to its existence. Thus, ideologies about racial or ethnic purity and contamination permeate community life and convey the implication of imminent danger. What I am proposing to add to this formula is that while power in the Peruvian Nikkei community entails notions of purity and danger, sustained through social relations based on generation, class, and regional origin, above all, power in the Peruvian Nikkei community is permeated in all of its manifestations by a masculinist worldview.

Dissent and dissidence are the great taboos of the Nikkei community of Peru. Racial intermixture is a clear example of one facet of this dissidence; although the 1989 census shows that one-third of all marriages in Peru involving a person of Japanese descent are mixed, little attention is paid to this issue, and there are no analytical essays or political speeches discussing it. It is as if a blanket of consensual indifference—or fear—were covering it. The truth is that racial intermixing is an uncomfortable and bothersome issue because it upsets accepted meanings and alters the idea of a unitary and cohesive community, at the same time bringing into question the assumed immobility and immutability of a symbolic universe.[20] Thus, it is preferable to speak of total cultural assimilation into the larger Peruvian society, and not of biological amalgamation via out-marriage, because 1) it does not put the defined borders of the ethnic community at risk, and 2) it allows the perpetuation of the standard mechanisms of control—including the ability to decide who to include or exclude—when new or threatening elements arise.

In every human group in which the idea of ethnic and racial cohesion prevails, notions such as personal and collective hygiene, purity, contamination, and dirtiness are inevitable. The Nikkei community is no exception, and it separates and classifies "others" in order to maintain an order that is easily recognizable and strongly limited. Racial intermixture, to the degree that it confronts and questions the idea of racial purity, represents disorder and a threat to the ethnic community because of its lack of definition and its unlimited capacity to expand. It necessarily implies a biological fusion, and, for a community based on continuity through blood ties, this fact is accompanied by implications of risk, threat, and even destruction. Intermarriage is, therefore, dangerous, and all contacts considered to be dangerous carry a symbolic load. Exogamy is a reminder that cultural margins are precarious and that the suggestion of contamination will quickly raise feelings of alarm.[21] The presence of an outside ethnic group implies a dangerous contamination and so becomes doubly evil, requiring disapproval; as Douglas would say, "first for crossing the line and second because it puts the others in danger."[22] Every transgression along these lines is a historical happening, in that such a transcendental act is composed of affirmations and negations, resistances and ruptures on both sides of the cultural dividing lines. Herbert Marcuse declared that order becomes liberty only if it is based and maintained by the free gratification of individuals.[23] Does out-marriage necessarily entail the rupture of an established order? Is the uneasiness about feminine and masculine stereotypes the reason why many Nikkei men and women cross the borders of their community and choose to remain outside the frontiers of the Nikkei universe? We will leave these questions unresolved for the time being.

Nikkei Identity: Biological or Symbolic?

In 1992 the crisis of the Alberto Fujimori–Susana Higuchi presidential couple brought the rigid patriarchal hierarchy of Nikkei families and the situation of their women into public awareness. Following the violent appearance of Nisei First Lady Susana Higuchi, in which she claimed her rights as a Peruvian citizen, the media raised the question, where is the submissive, obedient Japanese woman, the model person that everyone is so familiar with?[24] The stereotype of the Nikkei woman has definitely changed with the passing of time, arriving, toward the end of the twentieth century, at the point where a woman may publicly claim her rightful place in Peruvian society.

Like many social sectors of Peru that have been held back, the Nikkei sector aims to obtain full citizenship rights as an efficient tool for achieving integration into national society and approaching the ideal of a shared national identity, an aspiration that reflects many failed attempts in the history of Peru.[25] It would seem that the idea of racial integrity, as embodied in endogamy and the need for a closed community, has hindered that search. We see, in the example of Susana Higuchi—who preferred to risk discarding the stereotype of femininity, which had been symbolically constructed in the community from which she came—that she became a symbol for all Peruvian woman when she chose to express her concerns publicly. The majority of Nikkei men and women have not forgiven that act of dissent to this date, stigmatizing Higuchi as "disobedient," "scandalous," "impatient," a "traitor," and even "crazy." Such words suggest the transgression of the concept of femininity held by the community leading to ideas of boundaries, threats, limits being broken, and contamination, which imply threats and danger to the entire group.

As was stated at the beginning, grandiloquent and conventionally homogenized presentations concerning immigration and the Japanese community in Peru have hidden the complexity and diversity of a very rich symbolic universe. At the representational level, what in marketing is called "trademark identification" has been harmfully utilized, as sectors with little power, such as women and youth, are represented by a single stereotypical image created by the dominant sectors.[26] As has been shown, adapting to and becoming integrated into Peruvian culture has not entailed the same process for women as for men. However, oral and written analyses, such as historical research studies, have obliterated this fact and assumed a unilateral version, reconstructing and valuing only one of the possibilities, the masculine. All the other voices have been silenced under the weight of that one presumed truth. When we say "Nikkei identity," where, precisely, do those words lead us? To a picture of a powerful man and a submissive woman of Japanese origin? Or, even worse, do we only see a man?

I propose that any examination of Nikkei identity should not be a record of disarticulation or conflict, but should seek unification and reconciliation. This is only possible through acceptance of the diversity and contradictions that a human group presents. Democratic and inclusive practices, in both public and private spheres, become the only possible way to create less oppressive notions of masculinity and femininity. These in turn will make possible the construction of a Nikkei identity that is inclusive, and which, when the time comes for naming oneself and one's world, will be based on just and humane social relations as opposed to the memory of blood ties. In other words, I am proposing that "Nikkei" should become a more symbolic and less biological identity—all the more so, since the body is a source of inequality in a society of masculine overvaluations.

Many concerns remain unexplored, but with the ideas reflected in the present analysis I have tried to respond to the timely question raised by

Michel Foucault: "And what if power did not have the essential function of saying 'no,' of prohibiting and punishing, but rather of connecting cohesion, pleasure, and truth in an undefined spiral?"[27]

Notes

1. Benedict Anderson, "La comunidad imaginada," *Debate Feminista* 7:13 (1996): 100–103.

2. Susanna Rance, "Teorías vividas: el método auto/biográfico en los estudios de género," *Umbrales: revista del postgrado en ciencias del desarrollo* 4 (1998): 43–46.

3. María Ester Grebe, "Antropología del género en la perspectiva del paradigma cognitivo simbolico," unpublished manuscript. Grebe declares, "The cognitive-symbolic paradigm ... privileges the discovery of cultural meanings through the rescue of the symbolic perceptions, conceptions and representations of each woman."

4. Amelia Morimoto, *Población de origen japonés en el Perú: investigaciones* (Lima: Comisión Conmemorativa del 90 Aniversario de la Inmigración Japonesa al Perú, 1989), 178.

5. Norma Fuller, *Dilemas de la femineidad: mujeres de clase media en el Perú* (Lima: Fondo Editorial de la Pontifícia Universidad Católica del Perú, 1993), 17.

6. Editorial Perú Shimpo S.A., *Inmigración japonesa al Perú: 75 aniversario (1899–1974)* (Lima: Editorial Perú Shimpo S.A., 1974), 28

7. Mary Fukumoto Sato, *Migrantes japoneses y sus descendientes en el Perú* (Bachelor's thesis, Universidad Nacional Mayor de San Marcos, 1974), 84.

8. Doris Moromisato, "Ellas trajeron el Japon al Perú," *Perú Shimpo*, Mar. 4, 1999, 12.

9. *Revista Nikko commemorativa de los 80 años de inmigración japonesa al Perú* 26 (1989): 241.

10. Doris Moromisato, "Olla, Tortuga, Flor: nuestras inmigrantes se llamaban como la vida," *Perú Shimpo*, Apr. 7, 1999.

11. *Informe nacional del Perú para la conferencia de las naciones unidas para el medio ambiente y desarrollo* (Lima: Documento Oficial de la República de Perú, 1992). This study reports that it is necessary to take into account that Peru is a multiethnic and multicultural state with more than sixty linguistic groups in sixteen ethnic-linguistic families.

12. Elena Kishimoto de Inamine, *Tradiciones y costumbres de los inmigrantes japoneses en el Perú* (Lima: Centro de Investigaciones Historico Sociales de la Universidad Nacional Federico Villarreal, 1979).

13. This dialogue took place in the "Second-year Assessment and Planning Meetings" of the International Nikkei Research Project in Los Angeles, California, June 1999.

14. Norma Fuller, *Dilemas de la femineidad*, 14. Fuller writes, "This is probably one of the dilemmas of present feminine identity, the deep internalization of strong, kind and generous models from which they must keep a distance in order to conquer new spaces."

15. Judith Butler, *Gender Trouble: Feminism and the Subversion of Identity* (New York: Routledge, 1990).

16. Norma Fuller, *Dilemas de la femineidad*, 18.

17. Norma Fuller, *Identidades masculinas* (Lima: Fondo Editorial de la Pontificia Universidad Católica del Perú, 1997).

18. María Raguz, "Masculinidad, femineidad y género: un enfoque psicologico diferente," in Narda Henríquez, ed., *Encrucijadas del saber: los estudios de género en las ciencias sociales* (Lima: Pontificia Universidad Católica del Perú, 1996). Raguz (p. 55) writes:

> A distinction must be made between patriarchalism and machismo, since they are wrongly used as similar concepts. Patriarchy refers to societies where power is concentrated in men, to whose authority women, sons and daughters must submit themselves, and to whom they guarantee protection. ... [In] machismo, on the other hand, ... there is no responsibility towards women and children, they are not recognized, they are not protected. However, they serve to validate men's virility. ... The use of violence, abuse, abandonment, double standards are characteristic of machismo.

19. Mary Douglas, *Pureza y peligro: un analisis de los conceptos de contaminación y tabú* (Madrid: Siglo veintiuno eds., 1973).

20. María Emma Manarelli, "Cuerpo femenino y discurso médico," *Revista márgenes* 9:15 (1996): 73–99.

21. Mary Douglas, *Pureza y peligro*, xi.

22. Ibid., 163.

23. Herbert Marcuse, *Eros y civilización* (Barcelona: Ed. Seix Barral, 1971), 180.

24. Doris Moromisato and Irene Oyakawa, "Las mujeres Nikkei en el Perú: cien años de historia y discreción," *Revista Quehacer* 92 (Nov.–Dec. 1984).

25. Alexandra De Mesones, "Formas híbridas de identidad y mentalidad en el Perú contemporáneo: clase, género, etnicidad y generación" (Master's thesis, University of Salamanca, 1999).

26. Betzabé Andía, "Treinta años del movimiento feminista: visibilizando las estructuras," paper presented at the National Meeting of Organized Women, 1999.

27. Michel Foucault, "Un dialogo sobre el poder y otras conversaciones" (Madrid: Alianza Editorial, 1981), 25.

CHAPTER TWELVE

Migration as a Negotiation of Gender

Recent Japanese Immigrant Women in Canada

AUDREY KOBAYASHI

Japanese women currently make up about two-thirds of the immigrants from Japan to Canada. The majority are unmarried and in their late twenties or early thirties. They represent a very specific group of women, generally highly educated, inclined toward professional careers, and disinclined toward the role of the traditional Japanese housewife/mother. For these women, life in Canada represents a significant form of resistance toward the limitations placed upon women in Japan today. Once in Canada, these women display a number of characteristics related to their backgrounds. They tend to work in the arts or social services. The majority marry men of non-Japanese background. Understanding their circumstances helps us to understand that migration is not a random process, but one that is deeply tied to the social and cultural circumstances of both the sending and the receiving countries.[1]

This paper addresses the experiences of *shin ijuusha* (recent immigrant) women in Canada. Their story is a little told one, full of the contradictions involved in moving from one country to another, the excitement and pull of new experiences, the wrenching disruption of emotional ties, and the uncertainties of entering a new society where language, custom, and the comforting security of the everyday environment are different. This is the story of how the thirty-eight women who participated in this study have dealt with those differences, and how they have negotiated gender relations in the process of making a new place for themselves in Canadian society.[2]

Over the past several decades, Japanese immigration to Canada has stood at slightly under one thousand individuals per year, a very small fraction of the more than two hundred thousand immigrants who enter Canada in most years. Compared to most migrant streams, however, that from Japan has a decided gender imbalance, as about two-thirds of the immigrants are women. My analysis shows that the stream is clearly divided into two groups. One group is similar to immigrants from other countries. These women are members of immigrant families, married to male immigrants, who come to Canada primarily for occupational reasons. The others are women who are single, or who are married to men from non-Japanese backgrounds. From no other country in the world does Canada receive such a proportionately high number of such women.

This migration pattern is quite different from that of other Nikkei societies, for two reasons. First, single women who emigrate from Japan travel overwhelmingly to English-speaking countries, primarily to the United States and Canada, and in much smaller numbers to Britain, Australia, and New Zealand. Similar migration patterns do not occur, therefore, for the Spanish- and Portuguese-speaking countries of Latin America. Secondly, while an even larger number of single Japanese women emigrates to the United States, the relative numbers are much smaller than in Canada, where such women make up approximately 10 percent of the total Nikkei population.[3]

The circumstances of these Japanese women immigrants, therefore, are central to an understanding of the Canadian Nikkei and the ways in which the Canadian situation differs from that of other countries.

Characteristics of the Immigrants

An analysis of data based on a special run of the 1986–96 censuses shows that most of these women have settled in the large cities of Vancouver, Toronto, and, to a lesser extent, Montreal. They are highly educated, and the largest proportion is employed in the arts or human service professions (such as social work, community service, and teaching). Some originally came to Canada as students but stayed on in Canada as permanent residents after completing their degrees, discouraged by the bleak prospects of finding fulfilling jobs in Japan. Their average age of immigration is approximately thirty years. The majority marries in Canada, but only rarely to a partner of Japanese ethnicity. These statistics represent fascinating lives, and a fascinating story of how Japanese women have used emigration as a way of negotiating gender.

Escaping Japanese Patriarchy

Much has been written about the exceptionally high level of patriarchy in Japanese society. This characteristic needs to be understood in context as a manifestation of a particular set of social, economic, and cultural factors that have influenced Japanese society over at least the past century. Although Japanese women have always played a very important role in the workforce, and since the 1880s have made up nearly half of Japanese workers, Japanese visions of citizenship since the country began its major push toward modernization during the late nineteenth century have depended upon a definition of "woman" as primarily a subservient household member, whose role is to produce and protect the coming generation. On the whole, Japanese women view their major role in life to be a wife and mother, positions that, unlike in the West, are seen as a form of responsible employment. Japanese society could in many respects be described as a cult of motherhood.

Since World War II, although women have played an increasingly important role in the workforce, their position has remained largely subservient. Notions such as equal pay are not part of the Japanese philosophy of employment. The most distinctive aspect of the female workforce in Japan is the famous "M" curve, which shows high participation of women up to their early thirties, then a drop-off as women are encouraged, and in many cases even required, to quit their jobs during their childbearing years. A second peak in the rate of women's participation occurs from their mid-forties, as the demands of motherhood begin to drop off.[4] Because it is so difficult for women in Japan to find fulfillment through career development, many women retreat into the cult of motherhood, disdaining paid work as demeaning and establishing social outlets in their families or community activities.

The success with which women are able to use motherhood as a basis for social status (that is, to use complicity as a form of resistance) varies with class and other factors. As a general rule, the higher the socioeconomic class, the more women disparage work outside the home. In recent years the attitude that working mothers provide a poor upbringing for their children has waned considerably, but it still holds in more traditional settings.[5] But because the housewife/mother role is valued and seen by so many as more valuable than working outside the home, it is usually a much easier role for Japanese women to accept than it would be for women in most Western cultures. Nonetheless, as a system based fundamentally on inequality, it is bound to be unsatisfying for many. In recent years resistance has taken the form of political activity and limited but concerted efforts to bring about cultural change. As Patricia Morley suggests, "The mountain is moving."[6]

Those who choose migration as a form of resistance are small in number, but for the most part they leave because they reject the specific ways in which Japanese patriarchy is manifested. This rejection contrasts markedly with the attitudes of Issei women who emigrated from Japan prior to World War II.

For the earlier generation emigration was a means of fulfilling the obligations of wife and mother. Virtually all of the earlier emigrants were already married, or left Japan as "picture brides" in arranged marriages, understanding that they were obligated to work to support the household and to bear children to carry on the family.[7] Emigration in the earlier years was therefore a way of reinforcing, rather than escaping, tradition. The experiences of the shin ijuusha women, therefore, represent not only a break with Japan, but also a break with the established pattern in most Nikkei societies.

The Study Groups

Focus group sessions were conducted in Toronto, Ontario, with two groups of shin ijuusha women, the Mummies and Harmony International. The groups met in roundtable sessions, over coffee, as part of their monthly meeting routine. Each session lasted approximately three hours and was conducted primarily in Japanese. Although all the members speak English in their homes and workplaces, they felt more comfortable speaking about personal issues in Japanese. Moreover, because they speak English with varying levels of fluency, speaking in Japanese gave them the opportunity to participate equally.

The Mummies is a recently formed group, founded by young immigrant mothers as a support group. All of the participants had emigrated from Japan to Canada within the past ten years. Despite its name, only eight of the fourteen participants were mothers, and nearly all of these had only one child. They were born in the 1960s and early 1970s, with an average age of thirty-three. They were relatively well educated: ten had attended junior college, and three university. The majority worked in clerical, sales, and food service positions. There were also two homemakers, two students, and one journalist. A number of these women worked part-time while raising children. Except for one unmarried student, all were married to non-Japanese spouses.

Harmony International has been meeting for many years. Its twenty-four participants were born in the late 1940s and early 1950s, with an average age of forty-eight. Most of them came to Canada during the 1960s or early 1970s. Nearly all were mothers, and nearly all had two children. They had higher levels of education than those in the other group: three had postgraduate degrees, fourteen had graduated from university, seven from college or technical school. Three were homemakers, and the majority were employed in small business or professional positions. They included a dentist, an opera singer, a librarian, and a computer programmer. As the name of the group suggests, all were married to spouses of non-Japanese ancestry, although one was married to a Canadian-born Nikkei.

Although both groups are made up of women married to men of non-Japanese backgrounds, they are different in other respects, and representative of two types of shin ijuusha women. Those who came during the earlier years have higher education levels and professional aspirations. Some came to Canada initially to further their education, supported by their families in Japan. They stayed to work, eventually marrying Canadian men of non-Japanese backgrounds. Although I did not undertake research into their backgrounds in Japan, the leader of Harmony International believes that these women came from relatively well-off Japanese families, and thus had the means to leave Japan at a time when it was difficult for most young Japanese women to do so. They were not asked to provide information about their incomes either, but their dress and demeanor gave the appearance that they were relatively well-off.

In contrast, the Mummies members, more recently arrived, had lower educational levels and worked in part-time, lower skilled, or lower paid jobs. The leader of the Mummies told me that most of them were not well off. Approximately half of this group came to Canada initially on "Working Holiday" visas, which would indicate that they did not have the same means as the Harmony International members, only one of whom had come on such a visa.

Although this project focused on the groups of intermarried women, an interview was also conducted with the president of the Wa-on Club, another group of shin ijuusha women, most (but not all) of whom are married to shin ijuusha men. It may be useful to provide a brief description of this group to provide a sense of other aspects of the shin ijuusha population. Like the other two groups, this group meets once a month for conversation and mutual support, but their concerns are quite different. They are predominantly homemakers and mothers who find living in Canada very difficult. They do not speak English well, and they have difficulty negotiating with Canadian institutions such as the health care system. The leader of the group indicated that they lack confidence and feel culturally and socially isolated. Although I do not have sufficient information on the Wa-on Club to draw definitive conclusions, their leader claimed that they are much more concerned with maintaining "Japanese culture" than are others, and feel unwilling or unable to adapt to what they view as the foreign society in which they now live.

While the three groups show significantly different perspectives, for all of these women, the experience of migration has disrupted established human relations. New relations have been formed under circumstances in which they may feel at a disadvantage because of linguistic or cultural barriers. Ordinary human acts such as those involved in being a worker, spouse, mother, daughter, or citizen are cast out of an established context. For some this disruption was welcome; for others it was thrust upon them with perhaps bewildering suddenness. For all, however, there were unexpected results. During the focus group sessions, we held frank and often very revealing discussions of how new relations, including those of marriage and family, were forged, and of the difficulties that arose. The three forms of human relationship that dominated discussions among both focus groups were those with husbands, children, and parents.

Escaping Japanese Patriarchy

The focus group discussions began with the question, "Why did you leave Japan?" Although their answers took many forms, the participants fell into two basic categories: those who left because they were married and wanted to be with their husbands, and those who wished more freedom to live their lives according to their own choosing:

"I have also asked this question to many of my friends, and they say, 'it's freedom.' Yeah, because for them Japanese culture tells 'a girl should be this' in too many aspects. It's *kyu-kutsu* [rigid, narrow], they say. Then, after they come, they feel more freedom." (original in English)[8]

"Rigid ideas that 'Onnanoko [girls] should be like this' was also the reason for me. I had to carry the right bag; I had to wear the right clothes, a big name brand. But in Canada, I see some wearing a leather coat and others wearing short sleeves, all in the same season. [Others laugh]. In other words, they don't care how other people look at them. It's nice."[9]

"There was so much pressure to being a woman in Japan . . . every day, every day, I thought of the disadvantages I faced because I was a woman. When I came to Canada, I looked around and for the first time I saw a man putting out garbage . . . and thought, 'Wow, what a tough life men have here! What an easy life women can live here.' Well, I thought Canada was wonderful in this respect, but I had a tough time in many other ways."

Freedom also means finding work that allows one to be more than what one woman termed just an "accessory" to men:

In a big company, women's job is to *ochakumi* [make tea]. Even when they are given a real job, they earn poor wages, even if they do the same job as men. I thought it was unfair. But when I said so, my boss told me, "You are difficult, and it is difficult to deal with you. You should get married as soon as possible and quit this job." He tried to fire me.

Another had a slightly different perspective, but still found her Japanese routine unfulfilling:

I graduated from university, became an OL [office lady], and started serving tea. Then I came to Canada when I was twenty-six. The reason was not because my life as an OL was boring or meaningless. . . . Tea serving and cleaning were meaningful for me. . . . But I felt so comfortable living in Japan. I had never experienced something uncomfortable, so I wanted to seek something uncomfortable somehow. I wanted to put myself in an inconvenient place, and see whether I could manage it.

Each participant presented a slight variation on this theme, but all emphasized the fact that life in Japan meant getting on normative "tracks" from which it was almost impossible to get off without actually leaving the country. The pressure to conform was too great, and the opportunity to do something different too limited. Changing one's life meant changing one's place; only at a physical distance could they achieve freedom as they defined it.

Intermarriage

Freedom meant escaping the bounds of a traditional Japanese marriage, but not escaping marriage altogether. Intercultural marriage is a way of life for most Japanese women immigrants.[10] All the women spoke frankly about the circumstances of their marriages and their relations with their husbands. They were quick to use humor and to express empathy with those having marital difficulties. Those in the Mummies group were much more willing than those in Harmony International, however, to speak about difficulties.

I began the discussions about marriage by pointing out that when I looked at the census data on Japanese immigrant women, I was fascinated to find that the modal age of immigration of single women was twenty-nine years.[11] This observation garnered knowing laughter, and comments about the fact that those sitting around the table were a bunch of "Christmas cakes." A number of women in both groups stated that they had come at age twenty-nine, or just before. As the conversations progressed, it became apparent that for nearly all the women, pressure to enter a traditional Japanese marriage, which usually also involves quitting one's job, was a major factor in the decision to come to Canada.

The marriages follow three basic patterns. In the first, most common among the Harmony International group, young Japanese women had met Canadian men who had traveled to Japan to study or work, became involved, married, and returned with their new husbands to Canada. These husbands were described as generally enthusiastic about Japanese culture. Some speak a little Japanese, and they are eager to maintain links with Japan and Japanese relatives. One woman said, "I met my husband, who is Canadian, in Japan. He was working for a company. We decided to get married. I wanted a freer lifestyle, that's for sure. And, luckily, I met him and decided to take him."

In the second pattern, the women met men from a third country, including the United States, Britain, France, Poland, Germany, South Africa, and Sri Lanka. These couples made decisions to move to Canada, which was described by one woman as "neutral" territory, although in most cases it was the husband's job that dictated the destination. These women tended to have a strong sense of marital equality and confidence. An example:

The first reason I came to Canada was that the person I married was not Japanese. We decided to go to a third, neutral, country. . . . That's why we came to Canada. I was twenty-seven when I left Japan and went to Britain. . . . Twenty-seven was the age when I came under the most pressure to marry from people around me. They tried to arrange a marriage for me through *omiai* [introduction for the purpose of marriage]. I didn't want to get married for a while. I wanted to study, so I went to Britain.

In the third pattern, more common among the Mummies group, the women had come to Canada on their own, perhaps on a working holiday visa, and had met and married Canadian men. In general, women belonging to the third group expressed the greatest frustrations concerning lack of understanding on the part of their Canadian-born husbands:

I came to Canada with a working holiday visa. . . . In Japan, we have to go to a good *tandai* [two-year college] in order to find a job in a good company and a good husband and a secure life. That's what all my friends did. I followed the course, and ended up in a good company. . . . I found a nice-looking guy with a promising future, but he married my best friend. I tried a few more, but failed. My boss told me I was not a typical Japanese woman. He asked me when I would get married and quit that job. . . . Then I got a working visa so I could [come to Canada and] earn money. . . . Then I met my husband, who is a bit different from my dream.

Some women found that the degree of patriarchy in marriage was not significantly less than it would have been in Japan. They have become part of what I have elsewhere called the "Yoko Ono Syndrome," whereby Asian women have been exoticized in the imaginations of white Western men and treated as objects of a particularly patronizing kind of desire.[12] The conversation made it clear that while relations were extremely diverse, nearly all of the women felt that their husbands' needs, especially their career needs, took precedence over their own. They agreed that their husbands would not have had the same degree of cultural and linguistic adaptability that they had themselves, and therefore their husbands could not have adapted to life in Japan as they, the wives, had done to life to Canada.

Differences were expressed most strongly in relation to children. Many of the women wished their children to learn Japanese, but their husbands saw no need. They wanted their babies to sleep in the same bed, as occurs in Japan, but their husbands objected. In one case a mother-in-law also objected, and made it clear that such a practice is considered improper in Canada. Inevitably, the conversation returned after such revelations to questions of communication and understanding.

Communicating

Language is a significant factor in defining the degree to which women feel confident in their communication with husbands, children, and neighbors. One of the major reasons that the women's organizations exist is to provide a setting in which the members can lapse into Japanese and the comfort of expressing themselves without constant strain and possibilities of misunderstanding. For it is not simply being able to express oneself in English that presents the major challenge; it is being able to express oneself so that the entire context of one's speech act is understood. What these women expressed most strongly was the frustration of knowing that such total communication "from the heart" had been cut off in most of their everyday lives:

"What is the most difficult thing in Canada?"
"To get socialized with people—with neighbors, with people at school."
"Why? Language?"
"Well, I can't handle the language very well, but it's more. I think that face and ways of thinking are so different, so I feel that I cannot be very Japanese. I think, 'What do other people do in such a case?' and I cannot open my heart."

The language issue is less significant with husbands, even if the women felt unable to express themselves precisely:

"Sometimes it is good that we cannot understand the language. If you don't understand everything that he is saying, sometimes it makes our relations better, because you only think of the good things. It's mysterious. So, I don't think that language is such a problem. To me, it's culture, like what food to serve his relations. And he doesn't like rice. That's very, very bad. It's so much work to make potatoes."
"But in Japan, we can communicate without actually saying anything."

Communicating with children, however, is a bigger issue:

"After they have grown up, if we cannot communicate with each other, we'll have troubles, because I'm not very good at English."
"You won't have a problem. You're their mother."
"People who have jobs speak English better, but people like me who stay home all day are not exposed to English, and it will never improve."
"Don't you speak with your husband?"
"But the contents of my conversations with my husband are always the same. We just say, 'I love you,' that's all. My husband is very busy with his job, and he's never at home."

"You should throw him out. A Japanese husband would be better. Could you go to work outside again after your children have grown?"

"Yes, but by that time my brain will have atrophied."

The women spoke at length of their frustration with attempts to teach their children Japanese, or to send them to Japanese language school. Most of the children have learned to speak Japanese somewhat; some of them can speak three languages. But,

"It is impossible to have an adult conversation with them. So they talk about the world situation and other things all in English. . . . Even when they speak in Japanese, they have to add words in English when they talk about difficult issues. 'What do you want to eat today,' or 'What time did you come home yesterday?' do not mean real adult conversation between parents and children."

"Even if we speak in Japanese, how long do we speak in a day? 'Do you want some dinner?' 'You should study'—that's it."

The issues surrounding language clearly reflect a much deeper concern than simply whether the children go to Japanese language lessons. The women were very concerned that it was impossible to have meaningful relationships with their children without a common language in which they both feel fluent and emotionally secure. The gaps and silences represent gaps in their relationships that have caused deep anxiety for some of them. This issue was of much greater concern for the Harmony International group, most of whose children were young adults, than for the Mummies group, whose children were very young.

Most difficult of all, however, is communication with civil authorities, in particular about children's health or schooling. The experience can be humiliating:

"In Toronto, recently, [my child's] teacher said to me, 'I don't want to speak with you without an interpreter.' Then she turned her back on me. I said, 'I understand what you are saying, there is no trouble. I have studied here for ten years and have never had such a need. I can keep up with other people.' . . . But she says she won't talk to me without an interpreter. But that's her limitation, it's her problem."

The sense of communicative isolation has far-reaching implications. A little farther on in both focus group discussions, we came to the issue of discrimination. Both groups feel that they experience discrimination from other Canadians, although the older Harmony International group felt it much more strongly than did members of the Mummies. Most commonly, however, they spoke of the discomfort of not feeling at home, not knowing what to say in social situations, and not being accepted.

The issue of acceptance is crucial to their sense of identity, which is overwhelmingly "Japanese," not "Japanese Canadian" or "Canadian." They are certainly transnational and cosmopolitan, but their discussion reiterated in a variety of ways that they think of their husbands and children as Canadian and themselves as Japanese. This situation affects not only relations within the family, but the ways in which they construct themselves in relation to the wider society, as perpetual outsiders. The focus groups only scratched the surface of their senses of identity, but provided thought for much additional work on what it means not only to be shin ijuusha, but what it means to be an immigrant in a deeply racialized society.

The group members also talked at length about racism and the direct discrimination they have encountered. For most, the experiences are subtle. One woman joined a golf club where the white members continually challenged her scores and made her feel fraudulent as group member. Others spoke of epithets directed both toward themselves and their children, such as when "Chink" was called out on the street. Still others spoke of how it is sometimes "an advantage" to be a "Japanese" woman, because employers like Asian women, who are viewed as both compliant and efficient. But such orientalism is itself a form of othering that labels the immigrant woman as different. All these experiences contribute to the very strong feeling that, unlike their children, they cannot ever be or feel like full-fledged members of Canadian society.

Parents

The discussion concerning children was conducted with the greatest energy, but the discussion about parents was more emotional. Despite the fact that it is traditional in Japanese society for daughters to give up responsibility for their parents upon leaving the household, most of the women felt strong emotional bonds. They keep in touch with their parents regularly, the majority through weekly telephone calls as well as annual or semiannual visits to Japan. Whenever possible, they take their children, so that they can have a relationship with their grandparents. Nonetheless, the women express guilt about leaving Japan, where the ongoing relationship between parents and children is so bound by cultural tradition:

"I am the eldest, and I have one younger sister and one younger brother. [My mother] said, 'Okay, you can go.' She still has two left. But I still feel bad, because she invested so much time and money to make me. . . . But my mother and father are happy if I am happy. They would like me to be married to a Japanese man, living close to them in Japan, so they could see their grandchildren. That would make them happy. But if I can't be happy [doing that], then they couldn't really be happy either. That's what my mother said, and I think she understands me. But still, I feel guilty."

"I abandoned my parents and came to Canada in 1967. I didn't think about my mother's feelings at all, I only thought about my own happiness. When my own daughter left home and went to university, I finally realized a mother's pain. Then I decided to go back to Japan once a year, whatever happens. She is ninety-eight years old, but she is still alive. . . . Now I understand how hard it was for her."

The greatest difficulties arise as the parents age and face ill health, especially if they need extended care and do not have anyone in Japan to provide it. Members of both groups shared the difficult emotional experience of living through the ill health and eventual death of parents, of being unable to be there to support the other parent, or in some cases of traveling to Japan and feeling that they were neglecting their husbands and children in Canada. When one member of the Mummies group expressed her feelings about living through such a situation, the entire room was in tears:

"My mother is in the last stages of cancer, and this is a problem I am facing right now. Now, when it has finally come, I can't tell yet whether the fact that I came [to Canada] was right or not. It's useless to think about it. It's such a great distance, and it costs so much to get a plane ticket. I just can't see her very often. . . . I only found out about a month ago, and now I just can't make sense of it, but I'm beginning to understand what it means that I'm living in Canada, that I left her. . . . I should have stayed in Japan. . . . Well, I shouldn't even think about such a thing. . . . What am I talking about?"

"Do you want to be near her?"

"Yes. They told me that she might go at any time. I want the rest of her life to be as happy as possible. If I could do anything for her, I would. I am her only child. There must be so many things I could do for her. But she's so far away that I can only think about her. I should not be so far away. I think about it constantly."

This woman was quite young, in her early thirties. Among the older women, most of who had already gone through a similar experience, several spoke of the effects of distance in changing human feelings:

"I lost my mother two years ago. I came to Canada in 1981, so have lived here for seventeen [sic] years apart from her. After she died, I couldn't really feel that she was gone, because I was not with her. Even now I think of her as alive. . . . I can't feel too sad."

"My father is eighty-eight and my mother is seventy-four. They have various health problems. . . . I call them, and find out, 'Oh, your father is in the hospital,' and the next time, 'Oh, your mother is in the hospital.' I keep telling them, my father, my mother, my elder sister, and my younger sister, that if anything happens they should tell me as soon as possible, and I'll go back to Japan any time. But they don't tell me anything, so that I won't worry—then I call up and find out that they are in hospital!"

"My elder sisters always concealed the truth about my mother. You know, when our parents get older, they are often sick. And my sisters would say to my mother, 'Mother, you'll get better when [Mariko (pseudonym)] comes back. She is coming soon, and you'll be better again.' So they didn't tell my mother that she was going to die soon."

"My thinking has changed. I didn't think about it when I was twenty years old. I didn't even think about it when I was thirty. I thought about it for the first time when I was forty."

But, finally,

"You can't live two lives. Eventually, you have to compromise."

The Negotiation of Gender

Compromise is a good word to describe the ways that Japanese women, and Canadian shin ijuusha women, negotiate their gendered lives. The focus group participants were remarkably frank and open, and thoughtfully aware of the contradictions marking their extremely complicated lives. They think of themselves as strong, adaptable, and resilient, yet they know that they have left behind one form of patriarchy to become part of another. Their participation in Mummies and Harmony International provides a forum for bringing the contradictions of their lives to the surface.

It is clearly too simplistic to say that in escaping the traditional bonds of Japanese patriarchy they found the freedom of Western society, despite the fact that many say they left Japan in order to seek such freedom. Most of them lead much less structured lives in Canada, to be sure, with a much larger range of opportunities. They also lead much more contingent existences. In Japan, they would understand their place, as well as how much room they had to maneuver outside the bounds of convention. In Canada that understanding is often lacking, or achieved with great difficulty.

Their marriages involve a wide range of negotiations. There is no single, typical relationship, and gender roles are much more flexible than they would be in Japan. But flexibility can also lead to uncertainty, which seems to be a greater problem for the most recent arrivals than for the older shin ijuusha women. Uncertainty combines with loneliness, especially for the younger, more recently married women, who are less well established professionally than the older ones. Being less well educated, they tend to speak English less fluently. It is difficult for them to reach across the cultural, linguistic, and gender divides that separate them from husbands who, for their own part, are caught up in their work. This situation is, of course, one that is common in both Japan and Canada, and in marriages between partners of similar backgrounds, but the loneliness takes a particular form in situations of partial linguistic understanding, or interrupted discourse.

The most difficult uncertainties revolve around language issues. For some, especially the most recent arrivals, this means a continuous effort just to accomplish everyday tasks, and to establish some sense of social belonging across a linguistic divide. Even for those whose English is fairly fluent, however, there is a struggle to understand more about the subtle texts according to which people in Canada lead their lives. These subtle texts are manifest in fairly trivial ways that have huge implications for the degree of comfort they feel in Canadian society. For example, they see that Canadian women are not bound by the strict dress code that applies in Japan, and they interpret that situation as an example of greater freedom. Yet because of their unfamiliarity with the language and customs, they do not see that at least some of those Canadian women conform to dress codes that may also be strict, but are expressed in a language of which they are not aware. They understand the literal meaning of the words spoken in English by a child's teacher, but both because they do not understand the subtlety of the language, and because of the deep-seated discrimination in the teacher's attitude, they are unable to communicate fully.

The language issue, then, is not one simply of translating words, but of being part of the larger discourse through which gendered citizenship is negotiated. They tend to be excluded because the discursive strategies of many members of dominant Canadian society either fail to include them or express outright hostility, and because such practices of exclusion are amplified by the fact that the shin ijuusha women are not always aware of the subtle words and gestures that mark their exclusion. This situation speaks to the larger question of how immigrants are received in the dominant society, and raises questions of what needs to be done to alter the discourse around inclusion and the definition of who belongs. I have dubbed this interrupted discourse, because of the breaks and silences that condition immigrant women's lives.

While addressing this issue lies much beyond the scope of this chapter, it is important to note that associations such as Harmony International and Mummies play a significant role in this process. Their place within the larger Nikkei, and Canadian, society, therefore, deserves considerable attention. In recent years, the National Association of Japanese Canadians has taken on the task of addressing the needs of the shin ijuusha, who make up such a significant part of their community. They have held a national conference on new immigrants, regularly sponsor discussions, and take steps to ensure that shin ijuusha have representation on the national executive council. In 1996, they sponsored a series of community workshops on intermarriage in Nikkei communities across the country. These occasions provided an important opportunity for intermarried shin ijuusha and intermarried Canadian-born Sansei (third-generation) couples to get to know one another. In some communities, for example Vancouver, the momentum of the workshops has carried forward to establishing regular meetings of intermarried couples.

Negotiating gender, therefore, is also part of the larger institutional processes that define the Nikkei community. For the Canadian Nikkei, the challenge is to recognize the many ways in which gender differences occur within a community that is culturally, linguistically, and generationally diverse. Canadian Nikkei are active in addressing these issues but have a long way to go, both in understanding the situation of new immigrants and in developing community programs that will address their needs.

It is also important that we understand how the negotiation of gendered citizenship for Nikkei groups in Canada compares to experiences in other countries of the Nikkei diaspora. As mentioned above, the phenomenon of large numbers of single, and eventually intermarried, shin ijuusha women is unique to the developed English-speaking countries, and is more pronounced in Canada than elsewhere. Canada also likely has the highest rate of intermarriage throughout the Nikkei diaspora. But all Nikkei societies have new immigrants who face specific issues of adaptation and specific concerns in negotiating gender relations. Intermarriage is an issue for all Nikkei, as is the question of linguistic and cultural difference, among Nikkei and between Nikkei and non-Nikkei. Much further work needs to be done in each country to understand how those differences are negotiated. As Doris Moromisato's work points out, we struggle simply to name the issue of gender, to gain the collective power to recognize difference. Further work is also needed to understand in comparative terms how the varying circumstances from one Nikkei society to another condition the experiences of the Nikkei and, in particular, of the shin ijuusha. That understanding needs to occur in a context that recognizes the political, institutional, and intellectual environments in which diverse Nikkei live. The International Nikkei Research Project has set precisely that understanding as its major aim, so we may expect such work to emerge from this project.

Notes

I wish to thank the groups Mummies and Harmony International for cooperating in the development of this paper, and Natsuko Chubachi, who provided assistance in organizing focus groups and in transcribing and translating the results.

1. Data cited in this report are derived from reports of Citizenship and Immigration Canada or from the Canadian census. See also Audrey Kobayashi, *A Demographic Profile of Japanese Canadians, and Social Implications for the Future* (Ottawa: Department of the Secretary of State, Contract PCS-8-00374, 1989).

2. The issue of representation always arises when defining a small sample size for qualitative methods such as focus groups. The two groups, "Mummies" and "Harmony International," were selected because they are broadly representative of the population targeted for this study: i.e., Japanese immigrant women who are married to men from other ethnocultural backgrounds. Despite the small sample size, the demographic characteristics conform to the average characteristics available from census figures. In the future, this study should be extended to include more women,

and women from other places, such as Vancouver and Montreal. In addition, this chapter does not address those who come to Canada on "Working Holidays," a special category that allows young people to work for a period, often while taking courses in English. The latter make up a large percentage of Japanese workers in the service industry, particularly in restaurants. They often experience severe harassment and mistreatment on the part of employers.

3. This figure is an estimate, based on the fact that approximately 17 percent of the total Canadian Nikkei population was born in Japan, and over 60 percent of that group (two-thirds of whom are women) are intermarried. More exact information is not available through census figures, but 10 percent is, if anything, a conservative estimate. The proportion for Australia may be similar or even higher, but the absolute numbers are much smaller.

4. Sumiko Iwao, *Japanese Woman: Traditional Image and Changing Reality* (Cambridge, Mass.: Harvard University Press, 1993), chapter 6.

5. Ibid., chapter 5.

6. Patricia Morley, *The Mountain Is Moving: Japanese Women's Lives* (Vancouver: UBC Press, 1999).

7. Audrey Kobayashi, "Learning Their Place: Japanese/Canadian Workers/Mothers," in A. Kobayashi, ed., 45–72, *Women, Work and Place* (Montreal: McGill-Queen's Press, 1994).

8. Except where indicated, the transcripts are direct translations from the original Japanese. The original transcription was done by Natsuko Chubachi, and revisions are by Audrey Kobayashi. All the indented block text represents the words of the participants.

9. Dorinne K. Kondo, *Crafting Selves: Power, Gender and Discourses of Identity in a Japanese Workplace* (Chicago: University of Chicago Press, 1990).

10. According to Canadian census figures, the current rate of intermarriage is approximately 96 percent for Canadian-born Nikkei and over 60 percent for Nikkei born outside Canada.

11. Twenty-nine is the age traditionally considered the point beyond which a Japanese woman has no chance of getting married, and when those around her give up on the project of arranging a suitable mate. Women who are unmarried past the age of twenty-nine are referred to as "Christmas cakes," indicating that they are well aged.

12. Audrey Kobayashi, *A Demographic Profile of Japanese Canadians.*

CHAPTER THIRTEEN

Race, Gender, Ethnicity, and the Narrative of National Identity in the Films of Tizuka Yamazaki

NAOMI HOKI MONIZ

The Brazilian Japanese director Tizuka Yamazaki is one of the most important movie directors in Brazil today and, among the fourteen Brazilian women directors, the most famous and successful. In addition, she is a rarity among directors because of her predilection for making historical movies of epic dimensions with strong women main characters, including *Gaijin, Roads to Freedom* (1980), *Parahyba, Mulher Macho* (1983), and *Patriamada* (1984). Her last project, *Gaijin II*, is a work in progress that was scheduled for filming when I wrote this chapter in 2000. Her career can be seen as a study of the evolution of Brazilian social and political life during the past twenty years. This study will analyze the way she examines issues of race, gender, ethnicity, and national identity in her films. Yamazaki depicts the evolving negotiation of Brazilian national identity beyond the traditional Euro-based, patriarchally oriented model to include: 1) immigrants, 2) the political use of gender for the construction of state hegemony, 3) social movements incorporating feminism, Black militants, students, and workers, and 4) the transnational Brazilian Japanese *dekassegui* (guest workers) in Japan. Yamazaki's cinematic narrative moves from examining a nationalistic left-oriented, multiethnic workers' struggle in Brazil to defining a tropical cultural identity in Japan.

Before examining her movies, however, it would be useful to look at the interplay of race, gender, and ethnicity in the construction of a national identity in Brazil. Traditionally, the vision of national identity in the United States has been and continues to be based on an unspoken but accepted

Western norm of being white and Christian. In contrast, the Brazilian vision of national identity and consciousness has been based on the notion of racial diversity stemming from a shared past that is the repository of national essence. This past entails the ethnic roots of the three races that have become the foundation of the Brazilian people: Caucasian, Black, and Indian. As the movie critic Robert Stam notes, in the United States scholars have usually examined the discourse about national character in terms of the Puritan religious background of the first colonizers; or in terms of the frontier experience, emphasizing the rugged individualism of the national character; or by noting the democratic nature of the country's political institutions. The racial dimension of national identity in the Unites States, downplayed in the past, has only recently become dominant. By contrast, Brazilian intellectuals have always conceived of national identity in racially plural terms. They have been acutely aware of racial diversity in the formation of the nation. In fact, in Brazil, as in most of Latin America, there is broad recognition of the fact that the national culture is syncretic, hybrid, and mixed. As Stam notes, "The current Anglo academic discussion of post-colonial hybridity usually ignores and remains ignorant of the long history of such discussions in Latin American cultural criticism."[1] Yet these issues have been important in Brazil since colonial times, and have been at the center of the national discourse on identity, especially since the country achieved its independence from Portugal in 1822.

In Brazil, since the nineteenth century there has been an intellectual tradition devoted to the study of race and miscegenation, or, more precisely, of mestizo culture. Debates about the so-called uniqueness of race mixture, fundamental to the understanding of Brazilian national identity, evolved in different ways according to the different interpretations and constructions of scholars following different trends. Some promoted the literary use of the native Indian as a historical symbol of Brazil's cultural purity and nationalism. Some viewed the mixing of races as the reason Brazil was at a disadvantage with respect to other civilizations and preached a gradual whitening of the race, resulting in the eventual supplantation of Indian and African elements. Others presented theories of a progressive trend toward racial miscegenation, and some like Silvio Romero claimed that only a mestizo culture would be truly Brazilian. Finally, in the 1930s Gilberto Freyre—in opposition to earlier pessimistic studies—enthusiastically pioneered the theory that mixed cultures of the white, African, and Indian gave a mark of uniqueness to Brazilian culture and thus had to be cherished and preserved.

Earlier, in 1922, during the commemoration of the centennial of political independence from Portugal, the Modernist movement in Brazil rebelled against the Lusitanian Portuguese canon and declared its cultural independence. The so-called "Anthropophagic" movement launched its cry "Tupi or not Tupi, that is the question," a pun on the name of an Indian tribe intended to celebrate Brazil's Indian origins and also the cannibalization of a Portuguese bishop in the seventeenth century by native inhabitants who believed it appropriate to eat the enemy in order to acquire his power. The image also played on cannibalism as a rite with the purpose of assimilating strength and creating something new. One can thus say that multiculturalism, intertextuality, hybridity, or transnationality existed in Brazil significantly before these terms were conceptualized.

The intellectual, academic, and literary celebration of racial mixture as a metaphor of national unity would have an impact on the aspirations of a nationalist and homogeneous nation in the 1930s. It would also become an important argument in the debate about immigration that grew significantly, especially in the Brazilian south, after the abolition of slavery in 1888. Nationalists encouraged European immigrants who would help to "whiten" the Brazilian population, but who were desirable only as long as they were willing to mix with Brazilian mestizos and thus contribute to this national project of miscegenation. In the national immigration law project 391 proposed by Fidelis Reis, no more Africans were to be accepted into the country, and Asians would be limited to 5 percent of their total number already in Brazil. Some argued that both races, Negroes and Mongolians, were already represented by former slaves and the indigenous population. The immigration of Japanese became the focus of intense debate: some were in favor of and others against their presence. In the national assembly of 1934, questions were raised about the ability of Japanese people to mix with other racial groups. Popular at the time was the use of eugenics as a technology of knowledge and power to be applied in the social realm to advance the purification of race by regulating sexuality by regulating intermarriage between the existing population and new immigrants.[2] In this atmosphere it was noted that the Japanese formed what were referred to as "racial tumors," that is, they were of a race incapable of assimilation. Thus they came to be labeled "sulfur": like the chemical compound they were considered yellow and impervious to dissolution in the melting pot.[3]

Unlike the United States, with its racial segregation laws during that period, Brazil supported a project of imposed assimilation and nationalization in the effort to promote the development of a single national culture. The state repressed and banned any semblance of separatist or pluralist movements. The Constitution of 1934, article 121, paragraph 6, states that the entrance of immigrants into national territory would be subject to the restrictions necessary to guarantee ethnic integration. A few years later, in 1937, Getúlio Vargas declared "ethnic integration" an official policy of the dictatorship of the "New State." Using the same drive for an authentic national culture that represented Brazil's Luso-African and Indian roots, Vargas's populist government officially declared *samba*—an urban, regional dance associated with Rio de Janeiro—the homogenizing and hegemonic symbol of the cultural unity of the nation. It would celebrate the ubiquitous image of the *bahiana* portrayed by Carmen Miranda as representative of the charming and seductive Brazilian *mulata*.[4] The irony of the adoption of the image of the *bahiana* embodied by a white woman reconfirms the underlying paradox of gender, race, and class relations in Brazil. In this social and sexual economy, Black women were privileged as sexual objects, white women as wives, and gender and class inequality were perpetuated in the larger social structure.

Nevertheless, as in many Western countries, great changes were taking place in Brazil after World War I, including urbanization, industrialization, workers' unrest, and demonstrations by suffragettes. Thus urban upper- and middle-class women challenged patriarchal authorities at home and organized to achieve new roles in public. The phenomenon of the "modern girl" was ubiquitous, promoting new expectations and patterns of behavior that led to debates in many sectors of society. This was when intellectuals, medical doctors, psychiatrists, politicians, and eugenicists created a pseudoscientific discourse intended to support the improvement of the Brazilian race and women's essential role in this through marriage, sexuality, and maternity. While responding to the rising needs of women and creating opportunities for them, at the same time the government managed to preserve the institution of the family and, in so doing, to preserve existing levels of gender inequality.

In 1922, the vanguard Modernism movement had proposed a complete transformation and updating of cultural production in areas engaged in the construction of a true national identity, like music, the plastic arts, and literature. This radical effort of experimentation with *brasilidade* (Brazilianness) would be reaffirmed by the Cinema Novo ideologues. In the 1960s there was a reconfiguration of the notion of national identity among the left-oriented intellectuals that was more in tune with the anti-colonial wars in Africa and the rise of Fidel Castro in Cuba. The push for modernization started in the late 1950s and early 1960s, and the dominant media had become radio, television, cinema, the recording industry, and live shows that disseminated popular music. So a resistance was born against the American influence of rock and roll, Hollywood big budget movies, and what the Brazilians called imported *enlatado* popular culture (literally, "canned goods," referring to "ready-made" American movies, television series, and music). The objective of the New Cinema and MPB (popular Brazilian music) was to bring attention to and denounce Brazilian reality, the harshness of life in the backlands and the poverty of the slums. The goal was to produce an authentic popular and national art with a political mission to raise consciousness and offer liberation to the masses. Resistance to foreign influence and commercialization in the creation of cultural products was the order of the day. In contrast, *tropicalismo* appeared as a neo-anthropophagic countercultural movement that embraced all the elements considered nonnationalistic: the electric guitar, rock, pop music, and Caribbean influences that reflected postmodern transnational sensibilities.

This cultural battle took place during a military dictatorship that had its own nationalistic version of industrialization and progress: the Brazilian "economic miracle" that would bring the country recognition and establish it as a leader among emerging nations in the world. This government maximized the jingoism of Vargas's dictatorship and, through censorship, political repression, torture, and persecution, imposed a utopian vision of the nation's manifest destiny that was being built under the motto "*Brasil Grande*" (Great Brazil). In the same way that its predecessor, Vargas, had done, the military dictatorship that took over in 1964 placed great importance on the reaffirmation of patriarchy, which was important to the organization of social relations in the private realm and for the consolidation of absolute hegemony.

Because of the limited official space for social activism in the 1970s, there would be much development of grassroots civilian groups—including indigenous groups, labor groups, human rights groups, and groups of Afro-Brazilians, feminists, gays, and environmentalists—in alternative public spaces. All began to voice the discontent that would lead to the return to democracy after more than twenty years of authoritarian rule.

Tizuka Yamazaki, a third-generation Nikkei born in 1949, grew up in a town near the capital, São Paulo, and like most members of her generation, came of age under the dictatorship.[5] She was profoundly marked by this period, which was one of the most creative eras in Brazilian cinema with its Cinema Novo (New Cinema) movement. During the 1970s Yamazaki studied with and worked under Nelson Pereira dos Santos, one of the precursors of this movement. She also worked for its founder, Glauber Rocha, creator of the Third World cinema's "aesthetics of hunger" and director of the most representative films of the period. Yamazaki's career of producing long feature films began in 1980, after the end of this movement, but her works are informed by the tone set by these two great directors. From Santos she took her preference for natural settings and locales and her emphasis on popular culture, as well as a neo-realist style and themes. From Rocha she inherited a redemptive view of the multifaceted baroque country that is Brazil, with its multiple realities waiting for a revolution. Yamazaki adds other groups to her films, especially immigrants—what the historian Laura de Mello e Souza calls *desclassificados* (the omitted or the unrecognized)—who were excluded from the official national culture. She introduces a new voice, that of the woman immigrant, one that until then was not perceived as part of the symbolic reality or canonic history of Brazil.

Yamazaki directed her first movie in 1980, during the interregnum called the *abertura* (opening), the period of gradual return to democracy after twenty years of military dictatorship in Brazil. Her movies are informed by, and are also a response to, earlier polarized ideological-political struggles concerning national identity in a peripheral country going through a modernization process. As the film critic Ismail Xavier notes, the international and political conjuncture of the period allowed a significant affirmation of national cinemas in what seemed to be a first step toward an idealized new order, one more pluralistic in both the production and consumption of films. At the time, there were high hopes for drastic political and economic changes. Different and conflicting modes of change were advocated, ranging from guerrilla warfare to social democratic concepts to modernization in the capitalist framework, in either its social-democratic or conservative-authoritarian form. Despite these differences, everyone was willing to present an all-encompassing hegemonic view of historical changes and national identity.[6]

Much is said about Brazil's great racial diversity, but ethnicity in Brazil is often portrayed as a matter of the traditional distinctions—Black, white, and Indian, distinctions reinforced by the dominant discourse that embraces an ultimately Eurocentric national identity. Yamazaki's first movie, *Gaijin*, won many international prizes and was hailed as the first Brazilian motion picture to present a story about Japanese immigration in Brazil. The Nikkei director portrays the immigrants' role in an important period of Brazilian history, and in so doing shows them participating in the construction of the nation and the search for their own identity within it, thus challenging the conventional notion of Brazilian nationality and citizenship. The movie also presents the way minorities and other immigrants, along with Brazilian migrant sharecroppers, were marginalized and exploited as a cheap replacement for slave labor in the coffee plantations. Yamazaki subverts the common usage of the word *gaijin* among the Japanese living in Brazil as a term for anyone who is not ethnically Japanese (similar to the way *goyim* is used in Yiddish) by returning it to its original Japanese meaning: a foreigner. For her, the Japanese were marginalized twice: they were forgotten by their own Japanese government and excluded by the Brazilian elite.[7] Furthermore, this exclusion embraces all the heterolingual sharecroppers who work on the plantation. Japanese, Italian, and *nordestinos* (northeastern migrants), with their regional dialect, all become *gaijin*, left out of and alienated from the society in which they live.

Gaijin, Roads to Freedom thus has two narratives. First, it is the story of Yamazaki's own grandmother, Titoe, who was among the first Japanese immigrants to arrive in Brazil in 1908. Second, it is the story of the way the director presents the first story as she reflects on her own conflicts about her identity as a Nikkei. As a young woman Yamazaki had stayed as far away as possible from the *colonia* (Japanese community) and rejected her Nisei mother's demand that she *nihonjin-rashiku* (behave more like a Japanese). Distancing herself from her Japanese heritage, she avoided dating Nikkei men, went on to study in Brasilia, which had a minimal Japanese population, chose a career atypical for a Nikkei at the time, and also chose to become a single mother.

The movie opens with a view of modern São Paulo and the voice-over of the narrator who remembers her first years in Brazil in a flashback. Titoe, as the first person narrator, begins, "I was a young woman of sixteen ..." and relates how she immigrated to Brazil at her brother's request in an arranged marriage to his friend Yamada Kawada, a Japanese Russian war hero. Many groups of families were artificially put together to form the minimum requirement of three fit men to labor in the fields—popularly known as "three hoes" per family.[8] In this aspect, the requirements for Japanese immigrants to Brazil differed greatly from those applying to the United States, which allowed single men to immigrate alone.

Japanese immigrants to Brazil were attracted by promises of quick riches to be gained in the New World El Dorado, encompassing vast lands and wealth. The movie shows the way many immigrants arrived in the seaport of Santos and were taken to the immigration center in São Paulo. There, among European immigrants—mostly Spanish and Italian—they were separated into groups to be taken to different coffee plantations. Culturally and linguistically they were totally at a loss. Their sense of anomie and estrangement in the new country is contrasted with the gregariousness and communicative ease of the officially favored Mediterranean immigrants. The death of a child due to food poisoning during the long journey by train casts an ominous shadow over their lives and increases their apprehension.

Local authorities and the aristocratic plantation owner meet the immigrants at the train station in the interior with great pomp and a marching band. The plantation owner's comments reveal the reasons Japanese immigrants were chosen: all were dressed in Western fashion and were clean and disciplined. Above all, they were not troublemakers, an allusion to unruly, politicized European laborers. For the landowners, the immigrants are the favored labor replacement for slaves, who would hardly be able to compete with the often educated or more skilled new arrivals. Also, true to the Cinema Novo tradition, the movie implicitly criticizes the alliance between the coffee barons, who ruled the country, and Anglo coffee buyers, which perpetuated Brazil's economic dependence on foreign markets, at the same time demonstrating the way the Brazilian elite ignored the needs of the masses.

The long trip of Titoe's group in an oxcart slowly introduces a sense of the harsh realities of the new land, including the heat, muddy roads, miserable living conditions in old slave housing and, above all, the radical change from the Japanese diet to one they considered inedible: beans, manioc flour, and beef jerky. Hard work harvesting and clearing new land for coffee growing, carried out under the watchful eye of Chico, the foreman, is made more difficult by slavelike working conditions. After a few years of work they realize very little profit, due to the exorbitant prices charged for their supplies by the plantation-owned and -operated store.[9] An Italian immigrant decides to protest the working conditions and to organize the workers in a strike. Yamada, Titoe's husband, is revealed as being stubborn and incapable of change, unlike his wife, who is always observing and learning the ways of her new home.

As the Japanese father and husband, Yamada replicates the patriarchal order undergirding the plantation setup, the absolute power of the father/husband/boss. Women and children were subjected to social norms and values that reiterated men's power and domination. As the leader of the Japanese immigrant group, Yamada refuses to join the Italians in protest and has the Japanese keep themselves isolated from the troublemakers.

The head of the Italian family is beaten up by Chico and other assailants and then expelled by Brazilian government officials, accused of subverting the national order. The physical and psychological stress breaks the spirit of the farmers: Titoe's brother runs away from the farm, deserting his family, probably leaving to search for the young Italian woman he fell in love with; one of the women, homesick for Japan, commits suicide, and her husband becomes an alcoholic. When Yamada dies of malaria and leaves Titoe alone to raise their daughter she finally decides to take action and lead the group away from the farm.

Titoe embodies the experience of Japanese women in arranged marriages, *omiai kekkon*, the norm among Japanese of that period. Her role is a portrait of the complexities and difficulties facing a young woman who initially rejects her husband but eventually learns to be loyal, if not affectionate, to the father of her child. Yamazaki honors the Japanese women who had to leave their native country and move to foreign lands in arranged marriages with men they hardly knew. Like other *colonas*, or women sharecroppers, on the coffee farms they had two jobs: to work in the fields side by side with the men at a lower pay rate ("half hoe"), and then to prepare the food and take care of the children and home.[10]

Yamazaki was strongly criticized by some Japanese viewers for the way she portrayed the immigrants' experience.[11] One of the major criticisms was directed against the fact that she suggests an interracial romance between Titoe and Tonho, the farm bookkeeper. The director highlights sharp differences in relations between genders: Brazilian gallantry and romantic manners are contrasted to the violence and perceived coldness of a Japanese arranged marriage with no room for romance. But the criticism from Japanese viewers derived from the fact that such a relationship could not have developed because at that time the Japanese community condemned interracial marriages and ostracized those who married outside their race. The isolation of the Japanese community and its lack of interaction with other groups are not emphasized in the movie, and the director's choice represents the fact that interracial marriages have become more the norm than the exception for Nikkei nowadays, which she presents as desirable.

In the suggested romance between Tonho and Titoe there is also a discourse of class solidarity. Like Chico, Tonho was a poor boy educated by the plantation owners and put in charge of the administration of the farm. Unlike Chico, who abuses his power, Tonho sympathizes with the workers and eventually helps Titoe and her group escape from the farm. At the end of the movie, when Titoe is shown settled in the city with a job in a textile factory, she seems to have achieved independence as a working woman, and to lead a tranquil life with her daughter Chinobu. At Yamada's deathbed she had promised to return to Japan, but now with a Brazilian daughter she is determined to make a life in the new country. The movie ends with Titoe happily going for a rendezvous with Tonho, who has now become a union organizer and is speaking to an assembly of workers against the exploitation of all working people, including immigrants.

Thus, the movie finishes with the promise of a possible revolution, a moment when disenfranchised groups could form an alliance in their class struggle and in their search for a place in a harmonious multiracial workers' utopia. This scene is the director's response to the traditional isolationist position of Japanese immigrants, and suggests their need to work together to form a new and more just society in Brazil. Obviously, in the beginning, isolation was natural, due to language, cultural barriers, and especially, the geographical separation entailed in the agricultural setup. Nonetheless, deploying some sentimental clichés, Yamazaki focuses on the openness and warmth of Brazilian people who worked with immigrants: the migrant sharecropper who teaches them how to harvest coffee, or how to use homeopathic medicine, or the Black man who teaches Portuguese to the children. In fact, historically, poor workers and former slaves, who often helped immigrants in their adjustment to the cultivation of tropical crops and plants and to a new form of land management, were often perceived as inferior by the immigrants themselves. The Japanese did achieve social mobility and economic success at a level that has not been experienced by the Black or Indian population even today, an issue that is also raised by the movie. Nevertheless, Yamazaki presents a positive view of race relations, one based on Brazilian kindness and generosity toward others. The movie foreshadows ensuing integration and the love the Japanese and their descendants would come to have for their new home after World War II.

In her next two movies Yamazaki follows in the Cinema Novo tradition with a careful observation of Brazilian social reality, with a particular concern to show sectors that the system left out, especially during the dictatorship: feminists, environmentalists, workers, indigenous people, Blacks, and neighborhood groups. In Cinema Novo the idea of "nation" was central to framing the space where interactions between individuals and existing social structures took place, and the imprint of the director inevitably presented a totalized view of the country. This trend toward an allegorical mode in literature and cinema became typical of the period under dictatorship, as if to become an alternate to the reality censored by the government. Yamazaki addresses the problems created by the dominant nationalistic discourse, as well as the authoritarian frame of allegorical films speaking for the subaltern. She chooses to present a more fragmented view of reality: an autobiographic, feminist-constructivist perspective, or documentary-journalistic style, especially in her next two movies, *Parahyba* and *Patriamada*.

Yamazaki's movie *Parahyba, Mulher Macho* is based on a true story that happened in the late 1920s and early 1930s in the northeast of Brazil. It is a love story set during a pivotal political struggle, when the caudillo Getúlio Vargas, from the state of Rio Grande do Sul, wrestled power away from the old regional oligarchy dominated by São Paulo and Minas Gerais by forming alliances with governors in the northeast. In this political setting Yamazaki studies the anatomy of the patriarchal tradition, its rules governing love and sex, and its culture of violence. Patriarchy is one of the major moral ideological values in the northeastern part of Brazil, and the heroine of the story is a freethinker, a poet and a sexually liberated woman who defies this extremely traditional society. Anayde is the "macho woman" (liberated woman) who shocked society with her nonconformist ways and free sexuality. The daughter of a lower-middle-class family, she is a brilliant student who is denied a job at the school from which she graduated. Unable to teach in the convent school run for the benefit of the elite, she goes to teach villagers who fish for a living. Wearing short hair *a la garçonne* and the short dress of a flapper, she is the image of the modern woman, understood locally as an "easy" woman. As such, she is raped by a fisherman, but the director gives the episode a triumphant tone as the character goes to wash herself in the sea after the attack and comes out triumphantly, beautifully purified and metamorphosed by the water as a goddess, Venus Dyanomene, risen from the sea. In time elected a beauty queen, she gains access to the finest social clubs in the state capital, João Pessoa. There she flaunts her poetry and her beauty, and meets openly with her lover, the journalist Dantas. Politically he belongs to a conservative landowning family, and for this reason he has become an enemy of the state president, Epitácio Pessoa, a progressive and ally of Getúlio Vargas. Pessoa, in search of political revenge, has the state troops invade Dantas's house, and there a cache of letters and erotic poems exchanged between the lovers is discovered and made public. To defend Anayde's honor, Dantas kills Epitácio Pessoa, which becomes an excuse for Vargas to galvanize his allies and take over the presidency of Brazil.

In this fashion, the film explores the far-reaching cultural, sociopolitical, and economic changes in gender relations at the time. Brazil's deeply entrenched social hierarchy had undermined gender equality in subtle ways. Legal equality was ineffectual without transformations in social relations. Female radicals who refused to show deference to men were faced with hostility and rejection that often jeopardized their physical and mental health. In her film narrative, Yamazaki develops a broader understanding of political realities by establishing the relevance of gender in the construction of state hegemony in Brazil. The legitimation of Getúlio Vargas's dictatorial power depended in large degree on the reorganization of social relations in the private realm, specifically the restructuring of patriarchy that was promoted by the military government that ended in 1984. Dantas commits suicide in prison, and in real life Anayde would kill herself six months later. Yamazaki, however, didn't end the movie on this sour note and "wanted to make a positive statement" about the gains Anayde had achieved as a professional and a woman. The film closes with Anayde walking through the streets where the civil war was going on, oblivious to this "predominantly male world" of war, bombs, killing, and battles, finally standing alone but defiant amid the destruction.[12] This movie is a feminist reconstruction and an exemplary story of an earlier feminist heroine with allusions to what was going on in Brazil at the end of authoritarian rule and to the significant growth of the women's movement in Brazil.

Yamazaki's next film, *Patriamada* (Beloved Country), is a semidocumentary and a movie about the making of the movie itself during the great spontaneous and intoxicating popular demonstrations of 1984. These demonstrations in favor of direct elections after twenty years of dictatorship took place all over the country. Yamazaki goes back to the *cinema verité* techniques of Cinema Novo, utilizing portable equipment, with no mood music or voiceovers, so that the viewer is immersed in the moment. As in traditional epics, viewers are plunged in *media res* (the middle of the action) and have the impression that they are witnessing things as they happen. Thus they are forced to make sense of scenes and relationships, seemingly without manipulation of the "truth." Like Rocha in his last films, Yamazaki uses documentary-style camera work, giving the audience a feeling of being overwhelmed by events and of having a limited point of view, as if the ongoing events had not yet been interpreted through the agency of narrative.

The main theme is the "historical moment"—the long-awaited revolution and the massive public demonstrations taking place. The film unfolds through the narrative of a love triangle: the female interest is a young journalist, Carolina Diniz; her friend and lover, Goias, is a film director who is making the movie *Patriamada*; and the old and powerful Rocha, the scion of a traditional family, is an industrialist whose sympathies are with the demonstrators and who becomes a "a traitor of his class." The movie documents the force of the masses in the streets, in every corner of the nation; students, housewives, feminists, Indians, Black militants, gays, student activists, celebrities, neighborhood association leaders, and workers unite in their demand for the reestablishment of democracy. These *desclassificados* represent the fragmentation of the monolithic Brazilian national identity propagated by the military regime.

Patriamada begins and ends with a banner showing Saint George fighting the dragon, the same image that appears in the opening triptych of a movie by Glauber Rocha, *Antonio das Mortes*. Yamazaki honors and adopts Rocha's most cherished symbol of Brazil's potential for revolution and redemption: Saint George, the heroic saint fighting evil. In Rocha's movie, the icon functions as a mythical frame that precedes the movie's action,[13] and as an allusion to the revolution Antonio will lead against the internal enemy, the powerful landowners. The image of Saint George fighting the dragon is ubiquitous in every home in Brazil, and it also appears in Yamazaki's movie as a sculpture in the home of Goias, an admirer of Glauber Rocha and a movie director like him. Goias is in search of the Brazilians' "beloved country" and he goes into the streets, camera in hand, to all corners of Brazil to document the coming political change. There is another twist to the iconography of warriors in this movie: Saint George is replaced by the figure of Lina, a young, idealistic woman who fights evil with her words and the camera. She is a modern version of the woman warrior except that this time she is a witness documenting the masses as agents of their destiny as they demand the end of dictatorship in Brazil.

The hope for a complete return to democracy fails with the institution of the collegiate vote for the civilian president. Their hopes for a complete change deferred, the revolutionaries settle for some kind of personal and private happiness in a possible ménage à trois. As the trio watches another demonstration in front of a cathedral, they embrace each other happily, like a modern version of the sacred family covered by the banner of Saint George. Lina embodies the professional progress of women and the personal independence they have achieved. Women's sexual liberation is also presented as an important element in the movie, explored through another female character—Goias's Nikkei ex-wife, who comes back home to pick up their son after having left for Paris with her lover for a year. Goias is at a loss managing the house and the child, Ilya, played by Yamazaki's real son. Ironically, the only person who really takes care of Ilya is the maid. The director, who once declared that she could not be a housewife and a professional, subtly exposes class issues, as the liberation of women is often achieved at the expense of other women who have not benefited from the women's movement, in this case the maid.

Patriamada provides a bridge to Yamazaki's next project, *Gaijin II*, in which she examines the lives of *dekassegui*, Japanese-Brazilian guest workers in Japan who had to leave their "beloved country" in the 1980s. The project was begun in the late 1990s; Yamazaki wanted to start filming it in the spring of 2000. The narrative begins where it left off in the first movie, in the 1920s, and then covers six decades, bringing us to the 1990s. Chinobu, Titoe's daughter, marries and moves with her family to the state of Paraná, where they become landowners, the story of many Japanese pioneers in that region. In the 1940s, Chinobu's husband is killed by a Shindo Renmei terrorist.

The narrative then moves up to the 1970s, when Chinobu's daughter is married to a prosperous Spanish soybean farmer who loses his fortune and decides to emigrate to Japan. After three years without news of her husband, Titoe's granddaughter decides to travel to Japan with their two daughters in search of her husband. With this plot, Yamazaki wants to portray the dilemmas faced by these new sojourners: their difficulty in adjusting to Japan despite their ethnicity, the rejection they suffer, and their own prejudice against Japanese people and culture.

According to Yamazaki, the story of the *dekassegui* in Japan is a story of triumph, contrary to the popular image. From her point of view, they have been able to achieve a level of prosperity in Japan in ten years that took their ancestors seventy years to achieve in Brazil. According to her research, there are more than five hundred businesses established by Brazilian Nikkei in Japan, including newspapers in Portuguese and cable television showing Brazilian programs. She says that Brazilian Japanese have much to learn from and much to offer Japan and vice versa. She wants to show their ability to adjust and live in multicultural harmony, as they have done in Brazil.

In conclusion, Yamazaki has become an artist who has expressed a casually nonchalant attitude about race. She is an artist liberated by the feeling that she did not have to perform according to what was expected from her as a Japanese Brazilian. In fact, after directing *Gaijin* she didn't want to be limited to addressing Japanese themes. So she has mastered her profession, received accolades, and founded her own production company. Intellectually, she has entertained an intertextual dialogue with the national patriarchal discourse and Cinema Novo by recreating a new discourse experience based on her own experience as a female, as a Japanese descendant, and as a Third World artist in Brazil. Yamazaki has been careful to avoid what Foucault has called "the indignity of speaking for others," so common among Brazilian artists and intellectuals.

Yamazaki has expanded and reformulated representations of feminine identity, community, and nationalism to account for the complexities of race, class, ethnicity, and gender and for the issues of women in relationship to metaphoric and geographical space. Titoe in many ways represents the experience of women's silence or submissiveness. Often Yamazaki represents the experience of women's silence as a negative stereotypical trait of women in general, and of Japanese women in particular. She strategically deploys silence, problematizing the role of history and historiography and juxtaposing nationally endorsed versions of Brazilian history against silenced histories. Yamazaki's grandmother's oral narrative and the recovered history of Anayde, a woman who sees herself as a historical agent resisting forms of oppression through social activism, opened space that brought considerations of desire, pleasure, and sexuality into the public.

Patriamada shows how the political scene in Brazil had changed: how the earlier social divisions are less clear, and how authoritarian rule has become much subtler. Iconoclasm is no longer an option because there is no longer an image of strong authority to counter. It also reflects the rejection of the instrumentalization of culture for the left's political ends, as well as the adoption of an anarchism of identity whose most iconoclastic expression was embracing kitsch, and the looks and demands of Black and Indian power. In short, Yamazaki's films invite a radical mutation of our understanding of sexual difference, which epitomizes a profound and unprecedented transformation of the "man-woman" relationship.

In *Gaijin II*, Yamazaki examines the phenomenon of the *dekassegui*, a quarter million Brazilian Nikkei who didn't want to leave their beloved Brazil and consider themselves "economic exiles" in Japan.[14] In this movie, Yamazaki will have to examine the effects of the globalization of culture and economics, the rise of transnational power, and the consequent hollowing out of the nation-state that has presumed itself the vigilant guardian of national culture. There is no longer an identifiable *patriamada*, as Goias and Lina find out by revealing the diversity of voices and identities of Brazil.

Admitted to Japan because of their ethnic ancestry, once in Japan, the dekassegui differentiate themselves from the local population by reaffirming their Brazilian identity for a host of different reasons. Thus, in Japan the dekassegui have developed schools of samba and propagated indigenous and Afro-Brazilian carnival customs. As a consequence, subjective and national identities are negotiated in relation to questions of ethnoscapes, globalized mass cultures and visions of universal values, and ideoscapes of future possibilities of citizenship in Brazil and Japan.[15] It shows how the rational, integrated self is being replaced by a postmodern self that is decentered, multidimensional, and mutable. Yet it is also about an identity, *tropicalismo brasileiro*, that has been disarmed of its iconoclastic character and ability to "scandalize the Left." This newly developing identity has become pasteurized and suffused with kitsch, and it is an affirmation of an image of pseudo-Brazilianness intended to be consumed in a globalized economy.

In Japan, Nikkei are allowed to work as foreigners with favored status due to their ethnicity. They have faced severe housing and job shortages and national debates about their immigrant status, debates that now arise concerning international borders and migrant/immigrant identities. The hysterical rhetoric about or the silence surrounding the presence of the foreign worker among the Japanese reflects anxiety about national identity or even the sovereignty of states threatened by globalization. In response, dekasseguis have built thriving communities, businesses, and cultural centers, and have organized themselves to define community-based needs and develop courses of action around issues central to metropolitan and national discourse: education, housing, immigration, and anti-discrimination laws.

In sum, dekasseguis have negotiated complex differences of nationality, ethnicity, class, gender, and sexuality to forge new bonds of identity and community as they jostle for power and control over resources. By examining the varied ways dekassegui use terms like "family," "community," and "homeland," Yamazaki intends to expose how the processes of cultural reinvention of Brazilianness often exist in deep tension with dominant and assimilationist trends. As good Brazilian multiculturalists, they might well be in the vanguard, acting as cultural traders of the Brazilian *mestisaje*, of Asian tropicalism in Japan, as they participate in the transformation of the society diagnosed by Japanese officials as needing to become more open and more multicultural in the globalized world of the twenty-first century.[16]

Notes

1. Robert Stam, *Tropical Multiculturalism: A Comparative History of Race in Brazilian Cinema and Culture* (Durham, N.C.: Duke University Press, 1997), 17.

2. V. R. Beltrão Marques, *A Medicalização da Raça* (Campinas: University of Campinas Press, 1994).

3. Oliveira Vianna, *Raça e assimilação* (São Paulo: Companhia Editora Nacional, 1932), 201–5.

4. The irony that Carmen Miranda was a whitened version of the Black *bahiana* was not raised at the time. As a singer of sambas, Carmen Miranda disseminated a popular genre identified with poor Black *favelas* of Rio de Janeiro and was generally looked down upon by the Brazilian elite.

5. She lived in Atibaia, near the city of São Paulo, where her father was a vegetable farmer. Yamazaki began architectural studies but left to study cinema in Brasilia. When the school was closed by the government during student demonstrations in the late 1960s, she finished her degree in Rio de Janeiro. Biographical information about Yamazaki is available in Japanese in Shuhei Hosokawa, *Shinema-ya, Burajiru o iku: nikkei imin no kyoshu to aidentiti* (Tokyo: Shinchosha, 1999), 186–209; Saefuji Mifuji, "Tizuka to Yurika: Gaijin ni miru shimai no kento," in *Koronia geinoushi* (Tokyo: Koronia Geinou Shi, 1986), 280–84. Biographical and film information was also taken from personal interviews by the author in June 1998 and December 12, 1999.

6. See Ismail Xavier, *Allegories of Underdevelopment: Aesthetics and Politics in Modern Brazilian Cinema* (Minneapolis: University of Minnesota Press, 1997).

7. Saefuji Mifuji, "Tizuka to Yurika."

8. M. Sílvia C. B. Bassanezi, "Família e força de trabalho no colonato: subsídios para a compreensão demográfica no período cafeeiro," *Textos NEPO* (8) (Campinas: NEPO/UNICAMP, 1986).

9. The movie *Picture Bride* (1994), by Kayo Hatta, portrays the life of brides sent from Japan to Hawai'i, then a territory of the United States. Like *Gaijin*, the story is narrated by a woman who reminisces about her early days. The experiences of Japanese immigrants on the sugar plantations in the islands—the hardship and meager pay, and the personal and psychological difficulties in adjusting to a new land and to life with yet-unknown husbands—are very similar to the experience related in Yamazaki's movie.

10. M. Aparecida Moraes Silva, "De Colona a Boia-Fria," in *Historia das mulheres no Brasil*, Mary del Priore, ed. (São Paulo: Contexto, 1997; 2d ed.), 555–77.

11. Shuhei Hosokawa, *Shinema-ya, Burajiru o iku*.

12. Yamazaki, Tizuka, *Istoe cinema brasileiro 6*, ed. 1452 (São Paulo: Ed. Grupo de Comunicações Trés), 5.

13. Ismail Xavier, *Allegories of Underdevelopment*, 155–200.

14. Shuichi Watanabe and Katsutoshi Sato, eds., *Dekasseguis "os exilados económicos": A Realização de um Sonho* (Tokyo: Kashiwa Purano, S.A., 1995).

15. Arjun Appadurai, "Global Ethnoscapes: Notes on Queries for a Transnational Anthropology," in *Recapturing Anthropology, Working in the Present*, Richard Fox, ed. (Santa Fe, N.M.: School of the Americas Research Press, 1991), 191–210.

16. Doug Struck, "Think American: Japanese are Advised," *The Washington Post*, Jan. 20, 2000, 1, A18.

CHAPTER FOURTEEN

The Japanese-Brazilian
Dekasegi Phenomenon

An Economic Perspective

EDSON MORI

Originally the Japanese term *dekasegi* referred to a farmer who, during the harsh winters in Japan, migrated from rural to urban areas in pursuit of temporary work in manufacturing. At the end of winter he returned to the rural area. Over time, however, the meaning of the word has changed. Now it is used to refer to migrant workers in Japan who intend eventually to return to their native land, like the Brazilian-born Japanese who work in Japan and plan to return later to Brazil.

The contribution of the Japanese-Brazilians to the Brazilian economy has been tremendous during the fifteen years of the dekasegi migration phenomenon (1985–99). The figures are impressive. Every year during this period, Brazilians of Japanese descent working in Japan have sent back home an average of $2 billion in U.S. dollars. In terms of their income, Brazilian dekasegi in Japan represent one of Brazil's top three export items; in terms of balance of payments, they follow traditional export items such as coffee and iron ore and are equal to the value of manufactured steel products. Furthermore, these remittances paid for almost all of Brazil's imports of Japanese goods during the period. According to some sources, during the height of the expanding Japanese economy these figures could have reached $4 billion, which would represent more than 5 percent of the official estimated global volume of remittances ($71 billion in 1990).

The main objectives of the majority of the more than 200,000 Japanese-Brazilians temporarily working in Japan include supplementing the income of relatives back home, buying a house, and opening their own business. Most dekasegi left Brazil with the intention of returning when they had accumulated enough money. As of the end of 1998, Brazilians were the third largest foreign resident group in Japan, representing almost 15 percent of legal foreign residents in Japan. The other two major groups of legal foreign residents in Japan are Koreans and Chinese. The number of Japanese-Brazilians returning to Japan as temporary migrant workers in the fifteen years between 1985 and 1999 surpassed one quarter of a million, and has also surpassed the total number of Japanese citizens who have immigrated to Brazil since 1908.

Japanese immigration to the Americas was strong during the early part of the twentieth century. Presently, Brazil maintains the largest community of people of Japanese ancestry outside Japan. It is currently estimated that there are about 1.3 million Brazilians of Japanese descent, mostly concentrated in the states of São Paulo and Paraná.

Unlike agricultural migrant workers who travel from Mexico to the neighboring United States, the dekasegi migrant workers travel more than twenty thousand miles to get to their destination, a unique occurrence in the history of mankind. These Brazilian citizens of Japanese ancestry voluntarily travel to the other side of the globe for short periods of time in order to seek employment as temporary migrant workers. This form of mass migration has only become viable due to the globalization of the world economy.

The dekasegi phenomenon would not have occurred without the technological and economic advances of the global market economy. Such advances, however, are a double-edged sword. On the one hand, technological advances in transportation and communications have made the movement of people, information, and capital easier, cheaper, and faster than ever before. The dekasegi phenomenon became viable as the growing global market economy drove a significant decline of both airfares and telecommunication costs during the last fifteen years. But on the darker side, market capitalism in the late twentieth century has increased the income disparity between rich and poor countries. Clearly, the impetus for such mass migrations of workers has been the great disparity of income between Brazilian and Japanese economies.

This chapter examines the deskasegi phenomenon of the last fifteen years from an economic perspective. Focusing on the remittances sent by dekasegi workers from Japan to Brazil, I describe the macroeconomic benefits of this exchange and draw some conclusions about the dekasegi phenomenon on this basis.

The Beginning of the Dekasegi Phenomenon

Although documentation is scarce, there are some indications that the first dekasegi from Brazil arrived in Japan in 1985. There appears to be no one reason that can explain the beginning of the dekasegi phenomenon. It probably came about due to a combination of circumstances that had to do with macro- and microeconomic conditions, governmental policies, and changes in the labor market.

From the macroeconomic point of view, in 1985 the Japanese economy was experiencing an unprecedented economic boom with very low levels of unemployment (2.6 percent) and high levels of economic growth (6.6 percent). In contrast, the Brazilian economy showed record levels of unemployment (12.5 percent), a three-digit inflation level, and low liquidity deepened by the debt crisis in Mexico. The extreme contrast between the state of the two economies in 1985 was one reason the dekasegi phenomenon began.

From the microeconomic point of view, emerging economic opportunities in 1985 can be accounted for by looking at labor migration in terms of a cost-benefit analysis. The most tangible cost of relocating to Japan was airfare, whereas the concrete benefit was the opportunity to earn higher wages in Japan. The significant difference in wages between Japan and Brazil was exacerbated by the increased value of the yen vis-à-vis the dollar during the Plaza Accord in 1985 and the high devaluation of Brazilian currency vis-à-vis the dollar, reflected in currency exchange rates on the black market (see Table 14.1). Basically, the huge gap between the value of the yen and Brazilian currency created an unprecedented economic advantage for Brazilian workers in Japan. In addition, increased competition in the airline industry due to deregulation caused transport costs to decrease significantly. The cost of air travel from Brazil to Japan during this period decreased by more than half, further facilitating the high volume of migration.

Japanese governmental policies in 1985 were relatively benevolent toward the initial wave of Japanese-Brazilian migrants. Japanese immigration laws are very restrictive toward foreign laborers in general; however, in the case of foreigners with Japanese ancestry, renewable annual permanent visas were easily obtained as long as the migrant had relatives in Japan. This was one of the main reasons for Japanese-Brazilians to start migrating to Japan as temporary workers. The intent of this Japanese public policy was later confirmed with the introduction of the new Immigration Act in 1990, which established that all individuals with proven Japanese ancestry would be eligible for a permanent resident visa for up to three years. Such eligibility was also applicable to the worker's spouse, regardless of the spouse's ethnic background.

Finally, from the labor market perspective, the high growth of the Japanese economy in the 1980s led to a labor shortage in specific industries, such as construction and manufacturing. Construction firms were obliged to look for foreign labor, since Japanese workers were not willing to perform jobs considered by the Japanese as the "three k's": *kitanai* (dirty), *kitsui* (difficult),

TABLE 14.1

Macroeconomic Data of the Brazilian Economy, 1985–99

	1985	1986	1987	1988	1989	1990	1991	1992
GDP growth (%)	7.8	7.5	3.5	–0.1	3.2	–4.3	1.0	–0.5
GDP per capita in USD	1,598	1,905	2,057	2,196	2,893	3,219	2,764	2,694
Inflation (%)[a]	228	68	367	892	1,636	1,639	459	1,129
USD Premium[b]								
Black/Official rate (%)	30	60	28	53	106	29	10	13
Tourism/Official rate (%)[c]	n/a	n/a	n/a	n/a	n/a	n/a	n/a	n/a
Unemployment rate (%)[d]	12.5	9.8	9.0	9.7	8.8	10.0	11.6	14.9

	1993	1994	1995	1996	1997	1998	1999
GDP growth (%)	4.9	5.9	4.2	2.8	3.7	0.1	0.2
GDP per capita in USD	2,901	3,569	4,554	4,920	5,037	4,798	n/a
Inflation (%)[a]	2,491	1,173	23	10	4.8	–1.8	7.5
USD Premium[b]							
Black/Official rate (%)	22	1.0	0.5	3.4	5.9	6.7	7.0
Tourism/Official rate (%)[c]	n/a	0.8	0.8	1.1	1.0	2.1	n/a
Unemployment rate (%)[d]	14.7	14.3	13.2	15.0	15.7	18.2	20.0

SOURCE: Fundação Getúlio Vargas, *Conjuntura economica* 53, no. 8 (Aug. 1999).

[a]The index adopted was the IPC-FIPE, a Brazilian consumer price index.

[b]The premium measures the average of the year.

[c]The difference between black and tourism rates is that the latter is regulated and normally used for tourists who need to buy USD in the banks. The black market disappeared in 1999.

[d]The unemployment index adopted was the one that measures the rate in the Great São Paulo City (DIEESE).

and *kiken* (dangerous). These "three k's" were later joined by what the Japanese-Brazilian workers would label "the additional two k's": *kibishii* (demanding) and *kirai* (detestable). The decrease in the supply of laborers was due to the increase in the average Japanese standard of living. Manufacturing firms, mainly the automotive and electronics industries, also faced a labor shortage, not only due to the five k's, but also to the need to lower production costs to keep their products competitive as exports, a pressure that increased with the sudden appreciation of the yen in 1985. Under the Japanese *keiretsu* system, the demand from large automotive firms to decrease costs was passed through to small and medium firms, which were the ones that started absorbing a significant number of dekasegi.

The service industry has also seen an increase in the demand for Japanese-Brazilians in recent years in some labor-intensive subsectors. These include: 1) food preparation for traditional Japanese boxed lunches, or *bento*, in the metropolitan Tokyo area, 2) hotel attendants and maids for Japanese-style hotels, or *ryokan*, located in hot-spring areas (Nagano and Gumma prefectures), and 3) golf course maintenance and caddying. The common element in these jobs is that they require neither skilled workers nor Japanese language proficiency. Although there are no figures to confirm that the salaries of dekasegi were lower than those of Japanese—and that consequently the employer's average labor cost for a dekasegi was lower than that for an equivalent Japanese worker—there are some indications that such was the case. In practice, some indirect and direct benefits, such as access to private pension plans or payment of bonuses, were not extended to the dekasegi. In addition, migration studies show that upon entry to the host country labor market, migrants generally earn less than the native-born doing comparable work.[1]

Actually, all the factors described above, presented as reasons for the beginning of the dekasegi phenomenon, are consistent with the various theories attempting to explain the causes of international migration. Both national and individual perspectives are consistent with the neo-classical macro- and microeconomic theory on international migration. On the one hand, the macro perspective affirms that the major factor driving individual migration decisions is the difference in supply and demand for labor between the points of origin and the destination. On the other hand, the micro perspective affirms that the major driving force for the decision to migrate has to do with individual cost-benefit calculations.

The "new economics" theory of migration views migration as a group strategy to diversify sources of income, minimize risks to the household, and overcome barriers to obtaining credit and capital. Such a viewpoint is consistent with what happened in the latter stage of the dekasegi phenomenon, but not in the initial stage; initially, that is, migration was more of a serendipitous, rather than a planned, phenomenon. However, the above theory also holds that governments influence migration through their immigration policies (regulations), which indeed was a decisive factor in the case of the dekasegi.

Lastly, the labor market perspective is supported by the dual labor market theory that holds that to maintain low labor costs as a variable factor of production, employers seek low-wage migrant workers. One indicator supporting this thesis has to do with the high number of dekasegi initially engaged in labor-intensive activities such as construction and export-oriented assembling.

The Evolution of the Dekasegi Phenomenon

During the fifteen years of the dekasegi phenomenon, the initial conditions mentioned in the previous section that generated such a population movement might have been quite different from those that perpetuated it. This is because in the course of migration new conditions arose that came to function as independent causes themselves, making additional migration more likely. Technically such a process is known as "cumulative causation," and it is certainly observable in the case of the dekasegi, whose waves of migration from Brazil to Japan can be divided into at least three periods.

The first wave occurred between 1985 and 1989. Migrant groups were usually composed of single men, with ages distributed at the two extremes: either old, mostly Issei (first-generation Japanese immigrant) men, or young, mostly Nisei (second-generation) men who had relatives in Japan. Both groups had no fixed expectations about the period of time they would be staying, and had good prospects for making average yearly earnings of up to $60,000. Most of these men were engaged in the construction and manufacturing industries. Family ties, as well as a command of Japanese, were important; both were in fact essential for getting a work permit.

During the second period, from 1990 to 1995, migrants were typically single men and single women, with an age distribution from eighteen to sixty years old. Again, they were mostly Nisei and Issei, but this group expected to stay for a fixed period of one to two years and expected to make average yearly earnings of up to $60,000 for men and $36,000 for women. This was the boom period of the dekasegi phenomenon. During this period the range of activities started to diversify to service sectors, such as bento, ryokan, health care, and golf courses, with the admission of women dekasegi into the labor force. Knowledge of the Japanese language was less important than in the earlier period. The 1990 change in immigration law eliminated the requirement for family ties and instead allowed migrants simply to demonstrate their Japanese ancestry.

In the third period, from 1996 to the present, migrants included significantly more couples and families with children. Migrants usually ranged from eighteen to forty years old and included mostly Nisei, Sansei (third generation), and spouses without Japanese ancestry. This group came with the expectation of staying for more than three years and anticipated average yearly earnings of $42,000 for men and $36,000 for women. The main changes observable during this phase were the increase in migration of families with children of school age and, with both parents working, double incomes. The decision of most manufacturing companies to eliminate overtime work had severely reduced earning power and consequently affected the length of stay for most dekasegi. Knowledge of the language regained its importance, partly due to the restructuring process of Japanese companies and partly because families with children needed to enroll them in Japanese schools, given the lack of Brazilian schools in Japan.

Examination of these three periods of migration shows clearly that changes in the socioeconomic context created a feedback mechanism that encouraged additional movements of dekasegi, all of which supports the theory of cumulative causation.

Remittances Sent by Dekasegi to Brazil

The most concrete evidence of the expanded presence of Japanese-Brazilians in the Japanese labor market is the increasing volume of remittances sent back to Brazil (see Table 14.2). At the same time, the use of these remittances as savings is demonstrated by the increase in real estate activity and the number of new small businesses established in the home regions of those migrants. The official figures for remittances published by the Brazilian government reflect only a small portion of the total volume of yearly remittances.[2] This is due to several reasons, including economic disincentives to send money through official channels.

It is clear that transaction costs in the form of foreign exchange and transfer fees charged by banks located in Japan were an obstacle to using official channels for sending back remittances in the beginning. In the recent past, however, these fees have been lowered significantly. For instance, one Brazilian bank in Tokyo charges around $18 for each draft up to a limit of around $10,000. Beyond such fees, a capital gains tax is applied, and proof of the source of that income (a pay stub or some other invoice) is required, which in most cases causes the process to become difficult and slow. The volume of these official remittances is not trivial. It is worth mentioning that the impact of these remittances on the profitability of the Tokyo branches of

TABLE 14.2

*Estimated Amount of Remittances and
Number of Dekasegi, 1986–99*

Year	Total remittances (millions of USD)	Number of dekasegi
1986	300	13,400
1987	700	12,200
1988	1,000	16,700
1989	1,000	29,200
1990	1,000	56,400
1991	1,600	119,333
1992	2,000	147,803
1993	2,000	154,650
1994	2,000	159,619
1995	2,400	176,440
1996	1,900	201,795
1997	1,900	233,254
1998	1,700	222,217
1999	1,800	230,000

SOURCES: Banco América do Sul (estimates), Japanese Dept. of Immigration and Justice, Centro de Informações e Apoio ao Trabalhador no Exterior (CIATE).

Banco do Brasil and Banespa (both state-owned banks) led each of them to become the most profitable branches in their networks. The economic benefit of using the black market, where the premium had risen on some occasions to above 100 percent of the official rate, was the major economic reason for dekasegi *not* to make remittances through official mechanisms (see Table 14.1). In recent years, although not officially published, the volume of officially processed remittances has increased, primarily because the premium paid in the black market has lowered substantially. So, according to the economic figures (see Table 14.1), the premium paid on the black market after 1994 was very small, which stimulated dekasegi to transfer their remittances by official means, mainly through Brazilian banks such as Banco do Brasil, Banco América do Sul, and Banespa (see Table 14.2).

Brazilian macroeconomic conditions were very different prior to 1993, so many remittances were not made through official channels, but instead the dekasegi brought their accumulated savings with them personally when returning to Brazil. It has been difficult to document exact figures for the inflow of dekasegi earnings to Brazil for the following reasons: 1) until 1993, many of them preferred to bring the money with them in the form of cash, 2) some banks followed procedures that sent the money from Japan to its American branch and then remitted it from there to Brazil, which obfuscated the origin of the funds, and 3) high foreign exchange and transfer fees and bureaucratic paperwork required to justify the origin of funds created a disincentive for sending money through official channels.

Increases in the overall value of remittances on a yearly basis are very impressive since they illustrate how little was actually sent through official channels. The rule of thumb according to most of the existing research has been that each dekasegi was able to save on average about $1,500 per month or $18,000 per year. If we use this figure, we can infer that in theory the total amount of savings would be around $4 billion per year. According to the estimates by the Brazilian Ministry of Foreign Affairs the total volume of remittances in 1998 was about $2.5 billion.

According to one research paper, the maximum remittance level of foreign workers in Japan is approximately 70 percent.[3] Their study hypothesized that foreign workers who originally came with different spending habits tended to follow the spending styles of the average Japanese after living in Japan for some time. Their findings are in line with our own estimates, since according to some surveys made in 1991 and 1993, the average monthly wage used to be around $2,500.

The *Real* Plan in Brazil and the Economic Effects on the Dekasegi Phenomenon

The consequences of the downturn in the Japanese economy and the stabilization of the Brazilian economy were two parallel events that had a significant impact on the dekasegi phenomenon. In 1998, the stabilization of the Brazilian economy after the adoption of the *real* (unit of Brazilian currency) plan, together with a faltering Japanese economy and subsequent restructuring of Japanese industry, led to a decrease in the demand for dekasegi laborers for the first time in the history of this phenomenon.

The Brazilian *real* plan improved some economic indicators such as inflation and GDP growth, and it led to an unprecedented overvaluation of the *real* with respect to other currencies. The unemployment rate, however, did not decrease.

Despite *real* overvaluation in July 1994, during the period 1994 and 1995 dekasegi benefited greatly from the overvaluation of the yen—which reached its peak in 1994 at eighty yen per dollar—partially explaining the high volume of remittances for those years.

During the period after 1997, the economic incentives for migrating decreased mainly due to the deep recession of the Japanese economy (see Table 14.3). Recession hit all Japanese companies, obliging them to start to stop paying overtime and reduce their labor force. Overspeculation in real estate and the doubtful portfolio of loans that many Japanese financial institutions carried on their financial statements, collateralized by doubtful assets, have been pointed out as the major causes for the recession. The overall decrease in consumption in Japan was fueled by the specter of unemployment due to the prospect of imminent restructuring throughout most segments of the Japanese economy.

TABLE 14.3

Macroeconomic Data of the Japanese Economy, 1985–99

Year	GDP growth (%)	Unemploy- ment rate (%)	Exchange rate (yen/USD)	Year	GDP growth (%)	Unemploy- ment rate (%)	Exchange rate (yen/USD)
1985	6.6	2.6	238	1992	2.8	2.2	127
1986	4.7	2.8	168	1993	0.9	2.5	111
1987	4.9	2.8	145	1995	0.8	3.2	94
1988	6.9	2.5	128	1996	0.3	3.4	109
1989	7.0	2.3	138	1997	0.1	3.4	121
1990	7.5	2.1	145	1998	(1.9)	4.1	131
1991	6.6	2.1	135	1999	0.5	4.7	114

SOURCE: International Monetary Fund, *International Financial Statistics*, 1998.

The combination of these economic circumstances is reflected in the 1998 annual statistical report on migrants, which reveals a 5 percent decrease in the number of Brazilians (mainly dekasegi) living in Japan, a 38.4 percent decrease in the number of new visas issued for Brazilians, and a 35.5 percent decrease in the number of visas under the "resident" (*teijusha*) classification.

However, this decrease may not continue over the short term, mainly because of the high depreciation of Brazilian currency, which has dropped by 50 percent since January 1999. In addition, since mid-1999, the value of the yen has risen against the American dollar by 15 percent, going back to the levels of 1996. The effect of Brazilian currency devaluation was promptly reflected in the volume of remittances, which again showed a significant increase during the first quarter of this year. According to official data from the Brazilian Central Bank, there was an increase of 32.2 percent compared to the same period the year before. The deregulation of the Japanese financial system has allowed greater freedom for commercial banks operating with dollars, and has facilitated the dekasegi's ability to convert currency at their discretion. Some Japanese bank branches located in areas of high concentration of dekasegi and some Brazilian banks operating in Japan have reported a higher volume of foreign currency transactions by individuals on days following the appreciation of the yen.

The greatest threat to the continuing demand for dekasegi is the unprecedented level of unemployment in Japan, the highest since the end of the Second World War. Moreover, most Japanese companies have had to cut overtime remuneration, which used to be an important income source for dekasegi, not only in terms of immediate financial gain, but also as a means of allowing them to shorten their stay in Japan. The direct effect of this economic scenario has been a significant decrease in the dekasegi practice of constantly switching jobs, and it may lead to the necessity of the dekasegi lengthening their stay in Japan in order to achieve the same level of savings. In terms of future prospects, the number of dekasegi should not increase significantly, mainly due to the saturation level of the Japanese labor market given the perspective of the Japanese economy, in particular in the construction sector, and the trend of Japanese manufacturing to seek out cheaper labor markets.

Conclusion

On the whole the dekasegi phenomenon has benefited the temporary migrant workers, providing them with a quicker means of accumulating savings. It has also benefited Japan by supplying migrant workers at lower cost, and it has benefited Brazil as foreign exchange earnings have been remitted back to the country. My conclusion is based on the analysis of four variables and can be summarized as follows:

Economic benefits to the country of origin. The Brazilian government did not actively support or discourage the dekasegi phenomenon, but the Brazilian economy in the last fifteen years received a tremendous benefit in terms of hard currency remittances, which helped improve the balance of payments by about $30 billion (see Table 14.4). At the same time, the fact that a number of workers left the domestic labor market led to greater job prospects for those who remained in Brazil and were still unemployed. Even if the actual numbers of dekasegi are not that significant when compared to overall unemployment numbers, when analyzed by specific sectors such as farming, where there had been a high concentration of Japanese descendants engaged in such activity, the impact was considerable.

Income distribution. Remittances from Japan have been shown to play an important role in lowering inequality within the Japanese-Brazilian community, primarily for those workers earning less than $5,000 annually. On a macro level, within Brazilian society remittance income distribution may have been skewed toward the middle of the economy, as many Japanese-Brazilian households have incomes that are slightly above the average Brazilian household income. This seems to be one of the best benefits of the dekasegi phenomenon: the opportunity for lower-income Japanese-Brazilians to rise economically within the society where they were born and where they want to continue their economic lives.

Human capital development. From this perspective individual expectations to acquire technical skills and self-improvement were high, but the reality was much harsher. The demand in Japan was for unskilled workers; even skilled workers, therefore, had to take whatever jobs they could get. Japanese employers did not see the relevance of college or more advanced degrees from Brazil when hiring dekasegi to do the unskilled work that was available in Japan. Having Japanese language competence was considerably

TABLE 14.4

Trade Balance between Brazil and Japan, 1985–97
(millions of USD)

Year	Exports from Brazil	Imports from Japan	Trade balance	Year	Exports from Brazil	Imports from Japan	Trade balance
1985	1,398	613	785	1992	2,306	1,151	1,155
1986	1,515	979	536	1993	2,313	1,664	649
1987	1,676	939	737	1994	2,574	2,412	162
1988	2,274	1,058	1,216	1995	3,102	3,279	(177)
1989	2,312	1,322	990	1996	3,047	2,756	291
1990	2,671	1,357	1,314	1997	3,068	3,599	(531)
1991	2,557	1,350	1,207				

SOURCE: International Monetary Fund, *Direction of Trade Statistics Yearbook*, 1992; 1998.

more important in getting a job than years of education, although according to some studies, it seems that even fluency in the language did not influence wages. A significant portion of dekasegi are well educated and were formerly white collar workers in Brazil, but did not learn anything in Japan that enabled them to get better jobs upon their return to Brazil. Therefore, most dekasegi on their return to Brazil have no other option than to start their own small business since returning to their former or equivalent positions is very difficult. In that regard, the costs of forgoing career opportunities not only for well-educated dekasegi, but also for Brazilian society as a whole, might be very high.

Increased savings and entrepreneurship. According to a survey done by SEBRAE, a Brazilian agency that supports entrepreneurs who wish to open small businesses, the first priority of most would-be entrepreneurs is to acquire a home; the second is to start a small business. An increase in real estate activity, as well as in the number of new small business such as rotisseries, gasoline stations, coffee shops, video rental stores, and restaurants, established in areas where Japanese-Brazilians are concentrated, has confirmed the findings of the survey. The lack of reasonable capital to finance investments is reflected in the high domestic interest rates charged by Brazilian financial institutions. To overcome this, self-financing, through accumulation of savings, has been the only alternative.

Notes

1. B. C. Chiswick, "The Effect of Americanization on the Earnings of Foreign-born Men," *Journal of Political Economy*, 86 (1978), 897–921.

2. For the years 1990–95, total workers' remittances (in millions of U.S. dollars) were 527 (1990), 1,057 (1991), 1,719 (1992), 1,123 (1993), 1,834 (1994), and 2,891 (1995). Figures are from International Monetary Fund, *Balance of Payments Statistics Year Book* (1998); figures are unavailable for 1985–89 and 1996–99.

3. Saito Komomi and Saito Katsuhiro, "An Estimated Maximum Remittance Level by Foreign Workers in Japan," *Soka University Economic Essays* 24 (1995), 105–11.

CHAPTER FIFTEEN

The *Dekasegi* Phenomenon and the Education of Japanese Brazilian Children in Japanese Schools

MASATO NINOMIYA

According to information obtained by the Centro de Estudos Nipo-Brasileiros de São Paulo, the first announcements recruiting unskilled Brazilians for jobs in Japan were published in the main Japanese-language newspapers in Brazil in 1985. They were directed toward people of Japanese nationality in Brazil, after changes in Japanese laws had been passed permitting the entrance of nonskilled workers.[1]

This search for unskilled labor came from Japanese industrial companies, mainly small and medium-sized. Because of a shortage of unskilled laborers, these companies could not deliver their products, especially during the peak of Japan's so-called bubble economy. The reason for the shortage was that Japanese workers did not want to take the "three k" jobs, jobs they regarded as "tough, dirty, and dangerous" (*kitsui, kitanai, kiken*).

Mindful of the legal prohibitions against recruiting foreign workers, the heads of the companies' human resource divisions recalled that many Japanese nationals had emigrated to South America when the Japanese economy was in difficulty, before and following World War II. They knew as well that many Latin American countries were suffering severe economic crises.[2]

It soon became apparent, however, that the number of Brazilians of Japanese descent coming into Japan would not be enough to meet the heavy demand for laborers. It was not long, then, before a large number of Brazilian Nisei started entering Japan on tourist visas, which were later transformed into one-year visas—purportedly for the purpose of visiting relatives—that allowed Brazilian Nisei to go to work.

Once Japanese officials became aware of the number of descendants of Japanese immigrants living in South America, mostly Brazil, they realized that they might provide the solution to Japan's labor shortage. As a way of regularizing their situation, the Japanese passed a reform called the "Immigration Control and Refugee Recognition Act" in June 1990. The amended law created a new status for Japanese nationals and children and grandchildren of Japanese emigrants born abroad: "long-term resident." This law gave them a permit to stay in Japan for three years, with an option of renewal with no restrictions, which meant they no longer faced any barriers to employment.

The result could be seen immediately. According to statistics from the Ministry of Justice in Japan, 83,875 Brazilians of Japanese descent entered the country in 1991. The number of immigrants remained high in the following years, ranging from forty to sixty thousand. As of December 2000, ten years after this legislative reform, there were 254,394 Brazilians in Japan. If we add to that number the people that have dual nationality, the number of Brazilians who went to Japan might reach 270,000.[3]

Up until 1973, ships were the primary means of transport between Brazil and Japan. After that date immigrants began to travel by air. After a boom period from 1958 to 1962, numbers of immigrants decreased until 1993, when the Japan International Cooperation Agency (JICA), the government institution in charge of emigration, announced the ending of official support for emigration. At the time, the inverse flow had already begun.[4] Nonetheless, the Brazilians still represent the third major foreign resident group in Japan, after Koreans and Chinese.

We can point to both positive and negative consequences of the dekasegi phenomenon. On the positive side, as Edson Mori's chapter indicates, there has been a wide range of financial benefits for both the dekasegi themselves and for Brazil, to which the dekasegi remit their earnings and where they invest their money.[5] There have also been cultural gains and contributions. Although some deny it, living in Japan allows dekasegi to obtain a degree of knowledge about many aspects of Japanese culture, language, and technology, including familiarity with modern production control systems such as QC, TQC, and TPM, for those who have worked in factories. Although this last benefit seems to be economically less important than remittances for them, it is not difficult to imagine the additional value of knowledge acquired by years of living in an industrialized country.

Concomitantly, Brazilians have made valuable contributions to the internationalization and globalization of Japanese society. Contact with a foreign culture certainly helps to broaden the images Japanese hold about other societies and cultures. Brazilian culture was once little known in Japan, the understanding of it restricted to stereotypes about the Amazon region, carnival, soccer, and coffee. But there has been a great deal of change since the early 1990s. Brazilian music, dance, cooking, and language, as well as soccer, widely publicized in Japan just before the 2002 World Cup, have become more familiar to Japanese, and they have even become popular in some sectors of Japanese society.[6]

We must not, however, mention only the positive aspects. Although the great majority of Brazilians who live in Japan are happy, there are inherent problems in the presence of this sizable immigrant population. Many problems have been noted in the media in both countries, as well as in the international sphere. These problems include domestic troubles, employment issues, legal problems, crimes, imprisonment, and so forth.

Moreover, the Japanese economy has been facing an unprecedented crisis for the past seven or eight years. The economic bubble has burst, and Japan has fallen into a recession. This situation directly affects workers, especially foreign workers such as the Brazilians. Nevertheless, salaries in Japan are still higher than those in Brazil, with monthly averages of $1,500 to $2,000 for women and $2,000 to $2,500 for men (all figures are in U.S. dollars). These figures are far, however, from the $3,000 to $4,000 once paid to workers, which included wages for overtime, which is no longer being offered.

The above describes only some aspects of the varied dekasegi experience; it is not possible to examine the experience exhaustively in this chapter. Let us focus, then, on a crucial aspect: the education of Brazilian children of Japanese descent in Japan.

The Educational System in Japan

As in most countries, the education system in Japan can be divided into public and private systems. Compulsory public education lasts nine years. The first six years are for elementary school and the last three are for junior high school. Children normally enter the educational system at the age of six and finish at the age of fifteen. To discover a Japanese child's age it is enough to ask simply which year of school he or she is in. Students do not repeat grades in the compulsory public system, and advancement is based on having attended a minimum number of classes.

Japanese who do not send their children to school for any reason can be punished by law, but this requirement does not apply to foreigners. However, those Japanese-Brazilian parents who want their children to go to school can get them admitted, no matter whether classes are filled or not. Students are eligible to go to work after junior high school, but this seldom happens nowadays; almost all of them (96.5 percent) enter high school. Of

252 / MASATO NINOMIYA

these, 97.1 percent finish their courses, whether regular or technical (industrial, commercial, cooking, etc.), all of which are offered as night classes as well as day.[7]

Students who want to enter high school have to pass a difficult entrance examination. The score required on this examination increases according to the reputation of the high school the student aims to enter. Nonetheless, there are a number of foreign students, including Brazilians, who have been accepted into the more desirable schools. The cost per month to attend a public high school is approximately $110; at private schools tuition is $400 to $500.

Of the students who finish their high school studies, more than 50 percent enter two-year colleges or university programs lasting four years or more. Opportunities for students to attend colleges and universities, especially private schools, have increased recently because of Japan's dropping birth rate, and because some private schools do not require an entrance examination. This is particularly the case for two-year colleges, which may simply require candidates to present a record of high school classes and participate in an interview. Some colleges also require a letter of recommendation from the student's high school. Even for professional programs of four years or more (excepting medical schools), students are given easy entrance exams. Candidates may choose to take only one test, so someone who wants to study physical education, for example, might only need to show the ability to play a single sport such as soccer.

Competition for entrance to the most prestigious public and private schools, however, is still high, since the major Japanese companies recruit their employees from the twenty or thirty best universities in the country. Furthermore, competition starts long before the university entrance examinations, beginning when parents attempt to register their children at the best elementary schools at a very early age. Frequently, students in the final years of elementary school attend a second school that offers tutoring and extra classes to help them get into a good junior high school. Naturally, this process becomes labor-intensive and onerous as students advance in their education. From the high school level on, there are students who practice sports or participate in other kinds of activities proper to their age, as well as a great number who attend preparatory schools to help them prepare for entrance examinations so they might qualify for the best universities.

Education in Japan is free of charge only at public schools for elementary and junior high school. Private schools at all levels charge tuition, as do public high schools. Preparatory schools and extra classes in subjects like musical education and foreign languages must all be paid for, and only well-to-do families can support the cost. Research shows that the average annual income of the parents of those attending the best universities is as much as $100,000. Tuition for any program at a public university is about $7,000, while at a private university a specialization in the humanities costs around $10,000. Medical and engineering schools cost even more. These figures are relevant as a reflection of the obstacles faced by the children of Japanese-Brazilians, who usually earn from US$20,000 to $30,000 annually.[8]

The Presence of Brazilians in Japanese Schools

According to Portuguese-language newspapers in Japan, in 1999 there were about 40,000 Brazilian children under fifteen years of age, but only 7,500 were registered in Japanese public schools. The Brazilians' lack of knowledge of Japanese seemed to generate major difficulties. In the beginning of the dekasegi phenomenon, many Japanese children rejected Brazilian and other Latin American Nikkei, mainly in small and medium-sized towns in the interior of Japan. This rejection did not happen with the same frequency in large cities, where people are accustomed to seeing foreigners. Although Nikkei children had the same physical appearance as Japanese children, they could not communicate in Japanese. Rejection grew into discrimination, and quite often into *ijime*, or bullying of younger students by older children.

With the enrollment of Brazilian children in Japanese schools, other problems quickly appeared. Research verified that there was a marked contrast between the adaptation of children younger than ten and older children. Children born in Japan or who had arrived by the early years of elementary school were able to adapt without any problem, primarily because the Japanese children of that age were just starting their education, too. Children in any situation tend to be very adaptable, even given marked differences in social status, nationality, ethnicity, and faith. If we were to look at Japanese immigrants' children in Brazil when they first started school, it is obvious that, mutatis mutandis, similar things happened there.

In any case, we should not forget that, in the beginning, Brazilian children were not always accepted by their Japanese schoolmates. This is apparent from the occurrence of ijime. Japanese children were not accustomed to seeing other children with the same physical appearance but without the knowledge of Japanese language, customs, and social rules that had been ingrained in everyone who had attended elementary school in Japan. This treatment was similar to that experienced in the past by Japanese children who had spent some years abroad with their parents. After returning to Japan they started attending classes without any knowledge of social rules and suffered from discrimination by their classmates, just like dekasegi children.

Thus, it could have been anticipated that the majority would treat newcomers rudely.

For these reasons, in the early 1990s I was invited to give lectures to elementary-school teachers about the dekasegi phenomenon and the educational system in Brazil in order to emphasize the need for diversity within a homogeneous ethnic and cultural entity like Japan. The presence of Brazilian children in Japanese schools is certainly contributing to the internationalization of Japanese society.[9] Several times it was emphasized that the presence of the dekasegi in Japan would probably constitute an important tie with the rest of the world.

In general, Japanese of all ages and social status have some problems accepting different racial and ethnic populations. The main reasons involve problems of communication and different cultural expectations. In the past there were protests by nationals from neighboring countries relating to the discrimination they suffered in Japan, which they did not experience with Caucasians. It is not surprising, then, that Japanese-Brazilian children should face some antagonism in Japanese schools. Nowadays, however, we seldom hear about this kind of discrimination, and there are fewer problems of acceptance of Brazilian children by Japanese schools or children, as we have personally verified in some visits. Rather, there is a high degree of assimilation to the Japanese lifestyle on the part of the Brazilian children, which causes another serious problem: the loss of their mother tongue, Portuguese, and their Brazilian culture.

Let us turn to the problems of children and adolescents who arrive in Japan after the age of ten. According to the Japanese system, students are assigned to a grade level solely according to their age. A Brazilian child twelve years of age would be assigned to the sixth grade even though he or she may not know Japanese or be able to comprehend the lessons and the third grade might be more appropriate. An exception can sometimes be made in consideration of a student's foreign origin, and recently the Japanese Ministry of Education authorized the school principals to put a child back for two years. It is easy to imagine the difficult situation of a Brazilian child, even one of Japanese descent, with limited knowledge of the Japanese language, in a sixth-grade classroom.

The educational program in Japan is very different than the system in Brazil. At the request of a group of principals from elementary schools of Gamagori city, Aichi prefecture, who wished to know about the educational program in Brazilian schools, I started a campaign in Brazil to collect Brazilian books on subjects like mathematics, physics, and biology. From this experience we recognized how hard it is to compare curricula of such different countries as Brazil and Japan.

It is necessary to point out a basic difference between Brazil and Japan. In Japan students in public schools providing compulsory education do not repeat grades. Even if a student has not understood the lessons, he or she is automatically promoted to the next grade, depending, of course, on the availability of places. This might seem like a benefit for the older Brazilian children, but this is not actually the case. Lacking a real understanding of their coursework, children start to lose interest in attending school and eventually drop out. Note here that compulsory education in Japan is only required for its nationals. Entrance to schools is allowed to foreigners, but if their children choose to quit there is no way to oblige them to attend. Although the school administration or even their classmates might invite the Brazilian child to come back to school, after repeated attempts fail, everyone may give up. The parents might receive letters from the school administration or a visit from the teacher, but most of the time parents do not understand what is written, or have problems communicating with school personnel. All these efforts often prove useless, as the child is rarely convinced to return to school. This is the beginning of many problems. The spare-time activities of a child or adolescent whose parents work all day might lead to forms of juvenile delinquency that concern us all.

The Adaptation of Brazilian Children in Japan

Although the children of Brazilian families who live in Japan are sent to school, the need for them to continue learning Portuguese has been a matter of great concern. Some children—mainly those under the age of ten— become so completely assimilated that they forget Portuguese, refuse to study it, or even refuse to use it in conversation at home.[10] This situation occurs most often in families that do not have a fixed time limit for their stay in Japan, and therefore have no serious commitment to teach their children Portuguese. On the other hand, even if parents do have a plan to return to Brazil, it is quite natural for children to adapt to the place where they are currently living.

There have been efforts on the part of Brazilian authorities and Japanese-Brazilian communities to address this situation. As mentioned above, the teaching of the Portuguese language has always been a concern of the Brazilians domiciled in Japan, as well as of Brazilian diplomatic authorities. After all, the hope of the majority of Brazilians arriving in Japan is to save enough money to return home and realize the dream of purchasing land or expensive consumer goods, or even starting a small business. Some young people want to return to Brazil to continue studies interrupted due to the lack of financial support.

The arrival of the first groups of children in areas where a large number of Brazilians are concentrated—Oizumi town in Gumma prefecture; the Tokyo metropolitan area, encompassing Saitama, Kanagawa, and Chiba prefectures; and the Tokai area, which encompasses Aichi, Gifu, Shizuoka, and Mie prefectures—prompted increased concerns about registering them in elementary schools. Parents encountered many problems in registering their children, including communicating with teachers.

After parents register their children in Japanese schools, the problem is having them continue their study of Portuguese and maintain their educational level according to the Brazilian system, in anticipation of the family's return to Brazil. Brazilian children who study in Japan may have their degrees revalidated once back in Brazil if the Ministry of Education recognizes equivalence. The major concern, however, is the maintenance of Portuguese. Many dedicated persons—including some who had already been involved with education in Brazil and who graduated in education, philosophy, science, language and literature, and related disciplines—have spent time searching for solutions to these problems.

The establishment of so-called "Brazilian schools" in Japan happened naturally, in response to an urgent need. Its goal was the preservation of the Portuguese language and the fulfillment of Brazilian curriculum requirements so that students might continue their studies in Brazil without any setbacks. Within this context the *supletivo* projects were established, allowing students to take Brazilian examinations to obtain certificates of graduation from junior high and high schools. The first project along these lines was the Ceteban Project for Distance Education, which prepared a great number of students to take the required examinations.[11] In response to the requests of Brazilians living in Japan, the first examination outside Brazil was held on November 2, 1999. Three hundred candidates took the examinations, of whom 110 were approved for junior high school graduation certificates, 150 for high school certificates. The examination was held at the Brazilian embassy and consulates in Tokyo and Nagoya.[12] The second examination was successfully held in November 2000, and as this chapter was written another round was scheduled for the next year.

In addition, the Ministry of Education of Brazil acting jointly with the Brazilian embassy in Tokyo initiated research to investigate the educational situation of Brazilians residing in Japan. Their objective was to start proceedings to allow the opening of Brazilian schools in Japan. This study resulted in the "Opinion CEB/CNE n. 11/99," concerned with establishing rules for Brazilian schools located abroad, to be presented to the National Council of Education on June 7, 1999.

Before that opinion was presented, however, there were already some Brazilian schools functioning in Japan, like the ones belonging to Pitagoras group of Belo Horizonte.[13] This is an institution with almost 100,000 students in branches around the world. Its specialty is establishing schools for the children of company employees around the world who work in distant places. In Brazil there is a school in Serra dos Carajas, in Para state, near the iron ore mine, and abroad there was a school established in Iraq for the children of those who worked in railway construction there. Recently the Pitagoras group opened its first unit in Japan in Ota city, Gumma prefecture, in 1999; a second one in Hamamatsu city, Shizuoka prefecture; a third in Handa city, Aichi prefecture; and a fourth in Monca city, Tochigi prefecture. The last two opened in 2000. The enrollment of the two first units reached two hundred, and the third started with forty students. Each unit offers elementary-school education with almost all the teachers recruited from among qualified Brazilians in Japan. A notable difficulty is that the monthly tuition of about $350 is a high price for Japanese-Brazilian workers whose monthly incomes average $2,000 to $2,500, unless both husband and wife are working.

Conclusion

What we wish for the Japanese-Brazilians residing in Japan is the achievement of their goals in their search for happiness. These goals do not merely take the form of the acquisition of material goods. The education of their children is doubtless an important mission for parents, and is a major legacy that they can leave for their descendants.

In Brazil Japanese immigrants and their descendants ascended the social scale rapidly compared to immigrants of other nationalities, thanks to the efforts they directed toward education.[14] Families made great sacrifices to give their children the opportunity to study, and thus the number of students who have graduated is high. If we consider that Nikkei constitute less than 1 percent of the Brazilian population but 15 percent of the students at the University of São Paulo, and that 8 percent of staff of the university are of Japanese origin, we get an idea of the number of people from the Japanese community in Brazil that have reached a high level of education.

But turning to Brazilians residing in Japan, only 25 percent of their children go to school. Difficulties they experience when they attend often lead them to abandon their education. Failure to attend school is in turn related to the marginalization of Nikkei young people in Japan that concerns us all.

Comparing the educational achievements of the Japanese immigrants in Brazil and the Japanese-Brazilians in Japan, we may notice that the former were more successful. They were helped by the Brazilian education system that permits working while studying, allowing students to register for night courses with no disadvantage. It is premature to come to any definitive conclusions about the future of the education of Japanese-Brazilians in Japan. The obstacles they have faced up until now are not trivial.

The major variable related to achievement in education is the interest, understanding, and support of parents. Given this, we believe it is possible to overcome obstacles to their education once it is recognized that there are already some Brazilian students experiencing success, such as their acceptance in Japanese colleges. Another good option for students is to return to Brazil to continue their studies.[15]

What is to be feared most is Japanese-Brazilians continuing the life of dekasegi, who are often undecided about where to put down roots in their goings and comings between the two countries. An inevitable factor in their decision is the destiny of their school-age children. Experience shows that family separation is not good, and its consequences can be disastrous. If families decide to stay for a while in Japan, their children should take advantage of every opportunity that Japanese schools offer, even though there are many barriers for children older than ten years of age.

What is needed in order to keep these children from abandoning their education is a joint effort on the part of all interested parties. Possible solutions include insisting on their regular attendance at Japanese schools, searching for alternatives such as supletivo examinations, and promoting their enrollment in Brazilian schools like Pitagoras. Other solutions may be offered by the authorities of both countries and the Japanese-Brazilian community itself.

We are convinced that such efforts will help provide a solution to the problem of juvenile delinquency, a matter of concern for Japanese-Brazilian communities in Japan and in Brazil. And we hope that Brazilian workers now living in Japan might come back to Brazil bringing not only the savings they have been striving for, but also enough knowledge to contribute to strengthening the cultural exchange between the two countries and enhance the dynamic growth of the Japanese-Brazilian community in Brazil.

Notes

1. Annex I-2 of the Immigration Control and Refugee Recognition Act (Cabinet Order no. 319 of 1951; latest amendment, law no. 71 of 1990), article 2, 2nd and 19th paragraphs.

2. In Brazil, the salaries of Japanese-Brazilians were one-fifth of those paid to their similarly employed Japanese colleagues. In addition, Brazil suffered from a high degree of unemployment—almost 20 percent according to the trade unions, about 10 percent according to official statistics—and hyperinflation that had reached 2,000

percent in 1988. Center for Information and Support for the Worker Abroad (CIATE), *Questionnaires about Dekasegi: Centro de Informação e Apoio ao Trabalhador no Exterior*, Dec. 1999.

3. That figure equals the number of Japanese that came to Brazil in the first several decades of the twentieth century, in the period from the arrival of the steamship *Kasato Maru* in Santos seaport in 1908 to 1941, before the Pacific war, and from 1953 to 1973, after the war. The year 1973 is meaningful in this immigration history, since it marks the arrival of the final steamship carrying immigrants. The children of the Japanese born in Brazil acquire Brazilian nationality, according to the principle of *jus soli* states. They also are given Japanese nationality, according to the principle of *jus sanguinis*, fulfilling the conditions imposed by the Japanese Nationality Law of 1950. Once in Japanese territory, the government considers them Japanese and does not treat them as foreigners.

4. Minoru Yokokawa, *Sengo no taihaku iju* (Emigration to Brazil in the postwar period) (Tokyo: Associação Central Nipo-Brasileira, 1995), 144.

5. It is worth mentioning that Brazilians are able to accumulate savings from work in Japan that they might not be able to accumulate in Brazil. Workers often return to Brazil with enough capital to realize their dreams of owning real estate or purchasing high-priced consumer goods. Others use their savings as the initial investment needed to start up a small business.

6. We also should not forget the dissemination of the Portuguese language in Japan through these Brazilian residents and their press. Important weekly newspapers, magazines, a TV channel, and other media make a contribution that is unprecedented in the hundred-year history of relations between the two countries.

7. Masataka Katsura, *Questãoes atuis e futuras da reforma da educação e do ensino no Japão* (Curitiba: Associação dos Professores e Funcionarios da Província de Hyogo, 1994), 49 ff.

8. The average per capita income in Japan is $24,109 using current purchasing power parities (PPPs), or $30,025 using 1998 exchange rates, which means that the income received by Japanese-Brazilians is close to the Japanese average. Carlos Shinoda, "Japan 2000: An International Comparison," unpublished manuscript, 17.

9. Masato Ninomiya, "Burajiru kara mita Nihon-Nihon no shinno kokusaika wo kangaeru," lecture presented at the VI Japanese-Brazilian Symposium on Education, held at the 42nd Congress of Teachers and Schools: Employees of Hyogo Prefecture, in Yabu City, Nov. 13, 1992.

10. Statements of Brazilian children's parents in Carlos Shinoda, *Porutogaru go ga iya da!* (Learning Portuguese, certainly!) (São Paulo: Alianía Cultural Brasil-Japão, 1995), 67 ff.

11. Carlos Shinoda, *Educação: trabalhar no japão e estudar no Brasil* (Education: Working in Japan and studying in Brazil), unpublished manuscript, 13.

12. According to the weekly newspaper published in Portuguese in Japan, *International Press*, Feb. 5, 2000, A-13.

13. In addition to the schools of Pitagoras group there are others in different cities, including the Escola Alegria do Saber, in Toyota city, Aichi prefecture, and the Escola Brasileira of Hamamatsu and Yaizu, both in Shizuoka prefecture.

14. For further information see Ruth Cardoso, *Estructura familiar e mobilidade social: estudo dos Japoneses no estado de São Paulo* (São Paulo: Kaleidos).

15. Important statements about the problems of readaptation of children who returned from Japan are in *Zainichi Keiken Burajiru jin: Peru jin kikoku jido seito no tekio jyokyo ibunkakan kyoiku no shiten niyoru bunseki* (Adaptation of Peruvian and Brazilian children who arrived from Japan: Analysis from an intercultural vision), research report no. 10041003, Ministry of Education of Japan, Mar. 2000.

CHAPTER SIXTEEN

The Emigration of Argentines of Japanese Descent to Japan

MARCELO G. HIGA

Around the middle of the 1980s, the migration to Japan of Argentines of Japanese descent who had settled in Argentina over decades began to manifest itself. This phenomenon, usually known as *dekasegi* migration, signified the reopening of the migratory flow between the two countries and would have repercussions on all aspects of the lives of those involved, from the level of the community to the realm of the familiar and personal. For those born in Argentina, the migratory experience would be of fundamental importance in the formulation of a new type of link with Japan. This link would become the point of departure for a restructuring of identifying orientations within the collective and the individual.

This chapter aims to reflect upon the implications of this experience. First, I will examine the general context in which migration occurs, paying attention to the socioeconomic factors that frame and impel this movement, and emphasizing the influence of Japanese immigration legislation in the formulation of the category "Nikkeijin." Then I will look at how dekasegi migration transforms such ideas as "settlement" and "return" and indirectly alters traditional frames of reference in the construction of identities. Finally, I will try to evaluate the experience that, regarding the gestation of identities, is characterized by the emergence and consolidation of a new discourse organized around the concept of "Nikkei."

262 / MARCELO G. HIGA

The Socioeconomic Context of Dekasegi Migration

At the beginning of the 1980s, the migration of Japanese to Argentina had reached a high level of stability. The interruption of the immigration flow at the end of the 1960s, the growth of generations born in Argentina, and the relatively good socioeconomic access to the middle classes of society created a situation that favored the definitive adoption by Japanese descendants of the general values present in the society in which they developed. This produced a gradual distancing from the identifying markers of the country of origin and gradual incorporation of orientations and viewpoints dictated by the national Argentine ideology.

The majority of descendants of Japanese immigrants understood their so-called "collectivity" (*colectividad*) as a kind of subsystem inserted within Argentine society that operated as an intermediary or transitional space, but was basically framed by the receiving society. Nevertheless, the adoption of "Argentineness" as the first principle of identification did not imply the immediate nullification of "Japaneseness."[1] However, it is also true that Japan remained present in diverse spheres of daily life. Certain family and kinship references, native village-framed reciprocal relationships, culinary tastes, and attitudes toward elders followed customs or values interpreted as "Japanese heritage," although these were rather general and vague. And the community or institutional framework continued to be an important space for socialization through language schools, social and sports clubs, and regional groupings (prefectural, regional, or village), as well as through very extended practices like rotating-credit groups (*tanomoshi*), which remained popular both economically and socially even among the youngest generations.

But the general agreement was that the interpersonal relationships of immigrants and their descendants inevitably had to incorporate the established demands of an Argentine national identity. These demands were privileged over claims either openly or weakly "ethnic." In consequence, even within the ambiguity of daily practices, the discourse of identification of those descended from Japanese immigrants did not admit doubts. That is why, in the Argentine context, there did not even exist a descriptive term such as "Japanese-Argentine": one was "Argentine," a term that could be softened occasionally by adding the clarification "descended from Japanese."

The Emigration Phenomenon in Argentine Society

From the second half of the nineteenth century on, Argentina was fundamentally a country of immigrants. The image of Argentina, so widespread in the first decades of the twentieth century, as a modern country, prosperous and full of opportunities, makes it in certain aspects similar to the United States, with which it shares its identity as a melting pot of races. In spite of the original national optimism, however, there is no doubt that the socioeconomic condition of the country has been deteriorating for decades. And a little-mentioned or generally ignored aspect of this process has been emigration. The dekasegi phenomenon is not, in this sense, an isolated occurrence in a country that conceives of itself as fundamentally "immigrantist." Therefore, independent of the specific links that connect the Japanese descendant to the country of origin of parents or grandparents, it is possible to view the situation from within the rubric of the generalized movement of Argentine society.

By the mid-1980s, after decades of socioeconomic crisis, there was a consolidation of an "emigrant culture" in Argentine society. The contact with peoples different from their own, with a different history and different codes, routines, and languages, not only had an effect on the lives of those who had emigrated, but it also indirectly influenced those who had stayed in Argentina. And while it is certain that the difficulties of adaptation that all emigrants suffer served to increase the nostalgic longing and emotional attachment to the homeland ("there is no place like Argentina"), for some it is also true that direct contact with other places and people encourages a healthy dose of tolerance, an attitude of greater openness toward differences, making it possible to question the very notion of nationality as it was understood up until then.

With this consolidation as the basis, emigration took on a new look at the end of the 1980s, when Argentina experienced a sweeping economic crisis. At that time inflation had reached such a level that expressions such as "high inflation," "galloping inflation," or "terrible inflation" simply could not describe it and a new word came into being: "hyperinflation."[2] With hyperinflation, a massive new wave of emigration was unleashed, this time not only of professionals and specialized workers but also of anyone who had the opportunity to leave. "The only way out is Ezeiza [the Buenos Aires international airport]" became a popular expression that faithfully reflected the sentiments of the people. In a broken country, emigration was an escape valve. While it did not assure the immediate improvement of one's position, it was a hopeful move and served as a palliative when facing an economy in free fall. The years 1988–89 are remembered for their waves of raids on supermarkets and long lines at consulates, where people went to apply for the visas that would open the doors to emigration. Ironically, many opted to go to the very countries their ancestors had left decades before.

The migration of the descendants of the Japanese back to Japan can be traced to this last period. The dekasegi phenomenon, then, is rooted in the context of a society in which emigration had stopped being unusual and had become a common goal for many people.

Japan: The Reformulation of the Nikkei Category

In the 1980s Japan was beginning to see a trend inverse to the one occurring in Argentina.[3] That is, it went from being a largely emigrantist country to being one of the poles of attraction for immigrants in East Asia, an event without parallel in the country's postwar history.[4] Japanese law, however, did not allow foreigners without permanent residence in Japan to work as unspecialized labor.[5] But the reality was that in spite of their "illegal" status, it was not difficult for the new immigrants to find jobs in industries such as construction and in small and medium-size businesses of different sectors, which found it necessary to adapt to the demands of an economy in rapid expansion and suffered from the scarcity of versatile workers.

The presence of workers from South America in this initial flow of immigrants has already been observed. In many cases, persons of Japanese nationality were "returning" temporarily to work in Japan. Some had emigrated to Japan after the Second World War, either as young adults or as children accompanied by their families. Others born in South American countries had been registered by their parents in Japanese family registries (*koseki*) through consulates, and so were considered Japanese citizens as well as citizens of their birth country. For those with Japanese citizenship, there was no legal obstacle to finding employment in Japan. But there were also those who, although descendants of Japanese, were simply "foreigners," and as such could not legally engage in any type of unspecialized labor.

In the late 1980s, as the number of foreign workers in Japan rapidly increased, their legal status became the object of great debate. Their illegal status was only tacitly admitted, since there undoubtedly was a scarcity of labor, but the conflicting interests of different ministries within the government impeded the formulation of a clear political solution to the situation. A partial solution was achieved in June 1990, when changes in immigration laws finally went into effect, establishing a category ("spouses, etc., of Japanese"—*Nihonjin no haigusha nado*) that opened the doors to legal work in unspecialized occupations for foreigners who could prove their relationship to persons of Japanese nationality. In addition, by means of a "special authorization," relatives categorized as "residents," or *teijumin*, even when they weren't descendants of Japanese, were also authorized to work without restrictions. Those in these categories became commonly known as Nikkei-jin.

With the migration law reform, the Nikkei emerged as the principal source of legal foreign labor. Although the laws continued to forbid the entry of unspecialized workers, this measure served partially to resolve the lack of labor issue, thus ameliorating the problem of increasing illegal immigrant labor.

Although the term Nikkeijin does not figure explicitly in legal texts, the expression is used widely, academically and in the daily conversations of the people. Literally "of Japanese lineage," Nikkeijin at its broadest alludes to the descendants of Japanese born or settled abroad generally, although in its more restricted use it refers to the descendants of Japanese who emigrated from the Meiji period until approximately the 1960s. In actual usage, it would seem that, on one hand, those designated Nikkei do not differ greatly physically from the average Japanese. Their last names (tending to favor the paternal line) and the characteristics of their family relationships also link them to the Japanese. But on the other hand, their nationality, language, habits, and customs generally define them as "foreigners." One might emphasize that there are also well-defined differences within them: generational differences, differences of nationality, and even language, and all the differences related to the environment in which members were raised and educated.

Finally, it is curious that in the context of contemporary migration, in some cases (with a certain etymological logic) those very Japanese whose permanent residence is in South America, or even those family members who don't have a direct "biological" relationship with Japanese citizens, are included within the Nikkei classification. As such, we may say that from the perspective of Japanese society, today the Nikkei constitute a group heterogeneously composed of people from different countries who, according to circumstances, may be included in or excluded from, likened to or differentiated from, that which is considered "Japanese" or "foreign."

In the case of immigrant workers, it is clear that access to Nikkei status determines a fundamental difference: whether one has the opportunity to work legally or not. For them, being "Nikkei" became something more than a simple and subjective affirmation; it was the key to access to legal work and to the legitimization of their presence in Japan. From that point on, in many countries movements to recover "Japaneseness" intensified, and such an ethnic recognition became an area of wide dispute among those who wanted to emigrate. Japanese authorities took on the task of "certifying" the Japanese heritage of prospective emigrants among the descendants of immigrants in South American countries.[6]

The situation that I have described, specifically in relation to the phenomenon of emigration, reflects the achievements of a legislative reform in the formulation of identities. In this sense, it is clear that in the context of current Japanese migration, "Nikkeiness" has become as much a philosophical as a practical problem.

The Reestablishment of Migratory Flow

I have mentioned that, during the beginning stages of emigration to Japan from South American countries, the movement was largely composed of those who possessed Japanese nationality and so were not barred from legal employment. Among them (now immigrants to their own country) were those who returned to Japan for good, but in the majority of cases emigration was "temporary." They "returned" to their natal country, but left their families in Argentina intending to return to them after several seasons of work.

In the community of Japanese descendants in Argentina, this movement was not encouraged, at least at first. According to Japanese immigrants' values, employment in a factory or as a construction worker, to mention some of the most common dekasegi occupations, represented a serious social setback. Furthermore, the idea of returning as a dekasegi itself signified a certain kind of failure, or at least the frustration of the dream that had taken them to such faraway lands.

The great majority of dekasegi were persons who had previously worked in independent occupations, either rural or urban, and who were unfamiliar with industrial jobs. Japanese contemporary society was for them as new as it would be for any other foreigner. They had little knowledge of their new surroundings, but they did have advantages over other immigrant workers. In some cases they had legal advantages, and in others the advantage of knowledge of the language. Above all they benefited from their similarity of background and appearance. Although many of them were, legally speaking, "foreigners," their link to the Japanese, however remote, made them less vulnerable to criticism and official pressures and more accepted in public opinion.

Many employers quickly recognized the benefits of this potential workforce, made up in part of foreigners who "seemed" Japanese. Their numbers increased to include, first, those of dual nationality and those who knew some Japanese, then young single people, parents, women, and family members without any direct link to Japan, and finally, the near elderly.

If emigration had at first been viewed with some skepticism in Argentina, doubts disappeared as rumors about economic benefits became more and more concrete. Frequent comments in the Japanese press about salaries and savings were enough to rapidly erase initial doubts and fears. Hard work and sometimes humiliating sacrifice were compensated for and justified by high incomes. In Argentina, hyperinflation created havoc as the currency was devalued daily. Japanese currency, in contrast, grew stronger in relation to the dollar. As a result, during the final years of the 1980s and the early 1990s, Japan became the promised land. Now everyone wanted to go to Japan.

Work in Japan

According to official statistics, in 1986, before the beginning of massive emigration, the population of Argentine nationality in Japan was just 359 persons. Of these, 199 (or 55 percent) resided in Tokyo, and, notably, 62 (17 percent) in Okinawa prefecture. The rest were sprinkled throughout the country. Five years later, in 1991, the number of Argentines had increased by a factor of ten, to 3,366. Kanagawa was the prefecture with the greatest concentration (1,273; 37.8 percent), trailed by Tokyo (284; 8.4 percent), Gumma (258; 7.6 percent), Shizuoka (224; 6.6 percent), and Saitama (215; 6.3 percent).[7]

The greatest number of Argentines could be found in Kanagawa, in the area of Shonandai on the outskirts of Fujisawa. An important automotive factory was located there, as well as many small and medium-size auto parts businesses. The jobs available were usually press or machinery assembly-line work. Another popular field of work was construction. Some preferred it because it was less high-pressure than factory work, although the physical demands were greater. Weather conditions, however, affected the number of days worked on outdoor construction jobs, and there was a risk of being unemployed between projects. In any case, moves were frequent, as many immigrants tried to optimize their stay by taking the best-paid jobs available.

Women, who mostly migrated after their husbands were already settled, also found jobs in the auto parts businesses, and even more so in electronics plants and the food industry.[8] Older migrants found work in security, cleaning, and maintenance services at factories, hotels, and hospitals.

The daily routine of a modern factory was not easy for immigrants, with practically no prior experience in the industrial area or salaried labor in general, to bear. In addition to the physical demands workers had to endure permanently rotating schedules (alternating biweekly), overtime (called "optional obligatory"), and lack of rest. Overtime was reflected in their salaries and was often the motivating factor for changing jobs, which happened more frequently in times of greater demand. There is no doubt that these jobs were attractive economically, but the daily work routine was not always good for a worker's mental and physical well-being.

Return to Argentina and Reintegration

Shortly after legal reforms in Japan were instituted, the Argentine economy entered a period of great transformation. Around 1991–92, the government put a drastic economic policy into effect that stabilized the currency by fixing it to the dollar, and checked inflation. Those who returned to Argentina before or at the beginning of the economic recovery maximized the return on their savings. These immigrants achieved what they had set out to do by working temporarily and, on their return, they resumed their prior activities or found new work.[9]

There was also another type of emigrant, who left Argentina not due to immediate necessity, but rather to avoid lowering his standard of living. In these cases, savings were earmarked for improving the family business (as in the case of those who owned a cleaners, the most popular urban occupation among Japanese settled in Argentina), or perhaps for their children's education, or just as extra "security." In the youngest group, savings were a means of achieving independence by acquiring a small piece of property or starting an enterprise on their own. Among new businesses, small, independent types were favored (such as kiosks, bookstores, perfumeries, and taxis), realizing in this way one of the typical aspirations of the descendants of immigrants. There were also those who returned but, even if they intended to, as their resources were not sufficient to allow them to resettle to their satisfaction, once again they opted for emigration. Some freely ruled out the idea of return to Argentina, at least in the short term, and opted to settle in Japan.

If the lack of opportunities (real or imagined) in Argentina had negatively affected the process of return and resettlement, there were those who, unaffected by strict economic concerns, found reasons for staying in Japan. Salaried work, security and stability, and order were values that encouraged them to stay. It should be emphasized that among those who opted to stay were families with children, and families created or reunited during the stay in Japan. As during the period of immigration to Argentina, children's enrollment in schools was the motivating factor for some families to leave and others to stay. These last cases merit greater attention, because these children (possibly the Japanese-Argentine-Japanese of the future) experienced socialization as the children of immigrants in a setting different from that of their parents.

By the early 1990s the dekasegi migration had finished its first cycle. Whether this immigration is considered successful or not, after this initial experience, the links between Japan and Argentina had been definitively reestablished. Today Japan remains a place offering solid work opportunities and a community base of Argentines and other South Americans with the capacity to receive newcomers. Finally, while the economic shake-up played an important role in this phenomenon, now neither Argentina nor Japan seems to be the final destination point of a continuous movement. In any case, for Japanese descendants, regardless of the place in which they remain, the meaning of Japan has changed radically.

The Reformulation of Territorial Identities

In light of migratory phenomena in general, there is no doubt that globalism is not a recent event. With the emergence of the dekasegi, the migration circle, which had been considered forever closed after the settlement of Japanese in South American countries, was reopened.

The greatest difference between past migrations to the Americas and the current phenomenon is the shortening of time and distances. Thus, events affecting the lives of migrants become more immediate. Facility of movement now makes possible the continuity of more or less synchronic developments far apart from each other. Emigration no longer creates abrupt breaks in the lives of its protagonists. As legal and economic channels for migration remain established, social networks sustaining it have consolidated, the spirit justifying and impelling it has become accepted, and for a great number of the immigrants' descendants, the very idea of settlement at one or the other pole of migration is no longer definite.

Within this context, is it possible to frame the dekasegi phenomenon as what in classic terms would be called a "migration of return"? We have seen that in the majority of cases the Japanese experience was, personally and in terms of work, something absolutely new. The temporariness with which the stay in Japan was regarded and the conditions of the stay, however, leave open the notion of "return." The same could be said of later stages after "return" to Argentina. On the other hand, given that leaving again is always a viable option, this too may be a temporary situation. And above all, the immigrant returning to his own country is never the same person: if the physical act of "return" is possible, emotionally the individual can never be the same. With each migratory swing one faces a new experience that is taken back to the birth society. In this sense, the state of being an immigrant (and the adjustments that come with it) is no longer an exceptional experience, but rather a phenomenon ever more present in daily life.

How do these circumstances influence the subjective construction of identities? Let us take as an example the question of nationality. If a national identity continues to be a determining factor in the legal regulation of movement into and out of a country, territorial notions (as in the case of Argentina) and biological ones (as in the case of Japan), in which this identity is nourished and on which it depends for its expressions, are ever more fragile: one is born of diverse origins and spends one's life in various places, adopting the languages, tastes, styles, and moral and ethical norms of an infinite number of traditions. The same could be said of ideas such as ethnicity, at least in the context of immigrant communities. As with assimilation theories, the discourse in which ethnic claims are privileged in the attempt to recover supposedly localized values is crystallized into irremovable essences, absolute references. Paradoxically, such values are often framed territorially by the specific limitations of the state. In a world in which human and informational exchanges have speeded up, the construction of ethnicity in such terms ends up being a labyrinth of impossible resolution.

The dekasegi phenomenon provides evidence that throws the validity of traditional discourses of identity into question. When migration is no longer an exceptional situation but has become a generalized way of being, even if in latent form, the fixed referents of identity lose the force, certainty, and explanatory efficacy once attributed to them. As the individual confronts a multiplicity of situations with each migration, classical identifying discourses that create solidly localized identity foundations lose the referential effectiveness they once had, at least when a stable and prolonged stay in a country is understood as the basis for each individual's state of being. Under these conditions, the sense of belonging is no longer acquired "naturally." For the migrant person, identifying orientations are of a basically dynamic nature and, in spite of the tendency to crystallize them, and beyond individual needs and desires, they are in a perpetually dynamic state of gestation and transformation.

Evaluation of the Dekasegi Experience

For decades, for most descendants of Japanese, Japan was a symbolic referent, generally of vague content, that did not usually come under elaborate scrutiny. In Argentina, the social environment in which they lived did not demand such scrutiny from them. With the dekasegi phenomenon, however, the ancestral Japan, until then only a distant idea, an idealized reference to the past, suddenly became a real space, an alternative source of work, a concrete place where their lives could unfold. "To go dekasegi" was, in this sense, the visualization of a part of an experience that had surrounded them from infancy: Japan, or "that which was Japanese," had come to life in their own selves. In this way various alternatives opened to the descendants of Japanese and created new terms in which to understand one's relationships with the country of one's forebears.

In Japan, the descendants of Japanese would find that if they remained silent, they would pass without remark. This possibility to belong physically to the majority, the anonymity of the masses, was a new sensation. To understand this we must remember that among the morals most vigorously inculcated in the children of Japanese immigrants were what we might call "ideas of national honor." Expressions like "Don't tarnish the Japanese name," or "What are they going to think of the Japanese?" so common in the immigrant environment, show how, under the pressures of the predominating assimilationist ideology, concepts like "shame" dominated individual behavior and were transformed into a collective responsibility. The descendants of Japanese, once in Japan, found themselves unexpectedly liberated from this responsibility: the imperative to defend or affirm Japanese "honor" before outsiders no longer existed.

Emigration also meant the opportunity to look at one's own unknown past. In the case of those descended from migrants from Okinawa (the largest group in Argentina), a visit to the birthplace of one's parents and grandparents had its emotional moments. First, unlike in large cities, in Okinawa descendants of immigrants are easily recognizable social figures: nearly all residents of Okinawa have a relation or acquaintance abroad. Hence the presence of a visitor from South America, someone who in spite of his physical similarity cannot express himself in Japanese or understand prevailing social etiquette, is not considered strange. For the South American immigrant this familiarity created a feeling of intimacy not often experienced in other places in the country. In the villages, owing to the density of personal relationships, this recognition was felt with greater intensity: even when two or three generations had passed since the original emigration, the descendants of migrants continued to be perfectly identifiable according to traditions of family attribution. When names were not remembered, such associations as "child number such-and-such of this or that family who emigrated to this or that country" continued to serve to clearly place the position of the visitor in the village social structure. The feeling of "belonging" that this type of reception produces, and the recognition of vague geographies one has heard of since childhood, became restorative experiences that helped fill the empty emotional spaces that the descendants of immigrants carry around with them.

If the encounter with the past had a largely reparative effect, it is also undeniable that the drastic change of environment and process of adaptation to daily life had a different kind of repercussion on the immigrant psyche. The majority of immigrants did not speak the language fluently, found the work was not the kind to which they were accustomed, and were used to different foods and tastes, as well as habits and customs, both at work and away from it. They had to learn about and adapt to a new cultural environment. For many, the contrast between the Japan that they had heard about and the Japan in which they had to live, or the disillusionment that came with the reality, became intelligible, in solitude and isolation, only with the confirmation of differences. In these cases, the recognition of their own "un-Japaneseness" became relevant at the moment of justifying and understanding the new situation in which they found themselves. Hence, "I will never go back to Japan" was the most frequent comment regarding this type of experience. For such people, the current Japan ended up becoming another absolute, definitively an Other, further solidifying their closeness to Argentina, the country of their birth.

Argentines and Other South American Dekasegi Groups

Besides the encounter with Japanese society, another subproduct of the dekasegi experience was that the majority of Argentines in Japan made contact with groups of Japanese descendants from other South American countries: Brazilians, Peruvians, Bolivians, and Paraguayans. The relationships between these groups were extremely complex. Depending on the circumstances, the similarities stood out as much as the differences. There was, at first, a certain unity, like that which results from the designation Nikkei, which at its most neutral simply refers to a supposed common Japanese origin, but in the present context specifically alludes to the Japanese who emigrated to the Americas. In many situations, the relative proximity between Nikkeijin or "Latinos" with respect to "the Japanese" was obvious.[10] They were found in the same work and social spaces. Their common language facilitated personal relationships, which often took the form of friendships, engagements, and marriages. If culinary tastes were less uniform, there was still a certain familiarity with daily meals, either in seasonings or flavors handed down in the families of Japanese immigrants. There were also numerous instances of relatives born in different countries who finally met while in Japan.

All of these factors provided a certain common orientation in terms of the identity expressed by the term Nikkei. To assume a Nikkei identity was a way of standing apart from those included among the *Nihonjin*, or people of Japanese nationality with different levels of status, depending on generation, place of birth, socialization, and experience. In addition, being Nikkei would become a way of globalizing the emigration experience to the Americas, in which the Japanese and their descendants had to face adaptation and assimilation into societies radically different from those from which they came.

However, we cannot ignore the fact that differences often imposed them-

selves despite similarities of experience. In general these differences corre-
sponded to the traditional national discourses of each country. Differences
experienced in workplaces were attributed to supposed national characteristics. In the opinion of one Argentine, Brazilians are "nice" and therefore get
along with the bosses; Peruvians are "idle" because "they've always lived well
and aren't used to working"; Bolivians "are like the Japanese," because they
haven't adapted as much to South American habits or language. In fact,
many businesses gave preferential treatment to workers of one nationality.

But if nationality continues to function as a basic referent, it is also certain that the appearance of "illegitimates," or at least Nikkei of doubtful origin, produced an internal schism that put the idea of solidarity based on a
common nationality to the test. When questioning the legitimacy of the
Nikkei identity of a person, disputes took precedence over the bonds of nationality and took on an "ethnic" character. The case that stands out most is
perhaps that of the Peruvians, for whom "ethnic" identity often prevails over
nationality. The presence of those disparagingly called "*Nikkei chicha*" ("false
Nikkei") caused serious conflicts with both the authorities who required
them to prove their "Japaneseness" and Peruvians who consider themselves
"legitimate" descendants of Japanese. These Peruvians saw that their honorable status as "authentic Nikkei" could be tainted by the potential illegality
of some of their fellow citizens, and that as suspicion fell on both groups of
Peruvians they might be excluded from work opportunities.

Neither the notion of "Nikkei" nor the significance of "Japaneseness" has
been completely resolved. In the case of natives of Okinawa, given the conflicted historical relationship between the region and the Japanese state, the
issue of Japaneseness is especially delicate. In immigrant South American
communities there was always a clear distinction, both institutional and individual, between Okinawa natives and non-natives, which, although attenu-
ated, lasted through generations in the different countries where they settled.
It is not strange, then, that the conflict between Okinawans and *Naichi* (the
term used for natives of the rest of Japan) has been reproduced once again in
Japan via the South American immigrant experience, with the added complexity of having taken place in a Japanese environment.

In summary, a game of alliances of similarities and differences has ensued,
which, depending on the situation, has confronted or drawn together the
different groups, sometimes along national lines and sometimes in accordance with criteria of ethnic legitimacy, language, or level of integration into
Japanese society. This tells of the difficulties in applying the term "Nikkei" as
an ethnic category in Japan today: it is a term whose limits or boundaries are
the object of permanent dispute. It describes a supposed nucleus made up of

persons who are far from being a homogeneous entity and who reveal and retain amongst themselves as many differences as similarities. To be Nikkei, in this sense, is more than an unnameable essence; it is a multivalent state to which one strategically refers according to the circumstances.

The Situation at the End of the 1990s

In Argentina, the dekasegi emigration produced a vacuum similar to that created by the aging of a community. The absence of young people brought nearly all activities characterized as part of the social life of the collective community (social gatherings, sports events, etc.) to a halt. Institutionally, since the end of the 1970s the crisis had affected the main immigrant organizations (such as the Japanese Association and prefectural associations), which were marked as much by internal rivalries as by a lag in generational restructuring that made them less attractive to young people. The situation worsened with the wave of emigration.

With the slow return of recent years we find some signs of renewed activity, although the needs of institutions have changed and the attitude they should take when confronted with new situations has not yet been clearly defined. At any rate, it is evident that today, the great traditional organizations on which community life was founded lack the original binding power they once had. Instead, new meeting places have emerged, less structured and narrower in focus, less uniform and tending to be less traditional, but satisfying a multiplicity of needs generated by the people. There are clubs for older people that meet on weekends, professional associations, informal soccer championships, and dance or folk music groups. Among these new forms of association, the bilingual Japanese-Spanish primary and secondary schools (Instituto Privado Argentino Japones, Nichi-a Gakuin), operating with official recognition since the 1980s, deserve special attention. Their main function is educational, but through parent associations (largely made up of children of Japanese immigrants) they have formed an important means of social contact. In this environment, a new way of "being Nikkei" is emerging in Argentina.

Interest in learning Japanese is another phenomenon that has emerged within the last few years. It would seem that the positive attitude toward the language is more widespread currently than in former times. The dekasegi migration, directly or indirectly, has without a doubt contributed to the formation of a new understanding of the language among parents who don't speak Japanese but want their children to learn it. But we must also take into account the influence of factors such as changes in family structure, namely the presence of grandparents in the family group, as well as other well-known explanations for the so-called Sansei phenomenon. Finally, it is worth mentioning that the popularity of the Japanese language is linked to the general reevaluation of Japan and things Japanese in national and international contexts, and society's greater acceptance of positive attitudes about the immigrant past.

At the other end of the spectrum, the impact of immigration on Japanese society is a phenomenon that goes beyond the merely circumstantial insofar as it has had a profound overall impact on Japanese society. The beginning of the migratory wave was a response to the collective necessities of Japanese industry and the economic situation of the countries from which immigrants came, and was generally considered "temporary." But at the end of a decade there were a considerable number of foreigners settling legally and illegally in Japan. In the specific case of Japanese descendants from South America, migration had as its consequence the formation of a "Latin American collectivity" rooted around the most important industrial centers of Japan. Many official and private services emerged in answer to immigrants' needs. Consulting organizations have been formed to advise local governments on affairs related to foreign residents, although results have yet to be seen. Regarding the acquisition of the Japanese language, many towns now offer free courses to adults and support classes for children. There are also a great number of places of entertainment, restaurants, and travel agencies whose primary customers are Latin American workers, and there is even a weekly newspaper that is available in any of the large train stations.

But above all, the rapid increase of foreign workers in Japan created an issue that until then was nonexistent in apparently homogeneous Japanese society: coexistence with foreigners. What a short time ago was known as "the problem of foreign workers" (*gaikokujin rodosha mondai*) has become more widely known as "the foreign neighbor" (*tonari no gaikokujin*). The Japanese press and television discuss legal and economic aspects of this phenomenon with increasing naturalness. Topics include legal status, human rights, working conditions, and cost-benefit analyses of the introduction of foreign labor, as well as sociocultural issues such as the Latin American presence in community life, educational problems, and delinquency. In other words, there is a stable, recognized South American presence today in Japan. Hence it is possible to affirm that from the initial moment of the dekasegi phenomenon, new faces, clothing, and accents began to become part of the urban Japanese landscape, a novel event in the recent history of the country, and one that has had a definitive impact on contemporary Japanese society.

Final Remarks

In conclusion, let me restate briefly my initial question: How has dekasegi migration affected the formulation of new identifying orientations among Argentines descended from the Japanese? There is no doubt that the dekasegi period has had wide repercussions, both collective and individual, beyond its economic benefits. Obviously, a period of residence in Japan did not evoke the same degree of self-searching in everyone. But in each case, "having been there" provided a certain authority, a different kind of legitimacy, reflected in the loss of prejudice, possibly a greater degree of self-confidence, and, above all, a greater liberty to examine one's Japanese heritage. Direct contact with Japanese society has made it possible for Japan to be a permanent presence in the lives of the descendants of immigrants. Although in the context of Argentine society most of the time one's Japanese heritage had never been merely "information," now it was transformed into a real life experience. This experience served to redefine individual connections with Japan, relating as much to the present as to the immigrant past, and as such, mapping out a vision for the future and opening new possibilities for the elaboration of different identifying choices.

As far as those choices are concerned, a single trend cannot be pinpointed. None of the individuals with whom I have been in contact has expressed an attitude of primordially "Japanese" identity. Rather, choices are expressed in a range, from the reevaluation and reappropriation of certain elements perceived as belonging to one's Japanese cultural heritage (for example, the "discovery" of attitudes, feelings, or familiarities that up until then had not found expression or been verbalized and that subsequently found a place in the Japanese environment), to the negation of this heritage and reaffirmation of one's "Argentine" identity (in these cases, what is Japanese becomes the absolute Other). The phenomenon of "lo Nikkei" is seemingly more clearly delineated as a relative point, a simple refusal to identify with "the Japanese of Japan" but not completely assimilating as "the gaijin Argentine," and is found at the intermediary point of the range. This choice is more than just the lineal and objective product of a common past understood as race or origin. It creates a certain positioning and transmits it selectively, in agreement with certain codes that acquire meaning only in their projection onto the frame of current Argentine society. As such, we are dealing with a specific, newly localized identity in a permanent process of gestation, incorporating elements of the migrant experience of the parents as well as contemporary trends. Now differences that might have previously existed within the immigrant group tend to unify or nullify themselves, and a reinterpretation and reformulation of what is Japanese becomes part of an orientation toward the future.

Finally, the potential "international" character contained in "Nikkei" cannot be ignored. More and more Argentines are found in places distant from Argentina, and there are more and more contacts between Japanese descendants from different countries. The term "Nikkei" then acquires as many different meanings as the environments in which it is created. Japan, in this respect, has become a new point of investigation for identifying orientations of Argentines descended from the Japanese, many of them now immigrants themselves.

I must also clarify that the near and distant relationships schematically discussed here with respect to the Japanese, far from being static or closed, vary, are adjusted, intermix, and are relative to an infinity of other possible identifying orientations that each individual chooses. Therefore it is interesting that, given such new conditions for understanding the migration experience and the emergence of multiple possibilities for reinterpretation, the concept we have labeled as "Nikkei" is but one possible facet or orientation, in constant transformation, and constantly connected with others. All such possibilities are available to the descendants of the Japanese and even more so to those connected to them as they live out their lives in contemporary society.

Notes

1. We should note that exchanges (personal, material) with villages of origin were never abruptly cut off. Relatively fluid communications were maintained and, in some cases, even increased. In the case of Okinawa, the return of the islands in 1972 eliminated the until-then necessary procedures such as the need for a passport from the Ryukyu government. This, along with the popularization of air travel, made it possible to maintain relations between the two poles of migration that would prove to be fundamental when dekasegi movement began to emerge as a real option.

2. In 1986 annual inflation was already at 81.9 percent. In 1987 it reached 174.8 percent, in 1988 387.9 percent, and in 1989 4,923 percent. This phenomenon equally affected other South American countries that, like Brazil and Peru, were initially the source of large numbers of dekasegi workers.

3. In addition to Japan, other countries such as Canada and Australia were recipients of a large number of skilled Argentine personnel during these same years.

4. Before World War II there was a considerable migration (sometimes forced) from China, and especially from the colonial territories in the Korean Peninsula.

5. This situation affected persons of Japanese descent who, even if born and raised in Japan, did not have easy access to Japanese nationality. Compare the situation of Koreans and Chinese who have resided in Japan for generations yet are still identified as "residents of Japan" (*zai-nichi*).

6. It is interesting here to draw attention to the different shades of meaning in the generic Japanese word for foreigner (*gaijin* or *gaikokujin*). Until the middle of the 1980s, the term connoted "individuals of North American or European origin." Currently, the dichotomy between "Japanese" and "foreigner" is maintained, although "foreigner" has acquired other connotations (such as "foreigner not admitted," which in some cases could mean "Chinese not admitted," for example).

7. These data are drawn from Haruo Shimada, "Visiting Workers from Latin America in Japan," *Foreign Policy Review* 79 (1994): 26–27; Table 2.8.

8. In addition to allowing relatives of Japanese to work, a program of "technical training" for foreigners was created, which in practical terms entailed a kind of regulated immigration of workers.

9. Migration statistics clearly reflect the return trend to Argentina. Annual arrivals to Japan from Argentina peaked in 1991 at 6,322, but from then on numbers began to decline. This is clearly different from the case of Peruvian and Bolivian dekasegi, as their numbers continued to increase.

10. Paradoxically, the descendants of Japanese immigrants, usually identified as "Japanese" or "Oriental" in their countries of origin, have become "Latinos" in Japan. The word in Japanese—*raten-teki*—is related to terms such as happy, carefree, irresponsible, and romantic.

CHAPTER SEVENTEEN

The Nikkei Negotiation of Minority/Majority Dynamics in Peru and the United States

STEVEN MASAMI ROPP

The period of 1988–90 marked a critical turning point for Nikkei communities in the United States and Peru. In the United States, Congress approved H.R. 442, the redress and reparations bill, bringing to a close the long struggle for justice on behalf of Japanese Americans interned during World War II. In Peru, Alberto Fujimori emerged in 1990 onto the world scene as he soundly defeated novelist Mario Vargas Llosa in a second-round run-off for the presidency of Peru.[1] Fujimori capitalized on a wave of Nikkei activity in mainstream politics starting in the 1980s. These ventures by Nikkei into the national political arena of their countries are notable achievements in their own right. My interest here is to compare the two achievements in order to examine the interrelationship of ethnic and national formations. The groups in both countries share a common origin and immigration history, and yet they are characterized quite differently with regard to minority/majority relations. One group is considered insular, closed, and distinctly nonassimilated, while the other is generally seen as highly assimilated. Why would one produce a redress movement and the other a president? I will address this question through a comparison of Nikkei ethnicity in relation to the precepts of national belonging in Peru and the United States.[2]

Nikkei and the Minority/Majority Dynamic

In February 1999 I had the chance to observe and participate in an international Nikkei youth conference in Lima, Peru.[3] During a workshop on

Nikkei values, a simple but important point emerged: how Nikkei communities see themselves and are seen by the society at large varies from country to country and is largely a product of prevailing minority/majority dynamics.

This workshop broke into three groups, one Brazilian, one Peruvian, and the last mixed, with persons from Paraguay, Chile, Argentina, and the United States. Each group worked with the question, "As Nikkei, how do we see ourselves and how do others see us?" What I found striking was the decidedly positive or negative spin each group associated with stereotypical Nikkei characteristics. The important distinction that emerged was between Brazil and Peru on the one hand, and Argentina, Chile, and the United States on the other. In the case of Brazil and Peru, there was no real sense of a downside or negative consequences with regard to Nikkei stereotypes. Nikkei "characteristics," whether of a seemingly positive or negative nature, were a source of pride.

On the contrary, in the case of Argentina, Chile and the United States, there was a sense that even positive values, such as being hardworking, intelligent, and organized, could carry negative consequences. For example, the idea of the Nikkei as hardworking and industrious has a flip side in stereotypes of being uncreative and robotlike, of being good workers and followers but with limited managerial and leadership ability. In contrast, the Peruvian Nikkei included creativity among their strengths and, in general, there was an attitude that whatever the endeavor, whether in the arts, literature, sciences, business, or politics, Nikkei are capable, if not superior. This positive minority status has been noted in the case of the Brazilian Nikkei and appears to carry over to Peru.[4] The common denominator of the two appears to be a large non-European descent majority. In the case of the United States, Argentina, and Chile, Nikkei face a different majority/minority formula, one dominated economically and culturally by a European descent majority. Chile and Argentina, in the context of Latin America especially, see themselves as nations of primarily European descent in contrast to the Indianness of Peru and the Africanness of Brazil.

Given these types of distinctions, my goal is to approach Nikkei ethnicity as a negotiation of insider and outsider conceptualizations in the context of nationalist formations. In Peru, the Nikkei find themselves with a positive minority status among a predominantly nonwhite and disenfranchised majority. In the United States, they find themselves with a contradictory status as a model minority, lauded for their adaptability but always considered of questionable loyalty. Given that distinction, I will look at Nikkei in Peru and the United States as they make common reference to and put into practice "being" Nikkei. I am interested in how these claims, these formations of self and community, take form through the molding of content such as culture, history, race, gender, and family in the context of projects of nation building.[5] Projects are the parameters and goals of making and being made in those cases where competing groups negotiate position, belonging, and just rewards. The dynamic process of constructing individual and collective Nikkei identities in relation to the demands and parameters of nation building can be explored through a comparison of national level representations. These formations can then be analyzed as they emerge in dialogue with the products of nationalist precepts such as minority/majority dynamics and ethnic/mainstream distinctions.[6]

At a general level, my assertion is that Nikkei in Peru and the United States represent two distinct formations. On the one hand, among the Nikkei in Peru, one encounters a system of fluid hierarchies constituted through vertical relationships of social status and symbolic power that privilege race and class. In the United States, one finds a fixed flat formation constituted through horizontal relationships that privilege race and culture. To arrive at this conclusion, I discuss collective group formation, analyze significant differences between the two cases, and, finally, place each group formation in the context of citizenship, belonging, and nation building. By way of explanation, I discuss differences in the initial composition of the two communities, radical differences in local and national subject making (individual, citizen, minority) processes, and significant differences in geopolitical relations between the country of origin (Japan) and the country of residence.

In the following analysis I focus specifically on two events that took place in 1998. In the United States, I discuss the "Ties that Bind" conference (April 3, 4, and 5), the first national-level, community-based conference. In Peru, I focus on the 38th Annual Assembly of Representatives (November 27–28). This annual meeting brings together all Nikkei in Peru operating under the umbrella of the Japanese Peruvian Association. In each case I am especially interested in the official proclamations produced, organizational and personal interaction dynamics, and the key issues that emerged relating to identity, community composition, and internal politics. The overall goal is to examine how internal diversity is managed and organized and how that formation emerges in response to and in dialogue with minority/majority dynamics in the larger society.

Being Nikkei in Peru and the United States

Peruvian Nikkei

The annual assembly that I focus on here is the one that took place just as the main activities of the centenary (April 3, 1999) of Japanese immigration to Peru were getting underway. The Japanese Peruvian Association, or as it is referred to in Spanish, "APJ" (ah-peh-hota), organizes and hosts the annual assembly at its base of operations, the Japanese Peruvian Cultural Center located in Jesús María, a middle-class neighborhood in Lima. APJ is the central organization and power in the community. Everything relating to Japan and the Peruvian Nikkei community passes through APJ. Its mission to serve as the liaison between Japan and Peru, between Nikkei and the larger society, and to serve as the central point of decision making and the diffusion of power and resources in the community is clearly stated in the official goals of APJ. The Nikkei leaders that the two-day assembly brought together in 1998 included those of thirty-four organizations in Lima and ten from provinces outside Lima.

The actual business of the assembly is highly formalized and full of protocol. Most agree that real decisions are generally made prior to and outside the formal assembly. Long speeches, even longer protocol salutations, and sedate, repetitive reports from each and every representative are typical. The majority of the representatives, especially those from Lima, are part of an internal power structure and network that maintains and circulates control within a small number of individuals, a cadre generally referred to as *los dirigentes* (the leaders). The first day of the event this particular year was composed of the standard protocol ceremonies, a series of lectures on the history of the community on the occasion of the centenary, and, finally, reports from each of the major commissions and organizations. The second day began with everyone divided into thematic workshops, the topics for this particular year being institutions, business, and human resources. Later in the afternoon everyone reconvened, at which time designated officials from each workshop presented their group's findings and conclusions. This was followed by a series of rather long presentations on the topics of the workshops. The final results of the assembly were published a few days afterwards in *Perú Shimpo*, the primary Nikkei community newspaper.

Despite the formality of the event, there were two sources of excitement during the proceedings. The first of these was "the apology." During José Yoshida's speech on the "significance of the centenary of Japanese immigration to Peru," he expressed that on the occasion of the centenary it was important to acknowledge the history of discrimination and mistreatment of Okinawans. He acknowledged that immigrants brought with them ideas and practices that essentially gave second-class status to the Okinawans. Yoshida expressed his personal apology, "*lo siento mucho.*" This caught everyone by surprise, and immediately after the speech ended a reporter from *Perú Shimpo* rushed to gather opinions from the representatives of Okinawan organizations and well-known persons of Okinawan descent in attendance. The whole episode was interesting for a number of reasons.

The fact that a point of historical tension and division within the community surfaced in a public presentation by a high-ranking person in the community was semiscandalous. Reactions to the apology reveal some of the key internal dynamics of community politics. The most important of these is the maintenance of a united front for a common cause. Public sentiment tends to focus on this very characteristic, that the Japanese maintain a closed community. Internal politics tend to be handled off the record. Furthermore, differences of opinion tend to remain firmly entrenched within a structural framework and are rarely discussed and generally not well known outside the confines of the community. The apology created a buzz on an otherwise sedate afternoon because it was a moment of transgression, when the politely unspeakable was spoken. Not only was this historical discrimination openly referred to, but the protagonist also apologized for it. By apologizing, the protagonist, speaking on behalf of non-Okinawans, acknowledged a wrongdoing at the same time he invoked the power dynamic that made that discrimination possible in the first place. Damage control was interesting. The majority of those interviewed by *Perú Shimpo* expressed the opinion that it was a profound gesture, but perhaps unnecessary in this day and age, that discrimination is in the past. The one unqualified endorsement of the apology was by a leader of an Okinawan organization who stated that the apology was a just and appropriate acknowledgment of the discrimination that characterized the early history of the community.

It is interesting that in the case of Japanese Americans, homogeneity is often cited as a fundamental factor in their successful adaptation.[7] This explanation, often bordering on cultural essentialism, maintains that the Japanese brought with them a sense of common purpose and a value system that placed group survival above the individual. In Peru, the stereotype of the Japanese often focuses on this notion of an undifferentiated homogeneity. In reality, the eighteen thousand who arrived in Peru between 1899 and 1923 were anything but a homogenous group. As a whole, immigrants from the various regions and prefectures of Japan became Japanese through the immigration and settlement process,[8] and a sense of Japaneseness and common cause did emerge, but not without its tensions, sacrifices, and internal power struggles. In Peru, one of the principal forms of differentiation to be institutionalized right from the beginning, one that carries over to the present day, is this distinction between Okinawans and non-Okinawans.

The Naichijin, referring to those from Japan proper, often viewed the Uchinanchu, those from the prefecture of Okinawa, through the lens of that very nation-state building process credited with giving Japanese immigrants their adaptive edge. As other research in this volume points out, prior to its formal incorporation into the emerging Japanese nation-state in the 1860s,

Okinawa was an independent region, a tribute kingdom of Japan. The Meiji restoration and Japan's general reconfiguration as a modern nation-state necessitated new myths of cultural and racial homogeneity. Okinawans became one of a number of minorities, second-class ethnics in the homogenous Japanese body politic. This tumultuous period saw not only the initiation of Japanese immigration but also the creation of a Japanese cultural citizenship that would be carried to the Americas. Okinawa was a neo-colony within the Japanese nation-state and, as such, the Naichijin looked upon the Uchinan-chu as culturally, racially, and socially inferior, as second-class citizens, as not quite "real" Japanese, that construct being at once ancient in reference and modern in form. In Peru, intermarriage between the two groups was rare, and, institutionally, the Naichijin and their "Japanese" associations monopolized official power and definitions of community.

Today, discrimination against Okinawans is officially relegated to the past. In practice stereotypes and prejudices persist, although with generational change and intermarriage between the two groups they are much less deterministic. The power structure and its regulation of internal differentiation are expressed through events such as the annual assembly. APJ is the top of the pyramid, the apex of the power structure that encompasses all matters relating to the Nikkei community. APJ monopolizes activities, resources, and definitions, and in doing so incorporates all other institutions. Differences in origin, gender, culture, class, and social status are organized and managed within this hierarchical structure. In the case of specifically Okinawan associations, they are quite prominent, given that at least 50 percent of the Nikkei population traces some Okinawan descent. However, they exist as subsets, as lower rank-order specificities within the overarching hierarchy of Nikkeiness, a construct that supersedes all other differences and determines what role those differences will play and represent internally and externally.

The second source of excitement at the assembly after "the apology" was an exchange between Juan Kanashiro, president of APJ in Haucho, a small provincial town on the northern coast of Peru, and Geraldo Maruy, president of the Centenary Commission. This exchange illuminates some of the other important dynamics of community politics. Kanashiro raised an interesting question, both in his written report and during the debate. In rather oblique language he raised the issue of discrimination based upon generational distinctions as the source of two problems. First, young people, especially Yonsei (fourth generation), when encountering generational discrimination feel slighted and are subsequently less likely to participate in Nikkei institutions. Second, in his opinion the Sansei, Yonsei, and subsequent generations lack *personería*, a rather obscure term that translates as "solicitorship" or "legal capacity." Maruy, not understanding the comment, asked specifically "who is discriminating against whom," and what exactly is at stake with regard to personería. After some discussion it became clear that Kanashiro was actually referring to a special immigration category created in Japan in 1990 that allows for a person with a parent or grandparent who was a Japanese national to obtain a special visa in Japan.[9] His concern was that this legal status in effect defines who is and is not Nikkei. An exchange followed about how being Nikkei is about having pride, and that this is passed on from the parents. There was also an undercurrent in Maruy's comments that one is not Nikkei by virtue of sympathy for some perceived mistreatment, and that this "poor-me" attitude is antithetical to what being Nikkei is supposed to be about.

This exchange brings out certain internal dynamics, the most important dimensions of which are related to the tension between *los limeños y los de provincia*, that is, those from Lima and those from the provinces. Lima is the center of power in Peru and in the Nikkei community. This relationship between Lima and the provinces has historical, class, racial, and power dimensions. The historical dimension, for the Nikkei, derives from the initial immigration period that was characterized by two types of immigration, an initial pattern of contract labor and a subsequent pattern of free immigration from Japan. Specifically, with the end of the contract system in 1923, a *yobiyose* pattern became dominant. The yobiyose, those "called over," went directly to Lima and were able to bypass the difficult experience of contract and farm labor in the provinces.

In Peru as a whole, of the three zones, *selva, sierra, y costa* (jungle, mountain, and coast), the coast has always had a monopoly on power, status, and privilege, with Lima as the dominant center. Having origins outside Lima carries negative implications of culture, race (Indianness), class (poverty), and power (subjugated). This is reproduced in the Nikkei community. Nikkei *provincianos* are stereotyped as poor, multiracial, and completely Peruvianized, that is, distinctly "non-Japanese." Provincial Nikkei status is undermined by assumptions of cultural and language loss, lack of Japanese last names, and racial impurity. Provinciano identity claims are often viewed with much cynicism as being only economically motivated. In the end, Juan Kanashiro's attempt to address the status of young provincial Nikkei ran into two barriers: 1) APJ has no control over how Japanese immigration law defines Nikkei, and 2) sympathy is a scarce commodity, especially for provincianos.

Japanese Americans

"Ties that Bind," "a national gathering to explore the themes of identity, community, and diversity," was the first of its kind for Japanese Americans.

The motivations leading up to the conference and its goals emerged from and reflected new challenges and new realities. Consistently high levels of out-marriage since the 1960s, various types of postwar immigration from Japan, and the successful conclusion of the redress movement in 1988 were key factors. Questions of diversity and post-redress community organizing are still concerns in the community today. At the center, although often unspoken, is a tense and often painful undercurrent rooted in wartime internment, legal exclusions, racial discrimination, and all the contradictions and challenges of adaptation that Japanese Americans have faced in the United States. The overwhelming concern in this national-level dialogue was the question of the future of Japanese Americans as a distinct ethnic community. In this section, I will discuss some of the motivations leading up to the conference and the event itself, including organizational features and the framing of internal community dynamics. The declarations and directives of the conference are extensive and especially telling.

The stated goals of the 1998 conference were "To explore the dynamic changes occurring within the Japanese American community. Central themes to the conference are inclusion, diversity, and the developing of the new paradigm to define ourselves and our community."[10] The conference took place in Los Angeles and was planned, organized, and carried out by three groups: Little Tokyo Service Center (LTSC); the Japanese American Cultural and Community Center (JACCC), based in Los Angeles; and the Japanese Cultural and Community Center of Northern California (JCCCNC), based in San Francisco. These three organizations, along with the Japanese American National Museum (JANM), have recently initiated a national-level dialogue, primarily through these conferences but also through the establishment of the California Japanese American Community Leadership Council (CJACLC). In spite of these efforts, there exists no one umbrella organization. The community's previous experience with centralized leadership in the form of the Japanese American Citizen's League (JACL), pressed into a leadership role by the government during World War II internment, still carries much bitterness. "Ties that Bind" was the first national-level organizing effort not associated with either the Japanese American Citizen's League (JACL) or the redress movement. Since World War II, the JACL has remained the primary institutional voice for Japanese Americans on a national level. The redress movement and groups like the National Coalition for Redress and Reparations (NCRR) arose in the 1970s, and in many ways challenged the conservative accommodation politics of the JACL. The redress movement, in the opinion of many, became a truly unifying community-building force that bridged generations and pulled people together from across the political spectrum. Since the conclusion of redress in 1988, JACL membership continues to decline. The conference focused on the important question of what is left and what lies ahead for the Japanese American community.

Approximately five hundred people attended the three-day public event, the only requirement for participation being the payment of a registration fee. The first day consisted of tours, a program on the concentration camp experience, and a performance art program. The following day saw the main activities of the event. In the morning, opening remarks introduced the Japanese American experience and placed in it a social historical context. This was followed by an opening panel, "Who are Japanese Americans?" The next activity involved all participants and consisted of randomly assigned small group sessions with the task of defining various perspectives in the community, identifying what is important to different segments of the community, factors for nonparticipation or dis-identification, and, finally, solutions for strengthening community. This was followed by a panel presentation and discussion about values, in the search for "the glue that keeps our community together." Small topic-specific breakout sessions followed in the afternoon, covering a wide range of topics, from youth to the elderly, the church to Japantown, and language to out-marriage. The results of the breakout sessions were presented in a summary session on the morning of the third day, concluding the conference.

Certain issues that arose in the planning process for the opening panel, "Who are Japanese Americans?" present some interesting perspectives on the state of the community.[11] The intention for this panel was to have a moderator and four speakers, each one representing a particular segment of the community. Shin-issei (new, postwar Japanese immigrants), Nisei, Yonsei, and Hapa were the first-order categories identified by the planning committee. In addition, balance and representation in terms of gender, religion, and region were concerns. With these categories, lists of potential speakers were compiled. Each participant was expected to give a short exposition on their experience as a Japanese American and then on the experience of the subgroup. Through this process the community would be segmented into three major groupings. At the center was the official Japanese America found in social science studies and museums, a monoracial community ranked by generation and age. The unqualified terms Issei, Nisei, Sansei, and Yonsei always refer to a monoracial subject with roots in the initial immigration period, 1880 and 1924. The next two major groupings are add-ons, the sources of the "diversity" that the community must "struggle with," and these are postwar immigrants, the Shin-Issei and Shin-Nisei, and multiracial subjects, or, as they are referred to in conference literature, "mixed Japanese racial groups."[12]

288 / STEVEN MASAMI ROPP

In the process of composing this all-important and symbolic opening panel, the limits of diversity became apparent. A certain tension was evident with respect to the divide between the hegemonic core and the diversity segments. For this discussion, I will focus on the multiracial issue, although the question of postwar immigrants was equally important.[13] With regard to the multiracial segment, the question was initially framed as "How do we deal with the Hapas?" In one planning meeting the question of whether to address the issue at all was raised, with the suggestion that perhaps the Hapas would be offended at inclusion because it would seem their participation was sought only out of desperation. It is an interesting response to the "multiracial problem" when leaders and organizers do not want to be seen as so desperate as to have to include Hapas.

It is obvious that a serious generational and racial divide has emerged in the community. It is a problem that seems, at times, to inspire fears of civil rights–style protests and messy demands for equal participation and entry. Despite the fact that the current generation is multiracial and multiethnic and that future generations will be increasingly so, the ideal and the future remain distinctly monoracial.

The conference produced a list of five declarations and a rather extensive list of directives deriving from those declarations. The first proclamation was that "there will be a Japanese American community in the 21st century." The community is made up of a number of institutions and organizations, and with care and guidance the "ties that bind" will ensure the continuation of the community. This first declaration was a response to numerous prognostications of the imminent death of the community since the 1960s.[14] These death knells cite high out-marriage rates and cultural assimilation as cause and evidence of the eventual and inevitable complete amalgamation into the mainstream.[15] The second proclamation suggested that diversity is increasing. The generational distinction (Issei, Nisei, Sansei, etc.), the hegemonic core mentioned earlier, is no longer solely sufficient in capturing the reality of the present community. The proclamation further states that this diversity must be embraced and that all those who "wish to identify with the Nikkei community" should be allowed to do so. The diversity specifically named includes postwar immigrant status, gender, sexual orientation, and mixed heritage. A third proclamation stated that a Japanese American culture does exist. Although difficult to define, it is a dynamic formation with roots in community institutions. It includes elements of the culture brought from Japan and elements unique to the community in the United States. The fourth proclamation stated that there are, in fact, Japanese American values and that it is necessary "to discuss and selectively integrate them as a positive force as we claim our place in American society." The final proclamation stated that "historical experience is full of important lessons." Examples include internment and the many injustices the community has faced.

All of these statements, read in reverse, point toward dilemmas that Japanese Americans face as an ethnic/racial minority and the strategies employed to negotiate them. Insisting that, indeed, "Japanese American culture and values do exist" is a response to the contradictions of minority status in the United States. On the one hand, Japanese Americans were expected to leave behind Japanese culture and to assimilate.[16] Their eventual exclusion from entry and the denial of naturalization were based on the idea that they were incapable of such assimilation due to their racial difference, their non-European origins. Therefore, even as they tried to assimilate, they faced rejection and denial. The postwar period brought new possibilities due to the postwar economic boom and the civil rights movement, as racial barriers were broken down and prevailing minority/majority dynamics were challenged. However, as much as assimilation was challenged and ethnic pride became a possibility, national identity has firmly retained its European reference. The basic formula of race and nation did not change. "American" remains a metonym for white with a proliferation of sub-groups, x-Americans, y-Americans, z-Americans. In the case of Japanese Americans, traditional values and culture post–civil rights could be a source of pride, but only in the sense that they facilitated adaptation. A model minority is still a minority, outside the mainstream, different. In the 1980s, the limits of ethnic revitalization quickly surfaced. As Japan challenged American hegemony, Japanese Americans were once again confused with the enemy. As O'Brien and Fujita suggest in their account of the Japanese American experience, as long as they "look different," they will be outsiders, a marked ethnic minority.[17] Only with physical amalgamation, through out-marriage, will they escape this marked position. And herein lies the root of the contradiction. Out-marriage is the ultimate escape from discrimination, but it is also the demise of the community. It is no wonder that the increasingly multiracial and multiethnic character of the community generates concern, fear, and resentment.

The Influence of National Context on Community Structure

The Japanese Peruvian community is a pyramid structure based on vertical and hierarchical relationships. For example, although only 32 percent of the population is officially affiliated with a formal organization,[18] the reach of these organizations is much greater due to extended family connections and the *kenjinkai* system.[19] Each and every individual is tied in through an overlay structure of association and membership through family and extended family ties with the kenjinkai as the basic building block. The hierarchy itself is made up of a series of smaller nested groupings. Each person tends to have his or her own particular group and/or network, which may or may not coincide with a formal grouping. Particular types of groupings tend to have differential status within the overall symbolic hierarchy.

Participation and membership in the Peruvian Nikkei community is relatively open and flexible, but with limited upward mobility. This mirrors Peruvian society in general. Definitions of who is Peruvian, for example, are relatively porous, but upward mobility within that formation is extremely difficult.[20] In other words, a wide variety of people can associate with and identify with the Nikkei community, but the actual role that the person plays within the hierarchy depends upon certain status formulas. Origins in Lima, prominent family lines, business success, racial purity, and Japanese language and cultural skills are just some of the components of the Nikkei formula. It is relatively easy for a person who has only one Japanese grandparent and who does not appear phenotypically Japanese to claim and to some extent actualize a Nikkei identity. This person can join the formal institutions by virtue of a Nikkei last name, keeping in mind that Peruvian legal names consist of both the paternal and maternal last names. At the same time, multiple claims to various descent lines are common elements of Peruvian society. Race and social identities are not such either/or propositions as they are in the United States.

A Nikkei identity in Peru is pragmatic, providing a social network to optimize opportunity where opportunity is scarce. Finding work, getting into school, and finding a secure place to put money are all difficult propositions, and the slightest advantage, no matter how slim, is worth pursuing. Peruvian social identities consist of fluid forms of affiliation and identification, in contrast to the United States. There they remain relatively fixed, but at the same time each individual, rigidly defined within the parameters of the structural whole, has the power and rights associated with that particular category. As is evident from "Ties that Bind," diversity is a tremendous obstacle because of the fixed horizontal nature of identification and community formation. A person either is or is not Japanese American, and once you let someone cross that line, then they have full and equal access. By contrast, in Peru diversity is less of a challenge because identity and community formation is much more fluid and acceptance as Nikkei does not guarantee much of anything other than the chance to contribute to and perhaps draw some benefit from the community. In other words, if you ask someone who is Nikkei, they will provide a narrow definition.[21] In reality, social identities in Peruvian society are fluid and highly contested. Much of what passes for belonging can be attributed to sheer willpower and confidence.

In the Japanese American case, community is horizontal and relatively more individuated. I think it is fair to say that although in Peru a Nikkei identity has much to do with the search for opportunity in an extremely poor environment, in the United States, Nikkei identity involves much more of a search for self, for individual self-realization. A Nikkei identity is ultimately an attempt to reconcile on an individual level the contradictory search for acceptance in a society that sees them as perpetual foreigners. Internal dynamics tend to emphasize relatively egalitarian ideals, especially in interpersonal relations. While hierarchies of gender, race, age, generation, and regional origin certainly exist, there is an emphasis on giving equal time and space to differences within the construct as a whole (sexual orientation, generation, gender, multiraciality).

Nikkei and the Equation of Race, Nation, and Development

In this comparative analysis, I argue that significant differences exist in the formation of each community, although each shares and makes common reference to the same origins in Meiji-era Japan. The different outcome is a product of historical factors and specifics of the immigration experience and adaptation. I find these to be more compelling than essentialist and reductive cultural explanations of Japanese adaptability.[22] In this historical and national context, then, the question is, what are the demands of nationalism, and what strategies are employed at the individual and group level to meet those requirements?

At the heart of the minority/majority dynamic is an equation of race and nationalism. In Peru, a European descent minority took control in 1534 and has maintained rule through the subjugation and oppression of an indigenous majority. Whiteness is like a small island in a dark sea of racial inferiors. Modern Peruvian nationalism struggles with a contradiction, as the path to national development continues to be based on the denial and ultimate elimination of the Indian.[23] This is often expressed in the sentiment that the problem with Peru is Peruvians. The United States, on the other hand, has always constructed itself as a bastion of progress and whiteness. Racial and ethnic minorities are tolerated as second-class citizens, but America by definition is white. Peru, unlike countries such as Argentina and the United States, was never able to attract many European immigrants, and so had to settle for Asians. However, the Japanese presence quickly inspired fear among the small ruling oligarchy, thanks in part to a continent-wide yellow peril campaign by the U.S. government, which was fearful of Japanese encroachment in Latin America. In Peru, the local white elite feared that common racial origins would enable the Japanese to lead the indigenous majority in the overthrow of the white elite.[24]

Political participation in the United States has been predicated on a natural order in which ethnic and racial minorities accede and assimilate or remain on the margins. In reality, racial minorities can never really assimilate except by disappearing. As opposed to this strong nationalism, Peruvian nationalism is essentially a weak and negative construct. The racial mores and hence the cultural, social, and economic potential of the nation is low due to its racial composition, and for this reason immigrant groups entering Peru, especially but not exclusively from Europe, have had a window of opportunity. These immigrants, whether Italian or Japanese, can become Peruvian if they can demonstrate a contribution to the dual projects of *blanquemiento* (whiteness) and national development.[25] In spite of the common view that Peruvian nationalism is weak, it does exist, finding its primary expression in religion and culture.[26] By these two measures, Nikkei in Peru are extremely assimilated, especially when compared to the religious and cultural practices of Japanese Americans.[27] Practically all Nikkei are Catholic, and the majority embrace the predominant Creole culture, a hybrid of Spanish and indigenous cultures.

For Japanese Americans, historical circumstance and the strength of nationalist precepts helped Americanization win out as the dominant strategy employed from World War II onward. Redress was an acceptable social cause because while it contested the action of the federal government during World War II, it did so in a way that was completely consistent with the postwar strategy of being 110 percent American as a way to be accepted and to avoid a repeat of the internment, during which their loyalty and Americanness was distinctly challenged. Redress allowed Japanese Americans to stand up for and help validate the core principles of equality and justice under the law. The wartime experience was equally traumatic for Nikkei in Peru, and yet a redress movement has not emerged. For Japanese Americans, redress became a historical memory around which to organize and to construct community, at the same time that it was a fight to vindicate America's so-called democratic ideals. As redress came to a close in the United States and Japanese Americans faced the test of renewed Japan bashing, a very different political discourse emerged in Peru. This discourse depended on Japan's postwar rise and did not ask for an apology, but for the chance to lead the country. Nikkei politicians, Fujimori being the most prominent example, sought entry into national political and economic management of the country.

The different political participation in the two cases is a rather obvious outcome of Japan's emergence as the number-two economy in the world. As Japan reached its peak in the 1980s and the United States saw itself falling behind, Japanese Americans became scapegoats, as they had been during World War II, and perpetual foreigners. In contrast, in Peru, Japan and the

Asian Tigers—Malaysia, Singapore, South Korea, and Hong Kong—represented hope for a Latin America that has seen its fortunes diverge greatly from East Asia since World War II. For local Nikkei, this success opened up an opportunity to redefine the terms of Peruvian nationalism in a way that Japanese Americans could never do. A Japanese American running for president? Much less one who publicly speaks Japanese, distributes campaign photos of himself dressed as a faux samurai, and promises millions in Japanese aid? By the same token, a redress movement in Peru is equally unimaginable as poverty rages on, the economy grinds on servicing foreign debt but creating little employment, and the state remains as weak as ever. Basic survival is more important than the events, unfortunate as they are, of fifty years ago. In either case, these two Nikkei formations tell us less about an essence (cultural, racial) than they do about the circumstances of history and the persistence of a global rank-order system that ties race, nation, and development together.

Notes

1. See Luis Jochamowitz, *Ciudadano Fujimori: la construcción de un político* (Lima: PEISA, 1993); Joseph Contreras, "Peru: Looking for a Miracle, Japanese Style: Fujimori for President?" *Newsweek* 115 (Apr. 23, 1990), 36.

2. For my purpose what makes ethnicity distinctive is its function in marking difference from an unspecified mainstream in nationalist discourses and projects. The common view of race as imposed and ethnicity as claimed is insufficient for the purposes of comparative analysis in this particular case. The Nikkei identities that I analyze are neither solely imposed nor completely voluntary.

3. I spent one year in Peru doing dissertation fieldwork. This youth exchange program is approximately one week in duration and normally involves Nikkei youth and youth organizers ages fourteen to twenty-five from all over Latin America.

4. See for example, Takeyuki Tsuda, "Ethnic Preferences: Positive Minority Status of Japanese Brazilians and Their Ethnic Encounters with Other Minority Groups in Brazil," in Roshni Rustomji-Kerns et al., eds., *Encounters: People of Asian Descent in the Americas* (Lanham: Rowman & Littlefield Publishers, 1999), 209–22.

5. I want to draw attention to a number of different levels in saying that forms of identity and community emerge in response to "x." The "x" factor could be a racial formation, as in the United States, where a diverse group is molded into a homogenous racial category. It might be something like diaspora subjects, as in Japanese government preferences for Nikkei labor. The idea is to point out the constructivist and purposeful nature of social formations.

6. For the best discussion of race, ethnicity, and nationalism, see Brackette Williams, "A Class Act: Anthropology and the Race to Nation Across Ethnic Terrain," *Annual Review of Anthropology* 18 (1989): 401–44.

7. See for example, David J. O'Brien and Stephen S. Fugita, *The Japanese American Experience* (Indianapolis: Indiana University Press, 1991), 3–10.

8. See Amelia Morimoto, *Población de origen japonés en el Perú: perfil actual* (Lima: Centro Cultural Peruana Japonés, 1991); Amelia Morimoto, *Los inmigrantes japoneses en el Perú* (Lima: Taller de Estudios Andinos, Universidad Nacional Agraria, 1979); and C. Harvey Gardiner, *The Japanese and Peru, 1873–1973* (Albuquerque: University of New Mexico Press, 1975).

9. This is a consequence and further incentive for the massive *dekasegi* phenomenon, in which many Latin American Nikkei have returned to Japan. See other research in this volume on the dekasegi phenomenon.

10. Conference information can be found at http://www.janet.org/ties/.

11. As a board member of Hapa Issues Forum, a nonprofit advocacy group for multiracial Asian Americans, I became involved in planning committee meetings. My initial role was to help identify issues specific to multiracial Japanese Americans as well as potential speakers and participants.

12. The fact that the multiracial subjects are most easily understood as a distinct racial group(s) is all too indicative of the entrenchment of racialized thinking.

13. Due to space limitations I cannot say too much about the postwar immigrants, although the subject deserves much more attention than it generally receives in discussions of Japanese Americans. This group is often overlooked because of the focus on internment as a marker of group membership, the fact that a large part of this immigration was Japanese women who married American service men, and finally, the cultural and linguistic distance between the descendents of Meiji-era Japanese and the modern Japanese immigrants, usually students, businessmen, and their families. There were some interesting discussions in the planning meetings about things like having Japanese translations of publicity and conference materials since postwar immigrants from Japan may not be comfortable with English and what the role of this group really is in the Japanese American community.

14. See, among others, Harry Kitano, *Japanese Americans: The Evolution of Subculture* (Englewood Cliffs, N.J.: Prentice-Hall, 1976).

15. This idea that the multiracial and multiethnic character of the community is the major problem facing the community remains part of the everyday discourse of leaders and organizers in the community.

16. See Eileen H. Tamura, *Americanization, Acculturation, and Ethnic Identity: The Nisei Generation in Hawaii* (Urbana: University of Illinois Press, 1994).

17. O'Brien and Fujita, *The Japanese American Experience.*

18. See Amelia Morimoto, *Población de Origen Japonés en el Perú*, 176.

19. Kenjinkai is the Japanese language term for a prefectural association. In immigrant communities such as in Peru or the United States members of the same prefecture (or *ken*) in Japan formed these associations on the basis of common origins. In the case of immigrants from the prefecture of Okinawa, an even more specific system of *shi, cho, son* was used. These refer to the county, district, and neighborhood, and immigrants in Peru often belonged to both the Okinawa kenjinkai and also a *sonjin* or neighborhood association.

20. One discussion of Peruvian elites suggests that it is easier to come in from the outside than it is to move up internally. The elite ranks consist of names that go back to the initial Spanish conquest. Additions to this traditional oligarchy have come from outside—foreigners from Europe and, to a lesser degree, Asia. *Peru Elites*, http://geography.about.com/education/scilife/geography/library/maps/blperu.htm, 1992.

21. For example, Ayumi Takenaka, "Japanese Peruvians and Their Ethnic Encounters," in Roshni Rustomji-Kerns et al., eds., *Encounters: People of Asian Descent in the Americas* (Lanham: Rowman & Littlefield Publishers, 1999), 113–18, found Japanese Peruvian identity to be distinct and exclusive, and that only pure Japanese counted as Nikkei. In direct questioning, especially in the power centers of the community, this is indeed what people will say, but in practice I found "Nikkei" to be much more ambiguous and certainly more porous than Takenaka suggests.

22. Much worse than essentialism is the framing of differences between Japanese Peruvians and Japanese Americans by Stephen Thompson, "Assimilation and Non-assimilation of Asian Americans and Asian Peruvians," *Comparative Studies in Society and History* 21:4 (1979): 572–87. He concludes that Japanese Peruvians remain aloof, refusing to assimilate, unlike their more docile American cousins who know their place.

23. An *indigenismo* movement took place in the early twentieth century that tried to rectify this contradiction. Of two currents, one based on the recovery of a romanticized pre-Hispanic past, and the other rooted in the true empowerment of the indigenous majority, the romantic one had the most lasting impact. For an entry point on one of the most important figures of the movement, see Ciro A. Sandoval et al., eds., *José María Arguedas: Reconsiderations for Latin American Cultural Studies* (Athens: Ohio University Center for International Studies, 1998).

24. See June Kodani, "La 'amenaza' japonesa en los escritos sobre la inmigración," in *Primer seminario sobre poblaciones inmigrantes* (Lima: Consejo Nacional de Ciencia y Tecnología, 1988), 205–22.

25. For an important discussion of this nexus between immigration, race, and nation building, see Richard Graham, ed., *The Idea of Race in Latin America, 1870–1940* (Austin: University of Texas Press, 1990).

26. See Freya Schiwy, "Santa Rosa, the Contested Saint: An Early Attempt at Constructing National Hegemony in Peru," *Journal of Latin American Cultural Studies* 8:1 (1999): 49–62.

27. The role of religion is clear because those who criticize the Nikkei for their lack of assimilation always argue that Catholic religious membership and practices among the Nikkei are superficial and disingenuous. See Isabelle Lausent-Herrera, *Pasado y presente de la comunidad japonesa en el Perú* (Lima: Instituto Francés de Estudios Andinos, 1991); and Stephen Thompson, "Assimilation and Nonassimilation of Asian Americans and Asian Peruvians."

CHAPTER EIGHTEEN

The *Uchinanchu* Diaspora and the Boundary of "Nikkei"

MAKOTO ARAKAKI

There is no place in Japan with such deep historical ties to its foreign emigrant communities, and with these ties continuing to the present, as Okinawa.[1] However, with the identity crisis that developed in the 1980s following the prefecture's return to Japanese governance, discourse began on the concept of a worldwide *Uchinanchu*—a worldwide Okinawan community—and the early stages of the organization and policies of its network were developed.

This was a turning point in the relationship between Okinawa and the overseas Uchinanchu. Today this network, which was created to provide a form of administrative leadership, has partially relinquished its administrative role, and it has now been recreated as the Worldwide Uchinanchu Business Association (WUB), whose goal is to promote professional and economic relations among people and businesses. This organization was created to reach beyond the limitations of previous networks and to deepen the promotion of community relations between Okinawa and overseas Okinawan migrants. One of the objectives of this chapter is to investigate the dimensions of the Uchinanchu diaspora. As new narratives of Nikkei diaspora are formed, such as in this International Nikkei Research Project, the Okinawan diaspora in relation to the Nikkei diaspora inevitably becomes an issue. Another objective is to discuss how the position of the Uchinanchu intersects with that of the Nikkei.

The Birth of the "Worldwide Uchinanchu" Discourse

After the Second World War ended, and after twenty-seven years of American military rule, Okinawa was returned to Japan in 1972. But even after Okinawa was drawn in under Japan's "peace constitution," the goals of the withdrawal of the Americans from U.S. military bases and the recognition of the equality of Okinawans with the mainland Japanese were not achieved. Even ten years later, in 1982, impasses concerning the control of U.S. military bases, land development and environmental damage, and economic and industrial stagnation were deepening, and the contradictions developing out of the return of the bases were growing more apparent. While pursuing implementation of the measures of the return, Okinawans gradually lost confidence and became frustrated and disillusioned. In the midst of the impasse that the prefectural government was experiencing and the identity crisis that Okinawa was undergoing at the time, Okinawa's prefectural governor, Junji Nishime, stated that "even if Okinawa wanted to become Japanese, it could not."[2]

An Okinawan publishing company named Ryukyu Shimpo-sha organized a meeting of its staff. Together they decided to initiate a popular movement away from the assimilation policy, which had already become controversial and deadlocked. Rather, this group decided to push for eliminating the Yamato/Okinawa dichotomy and forming an Okinawan identity.[3] This new identity could serve as the basis for building an equitable relationship with the Japanese mainland. The following attempt at building such a relationship was not based on highlighting Okinawa's unsatisfactory relationship with Japan, but rather on recognizing and identifying with Okinawan immigrants who were active and successful around the world.[4] Ryukyu Shimpo-sha began publishing a long-term series entitled "The Worldwide Uchinanchu" on January 1, 1984, which ran until December 28, 1985, featuring 484 parts. The following year these articles were published as a book, which was frequently used in various public study groups and assembly bodies, such as seniors' clubs and women's groups, and as a textbook.[5] The message that can be seen in this worldwide Uchinanchu narrative is that the proud Uchinanchu of the world are active and successful, and that their special traits are flourishing, not in Japan, but rather overseas. The narrative intertwines memories of the Ryukyu kingdom and Okinawa's great era of commercial trading with references to the achievements of worldwide Uchinanchu, giving birth to a self-awareness of the positive role of Okinawans in international society.[6] The overseas migrants have maintained and are carrying the spirit of "the ocean people" into the present. The continuity of this spirit is proof that the Uchinanchu are an international people, and thus a positive identity for Okinawa in the present era of internationalization is being formed anew.[7]

Forming Policy for the Discourse about the Worldwide Uchinanchu

In considering Japan's international contribution, national interest in international exchange / internationalization heightened in the 1970s with plans for regional promotion and development of local self-government, for building roads, and for revitalizing small towns. Under the Okinawa Promotion Development Plan Okinawa was positioned to become a center for international exchange in southern Japan. Among the traits qualifying Okinawa to become that center was the progressive attitude of the prefecture's people and their historical experience in the area of international exchange—Okinawa's unique tradition and culture.

In this context, in 1990 the Okinawa prefecture announced the Worldwide Uchinanchu Network, which would work to expand and systematize ties with the Uchinanchu living around the world and lead in the building of relationships with the overseas Okinawan communities. Also in 1990 the first Worldwide Uchinanchu Conference was held, with the theme "Okinawa and Its People: Uniting all over the World." The second conference, held in 1995 with "Across the Seas, Across Language Barriers" as its theme, drew more than 3,500 participants to Okinawa.[8] This conference—the largest event yet for establishing policy for the worldwide Uchinanchu discourse—also included a project for showing the possibilities of a new Okinawa within a relationship with the overseas Okinawan community. This conference was also held as a way for the prefecture of Okinawa to build self-determination. The self-awareness of participating overseas Uchinanchu as worldwide Uchinanchu was heightened, and the relationships built there have since been maintained.

From around this time, exchange among the overseas Okinawan communities has been lively, and what began as a network formed by a prefectural administrative leadership has evolved into an independent entity.

The Worldwide Uchinanchu Business Association (WUB)

Since the first Worldwide Uchinanchu Festival in 1990, Uchinanchu in Okinawa and overseas have strengthened their ties and begun to discuss business partnerships among themselves. Initiated by Hawai'i, the Uchinanchu Business Association (HUB) and the Worldwide Uchinanchu Business Association (WUB) were formed in 1995. Today, WUB International, a nonprofit that makes decisions regarding the direction of ideas and operations, and WUB Investment, Inc., which often carries out the plans of the WUB International, are together referred to as the WUB. In the past there was no overseas Okinawan migrant organization established as an independent body operating without reliance on donations or financial assistance from outside. While the WUB had its beginnings in the Worldwide Uchinanchu Network that was formed for administrative leadership, initially through government leadership, now it is not under the control of any administration and continues to exist as an autonomous movement.

The WUB differs from previous *kenjinkai* organizations, social clubs whose members originate from the same prefecture in Japan. First, the main characteristic of the overseas WUB membership is that it consists mainly of the younger generation. This has not come about because of the natural transition of leadership through the generations. The presidents and members of the branches are in many cases second- or third-generation descendants of immigrants. Also, with the exception of some Latin American branches, the kenjinkai of those regions and the main operations of WUB members are conspicuously different. In contrast with regions like Hawai'i, with long histories of migration and where generational transitions in kenjinkai organizations go smoothly, in many places like Los Angeles, where recent immigrants are called Shin-Issei (or "new" Issei) and where the history of migration is relatively short, the main membership of the organizations consists of older persons who were born in Okinawa. The main motivation for joining such organizations is fellowship, and meetings are frequently conducted in Japanese. In such a situation the younger generations, who use the language of their country of residence as their everyday language, experience an undeniable sense of alienation. And although the language problem is a factor, the young professionals who are active in the host society would probably have no interest in participating in the previously existing kenjinkai. The younger generations, who have more or less assimilated into the mainstream society consider their parents' generation dark, cliquish, and inscrutable. In some cases this is very similar to the way that mainstream society views ethnic minority groups as cultural outsiders.[9]

The WUB has a more positive image among the younger generation than kenjinkai organizations of the past. Meetings proceed with translations into English, Spanish, Portuguese, and Japanese, and members can openly associate across borders of various regions, which was not the case in the old kenjinkai. Many WUB members feel drawn by the international connections that are generated from personal exchange with professionals. In contrast with the Issei, who are united by common memories of their native Okinawa, the younger generation feels an affinity with Uchinanchu of their same generation who are active in other regions. When the president of the WUB of North America (Los Angeles), Nolan Higa, visited Okinawa in 1995 for the second Worldwide Uchinanchu Festival, he was more moved by recognizing the existence of Uchinanchu like himself around the world than he was by having returned to the land of his ancestors. He says that he became aware of his identity. Even if the question of one's ethnic identity persists, the answer is not found in ties with the generation of one's parents; if the younger generation feels a spiritual separation from the word "Okinawa," they can find new meaning in the Okinawa of this diasporic space. Where attempts to assimilate in a given society's mainstream leave a nagging sense of dissatisfaction, the WUB network can provide opportunities that transform deficiencies into assets for the younger generation of Uchinanchu. This is where men and women can recognize themselves as unique individuals through the discourse of the worldwide Uchinanchu, "the ocean people," and the *Bankoku Shinryo no Tami.*[10]

The WUB and the Okinawa Diaspora

Okinawa is unique in Japan for building a world network that goes beyond the framework of the international exchange of overseas kenjinkai organizations and sister-city programs. One of the reasons for this is that Okinawa has the nation's highest rate of emigration relative to its population. Thus more of the prefecture's people feel an affinity for the outside world because they have relatives overseas, and there have been ongoing historical relations of mutual aid between Okinawa and the overseas migrant communities. But what best enabled the formation of a world network was the many years of identity politics occurring in Okinawa. The work of dispelling the Yamato/Okinawa dichotomy and of projecting a positive, independent identity by drawing on Okinawan history, including emigration, is still going on. Whatever authenticity this historical interpretation might have, stories relating to the collective memory of an "ocean people" populating an independent state called the Ryukyu Kingdom continue to be important. These memories may be brought forth in the harsh political and economic reality of present-day Japan, where internationalization is desirable. But in an international society, for a peaceful people striving to coexist, such a history becomes an extremely valuable foundation for discourse designed to form a positive self-image. Overseas Uchinanchu may be self-conscious about their origins, or feel dissatisfaction with their own processes of assimilation, historical memories of immigration, and their self-image as a minority in their host society. Derogatory expressions applied to Okinawan immigrants, such as *Japan pake* in Hawai'i and *Japan kanaka* in Micronesia, still persist in the collective memory, even if the younger ones do not feel themselves separate from other Japanese immigrants on an individual basis. For Uchinanchu in the process of forming an identity, this discourse brings a sense of identity, building on their ethnic background as "ocean people" and praising the men and women who make up the worldwide Uchinanchu.

The Yamato/Okinawa formula, expressed in many ways, not only in Okinawa but also in the destinations of migration, is preserved in the collective memory of the Japanese community as a whole.[11] Placing the Okinawan historical and political experience at the periphery of the Japanese state is homologous. Okinawan immigrant societies are typically positioned at the periphery of their host states or vis-à-vis the Japanese migrant societies.

The deepening exchange between Okinawa and Okinawan communities stimulates their jointly held memories of marginalization and exclusion. The successes achieved by mutual aid in the course of severe trials, as part of the "Uchinanchu spirit," make up a discourse that goes beyond time and space. And this discourse becomes the basis of the Worldwide Uchinanchu Network and identity. As Paul Gilroy described the Black Atlantic, the subject position is constructed through collective memories, narratives, and stories.[12] The subjectivity finds its position while avoiding essentializing itself. And conversely, this network functions to preserve the collective memory; putting the Uchinanchu spirit into practice goes hand in hand with recalling these memories, and the Uchinanchu identity is formed or reformed in the process.

The WUB rules do not impose any conditions for membership because the WUB naturally wants the organization to be open and inclusive so that the network can expand, and with it business opportunities. However, to maintain a system that is open to the outside, the meaning of the term "Uchinanchu" must be extremely fluid and open to revision. Considering the complex and diverse national identities, languages, cultures, and ethnic backgrounds of Uchinanchu worldwide, qualifying (and exclusionary) conditions for membership in the Uchinanchu community probably could not be established. A subtle expression often heard at WUB meetings is "Uchinanchu at heart." Although a person may have no direct connection to Okinawa, possessing the "Uchinanchu spirit" is a sufficient condition for membership in the group.

Consequently, rather than being a self-evident identity established by an a priori method, the Uchinanchu identity is confirmed by living according to a "traditional" practice arising from a spirit of mutual assistance among the network members. As Robert Nakasone, president of WUB International, expressed it, "compared to the Chinese or the Jews, the Okinawan worldwide Uchinanchu network members are few. But as a matter of background, the 'Uchinanchu spirit' means feeling the ties of familial bonds. ... What is important is that we are Uchinanchu. We overcome difficulties by means of the Uchinanchu heart, and thus we are able to build the organization."

Shinji Yonamine, president of the WUB Brazil, stated, "The *yuimaaru* heart is alive in the Uchinanchu of Brazil.[13] I would like to share the *yuimaaru* heart with Uchinanchu all over the world."[14] The term "Uchinanchu" can mean many different things, and maintaining the varied uses of the term is important in order to support the possibilities of continued growth and renewal.

In the context of the larger network, this kind of unqualified worldwide Uchinanchu identity begins to shake the centrality, cultural authenticity, and self-evident identity or privilege of the Uchinanchu living in Okinawa. It is not guaranteed that the region from which emigrants departed will remain the center to overseas migrant communities. This phenomenon has already appeared in the organizational structure of the WUB. In the WUB network, WUB Okinawa is simply one branch under the umbrella of WUB International (Honolulu), and in terms of power, it is no different from any other branch. Looking at economic influence, the potential of the overseas network for stimulating economic activity in Okinawa itself, and for generating business in new fields, is great. The accumulation and promotion of information- and telecommunications-related industries, and the importation of cutting-edge technology, are already being planned by the WUB, and these are some of the areas where Okinawa prefecture is also making efforts. Also, exports of health products and the expansion of healthcare businesses from Okinawa (where longevity is the norm) have already begun through the WUB network. Local industries that generally operated within the prefecture have received new opportunities for market expansion. For the opening of the Kyushu/Okinawa summit, strategies for the dispatch of information about Okinawa are being discussed from the perspective of overseas Uchinanchu, with the intent to project positive images of Okinawa prefecture. Furthermore, possibilities are beginning to appear for increasing political influence, including lobbying, about Okinawa's ongoing problems with U.S. military bases.

Relationships being woven in this network have become de-essentialized and decentered. Okinawa has felt the violence of exclusion and homogenization, existing as it has on the periphery of the nation-state of Japan. But now there is the possibility of an ongoing coalition that is inclusive rather than exclusive, existing within the space of the new transstate society created by Okinawa and its overseas populations. Morimasa Goya, the WUB Okinawa president, stated that "the WUB is creating a new diaspora, and attaining success is the most important issue. The conditions for this, maintaining openness and mutual trust, are difficult, but considering the nature of the prefecture's people, I believe they can be realized."[15] Currently the concept of the Okinawa diaspora is being enthusiastically discussed in the overseas Okinawan communities, and its realization has been advanced in the course of WUB movement activity.[16] Memories of the land war taking place on Okinawa, the U.S. military base problem, and the memories of sad stories from overseas Okinawan communities in many regions make up the various narratives supporting this concept. And though the accounts of historical experiences and memories may differ, overall the common historical trajectory of the Okinawans can be seen. In sum, if we consider both the Okinawans in Okinawa and the Okinawans overseas, it has been a difficult process to establish a mutual identity—even within the common discourse of having overcome the severe challenges posed within their collective history. According to Stuart Hall, "we have to live this ensemble of identity-positions in all its specificities."[17] Therein a new Uchinanchu status may be found. Such a possibility was foreseen when the WUB was established, bringing the Worldwide Uchinanchu Network to a new level. However, this effort has not yet been fully realized.

The Okinawa Diaspora and Identity Politics

Okinawa has been placed at the periphery of the modern Japanese state and exposed to the violence of such contradictions and exclusion. Even the Worldwide Uchinanchu Network, which has been trying break free of the curse of the Yamato/Okinawa dichotomy, is caught in deep contradictions. The first Worldwide Uchinanchu Conference, which opened to the sound of the Bankoku Shinryo bell, suggested the possibility of forming a transstate diasporic body. However, the meaning of the conference was expressed in this way:

The ways of internationalization and international exchange for our country have been discussed among the general public. For the Uchinanchu who navigated the waters between many countries in the past, the time has come to play a large role in internationalization of our country. The 270,000 Uchinanchu residing in various regions of the world, and the promotion of interaction with the countries of their residence, will contribute to the building of a base for our country's international exchange.[18]

To obtain 300 million yen for the conference budget, specified as Okinawa prefecture's international exchange business expense, it was probably necessary to wrap together the overlapping policies of the Japanese government and its Foreign Affairs Ministry. However, the Okinawan movement, which was trying to go beyond the Japanese state framework and form ties overseas, was restricted from the beginning within the definition of Japan's national interest. The objective of the third Okinawa promotion development plan, "the formation of our country's southern base for international exchange," indicates the central government's thinking. If the Worldwide

Uchinanchu Network and the Worldwide Uchinanchu Conference were extensions of the Japanese government's agenda for prefectural development, and there was no departure from that framework, the "transnational" project that had been an aim for rebuilding Okinawa's identity would be transformed into something ultranational.

Furthermore, this recalls the past when Okinawa, which once wanted to be part of the Japanese empire, reconciled the history of "the ocean people" with an imperial project called the *Nan-shin* (southward march).[19] When Japan—a great capitalist nation approaching international exchange with the Southeast Asian nations that had achieved rapid economic development—defines Okinawa as "our country's southern base for international exchange," it is extremely dangerous for Okinawa to invoke images of the "great trading era."

Many such possibilities and dangers exist in the identity politics of Okinawa as it tries to form its new identity. Many highly politicized problems involving Okinawan independence have been encountered in the progress thus far in rebuilding the Bankoku Shinryo no Tami and "ocean people" traditions. In 1981 Koji Taira called the overseas emigrant society a "common Ryukyu spiritual body," and projected international relations for a greater Ryukyu.[20] In 1997, when the Okinawan economic world was shaken by the "free trade plan," Hiroiwa Miyagi stated that "the equation for Okinawa's independence will not come into being in the perspective of a Japanese framework," and that "Okinawa's independence exists only 'beyond national borders.'"[21] He depicted a "free commerce city-state of Okinawa," and a "great maritime era" arising in a tide of internationalization. In recent years one cannot speak of doing work to build an identity for Okinawa without discussing the reconstruction of such traditions.

The main meeting place for the 2000 Kyushu/Okinawa summit is called the Bankoku Shinryo Hall, and there is much excitement among the Okinawa media about welcoming heads of government and the press in a spirit of hospitality from "the great trading era." Even the summit slogan, "facing the world and sending out the Okinawan heart," is in the Bankoku Shinryo spirit. However, the current acceptance of folk characteristics from more than five hundred years ago as self-evident, without engaging in self-criticism, might be considered a fairly reckless act. In such a reconstruction of a historical identity, this "Uchinanchu spirit" is partially serving as the basis for WUB's unity. In the process of putting that spirit into action, that "traditional spirit" itself is surely put to a severe test.

Now, what does the WUB mean by its depiction of the "Uchinanchu spirit," "the ocean people," and the "great trading era" in the context of the Okinawan diaspora? The WUB network, which has freed itself from governmental control, as did the previous Worldwide Uchinanchu Network, probably will not be involved in defining the national policies of the Japanese state. Here, however, the new issue of global capitalism arises. The "Ryukyu spirit republic" of Koji Taira, the "all-prefecture FTZ idea" of Miyagi, and the WUB's investment company are all projected as part of the global capitalist economy. The decentralization of the WUB may simply be entrusted to the flow of global capital. The WUB's first meeting was co-sponsored by the Hawai'i East West Center. Seeing the shadow of a great hegemony that involves a violent side of colonialism known as global capitalism is probably no delusion. Really, the WUB represents "nonaligned transnationalities struggling within and against nation-states, global technologies, and market resources for a fraught coexistence."[22] "While defined and constrained by these structures, they also exceed and criticize them."[23] But will this really be possible? This challenge has only just begun.

Japanese American Studies and Okinawan Americans

The current process of creating the Japanese American identity is, needless to say, quite complex. Even in dealing with the theme of Okinawa and Nikkei, the discourse produced from these Japanese American studies should not be neglected. During the late 1960s, when the discipline of ethnic studies was first being developed, the various ethnic minority groups that had lost their voices put a scalpel to the master narrative of sociology and humanities; they freed their own identities from the spell of exclusion, and began to retell their own histories. However, for many years, much of the Japanese American research indiscriminately included Okinawan groups in the term "Japanese." In the same way that migrants from mainland Japan, like Kumamoto or Hiroshima prefectures, were grouped together with other Nikkei, Okinawans were considered homologous with other Japanese American subgroups.

Among early immigrants and among the Issei generation there existed a strong contrast between Uchinanchu and Yamatonchu. The differences between the groups, however, have been made invisible, and there is a danger that Okinawan identity, which was formed in response to ongoing exclusion by the Nikkei community, will be buried in darkness. What is being ignored in this case is the continuing colonialism of the modern Japanese state toward Okinawa, and the issue of historical continuity continuing to emerge from a homeland called Okinawa.

According to the powerfully discriminatory discourse of American society, Okinawans were treated the same as the Japanese Americans, excluded from the mainstream and subject to exceptionally harsh treatment as people of an enemy country. Okinawans were discriminated against as "Japs" along with the Japanese, sharing the experience of being treated as an "other"; thus Okinawans shared the subject position as a minority group in the United States with the Japanese. And, sharing the minority identity formed as a consequence of these two common occurrences, Okinawans and Japanese Americans of the North American mainland inadvertently shared a subjectivity. However, what is important here is that the status of the identity of Okinawans in North America is not just the story of their position within a simple dichotomizing discourse of "American mainstream / Nikkei" or of "Okinawan/Yamato." Thus, it cannot be denied that, in the process of absorbing the Japanese American political and historical identity, the particular voice of Okinawa was being silenced.

Where Okinawa Diaspora Meets Nikkei Diaspora

The identity of Okinawans, who cannot be spoken of simply as Nikkei, was first discussed in the field of Japanese American studies in the early 1980s. An awareness began to arise that Okinawans and other Nikkei are not "simply different cultural and class groupings of the same ethnic group, but can be seen as two distinct ethnic groups."[24] Nonetheless, the issue is more complex. A remedy for the silenced Okinawan subjectivity should not merely be the creation of another ethnic category. The new category is always vulnerable to the trap of cultural relativism unless the issue of power is addressed. A key to solving the paradoxical equation "Okinawans are/aren't Nikkei" lies in history that goes back to the premigration, and how social memories of the history are dealt with. As the Nikkei diaspora has been much discussed, as in this International Nikkei Research Project, it is necessary to see how the Okinawan diaspora is included in the picture. Can there be any place where the Okinawan diaspora meets the Nikkei diaspora and the two co-exist peacefully?

Academic institutions play a major role in producing discourses on concepts such as "Okinawa," "Nikkei," and "diaspora." Also, as an institution conducting research relating to Nikkei issues globally, the Japanese American National Museum is not only comparable to academic institutions, but may be said to occupy an extremely important position by presenting such studies to the public by means of various media. Historical exhibits—visual presentations of stories—can no doubt have a powerful impact on people's understanding of such concepts.

One example of such an exhibit produced by the Japanese American National Museum is "From Bento to Mixed Plate: The Americans of Japanese Ancestry in Multicultural Hawai'i." Its first destination in Japan was Okinawa, and lack of Uchinanchu stories in the exhibit was a cause for concern and discussion among the staff members. Okinawan visitors from this prefecture, which incidentally has the highest ratio of emigrants, may respond with feelings of affinity for their overseas relatives in Hawai'i on seeing this display, but would find few things reflecting Okinawa. This issue was raised both in the Hawai'i Uchinanchu community and in Okinawa. Given that the exhibit is about Nikkei in Hawai'i, the question, once again, is how the Uchinanchu are included in this. The issue was not only whether or not the show was successful in Okinawa, but also whether Okinawan collective memories were articulated, and Okinawan stories were told apart from the Japanese experience. Eventually, adding stories of Uchinanchu to the exhibit—the spirit of aloha, the concept of the mixed plate, and a better understanding of the historical experience of Americans of Japanese Ancestry (AJAs) in Hawai'i—bridged the gap for Okinawan visitors.

Such collaboration and negotiation between Uchinanchu and Nikkei identities are crucial for real understanding and the betterment of the two. Also, imaging and creating a place where Uchinanchu and Nikkei meet has great implications for how we visualize the diaspora as a new and better social form. The challenge has just begun. The process of the negotiation is now underway.

Notes

1. In 1899, since the first emigrant departed for Hawai'i, overseas migration has had an important meaning for Okinawa. Okinawa, the "emigration prefecture," with the nation's highest rate of emigration, has a high level of economic dependence on overseas emigrants. In 1929, 66.4 percent of the prefecture's entire revenue consisted of funds sent from overseas. In 1937, Okinawa was the largest recipient of such money, surpassing other prefectures. After the devastation of World War II battles, when Okinawa needed help to recover, it was the Okinawan overseas immigrants who sent large quantities of goods and food. In return, Okinawa showed its appreciation by instituting a student exchange program, donating funds to assist in the construction of a *kenjinkai* hall, etc. On an individual and grass roots level, a relationship of mutual assistance between Okinawa and the overseas Okinawan community has been maintained in various forms.

2. The issue of Okinawa being a separate entity to be assimilated into Japan and thus eliminated was not raised for the first time until after the return. See Ichiro Tomiyama, *Modern Japanese Society and the Okinawan* (Tokyo: Nihon Keizai Hyronsha, 1990) and "Birth of a Nation and the Japanese Race," *Shiso* 845 (1994), 37–56. This is an issue of identity politics, called "Ryukyu management," faced by modern Okinawa since its absorption into Japan. The unease and distress produced by the structure of the dichotomized identity of Yamato/Okinawa has still not gone away.

3. Okinawans use the term "Yamato" to indicate ethnic Japanese, as opposed to ethnic Okinawans, within the Japanese nation-state.

4. Interview with Ansho Yamane, managing director of Ryukyu Shimpo-sha, August 28, 1999, in Okinawa.

5. This project gave an impetus for Okinawan TV series such as *Earthlings from Okinawa* (1986–96), *World Uchina Traveler's Journal* (1997–), and related projects succeeding these. Currently a series entitled *The Overseas Uchina Situation*, which carries overseas Okinawan community news, is being published in the weekly Monday evening journal of Ryukyu Shimpo-sha. And another local publication, the *Okinawa Times*, is devoting space to "Overseas Okinawa" in their weekly Saturday evening issue.

6. Makoto Arakaki, "'Uchinanchu Spirit': An Inquiry into the Identity of the Uchinanchu in Hawaii," *Emigrant Research Annual Report* 4 (1998), 20–40.

7. Also, for the Japanese state, which is striving for internationalization, this may be interpreted as an emphasis on Okinawa's own historical and unique ascendancy.

8. The third world conference is planned for 2001, the year after the Kyushu/Okinawa summit.

9. From the WUB Okinawa branch outline (1998). Interview with Ken Nakai, WUB Okinawa office chief, Aug. 27, 1999, in Okinawa.

10. "Bankoku Shinryo no Tami" expresses the pride and the spirit of the Ryukyu Kingdom, which flourished as a central point for trade among China, Japan, Korea, and the countries of Southeast Asia during the great commercial era of the fifteenth century.

11. Makoto Arakaki, "'Uchinanchu Spirit': An Inquiry into the Identity of the Uchinanchu in Hawaii," 24–34.

12. Paul Gilroy, *The Black Atlantic: Modernity and Double Consciousness* (Cambridge, Mass.: Harvard University Press, 1993), xi, 187–223; Stuart Hall, "Cultural Identity and Diaspora," translated by Hiroki Ogasawara in *Gendai shiso* 26, no. 4 (1998), 94.

13. "Yuimaaru" is a traditional Okinawan support system through which people in a community help each other in times of need.

14. In 1998, the Okinawa, Argentine, and Brazilian branches were established, and the second world conference was opened in Brazil. The following year the Tokyo, Taiwan, Bolivia, and Peru branches were established, and the third world conference was held in Los Angeles. "The WUB News," WUB Okinawa, 1999–2000, 1–10.

15. Interview with Robert Nakasone, WUB International president, June 26, 1999, in Los Angeles.

16. The Internet committee, the circulation committee, the construction committee, the real estate committee, and the G8 committee. Interview with Ken Nakai, WUB Okinawa bureau chief, August 28, 1999, in Okinawa.

17. Stuart Hall, "Cultural Identity and Diaspora," 29.

18. Interview with Nolan Higa, president of WUB North America, June 26, 1999, in Los Angeles.

19. Charles E. Morrison, secretary-general of this same center, visited Keiichi Inamine, governor, at the prefectural office on April 28, 1999, and suggested inviting young economists as trainees. Morrison also stated that he would like to strengthen ties further with Okinawa and suggested 1) the training of young economists, 2) the exchange of professors between universities, 3) aid and advice for Okinawa's coun-

terpart to the East-West Center in Honolulu, and 4) aid for building a worldwide Uchinanchu business network. *Ryukyu shimpo*, Apr. 29, 1999.

20. Koji Taira, "The Ryukyu Republic in a New World Perspective," *Shin Okinawa Bungaku* 48 (1981), 2–12.

21. Hiroiwa Miyagi, *Okinawa Free Trade Theory* (Naha, Okinawa: Ryukyu Shuppansha, 1998), 10.

22. James Clifford, "Diasporas," in *Cultural Anthropology* 9, no. 3 (1994), 302–38, translated by Ken Arimoto in *Gendai shiso* 26, no. 7 (1998), 120–56, at 151.

23. Ibid., 120.

24. Y. Scott Matsumoto, "Okinawan Migrants to Hawaii," *Hawaiian Journal of History* 21 (1982), 125–33.

CHAPTER NINETEEN

Nikkeijin and Multicultural Coexistence in Japan

Kobe after the Great Earthquake

YASUKO I. TAKEZAWA

On April 28, 1908, the *Kasato Maru* left Kobe for Brazil with 781 Japanese on board. Famous for its role in bearing Japanese emigrants to Latin America during the early twentieth century, the ship carried *dekasegi* workers who intended to return to Japan after achieving their dreams abroad. Today, nearly a century later, there are more than 254,000 registered Brazilians living in Japan, the majority of whom are the children and grandchildren of these Japanese who immigrated to and eventually settled in Brazil. There are also approximately 46,000 Peruvians and thousands more from other Latin American countries.

In the current age of globalization, transnational population movements have increased on a massive scale. Roland Robertson defines globalization as "the compression of the world and the intensification of consciousness of the world as a whole."[1] In fact, people can make transnational movements more quickly and less expensively than before, owing to technological developments in transportation and long-distance communications. Not only can they cross national boundaries more frequently than before, but through global mass media, they can also simultaneously share the lives of other people and make comparisons with their own lives. Yearnings for "different worlds" or potential new lifestyles that they envision through the media urge people to move. Nikkei dekasegi workers coming to Japan are no exception.

Nikkei workers from Latin America are generally considered to be *gaikokujin*, or foreigners, in Japan. In conventional usage, the term Nikkeijin refers to descendants of Japanese who reside overseas. The assumptions inherent in sharing Japanese cultural and perceived racial characteristics no longer satisfies the conditions we observe among Nikkeijin in Japan. Changes in the Immigration Control and Refugee Recognition Act that went into effect in June 1990 created a new category of visa in Japan called the *teijusha*, or long-term resident, visa. This visa specifically applies to first-, second-, and third-generation Nikkei, their spouses, and their children.[2] The new law allows Nikkeijin and their families to stay in Japan for up to three years with unlimited renewals and lifts restrictions concerning occupational categories. Although this law does not explicitly conflict with the Japanese government's long-standing policy of restricting entry to skilled laborers, in reality, the policy change was an attempt to address the serious shortage of unskilled labor that Japan was experiencing in the early 1990s. Because of the Nikkeijin's presumed racial and cultural similarities with native Japanese, and their presumed ability to adapt smoothly to Japanese society, they were the first foreigners to whom the Japanese government offered special immigration status.[3]

Yet contrary to the government's original expectations that the Nikkeijin from Latin America could assimilate into Japanese society more smoothly than other immigrants, these people are now the focus of various social and cultural services developed for foreigners in cities and towns with high concentrations of migrant workers. Elsewhere in this volume, Harumi Befu discusses the dispersal of the Japanese prior to World War II. Edson Mori presents the dekasegi phenomenon's economic and social benefits to Brazilian society, and Masato Ninomiya sheds light on their educational situation in Japan and the way dekasegi parents cope with the problems faced by their children. In this chapter, I will explore the arenas in which the flow of Nikkeijin from Latin America has generated conflicts, negotiations, changes, and new social dimensions in Japan, using the city of Kobe as a case study.[4] The primary focus of this chapter, therefore, is to illustrate how these conflicts, negotiations, and changes have occurred through Kobe's responses to the social needs of Latin American Nikkeijin. This chapter suggests that these Nikkeijin have been the primary force in promoting the concept of *tabunka kyosei*, or multicultural coexistence.

Kobe provides a unique model for twenty-first-century Japan because the term tabunka kyosei arose from the aftermath of the Great Hanshin-Awaji (Kobe-Osaka-Awaji) Earthquake, which occurred in the Kobe area in 1995. The term has been gaining popularity in domains involving the presence of foreigners throughout Japan. Furthermore, although there is already an abundant scholarly literature on the motivations, backgrounds, and employment patterns of Nikkei workers in many other areas of Japan, very little research has been conducted on the Nikkeijin in the Kobe area.[5] I will show that Kobe presents an instructive contrast to the Kanto and Tokai regions, where there are high concentrations of Nikkeijin. Ultimately, analyzing the interesting theoretical implications of the Nikkeijin–native Japanese relationship will help to advance our understanding of the changing nature of boundary making among native Japanese in Japan.

An Overview of Nikkei Immigrants in the Kobe Area

The wave of globalization that has swept other parts of Japan has certainly reached Kobe. A significant portion of newcomers today consists of Nikkei workers from Brazil, Peru, and other parts of Latin America, most of whom provide unskilled labor to small or medium-size factories. These newcomers have enhanced the cosmopolitan character of Kobe by adding to its preexisting population of "old-comer" Europeans, North Americans, Indians, Koreans, and Chinese who have settled since the late nineteenth century.[6]

Since opening its port to world trade in 1868, Kobe has enjoyed a reputation as one of the most international and cosmopolitan cities in Japan. Currently forty-four thousand people of approximately one hundred different nationalities make up 3 percent of Kobe's population of 1.5 million. Two-thirds of the foreigners are Korean and one-fifth are Chinese. Since 1957 the city government has encouraged internationalization activities such as sister-city relationships (with Seattle being the first), providing assistance to countries in need, and welcoming foreign students. However, most of the municipal government's efforts were directed outside Japan toward enhancing relationships with foreign countries, rather than addressing the situation of foreigners residing in Japan.

The implementation of the new immigration law in 1990 catalyzed a sudden increase in Nikkei migrants from Latin America. The number of Brazilians in Japan skyrocketed from 4,159 in 1988 to 56,429 in 1990, and then to 254,394 by the end of 2000. Brazilians now comprise the second largest newcomer ethnic group, following the Chinese, and the third largest group of residents without Japanese citizenship, following Koreans and the Chinese.[7] Peruvians are also a significant presence among newcomers, being the fifth largest group. Nikkeijin are estimated to constitute 94.1 percent of Brazilians in the combined categories of "teijusha" (137,649) and "spouses of Japanese, etc." (101,623), and the estimated percentage of Nikkeijin among Brazilians has remained stable since the early 1990s.

In general these immigrants have provided unskilled labor mainly in the manufacturing and construction industries.[8] The 1990 immigration law changes are evidently responsible for a definite shift in preference toward Nikkei workers and away from unregistered migrants, pushing non-Nikkei workers out of these industries.[9] According to Komai, Nikkeijin composed the highest-paid ethnic group among newcomers, followed by Iranians, Bangladeshi, and Chinese, as of 1998.[10]

The Nikkei workers started to move into the Kobe area around 1991, apparently as a consequence of the revised immigration law. Initially, many Nikkeijin residing in the Kobe and Osaka areas did not come directly from Brazil or other Latin American countries, but rather through agencies located in Japan's Tokai region and Gunma prefecture in the Kanto region with high Nikkeijin concentrations. Nikkeijin, including many dismissed by employers elsewhere because of the recession, became a visible presence in Kobe around 1994.

In Hyogo prefecture, in which Kobe is located, Brazilians follow Koreans and Chinese as the third largest group of newcomers, and Peruvians rank eighth.[11] Other cities within Hyogo prefecture, such as Nishinomiya, Amagasaki, Himeji, Akashi, Kasai, and Sasayama, also have sizable Nikkeijin populations. In Kobe, Brazilians are the sixth largest group of residents without Japanese citizenship, following Koreans, Chinese, Americans, Indians, and Vietnamese. As of October 31, 2000, 911 Brazilians, 219 Peruvians, and more than 100 people from other Latin American countries were legally registered as foreigners with the Kobe city office.[12] If "overstayers" (those whose visas have expired) and unregistered residents are included, the number is probably significantly higher. Most of these people are Nikkeijin and their families, although it is said that many non-Nikkei Peruvians entered Japan disguised as Nikkeijin.

Mainly because of the food-processing industry in that area, 575 Brazilians and 55 Peruvians reside in Higashinada ward in the east end of Kobe. There are five food-processing companies in Higashinada ward, some of which have hired more than one hundred Nikkei Brazilians and their spouses. Until recently these companies provided migrant workers with living accommodations and offered bus service between the factories and the dormitories. The result was an extreme limitation of social interaction between these workers and the outside world. Recently, however, due to financial problems, these company-sponsored accommodations and other services were closed down. Most of the migrant workers were able to move into government-subsidized housing, as they, having suffered the Great Earthquake, were qualified for residence in this subsidized housing. Many Nikkei women in Kobe are engaged in janitorial work or *bento* (boxed lunch) processing. In general, Nikkei women are seen as friendly and caring and enjoy a reputation as good workers.[13]

For many surviving first-generation Nikkeijin, Kobe is a memorable place. It is from this port that an estimated 400,000 out of a total of one million emigrants left Japan for foreign destinations. In 1928 the National Center for Emigrants was established to provide information and training programs to departing emigrants. Recently, there has been a campaign to preserve the original center building to commemorate the emigration. Some advocate the use of the building as a center to provide Japanese language classes for Nikkeijin and other migrants from Latin America. Furthermore, a ceremony was held on April 28, 2001 to commemorate the first emigration from Kobe to Brazil, and to dedicate a new monument at the edge of the port.

The Great Hanshin-Awaji Earthquake and Nikkeijin

The Great Hanshin-Awaji Earthquake of January 17, 1995 took more than 6,400 lives and damaged more than half a million homes. According to the Hyogo Prefectural Police Department, among the victims were 173 non-Japanese residents, 151 of whom lived in Kobe.[14] Some non-governmental organizations (NGOs) estimate the number of victims to be more than two hundred. Although Koreans and Chinese constituted 90 percent of the total number of non-Japanese victims, there were eight Nikkei Brazilians and one Peruvian, most of whom resided in Kobe. About eighty thousand non-Japanese residents were affected in some way by the earthquake, and its destructive impact on residents' lives drew attention to the presence of ethnic minorities and new migrants such as Vietnamese and Brazilians.

Among an estimated 1.2 million volunteers active in Kobe following the earthquake, many groups from established local NGOs, as well as individuals concerned about the welfare of foreigners, formed relief organizations and quickly initiated various services to foreigners in the area, regardless of visa status. One organization concerned with the situation of foreigners was the Foreigners' Earthquake Information Center (FEIC), which later changed its name to the Center for Multicultural Information and Assistance (CMIA). This group was organized in Osaka five days after the earthquake to provide telephone hot line consultation services and distribute short newsletters containing official government information on survivors. These newsletters were translated into thirteen languages, including Spanish and Portuguese. This group also provided services such as the condolence fund, financial assistance, and other programs.

In February 1995, a few weeks after the earthquake, the FEIC joined several other organizations to form the Network for Foreigners' Assistance Kobe. In April, three months after the earthquake the radio station FM Yu-men started broadcasting information in five languages, including Spanish. In July, Yu-men combined with a station broadcasting in Korean and Japanese to start FM YY, which gradually added three more languages, including

Portuguese. Ethnic music was also broadcast to lift the spirits of the non-Japanese segment of the population.

Major municipal facilities either collapsed or were extensively damaged in the earthquake. Information services aimed at foreign residents, particularly those who didn't speak English, were substantially delayed.[15] By contrast, NGOs and volunteer groups took the lead in immediately responding to the need for multilingual services. Catholic churches functioned as the initial shelters for many people from Latin America, although they later moved to officially designated public shelters where food, daily necessities, and various services were provided. Acting upon a request by the Committee for International Cooperation under the Osaka Catholic Archbishopric, a Catholic nun, who was a committee member, and her associates engaged in assistance activities such as confirming the safety of foreign individuals by visiting each shelter by bicycle. This particular service played a significant role that would have otherwise been assumed by foreign consulates, some of which had been damaged and were forced to close down after the earthquake. This group later assisted foreign victims with the complicated official procedures required to receive condolence money and financial aid.

Non-Japanese victims of the earthquake included eight Nikkei Brazilians and one Peruvian. The Peruvian's short-term three-month visa had just expired and did not list a permanent residence. Although no official statistics regarding the number of injured non-Japanese residents are available, the FEIC reported a total of twelve critically injured foreigners who were hospitalized after the earthquake. Among the twelve foreigners were four Brazilians and three Peruvians.[16]

One issue that became a subject of debate between NGOs and local and national governments was the definition of "local resident," a term used in the law governing the distribution of condolence money to the bereaved after the disaster. The national government offered all legal foreign residents financial aid on a par with Japanese citizens, paying 5 million yen (US$45,000) as compensation for the death of a family breadwinner, and 2.5 million yen for the death of a dependent.[17] However, overstayers, unregistered residents, and travelers were denied such aid.

A similar issue surfaced in February 1995. Immediately after the earthquake, victims, regardless of status, received free care at emergency medical centers. After the emergency period, however, foreigners who had been living in Japan less than one year and "overstayers," ineligible for the government health insurance available to other foreign residents, had to cover their own medical expenses. Their cause was taken up by various NGOs and local organizations that stepped in to lobby for foreigners who did not qualify for government-provided condolence money. The Network for Foreigners' Assistance Kobe made an appeal that "all victims of the disaster are equal," regardless of whether they were Japanese, registered foreign residents, unregistered foreign residents, or tourists. It should be underscored that after many days of discussion, the term "tabunka kyosei" emerged.

Although the Ministry of Health and Welfare did not change its policy regarding this issue, neither the city of Kobe nor the Hyogo prefectural government made a distinction between Japanese, foreign residents, unregistered foreigners, and overstayers in dispersing condolence money to those whose houses were damaged. The requirement was proof of residence, as demonstrated by such documents as receipts for utility bills or mail.[18] The Hyogo branch of the Japanese Red Cross ignored visa status in offering 50,000 yen (US$450) to uninsured individuals who were hospitalized or had to make repeated outpatient visits to a hospital for a month.[19] The Network for Foreigners' Assistance addressed the problem by paying one million yen (US$9,000) drawn from donations for bereaved foreigners who were officially ineligible for the condolence fund. It also established the "Medical Expenses Subrogation Fund," which temporarily paid the medical bills of foreigners who were hospitalized but unable to cover their medical expenses. They later convinced the prefectural government to pay the remaining medical costs of those foreigners. It should be mentioned that Nikkei communities in Brazil contributed condolence money totaling 90 million yen (US$820,000) to Hyogo prefecture and other prefectures hit by the earthquake.

NGO leaders claimed that the national government maintained restrictive definitions of citizenship and permanent residence, whereas local governments were more flexible in adopting NGO proposals. NGOs were successful in pressuring local governments to consider most, if not all, of the difficulties faced by foreigners in the aftermath of the earthquakes. It is also noteworthy that as discussions continued between NGOs and the city and prefectural governments, an informal study group called GONGO (Governmental Organizations and Non-Governmental Organizations) was formed. GONGO ensured that unpaid medical expenses were paid by the municipal government. GONGO also promoted multilingual street signs, educational programs for immigrant children, and other services related to multicultural and multilingual needs in Kobe.

Compared to government officials, local Japanese residents made hardly any distinction in their post-earthquake treatment of Japanese and non-Japanese. According to a number of sources, including leaders of minority groups, Japanese of all ages, both victims and volunteers, made no distinction between native Japanese and non-Japanese in distributing and sharing goods and in extending assistance. Nikkeijin, whether Japanese in appearance or not, were no exception.

Since the earthquake, NGOs and local governments have cooperated to initiate a variety of projects that address the increasing diversity among Kobe residents. One recent highlight is the creation of a multilingual web site intended to provide information in the event of a disaster. Four organizations, including FM YY, created this web site that reflected the lessons learned during the Kobe' earthquake, when the lack of multilingual information caused an extraordinary amount of anxiety among newcomers without Japanese language ability.

Nikkeijin and Their Relationship with the Japanese

Despite the fact that they are referred to—and identify themselves as—"Japônes" in Brazil, Brazilian Nikkeijin in Japan are considered foreigners and referred to, in general, as Brazilians. Such categorizations seem to derive from two social domains. One is the domain of daily interactions between Nikkeijin and Japanese, in which some Japanese have formed ideas of linguistic and cultural "differences" between Nikkeijin and Nihonjin. The other is the public domain of media and service organizations in which Nikkeijin are viewed as "foreigners" needing services, such as Japanese lessons, guidance, and legal consultation. As a result, in the eyes of native Japanese, there is a clearer boundary between Nikkeijin and Nihonjin than between Nikkeijin and other foreigners.

Nikkeijin who came with their spouses or families usually have precise plans for when they will return to their home country, expressed in such terms as "I will go home when I have saved enough to buy a home," "to establish a company," or "when my children reach middle school age." This has made their adaptation to Japanese society rather difficult. By comparison with other newcomers, their efforts to adapt are often haphazard and their command of Japanese often fails to improve, despite several years of residence. Since many Nikkeijin work weekends or night shifts, which pay better than regular working hours, little time is left for socialization. Even in factories they often simply stand and work in lines, giving them few opportunities to talk with colleagues. Of course this works both ways: Japanese in general do not make extra efforts to be friends with these gaikokujin. When not working, Nikkeijin typically relax at home or visit their friends' apartments. Despite active mutual support and assistance, such social activities rarely develop into formal organizations. After the earthquake, heavily subsidized, unrestricted public housing became available to newcomers in Kobe, and public organization staff urged migrant workers to take advantage of this opportunity in order to lessen the power of the brokers and employers over employees. Public consultants say that this has the effect of reinforcing the power of brokers and employers.

The majority of Nikkeijin working in Japan have more or less limited Japanese language ability. Some of the most common problems in the initial period of Nikkei migration included visas, labor conditions, housing, and medical care. Especially in this initial period, when working conditions were not clearly specified, misunderstandings and suspicions arose on both sides. For example, some workers engaged in dangerous work and suffered serious injuries, for which they often went uncompensated. This left many Nikkei workers concerned about work safety. Nikkeijin often had high expectations about their work conditions based on what they were told by brokers. For instance, in some cases they were told that their daily pay would amount to 10,000 yen (US$90), or 17,000 yen (US$150) for skilled work or work at established companies. Some Nikkeijin were told that they would receive about 300,000 yen (US$2,700) per month. However, they were not told that their salary could be half that amount in the event of consecutive rainy days. Others clashed with their Japanese employers over the issue of utility bills. Some employers have complained that there are workers who take advantage of the free electricity in company-provided housing, indiscriminately using costly amenities such as air-conditioning. As both Nikkei workers and Japanese employers have grown accustomed to each other's expectations and behavior, terms of employment have become more explicit and, with the help of various public and NGO services, the aforementioned frictions have decreased.

Despite many conflicts and misunderstandings, Nikkei workers are given high evaluations by Japanese employers. Men are willing to do jobs that require hard physical labor, and women have the reputation of being friendly and caring, and are popular among nursing and golf-related employers. It should be noted that when Nikkeijin or Japanese with some knowledge about Latin America mention these characteristics, in their discourse they attribute these characteristics to the overall attitude of "Latin people," not Nikkeijin. For example, I was told that "in Latin America, physically bigger men should do more physically demanding jobs," and "Latin people highly respect elderly people, so the elderly in hospitals are fond of these Nikkei women from Latin America."

With the increase in the number of Nikkei who prolong their stay in Japan, another serious problem has arisen: the nonenrollment and dropout rate among school-age children. Under Japanese law, irrespective of the legal status of the parents, anyone of school age is entitled to receive free public education in elementary and junior high schools. Parents receive information on public schooling when they register at a city office. However, unlike for Japanese children, education is not compulsory for non-Japanese children. According to statistics gathered by the Kobe City Board of Education in 2000, only twelve Portuguese-speaking and four Spanish-speaking students are enrolled in the city's public schools.[20] These figures seem significantly low considering the population of these two foreign groups. Such figures may indicate that a significant portion of school-age children from Latin America are not in school. This phenomenon seems to be the result of a number of factors. One is the "sojourner mentality" among parents who plan to send their children to Brazilian schools or colleges in the future. Also, among some families, children are needed at home to care for their younger siblings. Some children lack or lose interest in Japanese schools because of the language barriers, curriculum differences, feelings of isolation from Japanese classmates, or other reasons. Furthermore, different cultural attitudes toward school attendance and education may also be a factor. The dropout rate of Brazilian schoolchildren in Brazil is significantly higher than that of Japanese schoolchildren in Japan, where nonattendance is rare. One may estimate that roughly one-half to two-thirds of Brazilian students of elementary and junior high school ages do not go to Japanese schools.[21] The president of CETEBAN, a correspondence education course in Brazil, warns that unless immediate measures are taken, an increasing number of Nikkei children will end up in juvenile reformatories.

Today divorce and marital difficulties have also become serious problems among Nikkeijin, partially due to their prolonged stay. It is suspected that a number of Latin American Nikkeijin living in the Kobe and Osaka areas have not documented their marriages or their children's births. This is partly due to the distance and expense of a trip to Nagoya, where the General Consulate of Brazil is located, and to complex paperwork and the cost of wedding ceremonies. In an extreme case, one couple did not document their marriage or the births of any of their five children. As a result, these children will not be eligible for work permits when they become adults. Unformalized marriages are one factor that precipitates divorce and family breakups.

Multicultural Coexistence Following the Great Earthquake

The Hyogo-Osaka area hosts one of the largest concentrations of Latin American Nikkeijin in western Japan. These Nikkeijin gather at Catholic churches, stores, restaurants, and bars featuring Latin music. It is said, however, that Nikkei workers rarely seek assistance from Japanese for fear that they may lose their jobs if their complaints are leaked.[22] At present, Nikkeijin in this area are characterized by their dispersal and the virtual absence of any formal organizations initiated by newcomer residents. Under such circumstances, socializing with, or even meeting, other Nikkeijin is difficult. However, a number of organizations provide social services for Nikkeijin and other foreigners and act as cultural and social brokers between native Japanese and Nikkeijin. It is noteworthy that almost all of these organizations were formed after the Great Earthquake. In this section, I will describe the needs and problems of Nikkeijin and the ways in which these organizations have responded. I will also describe some new phenomena that illustrate the new multicultural sensitivity that has emerged through such interactions.

Despite the presence of Latin American migrants in the Kobe area, for many years there were no public consultation services available in Spanish or Portuguese. Since 1993, however, the Hyogo International Association, Information and Advisory Service, run by the Hyogo prefectural government, added consultation services in Spanish and Portuguese to those already available in English and Chinese. During the 1999 fiscal year (from April 1999 through March 2000), it dealt with 1,796 cases in Spanish and 818 in Portuguese, two-thirds of the total non-Japanese-language caseload. Services in Spanish and Portuguese were partially in response to a special request from a Nisei Argentine woman, who for several years had advised Nikkeijin and other workers from Latin America on a personal basis. The association's activities now include free consultations on laws, employment, housing, and other issues concerning daily life. Currently, three staff members, including one Nisei Brazilian, provide consultation services in Portuguese or Spanish. The organization also publishes bulletins in Portuguese, Spanish, and Korean containing detailed information on daily life and public services. The association offered a Portuguese and Spanish FM-radio broadcast program entitled "Hyogo Mi Amor," which, from 1994 to 2000, provided information on social welfare activities, visas, health and sanitation, banking, and traffic.

The NGO Network for Foreigners' Assistance Kobe, which was formed after the earthquake, offers telephone hot line consultation services in nine languages, including Spanish and Portuguese. Among the sixty-nine cases filed from August to October 2000, two-thirds were by those from Latin America, mostly Peruvians. Many consultation cases involve visa problems associated with marital relationships. Others concern job loss, governmental aid, and housing.[23]

According to a survey conducted by the Network for Foreigners' Assistance, a substantial portion of Brazilians and Peruvians search for jobs through personal networks rather than Hello Work, a public job placement office. This is especially true in comparison with other newcomer groups such as the Chinese and Vietnamese. The survey found that only 7.5 percent of Brazilians and 22 percent of Peruvians had visited Hello Work in search of employment, compared to 40 percent of Chinese and 50 percent of Vietnamese. Moreover, 58 percent of the Brazilians and 68 percent of the Peruvians surveyed responded that they had no knowledge of Hello Work. These are significantly higher figures than those for Chinese (26.7 percent) and Vietnamese (26.1 percent). Interestingly, responses seem to have no correlation with their language abilities.[24]

The Center for Multicultural Information and Assistance Kobe opened in April 1998. It initiated the World Kids Community project, which was based on the idea that promotion of multicultural education, rather than homogenous assimilation-oriented education, will benefit not only foreign children, but also Japanese children. It placed particular emphasis on various educational and cultural programs for children from Brazil. One of its first projects cooperated with city- and prefectural-operated agencies in February 1999 to offer an orientation program for school entrance, with the primary target being migrants from Latin America. They provided illustrated bulletins and information in Portuguese, Spanish, and English in preparation for children's entrance into elementary school. Topics included Japanese customs unfamiliar to migrants from Latin America, such as the school entrance ceremony, the parent and teacher contact notebook, home visits by teachers, parents' visiting days, and the preparation of school materials such as pencil boxes. In June 1999 the center organized Fiesta Junina, a major winter festival in Brazil, with the assistance of a Nikkei Brazilian woman. It was likely the first Brazilian cultural event held in Kobe targeted at Brazilian participants, attracting approximately 170 participants. This event also served as a networking opportunity for the otherwise invisible Nikkei Brazilians in the Kobe area. By collecting the names and addresses of attendees, the center slowly expanded the network of Brazilians, most of whom were Nikkeijin, in the region. Meanwhile, the Fiesta Junina attracted about three hundred people in 2001.

One urgent need voiced by Brazilians at the festival was the exchange of information. In response to this request, the first community newsletter for Brazilians was introduced in the fall of 1999. The center attempted to reach Brazilians by delivering or sending bulletins to Brazilian restaurants and factories that employed a significant number of Nikkei Brazilians. A Brazilian grocery truck that regularly visited Higashinada was also involved in distributing bulletins.

The center also organized free Portuguese classes for Brazilian children in Kobe and Akashi, a city adjacent to Kobe. Communication between parents and children was becoming a serious problem in many Nikkei families. These classes aim to facilitate communication between Brazilian parents and their children, who had quickly acquired Japanese language ability but had lost their Portuguese. At present, there are two dozen children attending classes. The center also started free Japanese language classes in Higashinada, mainly targeting Nikkei workers in the area.

The CMIA Kobe was closed in March 2000, and programs it offered have been taken over by a number of independent organizations. A new organization called Facil, located at the Takatori Community Center in Nagata ward, is one of them. Run by the former director and staff members of the CMIA Kobe, Facil is an NPO (non-profit organization) that aims at financial independence for foreign residents and provides fee-based translation and interpretation services in several languages, including Spanish and Portuguese. The need for financial independence among Nikkeijin and other newcomers has long been recognized, and this new support organization is expected to make advances in organizing mutual support networks to foster leadership among migrants. Following the closure of CMIA Kobe, the Japanese language class in Higashinada was assumed by another NGO, the Higashinada Japanese Class, and the medical coverage program was taken over by the Center for Multicultural Information and Assistance Hyogo.

One product of network building among migrants from Brazil has been a soccer team that was formed in Kobe in March 2000, consisting of a dozen (mostly Nikkei) Brazilian youth ranging in age from thirteen to twenty-one. They gather every Sunday to practice, and occasionally play games with Japanese teams and other teams composed of non-Japanese. The formation of this team was initiated by Facil and is expected to build networks among parents via the youth who play on the team.

Among some Nikkeijin who live in areas where mass services are available, Catholic churches serve as a core of their personal networks. In Kobe, only one church in Higashinada provides masses in Spanish. These are held every Saturday night by a Mexican Nisei priest. On special occasions, combined bilingual masses are conducted on Sundays. Japanese lessons or "catch-up lessons" are also offered by members and volunteers on weekday evenings. The Osaka archbishopric, which covers Osaka city and Hyogo and Wakayama prefectures, has only one Portuguese-speaking priest. As a result, six days each month this priest visits ten different locations in the Osaka-Hyogo area. This means that attendees receive mass services only once a month, making it difficult for them to maintain their relationship with the church. The priest has noticed a drastic fluctuation in the number of Nikkei attending services. For example, at Sasayama, a medium-size town in Hyogo where ten people usually attend, more than thirty people appeared one month and then just sixteen the next month. Such fluctuation, he says, is typical among gathering places for Nikkei.

The radio station FM YY broadcast a program entitled "Tabunka Kodomo World" (The multicultural world for children) that was hosted by two girls, one a Brazilian Nikkeijin and the other Vietnamese, from October 1998 through October 2000. FM YY also aired a world-music program featuring Latin music and offers Spanish- and Portuguese-language programs twice a week.

In 1999, the Hyogo Prefecture School Board of Education distributed a short pamphlet entitled "Follow-up Services" concerning foreign schoolchildren. The pamphlet was based on lessons learned from experiences of the Great Hanshin-Awaji Earthquake, after which mutual aid crossed ethnic and national boundaries.[25] Year 2000 guidelines advocated the "development of a spirit of multicultural coexistence" as one of four basic principles. The specific goal was "to foster students' interest in different cultures through opportunities to study Asian and Latin American cultures based on students' daily lives."[26]

Since 1991, yearly reports by the Japanese Ministry of Education show that Portuguese-speaking students (the vast majority of whom are Nikkeijin from Brazil) consistently constitute the largest group of foreign students requiring supplementary Japanese instruction. In 2000 they comprised 40.3 percent (7,425 out of 18,585) of so-designated students in public elementary, junior high, and high schools and schools for the disabled, followed by Chinese- and Spanish-speaking students (29.5 percent and 11.3 percent, respectively). The report explicitly stated that the ministry's investigation was prompted by "the increase of foreigners staying in Japan (including Nikkeijin), through changes in 'the Immigration Control and Refugee Recognition Act'" of 1990.[27]

Both the Kobe city and Hyogo prefecture boards of education now sponsor programs that provide elementary and junior high schools with part-time teaching assistants to assist non-Japanese students requiring Japanese language guidance. Again, the most frequent participants in these programs have been Latin American children, most of whom are Nikkei Brazilian.[28] The state-sponsored assistants help non-Japanese students by providing curricular support in their native languages, and the program is highly regarded because it promotes better communication between both teachers and students, and teachers and parents. Furthermore, the assistants play an important role as consultants who can talk to foreign students in their native languages.

A survey conducted among teaching assistants in the prefectural program who speak Portuguese, Spanish, Chinese, and Vietnamese reveals some instructive cross-cultural approaches and attitudes. Among Portuguese- and Spanish-speaking teaching assistants, those who indicated that differences in the education system and curriculum content were particular concerns for non-Japanese students were higher than the percentages for Chinese- and Vietnamese-speaking teaching assistants.[29] Furthermore, higher percentages of Latin American language assistants felt that differences in customs and ways of thinking were important factors (60 percent among Portuguese- and 50 percent among Spanish-speaking assistants). By contrast, Asian language assistants felt such differences were less important (10 percent among Chinese and 28.6 percent among Vietnamese-speaking assistants). Other comments from Portuguese-speaking assistants illuminate the perceived differences among Nikkei schoolchildren. Concerns of Nikkei schoolchildren included being disliked for their body odor after physical education classes, problems with the standard school lunch and green tea, public bathing with classmates during overnight school trips, and difficulty in the study of Chinese characters.[30]

As we have seen, in Kobe, various kinds of services and programs have been provided for immigrants from Latin America. In spite of the fact that there are several other ethnic groups who are numerically larger than Brazilians in Kobe, Brazilians are the most visible group among newcomers in terms of multicultural and multilingual programs and services. Organizations and public agencies make no distinction between Nikkeijin and other immigrants from Latin America in their services. The physical or cultural similarities between Nikkeijin and native Japanese are not a factor. A few times in my research, through NGO staff, I came across discourse from ordinary Japanese like "in the beginning I thought they had the same blood as ours." Nikkeijin are categorized as "foreigners," both among Japanese engaged in providing social services and those having first-hand interactions with them.

The Issue of Racism against Nikkeijin

The issue of racial prejudice or discrimination against Nikkeijin is rather complicated and cannot be simply attributed to native Japanese discriminating against Nikkeijin. Some Nikkeijin have experienced explicit or implicit labor exploitation or prejudice by native Japanese, often by small business employers or direct superiors. A typical example of racial prejudice is associating the Nikkeijin's limited Japanese language ability with childishness, resulting in condescension such as calling Nikkeijin "stupid" behind their backs. More serious conflicts included the failure of small factory owners to pay compensation for injuries. It is not clear, however, whether these issues involve race or not.

Interestingly, almost all of the Nikkeijin from Latin America and the one European long-term resident of Brazil who assists migrants from Latin America insist that there is hardly any racism or racial discrimination against people from Latin America in Japan (at least compared to the situation in their own countries). Instead, they argue that Nikkeijin and their families tend to quickly attribute common misunderstandings to racial prejudice or discrimination. For example, on a certain garbage collection day, one Nikkei found his garbage left at the collection site and blamed it on racism. A Nikkei consultant explained that it was because he had not followed regulations regarding the separation of flammable and inflammable refuse. Another typical example involves behavior when calling on Japanese homes. Japanese in general do not invite unexpected visitors into their homes. However, since Brazilians often invite visitors inside their homes, the Japanese behavior is interpreted as a sign of prejudice. However, among Nikkei schoolchildren *ijime*, or bullying, is a common problem that they face at school, as Ninomiya discusses in this volume. A typical event is receiving such comments as "Why can't you speak Japanese in spite of having a Japanese face?" Their *difference*, either in language, appearance, customs, or in other respects, often invites ijime in an explicit or implicit way—especially by children who are shy, have difficulty making friends with Japanese classmates, and therefore wind up feeling isolated.

On the other hand, there have been cases in which native Japanese demonstrate feelings of distrust or "difference" toward Nikkeijin after having close interactions with them and construct generalized images concerning them based on such cases. For example, a nun living in a medium-size town on the outskirts of Kobe shared the following story: When a Nikkei Brazilian couple lost their only child to a fatal disease, they said they had no money to conduct a funeral. She talked to people in the church and community who immediately donated money, materials, and services needed to carry out a funeral for their son. When the couple's apartment was subsequently broken into and one million yen (US$9,090) in cash was stolen, they again came to ask her for money. She says that she felt betrayed according to "our way of thinking," and that the incident reaffirmed the sense of difference between Nikkeijin from Brazil and native Japanese.

It is well documented that Nikkeijin change workplaces for even slightly higher wages. This is not surprising, since Nikkei workers generally aim to earn the maximum amount of money in as short a time as possible. Their employers, often small family businesses, feel disappointed, since "we did everything for them." These employers expected loyalty in return for their care and protection. They come to feel that what they thought was a reciprocal relationship was, after all, only one-sided.

At this point it is difficult to identify what forms of and to what degree discrimination against Nikkeijin exist. However, as sources of information increase in both quantity and quality, there has been a clear reduction in culture-based friction with native Japanese. In an interesting new development, a polarization is occurring between Nikkeijin who have integrated themselves into Japanese society and those who have been left out. The relationship between Nikkeijin and native Japanese is entering a new phase.

Conclusion

Kobe has taken the lead in promoting the idea of multicultural coexistence, or tabunka kyosei, an indigenous version of multiculturalism, and it is clearly becoming a society more sensitive to multicultural settings. It should not go unnoticed that such transformations were built on the decades-long struggles and achievements of old-comers, and Koreans and Chinese in particular. Furthermore, the formation of various NGOs, local government social services, multilingual radio stations, Japanese lessons, and such are all efforts made by an increasing number of native Japanese who deeply care about their neighbors and partners in a society that they want to make multicultural. The largest force for such social change is Nikkeijin from Latin America.[31] The sudden influx of Nikkeijin from Latin America after the amendments in the 1990 immigration law, compounded by the effects of the 1995 Great Hanshin-Awaji Earthquake, have prompted the rapid development of various multilingual and multicultural programs for non-Japanese. Many have been aimed at Nikkeijin from Brazil.

The massive influx of Nikkeijin into Japanese society seems to have brought about another change, namely the blurring of a boundary once believed to be fixed and essential, the boundary between "Japanese" and "non-Japanese." In spite of the fact that Nikkeijin from Latin America were singled out for opening the door to unskilled labor because of their assumed cultural and racial similarities, through direct encounters with native Japanese, they have come to be included in the larger category of gaikokujin, or foreigners. This, in turn, demonstrates that the ideology of sharing the same "blood" is losing its importance in determining how Japanese people determine "Japaneseness" and perceive difference.

The case of Kobe reflects features that are both unique to Kobe and common to many other cities and towns in Japan. Here I would like to emphasize the significant effects of the Great Hanshin-Awaji Earthquake in changing native Japanese consciousness toward nonnative Japanese. The appeal that "all victims of the disaster are equal" emerged among local NGO leaders in response to the government's treatment of some foreign victims in life-or-death situations during the aftermath of the earthquake. One drastic change involves an emerging consciousness of tabunka kyosei, or multicultural coexistence, a term that describes the new concept of society held by many Kobe residents.

An editorial entitled "Foreign Residents' Suffrage Needed for Rebuilding,"

published in the March 20, 1995, edition of *Kobe Shimbun*, discusses this issue:

Why is it that among Kobe's and Osaka's citizens, there is a consciousness, a kind of
affinity that they can engender toward Koreans, Chinese, and Filipinos? It is because
people of any country are their neighbors in their daily lives. Without mixing with
people from other cultures and experiencing their cultures, we cannot find uniqueness and strength in cities like Kobe and Osaka. ... In order to reconstruct our cities,
we need to build a new society of coexistence and, together with our foreign residents, choose a path of reconstruction.

It is in the process of rebuilding after the earthquake that the basis of boundary making seems to be changing to a more community- or neighborhood-
oriented than nationality- or race-oriented stance, among some, if not all,
Japanese residents in Kobe. As an old Japanese saying says, "Close neighbors
are more dependable than distant relatives."

On the other hand, many other cities and towns with sizable populations
of migrant workers, many of whom are Latin American Nikkeijin, have been
experiencing similar transformations. These changes have been brought
about by addressing the needs of Latin American Nikkeijin in response to
their sudden influx and perceived cultural and language differences. In that
sense, Nikkeijin from Brazil and other Latin American countries have represented a force for change in Japanese society.

Although it is too early to redefine the concept of "Nikkeijin," given their
brief history of migration to Japan and the tentative formation of their Ja-
pan-based community, the situation of Nikkeijin in Japan certainly defies
and may eventually change the term's conventional usage.

Notes

1. Roland Robertson, *Globalization* (London: Sage, 1992), 8.

2. As of January 1, 2000, 117,500 Brazilians held teijusha visas, and they accounted
for 54.5 percent of the total number of registered foreigners holding such visas. Brazilians and Peruvians combined accounted for two thirds, or 64 percent, of the total.
Old-comers such as Koreans and Chinese, if not naturalized, have the status of *ei-
jusha* (permanent residents) in Japan.

3. For details see Takeyuki Tsuda, "The Motivation to Migrate: The Ethnic and
Sociocultural Constitution of the Japanese-Brazilian Return-Migration System," *Economic Development and Cultural Change* 48, no. 1 (1999).

4. This chapter is based on my field research, which includes frequent personal
interviews with NGO leaders, local government staff, counselors, and other service-
related people, including Nikkeijin, in Kobe and its vicinity between February 1997
and January 2000, and follow-up research in November and December 2000.

5. See, for example, Hiroshi Komai, "Immigrants in Japan," *Asian and Pacific Migration Journal* 9 (2000); Takeyuki Tsuda, "The Permanence of 'Temporary' Migra-

tion: The 'Structural Embeddedness' of Japanese-Brazilian Immigrant Workers in Japan," *Journal of Asian Studies* 58, no. 5 (1999): 687–722; Yoko Sellek, "The U-Turn Phenomenon among South American–Japanese Descendants: From Emigrants to Migrants," *Immigrants & Minorities* 15, no. 3 (1996): 246–69; Takamichi Kajita, "Toransu nashonaru na kankyo ka deno aratana ijyu purosesu: dekasegi 10-nen wo heta Nikkeijin no shakaiteki chosa hokoku," Hitotsubashi University, 1999.

6. Following its usage in the literature concerning migrant workers in Japan, "newcomers" here refers to immigrants whose migration wave began in the late 1970s. "Old-comers" is a contrasting term that is primarily used to denote those ethnic groups (mainly Koreans and Chinese) who voluntarily or involuntarily migrated to Japan during the Japanese colonial period and immediately following World War II. Therefore, unlike other migrant/minority groups in Japan, the influx of Chinese and Koreans to Japan has tended to occur in waves depending on time and rationale. In this manner, Chinese and Koreans can be both "newcomers" and "old-comers."

7. Population statistics for "foreigners" (gaikokujin) are based on nationality alone; no government census measures ethnic background itself. The background-specific numbers of naturalized people and their descendants can therefore only be estimated.

8. According to the Employment Service Center for Nikkeijin in Tokyo and Nagoya, among 5,469 posted openings in 1997, 69.7 percent were in the manufacturing industry, and 85 percent of the employers were categorized as small or medium-size companies with fewer than three hundred employees. Kokusai Jinryu editorial board, "Employment and Educational Issues," Special Issue on Nikkei Brazilians Today, *Kokusai jinryu* (1998): 7–16.

9. Takamichi Kajita, *Gaikokujin rodosha to Nippon* (Foreign migrant workers and Japan) (Tokyo: NHK Books, 1994), 153.

10. The prolonged economic recession in Japan has affected Nikkei workers in various respects. Not only their daily wages but also overtime hours were substantially cut. Komai reports that the percentage of newcomers in the wage category of less than 7,000 yen per day increased from 25.6 percent in 1992 to 34.1 percent in 1998. See Hiroshi Komai, *Nihon no gaikokujin imin* (Foreign immigrants in Japan) (Tokyo: Akashi-shoten, 1999), 64; 160. This situation has even deteriorated recently.

11. As of December 31, 2000, there were about 3,862 people from Brazil, 881 from Peru, more than 149 from Bolivia, and nearly two hundred from other Latin American countries who were registered residents in Hyogo prefecture.

12. In the late 1990s, in addition to Japan's more than 600,000 old-comers, the total number of "newcomers" had reached approximately one million, a combination that represents 1.3 percent of the entire population in Japan.

13. Based on her research conducted in the Tokai region, Yamanaka classified Nikkei women into three categories: "Senior *Nikkeijin* women," "Junior *Nikkeijin* women," and "Brazilian wives." She identifies convalescent attendant as the primary occupation in Japan for senior Nikkeijin women, whereas factory work is the primary occupation for junior Nikkeijin and Brazilian wives. Keiko Yamanaka, "Return Migration of Japanese Brazilian Women: Household Strategies and Search for the 'Homeland,'" in *Beyond Boundaries*, Diane Baxter and Ruth Krulfeld, eds. (Arlington, Va.: American Anthropological Association, 1997).

14. See as the best source regarding the situations of foreigners affected by the great earthquake, Gaikokujin Jishin Joho Senta (Foreigners' Earthquake Information Center), *Hanshin Daishinsai to gaikokujin* (The Great Hanshin Earthquake and foreigners) (Tokyo: Akashi-shoten, 1996).

15. For instance, the Hyogo prefectural police opened "consultation services for foreigners" two days after the quake.

16. German T. Velasquez, "Situation of Foreigners Affected by the Disaster," in *Japan, Comprehensive Study of the Great Hanshin Earthquake*, United Nations Center for Regional Development, Nagoya, Research Report Series No. 12, 1995, 219.

17. In the case of injuries resulting in serious disability, 2.5 million yen was paid for such injury to the breadwinner, half of this amount for any other family member.

18. The Hyogo prefectural government provided 100,000 yen to those residents whose houses had "totally collapsed or burned down" and 50,000 yen for those whose houses were "half collapsed or burned down." In addition, the city of Kobe paid 40,000 yen to its residents in the former category, and 20,000 to those in the latter category. Payments were problematic, however, because many unregistered foreign residents did not have a stable residence, and therefore had great difficulty in producing the necessary documents.

19. German T. Velasquez, "Situation of Foreigners Affected by the Disaster," 221.

20. Although there are a number of private junior high schools in Kobe and the numbers of foreign children enrolled in private schools are unclear, the entrance fees and tuition are expensive, so the numbers are estimated to be extremely low, if there are any foreign students enrolled at all.

21. As of the end of 2000, there were 11,005 Brazilian children between five and nine years of age, and 10,210 between ten and fourteen years. However, according to the Ministry of Education and Science, as of September 1, 2000, there were only 5,241 elementary and 2,056 junior high students whose native language was Portuguese and who were classified as students who required special Japanese language classes. Although the ages do not necessarily match each other—and we also need to take into account a small number of students who do not need special classes, those who go to private schools, and those who go to so-called Brazilian schools—somewhere between one-third and one-half of Brazilian students at the elementary and junior high levels go to Japanese schools.

22. According to a survey conducted at Hamamatsu, when asked who they talk to when they are in trouble, 48.5 percent of Nikkeijin responded "family members," 28.2 percent "Nikkei friends," and only 2.5 percent and 3.5 percent responded that they talk to "employers" and "Japanese friends," respectively.

23. NGO Network for Foreigners' Assistance Kobe, "Hot Line Report for September 2000," unpublished memorandum. Also see Hiroshi Komai, ed., *Shinrai-teiji gaikokujin siryoshusei* (Data book on Newcomers and resident foreigners in Japan) (Tokyo: Akashi-shoten, 1998), 652.

24. NGO Network for Foreigners' Assistance Kobe, "Hyogo kennai niokeru gaikokuseki jumin no kyushoku nikansuru anketo chyosa" (A survey regarding job search among residents with foreign citizenship in Hyogo Prefecture), 2000, 16–19.

25. Hyogo Prefecture School Board of Education, "Gaikokujin jido seito ni kaka-

waru kyoiku hoshin" (Educational policies concerning foreign schoolchildren), 2000, 1.

26. Hyogo Prefecture School Board of Education, "Gaikokujin jido seito ni kakawaru kyoiku Hoshin," 3.

27. Ministry of Education and Science, "Heisei 12 nendo Nihongo shido ga hitsuyona gaikokujin jido seito no ukeire jokyo ni kansuru tyosa no kekka" (An investigation report regarding admission of foreign children in need of Japanese language guidance during the 2000 fiscal year), http://www/monbu.go.jp/news/00000459.

28. As of December 2000, nearly one-third of the schools enrolled in this program registered Portuguese-speaking teaching aids.

29. Among Portuguese- and Spanish-speaking assistants 46.7 percent and 33.3 percent, respectively, in contrast to 10 percent and 14.3 percent among Chinese- and Vietnamese-speaking assistants, respectively.

30. Department for Promotion of Human Rights Education, Hyogo Board of Education, "Gaikokujin jido seito sido hojoin setchi jugyo dainiki gakko chyosa-shukei kekka" (A report of the survey conducted among the second-term teaching assistants for foreign students), unpublished document, September 2000. The number of respondents was rather small (fifty in total), and the results should be interpreted as a general view.

31. Although Chinese compose the largest segment of newcomers in Kobe (and throughout Japan), they have recourse to far more established organs of assistance, such as community organizations and personal networks. More recently Vietnamese have surpassed Brazilians in Kobe, and it should be pointed out that their needs are not yet sufficiently addressed in Kobe.

PART IV

Retrospect and Prospects

CHAPTER TWENTY

Retrospect and Prospects

LANE RYO HIRABAYASHI

AKEMI KIKUMURA-YANO

JAMES A. HIRABAYASHI

Retrospect

We will begin by recapitulating a few points. Our decision to utilize globalization theory in order to analyze the case studies in Parts Two and Three was strategic. On the one hand, we were confident that the INRP researchers would find evidence of the reproduction of Nikkei identities in the Americas, and indeed, half did. On the other hand, we did not expect other INRP researchers to be adamant that new identities were emerging among people of Japanese descent in the Americas, and among Latin American Japanese working in Japan—identities that did not seem to fit under the rubric "Nikkei." In order to be fair to both of these perspectives, and yet put them into a context in which both might be assessed, globalization theory as an analytic framework seemed especially appropriate. So, having considered eighteen substantive case studies, what can we conclude about the five propositions relating to possible outcomes of globalization presented in Chapter 2?[1]

The Five Propositions

First, we maintain that it would be impossible to argue that globalization has had no tangible impact on Nikkei identities or communities. Masato Ninomiya's chapter, which discusses dekasegi parents' dilemmas with regard to educating their Brazilian children of Japanese descent in Japan, makes this clear enough.[2] Moreover, as Makoto Arakaki shows, Okinawans in diaspora have a plethora of connections to each other, as well as to communities and compatriots back in the home prefecture in Japan. Such cases clearly illustrate that new identity formations are evolving, and that these go well beyond the concept of Nikkei identities as we ordinarily think of them. We will cite additional data to contradict further the "no impact" proposition when we cover the disjunctures revealed in other case studies. For now, mentioning these two chapters should suffice to put the validity of such a claim in doubt.

Second, there may be evidence to support the second proposition: that globalization has intensified Nikkei identities and community formations. It is difficult to assess the veracity of this claim because, in point of fact, the evidence is mixed. On the one hand, Steven Masami Ropp's, Doris Moromisato Miasato's, and Audrey Kobayashi's chapters appear to support the second proposition. These chapters indicate that, whether we look at the situation domestically or internationally, increasing levels of intercultural contact have led to the breakdown of patterns of endogamy. Increasing rates of interracial marriage and larger numbers of children of bi- or multiracial descent have become a point of some contention among people of Japanese descent in the Americas. According to Ropp, the ostensible weakening of ethnic boundaries of Nikkei communities in countries such as Peru and the United States is worrisome to some community leaders. It even periodically generates apocalyptic rhetoric about the impending "death" of the Japanese American community in the latter country.[3] The point here is that in at least some community settings interracial couples and their children are sometimes perceived as a threat. In reaction to this supposed threat, gatekeepers of "pure" Japanese descent are sometimes hostile to interracial couples and their children and challenge their right to participate, or even claim membership, in the ethnic community. This would be an example of how if changes are sometimes threatening they can reinforce traditional identities even as the ethnic constituency is evolving in new and unexpected ways.

On the other hand, and at a number of different levels, people of Japanese descent in the Americas certainly seem to be more willing of late to explore the linkages that they may share with compatriots beyond the narrow boundaries of an immediate locality. The chapter by Steven Masami Ropp also illustrates this point. Historically speaking, both the Buddhist and Christian churches, as well as Nikkei sports leagues, have long held conferences or tournaments that have brought Nikkei from different cities, regions, states, and countries together. However, in the 1980s and 1990s a series of endeavors indicated a broader set of concerns. Ropp, himself one of the cofounders of the Hapa Issues Forum, discusses the "Ties that Bind" conferences that have attracted participants and attention across the United States.[4] While such organizations and their activities do not reflect a universal orientation per se, they certainly suggest that Nikkei may be more willing than ever to consider whether or not they have agendas similar to other Nikkei, ir-respective of local community, state, or nation.

Concomitantly, Edson Mori's chapter indicates new levels of openness. Perhaps because the dekasegi bring both money and new skills back home with them, there is no real indication that when they return to Brazil they face any special resentment or resistance as they try to reintegrate back into the Japanese Brazilian community. In other words, direct exposure to deka-segi, who have been profoundly affected by globalization, doesn't seem to generate backlash or resistance on the part of Brazilians of Japanese descent who have chosen to remain in Brazil.

In sum, because the evidence on the second proposition is at best mixed, we would argue that each case must be assessed on its own merits.

Because there is clear evidence of continuity and reproduction, it seems hard to argue that globalization has uniformly eroded Nikkei identities and communities—the third proposition—at least to date. In this light, it is worth attending for a moment to the chapters regarding gender. Certainly, it can be asserted that feminism, in the form of world conferences on women's issues and various struggles for the empowerment of women in formal poli-tics, economics, health, and other spheres of public life, has had a marked impact throughout the world and in a wide variety of ways.[5] And as Doris Moromisato Miasato's chapter indicates, feminist criticism has been a defi-nite resource in attaining her goal, raising unresolved issues revolving around gender hierarchy and power within Peruvian Nikkei families and in terms of the leadership and decision-making setup within community-based organizations.

Still, feminist critiques of sexism in Nikkei families and communities may not exemplify an erosion of Nikkei identities per se. Rather, feminists seem to be questioning a particular dimension of that identity. From a feminist perspective, gender roles and hierarchies are seen as atavisms, rooted in feu-dal Japan, that have been reproduced in new settings where they are neither appropriate nor salubrious. In the end, it is this specific dimension of Nikkei identities that Moromisato Miasato insists be revisited and revised.

At this juncture, we can address a related issue. In encouraging us to as-sess the full impact of patriarchy in Japan and the Americas, Audrey Kobaya-shi and Doris Moromisato Miasato raise an intriguing question: do women of Japanese descent leave Japan or eschew Nikkei identities and communities in order to escape sexism (especially in the form of sanctioned gender roles and constraints)? The answer to this question has not been determined to date. Lane Ryo Hirabayashi observes that, in terms of the Americas, Hawai'i has been an especially supportive setting for women of Japanese descent who have aspired to political offices and careers. He asks if there is something we can learn from the case of Hawai'i that would enable other Nikkei to foster the leadership potential of the women in their communities.[6]

The reasons for Nikkei women's disaffiliation leads us to a related point. There is a sizable number of people of Japanese descent in the Americas who appear to be disaffiliated from their ethnic compatriots, and this number does not just include women. Among the disaffiliated, for example, are 1) those who do not particularly self-identify as being of Japanese descent, even though they could, 2) those who decide for some reason not to become involved in the ethnic community, and 3) those who seem to prioritize variegated links to others in the host country or to the global ecumene on the basis of ties that do not revolve around ancestry or heritage. We know of little research that has tried to assess the seemingly disaffiliated persons of Japanese descent (but see Harumi Befu's comments in chapter 1), so we really do not know if they feel themselves to be Nikkei or not. Nor are we able to say with any certainty whether such disaffiliation is a subjective matter, whether it is a matter of assimilation over the course of three or more generations, or whether it is in fact a true reflection of the breakdown of cultural identities that Hall and others have hypothesized is a product of globalization. Research that focuses in detail on this matter would be of interest and use.

There does not seem to be strong evidence for the fourth proposition: that globalization has produced a marked trend among Nikkei away from their ethnic identities and toward a greater concern for and identification with the world as a whole. We note a possible exception, however, in the case of elite families and individuals—scholars, businessmen, activists, and artists (such as Tizuka Yamazaki, whose films are the focus of Naomi Hoki Moniz's chapter)—whose work, travel, and reputation make them international figures. We know of little research that has considered how being an internationally recognized figure might impact the consciousness of Nikkei elite.[7]

In terms of the fifth proposition about the impact of globalization, the chapters in Part Three indicate that there is a series of new, hybrid identities that began to emerge markedly in the 1980s and 1990s, and that have been fueled in part by globalization processes. Apart from Nikkei women, the three groups that most strongly illustrate this point are those in interracial marriages and their children, Okinawans in global diaspora, and Latin Americans of Japanese descent who became dekasegi. Below we offer a brief comment on each of these populations.

In almost every country throughout the Americas there is a great deal of interracial marriage going on, especially among the third and subsequent generations, as INRP meetings in 1998 and 1999 revealed. Unfortunately, this is basically an unstudied topic in Latin America. Even so, as Steven Masami Ropp observes in terms of the United States, and Doris Moromisato Miasato in terms of Peru, more traditional members of Nikkei communities seem ambivalent about the increase in and the status of interracially married couples and their children. It is not clear at this point whether the parents and children of these mixed marriages are retaining connections to other persons of Japanese descent, or to the larger ethnic community in their area, if indeed there is one, or whether they might reject such associations because of how they are received, lack of interest, or both. But, in any case, as Audrey Kobayashi indicates, since out-marriages are prevalent among people of Japanese descent, how this is handled and resolved by all parties involved is an absolutely essential matter in terms of the very survival of Nikkei communities.

Second, because of a history of colonial domination by mainland Japan, Okinawans have had a somewhat different experience and trajectory in the Americas, as Makoto Arakaki, Jeffrey Lesser, and Steven Masami Ropp note. Okinawans may be less hampered by negative stereotypes and marginalization than they were before World War II. Nevertheless, the strong Okinawan ethnic revival in Hawai'i, the United States, and Brazil, among other countries, demonstrates the development of a separate subcultural identity, as well as a stronger connection to Okinawa and things Okinawan than the concept "Nikkei" would generally imply.

Third, at least one chapter on the South American dekasegi suggests that, under the particular circumstances of temporary return migration to Japan, dekasegi can develop a unique consciousness similar to that of Nikkei in, say, the United States or Peru, as opposed to identifying with Japan and the Japanese proper. According to Naomi Moniz, this has happened among the Japanese Brazilian dekasegi living and working temporarily in Japan. We also have to acknowledge, however, that this does not always seem to be the case. Marcelo Higa, for example, argues that there is a great deal of heterogeneity among Latin American dekasegi in Japan. His chapter portrays a tremendous mixture of people and experiences that appear to defy characterization as Nikkei. Moreover, as Higa points out, dekasegi recognize differences between themselves as citizens of distinct Latin American countries. Higa's thesis is supported by the fact that none of the authors who studied the dekasegi in Japan (Edson Mori, Masato Ninomiya, Marcelo Higa, and Yasuko Takezawa) reference any situations in which the dekasegi as a whole have come together in order to struggle for their rights in common cause— irrespective of their different Latin American nationalities—despite the prejudice and discrimination that they face in Japan.

At this juncture, we must fully acknowledge that a number of chapters (especially those by Marcelo Higa, Makoto Arakaki, and Yasuko Takezawa) indicate that the term "Nikkei"—as a concept that could appropriately be applied to people of Japanese descent in the Americas, and of Latin American descent in Japan—has been stretched to the breaking point in the new millennium. People of Japanese descent in the Americas and beyond have now become so diverse, in myriad ways described in this book, that there should be little wonder that the INRP scholars, collectively and individually, had to stop periodically in order to reassess the validity of the concept "Nikkei."

The "Triadic Framework"

In the next sections, we will examine in more detail the conditions that favor the conjunctions of Nikkei identities—conditions that enable their re-production as such. A corollary section will identify conditions that have caused disjunctions. We will indicate how globalization has impacted both of these outcomes.

Before we do this, we note here that, at a methodological level, it is some-times difficult to calibrate the interface between macrolevel processes inten-sified by globalization, on the one hand, and regional- and micro-level proc-esses that the case studies in *New Worlds, New Lives* highlight, on the other hand. For this reason it is useful to introduce what we call a "triadic frame-work" of analysis, which we will explain below.[8]

In calculating the impact of globalization on Nikkei identities, it strikes us that the significant contextual relationships are often triadic, which is to say that they involve interactive relationships between the home nation, Japan, and the Nikkei community formation, if indeed one exists. As is made clear by the chapters in Part Three, today these transformational processes operate through a series of linkages spanning the individual/family and the commu-nity, the national and the international levels. Of course, as Teruko Kumei's chapter in Part Two indicates, triadic relationships have had a long history of impact on Japanese immigrants and their progeny overseas. We submit, how-ever, that these processes have intensified within the context of global capital-ism. Thus, assuming a triadic context as we pursue an understanding of the impact of globalization on cultural identities is essential, methodologically speaking.[9] We think of this triadic framework as kind of a meso (or mediating) level that helps one understand the articulation of the macro/global versus the micro/local.[10]

In point of fact, most of the chapters in *New Worlds, New Lives* indicate that a triadic perspective is key to understanding how globalization is mani-fested "on the ground" in the late twentieth and early twenty-first centuries. Nikkei identities in any given setting are clearly not static entities determin-ing the behavior of adherents, but rather cultural, historical, and political constructions that are shaped by a range of macro and micro conditions. This dimension of Nikkei identities is nicely illustrated by Ropp's chapter, which shows how the construction of Nikkei identities differs in the United States and Peru because processes of racialization have predominated in the former country, while in Peru, hierarchies are more deeply affected by class than by race. The construction of race in terms of the Nikkei in Peru is also distinctive, given Japan's superior positioning in terms of the global economy relative to their host country. (It would be interesting to see to what extent people of Japanese descent in Peru see themselves as superior to Peruvians of indigenous, mestizo, or even European backgrounds.) In any case, Ropp is right to remind us of how profoundly the national and international context can impact formulations of Nikkeiness. This is a comparative issue that clearly deserves sustained investigation.

A triadic approach is thus essential for careful analyses of the substantive, idiographic aspects of case studies. In other words, the triadic approach allows us to identify and explain contradictory aspects of "new" identities that Hall's framework does not fully account for. A recapitulation of some of the case studies will indicate how and why this is so, and also illustrate the point that, even while reproduction of Nikkei identities continues, differentiation and diversification are proceeding apace.

Conditions Favoring Conjunctures in Nikkei Identities

It is worth noting that there is actually a good deal of evidence presented in *New Worlds, New Lives* that the term "Nikkei" can be applied to people of Japanese descent in many different countries of the Americas—Bolivia (Kozy Amemiya), Brazil (Jeffrey Lesser), Canada (Audrey Kobayashi), Peru (both Raúl Araki and Amelia Morimoto), Paraguay (Emi Kasamatsu), and the United States (both Steven Masami Ropp and Lane Ryo Hirabayashi)—and even on a global basis (Harumi Befu). Given that this is the case, one can argue that the term "Nikkei" is valid not only conceptually, but also at an experiential level, since the populations in the countries listed above are apparently comfortable with the term and utilize it themselves.

In the chapters that identify and discuss conjunctures of ethnic reproduction, Nikkei identities are best conceptualized as symbolic social constructions (Doris Moromisato Miasato). They are negotiated by individuals and communities and arise out of a feeling of affinity derived from people interacting with each other in the context of a shared lifestyle (Jeffrey Lesser, Teruko Kumei, Emi Kasamatsu). Communities develop based on social networks in various spheres of life, including familial, economic, educational, and sociopolitical; these networks are domestic, but in some instances can also take on a transnational configuration (see Raúl Araki for an example of the former, and Kozy Amemiya and Masako Iino in terms of the latter). These may become institutionalized over time, but in any case they provide the context within which future generations are socialized into both the Nikkei community and the national society (Lane Ryo Hirabayashi). A sense of affinity and common ethnic identity thus arises out of this mutual participation in the arenas of the local community and the nation (Amelia Morimoto, Steven Masami Ropp). In this sense, Nikkei identities are the result of a continual negotiation, incorporating and adapting sociocultural resources in response to contemporary realities (Harumi Befu). Given these points, it is clear that the reproduction of Nikkei identities continues into the new millennium, even despite the exigencies of globalization. It is useful to delineate two key conditions under which this reproduction occurs.

In considering the INRP scholars' contributions, one central condition supporting the reproduction of ethnic identity is a matter of generation, and this suggests the need to take a historical perspective on generational cohorts. We can begin with the observation that Japanese immigrants, then and now, typically have a strong sense of ethnicity as Japanese proper. In this sense, Jeffrey Lesser's findings about Japanese immigrants in Brazil are supported by Marcelo Higa and Kozy Amemiya: that in many of the South American countries, Japanese immigrants tend to retain their identity as Japanese and even, in the majority of cases, their Japanese citizenship. Japanese immigrants may indeed become true settlers (and Nikkei) over time, but it is not clear exactly when and how this transition takes place, or even how it can be measured.[11] This is an issue that must be studied further in order to clarify it.

As we have seen in each of the chapters in Part Two, if and when there are enough of them in one place, first-generation immigrants typically lay down the institutional foundation for the ethnic community over time. Great effort and expense are usually entailed, and ties of affinity and solidarity are of critical importance in garnering the resources for community building (see, for example, Lesser, Araki, and Hirabayashi).

It is significant that Nisei are the ones who are most likely to exemplify strong manifestations of Nikkei identities. It is necessary, however, to analyze this in terms of a triadic perspective. Through their Japanese parents, the second generation has a vital linkage to their Japanese heritage, although this may be in part a matter of collective memories concerning the history and culture of the ancestral homeland (Kasamatsu). More generally, contact with the first-generation parents, in the context of the family, ensures that Japanese language, worldview, and interpersonal style are transmitted to the second generation on a day-to-day basis. Under certain conditions, these may be strong enough to generate ties of affinity that extend across national boundary lines, both in terms of Japan as well as in terms of Nikkei from other countries (Iino). In contrast to what we know of the first and second generations, however, by the time we get to the third and fourth generations, INRP scholars suggest that things are likely to change (Ropp). As is evident in the chapters having to do with education, these younger generations may have much less in the way of Japanese language abilities and exposure to Japanese values and lifestyle. They may be much more fully acculturated, if not assimilated, to the host country. In Part Two a number of the chapters, including those by Jeffrey Lesser and Amelia Morimoto, provide evidence along these lines. Not surprisingly, as a result, the orientation and focus of people of Japanese descent may shift more fully or even completely toward the host country by the third generation—especially if and when Nikkei are treated equally and thus achieve parity with members of the dominant society. This is why we think that generational cohorts have a great deal to do with the reproduction and strength of Nikkei identities, although we will note a caveat below.

Globalization has impacted the generational mix of populations of Japanese descent in the Americas in a number of ways. One has to do with the staggered arrival of postwar Japanese immigrants to the Americas. The chapters by Amemiya and Kobayashi give us two different examples of this. Another has been produced by shifts in the global economy that brought Latin American dekasegi to Japan. There are long-term implications for the host nations as the dekasegi return home, as both Mori and Ninomiya suggest. Yet another has to do with a relatively understudied phenomenon that none of the INRP scholars chose to focus on: first-generation Japanese expatriates who have lived in the Americas for many decades, but who have decided to retain many features of their original lifestyle as well as their Japanese citizenship. As has often been observed, this stance must be seen in light of Japan's position as a world power, especially vis-à-vis home countries that might not be as rich or as prestigious.[12]

It is clear from the INRP scholars' research that community formation is a second key condition that supports the manifestation and reproduction of distinctive Nikkei identities.

The group orientation has long been recognized as an organizational feature of Japanese society.[13] All the chapters in Part Two indicate that this orientation characterizes the strong inclination to form Nikkei communities, when numbers permit, throughout the Americas. Even so, community formation has certain basic preconditions, which include having enough people at hand and their concentration within a delimited geographical area. Community formation is also impacted by certain triadic conditions. Ethnic community formation can be impeded, for example, if there is heavy pressure from the host society to assimilate. This has been the case in countries like Mexico and the United States during specific historical moments—even apart from periods of outright oppression, such as occurred during World War II.

In addition, although they bear an air of similarity (as the chapters by Araki, Amemiya, Lesser, and others illustrate), the specific kinds of organizations and groups described in the chapters vary over time and according to the time of arrival, the composition of the immigrants, conditions in the host country, and the setting, from rural to urban. It is worth pointing out that, while we can identify conditions such as generation and community formation as supporting the reproduction of Nikkei identities, it seems unlikely that the essence of being Nikkei could ever be fully defined in terms of content per se, since there has been so much variation in terms of what cultural items have been reproduced, and how they have been reproduced. Even when similar institutions have been built by people of Japanese descent in the Americas, such as Japanese language schools, their focus has varied a good deal. This is clear when juxtaposing the chapters by Teruko Kumei and Emi Kasamatsu. Because of their feeling of vulnerability in the early twentieth century, Japanese immigrants on the U.S. mainland decided to downplay the reproduction of a Japanese identity proper. In the 1980s in Paraguay, however, Kasamatsu suggests that the inculcation of a Japanese orientation, if not identity, was a principal objective of Nikkei-organized Japanese language schools.[14]

In the end, what we are proposing here about ethnic community is fairly straightforward. In those places, times, and settings where community formation was not possible, one finds less in the way of connection, cooperation, or large projects that might enhance feelings of affinity toward, and efforts on behalf of, the ethnic group as a whole. In this sense, the community provides a vehicle for ethnic reproduction in ways that a nuclear or an extended family alone cannot replicate.

In fact, when and where community formation has been realized, and where there is a range of different institutions within a given Nikkei community, the possibilities for strengthening Nikkeiness as a distinctive (yet not separate) identity are greatly enhanced, even for the third, fourth, and fifth generations. It is worth emphasizing that a strong and dynamic community formation can offset the attrition of ethnic identity through the generations.

Conditions Favoring Disjunctures in Nikkei Identities

A triadic analysis of disjunctures reveals a set of variables and dynamics that are almost a reverse image of those variables and dynamics that generate continuities. In some cases, triadic linkages result in situations that actually reinforce a reidentification with Japan. This dynamic is most clearly captured in Kozy Amemiya's description of aid from Japan to Nikkei farmers in Bolivia, or Emi Kasamatsu's discussion of Japanese language education in Paraguay, which has also been heavily subsidized by the Japanese government. While this may be a historical phase that will pass—especially as governmental programs like the Japan International Cooperation Agency (JICA) curtail international aid to Latin Americans of Japanese descent—linkages along these lines seem to hinder the development of a Nikkei identity. These cases illustrate beyond a doubt that Japan itself has played, and will continue to play, a role in the formulation of Nikkei identities in the Americas. Japan's position in the structure of global international relations, as well as its ties to host countries and Nikkei communities, must all be considered in any analysis of the impact of globalization on people of Japanese descent.[15]

Similarly, Makoto Arakaki's research on Okinawan identities in diaspora seems best conceptualized in terms of a triadic framework. On the one hand, Okinawans may identify themselves as a distinct subculture within the larger Japanese American community in a site like Hawai'i, and in relation to immigrants from Naichi (mainland Japanese) backgrounds. On the other hand, the importation of teachers from Okinawa into overseas Okinawan communities in order to teach the Okinawan language, arts, and culture can reinforce new linkages to the home prefecture, as well as the reidentification with Okinawa proper. As is clear from Arakaki's text, the prefectural government of Okinawa itself has been very active in facilitating networks of Okinawans overseas, but also in promoting the direct identification of Okinawans overseas with the home prefecture. The exact outcome of these processes, including whether they will generate a cultural identity separate from, or related to, other Nikkei identities, is yet unclear. Either alternative seems possible.

A triadic approach is needed with the dekasegi case studies, too. As Edson Mori makes clear, when Japan's so-called bubble economy was flourishing as the economies and polities of many Latin American countries were in perpetual crisis, the material conditions framing dekasegi movement back to Japan were set in place. Even though many Latin American Japanese dekasegi had the backgrounds and even the language skills to adapt, tough laws and social conventions made foreigners' new lives very difficult indeed.[16] Masato Ninomiya's chapter discusses dekasegi educational dilemmas in terms of conditions in Japan and vis-à-vis the eventual return to Brazil. Dekasegi are clearly thinking of all three dimensions of the triad, so to speak, as they try to determine how best to address their needs—past, present, and future.

In a related and yet unique case, Yasuko Takezawa reports that the great earthquake disaster in Kobe generated new intergroup linkages and thus a new consciousness about identity/identities. Takezawa documents the emergence of a new multicultural awareness no longer revolving around Japanese heritage per se, or even the unique experiences of the Latin American Japanese dekasegi. This awareness was the product of triadic relations between Japan, Latin American home countries, and the dekasegi and, according to Takezawa, it impacted the people of Kobe in a profound manner, whatever their original backgrounds or actual nationalities.

Finally, returning to the topic of feminism, here too it seems that globalization and a triadic perspective go hand in hand in framing an appropriate perspective for study and analysis. When examining gender dynamics and gender issues in Nikkei families and communities, it must be acknowledged that these are also impacted by corollary aspects of patriarchy embedded in the Spanish/Mediterranean or Anglo-Saxon traditions. Thus, a study of patriarchy among people of Japanese descent in Latin and North American countries must encompass 1) Japanese roots, and 2) Nikkei revisions of these roots, but also very much 3) gender stereotypes and manifestations of sexism that are extant in the host societies. Doris Moromisato Miasato's chapter provides some analysis along these lines, but this could be systematically developed and might become the basis for an innovative research program.

Prospects

At one level, *New Worlds, New Lives* demonstrates that ethnicity is inherently and necessarily an emergent social construction. Nikkei are a result of a sociohistorical process in which ethnic categories are created, embodied, and continually transformed. The past plays a role in the construction of ethnicity to be sure, but transformations reflect the changing conditions that shape the content and expressions of a sense of peoplehood through time and space. Moreover, Nikkei identities do not exist in isolation. All Nikkei have multiple identities. These identities are fluid as well and, at times, are in a state of renegotiation in larger national and international settings. Whether it is deployed subjectively or analytically, the concept of "Nikkei" is necessarily characterized by flexibility and soft boundaries.

Nikkei identities are in flux at this moment because globalization has intensified certain ongoing dynamics having to do with diversification within the population of Japanese descent overseas. We propose, however, that globalization must be assessed vis-à-vis a triadic framework, the better to gauge the dynamic interplay between macrolevel forces, nation-states (including at least the points of origin and destination), and Nikkei communities and individuals. We believe that this same approach can also offer new insights into how to approach Japaneseness, as this too, as Takezawa indicates, is undergoing recalibration in the new millennium. As the chapters in Part Three demonstrate, the dynamics of globalization and triadic relations that frame the construction of the ethnic identities of overseas Japanese immigrants and their descendants are reverberating ever more strongly in Japan itself.[17]

Returning, finally, to a question posed in the preface: what light does an examination of people of Japanese descent in the Americas shed on Japanese (North) Americans? First, it is quite clear that these two are not the same and, second, while there appear to be many parallels between Japanese Americans on the U.S. mainland and Canadians of Japanese ancestry, these experiences should not and cannot be projected onto people of Japanese ancestry in the state of Hawai'i or throughout Latin America. Japanese Americans on the mainland and Japanese Canadians were, after all, tiny, disenfranchised minority populations—at least before and immediately after World War II.

It also strikes us that mainland Japanese Americans and Canadians were more systematically and intensively racialized, in a highly negative fashion, by the dominant society, although some caveats are appropriate. While the racialization of people of Japanese descent in Latin America was also quite intense and negative during World War II, this was characteristic of some nations (e.g., Peru), but not of others (e.g., Argentina).[18] Moreover, since key Latin American nations such as Brazil, Peru, Bolivia, and Mexico have large indigenous and mestizo populations, the racialization of people of Japanese descent differed from that found on the U.S. mainland, partly because of Japan's postwar status, which was higher than that of most Latin American nations.[19]

One of the results of intensively negative racialization and the trauma of mass incarceration has been—individually and collectively—deracination, especially on the part of members of the second and third generation of Japanese Americans and Japanese Canadians. Although there are certainly many Japanese Brazilians and Japanese Peruvians who have assimilated, the core of these communities, and the newer communities such as those described by Emi Kasamatsu and Kozy Amemiya, have retained a Japanese orientation—culturally and linguistically—to a greater degree than have their northern cousins. Similarly, because incarceration was visited upon only a small number of Japanese Americans on the Hawaiian Islands, Americans of Japanese ancestry there faced much less in the way of the destruction of culture and community.[20]

We would like to reemphasize, then, that community formation has been one of the central conditions that allows and promotes the reproduction of ethnic identities on the part of people of Japanese descent overseas. As globalization continues apace, the survival of Nikkei identities will surely revolve around the question of how "community" is defined in the twenty-first century. Our findings in regard to globalization indicate that community boundaries must be drawn in an ever more open and inclusive fashion so that new affinities and linkages can be explored. If so, Nikkei identities themselves may have more than just a passing chance to continue and to evolve.

Notes

1. Again, we think that this is a reasonable sample for our purposes here because, although we expressed interest in identity and community, we asked each scholar to select what they thought was a relevant topic and "tell it like it is," based on their intimate knowledge of a given population. The fact that more than half of the participants chose to focus on disjunctures of Nikkei identities is, to us, a sign of what is going on, and presented a challenge that we needed to face squarely in terms of analysis. Because we hadn't really expected this, we went back to the drawing board with regard to theory. We ended up thinking that the literature on globalization, and how globalization is supposed to impact cultural identities, would be a fair way to assess both conjunctures and disjunctures, as well as a way, in the end, to account for the patterning of both.

2. For a complementary piece that sketches in particular the relationship between restrictions on foreign workers and historically shaped patterns of racial ideology in Japan, see John Lie, "The 'Problem' of Foreign Workers in Contemporary Japan," in Joe Moore, ed., *The Other Japan: Conflict, Compromise, and Resistance Since 1945* (New York: M. E. Sharpe, 1997), 288–300.

3. Although Harry H. L. Kitano may not have used this exact terminology himself, the banner for an article describing a talk given by this Japanese American scholar read "The Death of the Japanese American Community?" See *Asian Week*, Feb. 14, 1987, 1. The substantive data that Kitano presented in his talk had to do with the high out-marriage rates of Japanese Americans.

4. At another level, the Pan-American Nikkei Association's and National/International Nikkei Youth Exchange's conferences throughout the Americas are efforts to establish a common ground to discuss common issues. On the latter, see J. K. Yamamoto, "Linking North and South: Toward a Pan-American Nikkei Youth Movement," *Hokubei Mainichi*, Jan. 1, 2001. The then upcoming conference in Lima, Peru, was being sponsored by MOVI (Movimiento de Menores) from January 18 to 27, 2001, and a group of Japanese Americans was planning to attend.

5. See Amrita Basu, *The Challenge of Local Feminism: Women's Movements in Global Perspective* (Boulder, Colo.: Westview Press, 1995). A general overview that describes how globalization has impacted women is available in "Challenging a Gendered World," in Robin Cohen and Paul Kennedy, *Global Sociology* (New York: New York University Press, 2000), 305–20.

6. Since Japanese American families on the Islands appear to be no less patriarchal than those elsewhere, why women of Japanese descent in Hawai'i have made substantial inroads into electoral politics is something that only additional research

can resolve. The anthropologist Brackette Williams suggested that one variable to be considered in this regard might be the status of native Hawaiian women in local families and communities (personal communication, June, 2001).

7. An interesting figure in this light would be world-famous artist Isamu Noguchi. Born in Los Angeles in 1904, Noguchi was biracial. He was brought up in Japan, but sent by his mother to study in Indiana in 1918. His studies took him around the world by the time he was forty. See the entry "Noguchi, Isamu," in Brian Niiya, ed., *Japanese American History: An A-to-Z Reference from 1868 to the Present* (New York: Facts on File, 1993), 269–70.

8. Our thoughts about the importance of a triadic framework were inspired, in part, by the work of Shigeru Sugiyama. See his paper, "Trilateral Relations between the United States, Mexico, and Japan and Shrimp Fisheries off the Mexican Northwest Coast in the late 1930s," which should be published in the near future. In addition, the framework put forward by Barbara Stalling and Gabriel Szekely, eds., in *Japan, the United States, and Latin America: Toward a Trilateral Relationship in the Western Hemisphere* (Baltimore, Md.: Johns Hopkins University Press, 1993), is useful. What differentiates our approach (and this is why we call it "triadic" instead of "trilateral") is the observation that ethnic communities themselves can play an important role in the mediation of relations between Japan and any given host country. Subsequently, we came across a recent article by Eriko Yamamoto, "Cheers for Japanese Athletes: The 1932 Los Angeles Olympics and the Japanese American Community," *Pacific Historical Review* 69 (2000): 399–420, which makes an analogous proposition.

9. Note, here, that we don't propose a triadic perspective is necessary in every case; rather, our point is that it needs to be considered in every case because a number of chapters herein indicate that it can be profoundly relevant for comprehensive analyses.

10. For a discussion of the three different, but linked, levels of analysis—macro, meso, and micro—see Thomas F. Pettigrew, *How to Think Like a Social Scientist* (New York: HarperCollins, 1996), 113–15; passim.

11. Historians Yasuo Sakata and Yuji Ichioka are two of the pioneers of this research endeavor, focusing on the lives and perspectives of the early Japanese immigrants. An example of the tremendous number of Japanese-language documents that they have collected and perused is available in a volume that they co-authored, *The Buried Past: An Annotated Bibliography of the Japanese American Research Project* (Berkeley: University of California, Press, 1974).

12. The literature on people of Japanese descent in Latin America has many references to the fact that the latter see themselves as a "superior people," and thus are reluctant to associate too closely with "locals." Besides considering the chapters herein (for example, Kozy Amemiya's), interested readers can see two examples in Stephen I. Thompson, "Separate but Superior: Japanese in Bolivia," in George L. Hicks and Philip E. Leis, eds., *Ethnic Encounters: Identities and Contexts* (North Scituate, Mass.: Duxbury Press, 1977), 89–101; and Christopher A. Reichl, "Stages in the Historical Process of Ethnicity," op. cit., 36.

13. See Chie Nakane, *Japanese Society* (Berkeley: University of California Press, 1972).

14. It is interesting that Kasamatsu introduces no data to indicate that these

schools address children's identities as Japanese Paraguayan (as opposed to people of Japanese descent who happen to reside in Paraguay, even after two or three generations), although, to be fair, in other contexts she has raised this point.

15. Yukiko Koshiro provides an instructive picture of Japan's attitude toward "development aid" in Latin America in her recent study, *Trans-Pacific Racisms and the U.S. Occupation of Japan* (New York: Columbia University Press, 1999).

16. Consider the case of Ana Bortz, a Brazilian reporter who was ejected from a jewelry store in Hamamatsu, Japan, because she was a foreigner. She sued and won $47,000 in damages; *New York Times*, International edition, Nov. 13, 1999, A1, A14. This article, by Howard W. French, "'Japanese Only' Policy Takes Body Blow in Court," suggests a change in the air: "if they can do nothing about the famous Japanese standoffishness toward outsiders, they can at least insist on equal treatment before the law" (A14). My thanks to Professor Evelyn Hu-DeHart for sharing this article with me.

17. A useful overview can be found in Michael Weiner, ed., *Japan's Minorities: The Illusion of Homogeneity* (New York: Routledge, 1997). And as has been reported for more than two decades now, Japanese nationals, especially children, who are socialized and educated overseas may find it rough going when they return to Japan. For a recent report that indicates that this has not changed, see Howard W. French, "Japanese Unsettles Returnees, Who Yearn to Leave Again," *New York Times*, International edition, May 3, 2000, A1, A12, A13.

18. See *New Worlds, New Lives'* companion volume: Akemi Kikumura-Yano, ed., *Encyclopedia of Japanese Descendants in the Americas: An Illustrated History of the Nikkei* (Walnut Creek, Calif.: AltaMira Press, 2002) for more details concerning this point.

19. Koshiro, *Trans-Pacific Racisms and the U.S. Occupation of Japan.*

20. In terms of almost 158,000 persons of Japanese ancestry in Hawai'i at the end of 1941, those who were initially incarcerated after Pearl Harbor were given individual loyalty hearings. In the end, fewer than two thousand (that is, approximately 1 percent of the total population of Japanese descent on the Islands) were deemed suspicious enough to detain and ship to camps on the U.S. mainland. See the report of the Commission on Wartime Relocation and Internment of Civilians, *Personal Justice Denied* (Washington, D.C.: U.S. Government Printing Office, 1982), 261.

Index

Index

In this index an "f" after a number indicates a separate reference on the next page, and an "ff" indicates separate references on the next two pages. A continuous discussion over two or more pages is indicated by a span of page numbers, e.g., "57–59." *Passim* is used for a cluster of references in close but not consecutive sequence.